Communications
in Computer and Information Science   1708

Rationale
The CCIS series is devoted to the publication of proceedings of computer science conferences. Its aim is to efficiently disseminate original research results in informatics in printed and electronic form. While the focus is on publication of peer-reviewed full papers presenting mature work, inclusion of reviewed short papers reporting on work in progress is welcome, too. Besides globally relevant meetings with internationally representative program committees guaranteeing a strict peer-reviewing and paper selection process, conferences run by societies or of high regional or national relevance are also considered for publication.

Topics
The topical scope of CCIS spans the entire spectrum of informatics ranging from foundational topics in the theory of computing to information and communications science and technology and a broad variety of interdisciplinary application fields.

Information for Volume Editors and Authors
Publication in CCIS is free of charge. No royalties are paid, however, we offer registered conference participants temporary free access to the online version of the conference proceedings on SpringerLink (http://link.springer.com) by means of an http referrer from the conference website and/or a number of complimentary printed copies, as specified in the official acceptance email of the event.

CCIS proceedings can be published in time for distribution at conferences or as post-proceedings, and delivered in the form of printed books and/or electronically as USBs and/or e-content licenses for accessing proceedings at SpringerLink. Furthermore, CCIS proceedings are included in the CCIS electronic book series hosted in the SpringerLink digital library at http://link.springer.com/bookseries/7899. Conferences publishing in CCIS are allowed to use Online Conference Service (OCS) for managing the whole proceedings lifecycle (from submission and reviewing to preparing for publication) free of charge.

Publication process
The language of publication is exclusively English. Authors publishing in CCIS have to sign the Springer CCIS copyright transfer form, however, they are free to use their material published in CCIS for substantially changed, more elaborate subsequent publications elsewhere. For the preparation of the camera-ready papers/files, authors have to strictly adhere to the Springer CCIS Authors' Instructions and are strongly encouraged to use the CCIS LaTeX style files or templates.

Abstracting/Indexing
CCIS is abstracted/indexed in DBLP, Google Scholar, EI-Compendex, Mathematical Reviews, SCImago, Scopus. CCIS volumes are also submitted for the inclusion in ISI Proceedings.

How to start
To start the evaluation of your proposal for inclusion in the CCIS series, please send an e-mail to ccis@springer.com.

Luís Ferreira Pires · Slimane Hammoudi ·
Edwin Seidewitz
Editors

Model-Driven Engineering and Software Development

9th International Conference, MODELSWARD 2021
Virtual Event, February 8–10, 2021
and 10th International Conference, MODELSWARD 2022
Virtual Event, February 6–8, 2022
Revised Selected Papers

 Springer

Editors
Luís Ferreira Pires
University of Twente
Enschede, The Netherlands

Slimane Hammoudi
ESEO, ERIS
Angers, France

Edwin Seidewitz
Model Driven Solutions
Herndon, VA, USA

ISSN 1865-0929 ISSN 1865-0937 (electronic)
Communications in Computer and Information Science
ISBN 978-3-031-38820-0 ISBN 978-3-031-38821-7 (eBook)
https://doi.org/10.1007/978-3-031-38821-7

This Springer imprint is published by the registered company Springer Nature Switzerland AG
The registered company address is: Gewerbestrasse 11, 6330 Cham, Switzerland

Preface

The present book includes extended and revised versions of a set of selected papers from the 9th and 10th International Conferences on Model-Driven Engineering and Software Development (MODELSWARD 2021 and MODELSWARD 2022), which were exceptionally held as online events due to the COVID-19 pandemic. MODELSWARD 2021 was held from 8 to 10 February 2021, and MODELSWARD 2022 was held from 6 to 8 February 2022.

MODELSWARD 2021 received 62 paper submissions from 24 countries, of which 8% were included in this book, while MODELSWARD 2022 received 59 paper submissions from 24 countries, of which 10% were included in this book.

The papers in this book were selected by the event chairs and their selection is based on a number of criteria that include the classifications and comments provided by the program committee members, the session chairs' assessment and also the program chairs' global view of all papers included in the technical program. The authors of selected papers were then invited to submit a revised and extended version of their papers having at least 30% innovative material.

The purpose of the International Conference on Model-Driven Engineering and Software Development is to provide a platform for researchers, engineers, academics as well as industrial professionals from all over the world to present their research results and development activities in using models and model-driven engineering techniques for System Development. Model-Driven Development (MDD) is an approach to the development of complex (software) systems in which models take a central role, not only for analysis of these systems but also for their construction. MDD has emerged from modelling initiatives, most prominently the Model-Driven Architecture (MDA) fostered by the Object Management Group (OMG). In the scope of MDA, a couple of technologies have been developed that became the cornerstones of MDD, namely metamodelling and model transformations. MDD relies on languages for defining metamodels, like the Meta-Object Facility (MOF) and Ecore (developed in the scope of the Eclipse Modelling Framework), and transformation specification languages like QVT and ATL. MDD has already been around for some years and is becoming common in system development due to its benefits (reduction of development costs, improvement of software quality, reduction of maintenance costs and support for controlled evolution of IT systems). MDD has also been applied in many application areas, such as real-time and embedded systems and telecommunication systems, and to the development and integration of enterprise information systems. Currently, the MDD research community is exploring the bounds of MDD, by investigating new application areas and combinations with other emerging technologies, like, for example, pervasive context-aware systems, semantic web, semantic web services, service-oriented architecture, cloud computing, ontologies and artificial intelligence. MODELSWARD aims at fostering the further development and application of MDD techniques for complex (software) systems.

The papers selected to be included in this book contribute to the understanding of relevant trends of current research on Model-Driven Engineering and Software Development, including: Model-Driven Development of Cyber Physical Systems, Model-Driven Software and Services Infrastructures, Systems Engineering, Model Execution and Simulation, Automated Code Generation, Multi-level and Multi-view Modelling, Model-Driven Architecture, Model-Based Testing and Validation, Model Transformation and Metamodelling: Foundations and Tools.

We would like to thank all the authors for their contributions and also the reviewers who have helped to ensure the quality of this publication.

February 2022   Luís Ferreira Pires
                                                            Slimane Hammoudi
                                                              Edwin Seidewitz

Organization

Conference Co-chairs

2021

Richard Soley (Honorary)   Object Management Group, Inc., USA

2021 and 2022

Edwin Seidewitz   Model Driven Solutions, USA

Program Co-chairs

Slimane Hammoudi   ESEO, ERIS, France
Luís Ferreira Pires   University of Twente, The Netherlands

Program Committee

Served in 2021

Achiya Elyasaf	Ben-Gurion University, Israel
Alberto Rodrigues da Silva	IST/INESC-ID, Portugal
Alex Groce	Northern Arizona University, USA
Alexey Khoroshilov	ISPRAS, Russian Federation
Ambra Molesini	Alma Mater Studiorum - Università di Bologna, Italy
Andrea D'Ambrogio	Università di Roma "Tor Vergata", Italy
Andrea Enrici	Nokia Bell Labs, France
Andrzej Niesler	Wroclaw University of Economics and Business, Poland
Ansgar Radermacher	CEA, France
Bülent Adak	Aselsan A.S., Turkey
Beatriz Marin	Universidad Diego Portales, Chile
Christelle Urtado	EuroMov Digital Health in Motion, Univ. Montpellier, IMT Mines Ales, France

Christiane Gresse von Wangenheim	Federal University of Santa Catarina, Brazil
Ethem Arkin	Hacettepe University, Turkey
Fabian Gilson	University of Canterbury, New Zealand
Giovanni Denaro	University of Milano-Bicocca, Italy
Hao Wu	National University of Ireland, Maynooth, Ireland
Huaxi (Yulin) Zhang	University of Picardie Jules Verne, France
Ioannis Stamelos	Aristotle University of Thessaloniki, Greece
Jean-Sébastier Sottet	Luxembourg Institute for Science and Technology, Luxembourg
Juan Boubeta-Puig	University of Cádiz, Spain
Kevin Lano	King's College London, UK
Klaus Havelund	Nasa/Jet Propulsion Laboratory, USA
Lior Limonad	IBM, Israel
Marcos López-Sanz	Rey Juan Carlos University, Spain
Marianne Huchard	Université de Montpellier, France
Matthias Tichy	University of Ulm, Germany
Sophie Ebersold	IRIT, France
Vladimir Estivill-Castro	Universitat Pompeu Fabra, Spain
Yassine Rhazali	Moulay Ismail University of Meknes, Morocco

Served in 2022

Alexander Raschke	Germany
Antonio Brogi	Università di Pisa, Italy
Beatriz Marín	Universidad Politécnica de Valencia, Spain
Eda Marchetti	ISTI-CNR, Italy
Katharina Juhnke	Ulm University, Germany
Sophie Ebersold	Université Toulouse II-Le Mirail, France
Stephanie Challita	University of Rennes 1, France
Vladimir Estivill	Universitat Pompeu Fabra, Spain
Wolfgang Reisig	Humboldt-Universität zu Berlin, Germany

Served in 2021 and 2022

Albert Zündorf	Kassel University, Germany
Alexander Kamkin	ISPRAS, Russian Federation
Alin Stefanescu	University of Bucharest, Romania
Ana Paiva	University of Porto, Portugal
André Miralles	INRAE - National Research Institute for Agriculture, Food and Environment, France
Anthony Simons	University of Sheffield, UK

Antonio Cicchetti	Mälardalen University, Sweden
Arnon Sturm	Ben-Gurion University of the Negev, Israel
Assaf Marron	The Weizmann Institute of Science, Israel
Aurora Ramirez	University of Córdoba, Spain
Christian Bunse	University of Applied Sciences Stralsund, Germany
Clémentine Nebut	Université de Montpellier, France
Colette Rolland	Université De Paris 1 Panthèon Sorbonne, France
Dana Petcu	West University of Timisoara, Romania
David Lorenz	Open University, Israel
Der-Chyuan Lou	Chang Gung University, Taiwan, Republic of China
Dickson Chiu	University of Hong Kong, China
Dimitris Dranidis	CITY College, University of York Europe Campus, Greece
Dongxi Liu	CSIRO, Australia
Dragan Milicev	University of Belgrade, Serbia
Elke Pulvermüller	Osnabrück University, Germany
Emilio Insfran	Universitat Politècnica de València, Spain
Frederic Mallet	Universite Nice Sophia Antipolis, France
Gereon Weiss	Fraunhofer Institute for Cognitive Systems IKS, Germany
Guglielmo De Angelis	IASI-CNR, Italy
Gustavo Rossi	LIFIA, Argentina
Guy Katz	Hebrew University of Jerusalem, Israel
Haiyan Zhao	Peking University, China
Hamed Taherdoost	University Canada West, Canada
Holger Eichelberger	Universität Hildesheim, Germany
Husnu Yenigun	Sabanci University, Turkey
Iris Reinhartz-Berger	University of Haifa, Israel
Jan Tretmans	TNO-ESI and Radboud University, Netherlands
Jean-Guy Schneider	Monash University, Australia
Jose Raul Romero	University of Cordoba, Spain
Jun Kong	North Dakota State University, USA
Kamil Zyla	Lublin University of Technology, Poland
Ludovic Apvrille	Télécom Paris, France
Ludovico Iovino	Gran Sasso Science Institute, Italy
Luis Llana	Universidad Complutense de Madrid, Spain
Marc Zeller	Siemens AG, Germany
Marco Autili	University of L'Aquila, Italy
Maria Jose Escalona	University of Seville, Spain
Marjan Sirjani	Mälardalen University, Sweden

Mykola Nikitchenko	Taras Shevchenko National University of Kyiv, Ukraine
Naoyasu Ubayashi	Kyushu University, Japan
Olaf Owe	University of Oslo, Norway
Olena Chebanyuk	National Aviation University, Ukraine
Omar Badreddin	University of Texas El Paso, USA
Paola Giannini	University of Piemonte Orientale, Italy
Pierre Laforcade	Le Mans Université, France
Pingaud Hervé	Institut National Universitaire Champollion, France
Stamatia Bibi	University of Western Macedonia, Greece
Stefan Naujokat	TU Dortmund, Germany
Stephan Flake	S&N CQM Consulting & Services GmbH, Germany
Steve McKeever	Uppsala University, Sweden
Sylvain Vauttier	EuroMov Digital Health in Motion, Univ. Montpellier, IMT Mines Ales, France
Ulrich Reimer	Eastern Switzerland University of Applied Sciences, Switzerland
Wieland Schwinger	Johannes Kepler University, Austria
Yuting Chen	Shanghai Jiao Tong University, China

Additional Reviewers

Served in 2021

Khandoker Rahad	University of Texas at El Paso, USA

Served in 2022

Somedev Chatterjee	University of Texas at El Paso, USA
Saif Mahmud	University of Texas at El Paso, USA
Maria Teresa Rossi	Gran Sasso Science Institute, Italy
Gijs van Cuyck	Radboud University, The Netherlands

Served in 2021 and 2022

Ievgen Ivanov	National Taras Shevchenko University of Kyiv, Ukraine

Invited Speakers

2021

Schahram Dustdar	Vienna University of Technology, Austria
Ralf Lämmel	University of Koblenz-Landau, Germany
Jim Logan	No Magic, Inc., USA

2022

Simon Brown	Architects Limited, Jersey
Gabor Karsai	Vanderbilt University, USA
Hans Peter de Koning	DEKonsult, The Netherlands

Contents

A Digital Twin Description Framework and Its Mapping to Asset Administration Shell

Bentley James Oakes[1,2](✉) , Ali Parsai[3] , Bart Meyers[3] , Istvan David[2,4] ,
Simon Van Mierlo[5] , Serge Demeyer[5] , Joachim Denil[3,5] ,
Paul De Meulenaere[3,5] , and Hans Vangheluwe[3,5]

[1] Polytechnique Montréal, Montréal, Canada
bentley.oakes@polymtl.ca
[2] Université de Montréal, Montreal, Canada
{bentley.oakes,istvan.david}@umontreal.ca
[3] Flanders Make vzw, Lommel, Belgium
{ali.parsai,bart.meyers}@flandersmake.be,
{joachim.denil,paul.demeulenaere,hans.vangheluwe}@uantwerpen.be
[4] McMaster University, Hamilton, Canada
davidi3@mcmaster.ca
[5] University of Antwerp, Antwerp, Belgium
serge.demeyer@uantwerpen.be

Abstract. The pace of reporting on Digital Twin (DT) projects continues to accelerate both in industry and academia. However, these experience reports often leave out essential characteristics of the DT, such as the scope of the system-under-study, the insights and actions enabled, and the time-scale of processing. A lack of these details could therefore hamper both understanding of these DTs and development of DT tools and techniques. Our previous work developed a DT description framework with fourteen characteristics as a checklist for experience report authors to better describe the capabilities of their DT projects. This report provides an extended example of reporting to highlight the utility of this description framework, focusing on the DT of an industrial drilling machine. Furthermore, we provide a mapping from our description framework to the Asset Administration Shell (AAS) which is an emerging standard for Industry 4.0 system integration. This mapping aids practitioners in understanding how our description framework relates to AAS, potentially aiding in description or implementation activities.

Keywords: Digital twins · Digital twinning · Digital twin experience reports · Digital twin framework · Asset administration shell · Industry 4.0

1 Introduction

The *digital twinning* concept is now prevalent in multiple domains and industries [12, 30]. This is due to *digital twins* (DTs) allowing system designers, manufacturers, busi-

---

B. Oakes carried out the majority of this work at the University of Antwerp.
S. Van Mierlo is now employed at EP&C Patent Attorneys, Belgium.
A. Parsai is now employed at Agfa Offset and Inkjet Solutions, Belgium.

L. F. Pires et al. (Eds.): MODELSWARD 2021/2022, CCIS 1708, pp. 1–24, 2023.
https://doi.org/10.1007/978-3-031-38821-7_1

ness stakeholders, and other users to explore possibilities in digital versions of their *system-under-study* (SUS).

For a useful definition of DTs, we point to Madni *et al.*, who state "a DT is a virtual instance of a physical system (twin) that is continually updated with the latter's performance, maintenance, and health status data throughout the physical system's lifecycle" [20]. This is an expanded definition from the original of Grieves *et al.*, who focused on *product life-cycle management* where the DT represented either the pre-manufactured product or the product in usage [10].

These DTs can be at multiple scales, such as monitoring air quality with a few sensors [9], representing individual machines in a factory [24], or monitoring the energy management of an entire district in Helsinki [32]. These DTs can be implemented to reason about the behaviour of a SUS in the past, present, or future in various conditions, allowing for unprecedented exploration of a system's dynamics. For example, usages of DTs can include automatic scheduling of maintenance [41], anomaly detection and prediction, visualisation, and system optimisation [30].

Describing Digital Twins. Our previous work has shown that both academic and industrial experience reports omit crucial information, such as the time-scales or automatic nature of activities [28] This leads to confusion about the capabilities and classification of the DTs.

For example, Kritzinger *et al.* define three categories of DT: *digital model* (DM), *digital shadow* (DS), and *digital twin* (DT). The criteria is whether the communication between the SUS and the DT is manual or automatic. In a *digital model*, data is not automatically sent from a SUS to a DT, and any *actions* from the DT to the SUS are manually performed. A *digital shadow* has an automatic data connection from the SUS to the DT, and a *digital twin* (as defined by Kritzinger *et al.*) has automatic transfer of data and automated commands from the DT to the SUS.

Our earlier paper showed that even this simple classification cannot be determined in some experience reports, leading to uncertainty about the capabilities of the DT solution [28]. The example in our earlier paper is a DT for a "human-robot collaborative work environment" [22], where robot control instructions are generated to prevent collisions between the robot and their human co-worker. However, it is unclear whether any code or instructions are automatically uploaded to the robot when analysis is performed. Thus, it is unclear whether the report describes a *digital shadow* or a *digital twin*.

To address this issue of imprecisions in experience reports, our earlier work suggests fourteen characteristics to describe in experience reports about DTs [28]. This structured approach allows for greater insight and clarity about the capabilities of DTs and their development. In particular, we wish authors to clarify their expectations about the term "digital twin", whether it is real-time control [46], an enhanced tracking simulator [41], or a high-fidelity model [23]. Five experience reports from the literature are presented with these fourteen characteristics, with a further fifteen reports in an online table [26]. Of particular interest is that we found six reports where the classification suggested by our characteristics differs from those of [14] and [8].

Paper Contributions and Structure. In this work, we further expand the presentation and applicability of our earlier paper. In particular, we present a DT of an industrial drilling machine with "smart clamp" suction cups [4] in Sect. 2. The capabilities of this DT is expressed using the characteristics of our description framework [28] in Sect. 3. This assists with the understanding of each characteristic and provides an example of their use in understanding a DT's capabilities. We also add an relevant detail to our list concerning whether a usage of a DT focuses on mainly *historical* information from the past of a SUS, on *streaming/live* information from the present time, or both [27].

To demonstrate the utility of our framework, we map it onto the Asset Administration Shell (AAS) in Sect. 4. The AAS provides standardized techniques to describe digital assets in a hierarchical fashion, but mostly focuses on the lower-level implementation details such as data and functions. In contrast, our framework enables describing high-level capabilities in a less formal, narrative-based fashion. Mapping our framework onto AAS serves two reasons: a) to allow authors who have a DT implemented in AAS to better express the characteristics by our description framework; and b) to offer a high-level starting point for AAS concepts.

Section 5 then concludes and provides directions for future work.

2 Running Example

This section describes the running example for this paper: an industrial drilling machine, augmented with a Digital Twin (DT) to improve drilling performance, monitor tool wear, and provide real-time feedback on the machine's operation. This complex cyber-physical system has been developed as a demonstrator and research platform by Flanders Make[1], the strategic research center for the Flemish manufacturing industry.

First Project Phase: Smart Clamp Drilling. As described by Bey-Temsamani *et al.* [4] the impetus behind the *smart clamp* project was to investigate innovations for improving drilling performance in composite materials which are useful for applications such as aeronautics. When the drill is forced against the plate and when exiting the material, there are significant forces applied to the plate due to the strength of the composite materials and the plate will move (*deflect*). This can ruin the surface coating (lamination) and circularity of the hole which directly affects the ability for plates to be fastened together.

Clamps can be used to secure the plate during drilling, preferably custom clamps designed for each piece to be secured. However, the clamps are time-consuming to construct and attach, and they must be very close (<80 mm) to the drill to properly secure the plate [4]. Therefore, the first improvement developed by Bey-Temsaman *et al.* is a patented *smart clamp* that uses suction cups which compensate in real-time for the drill and plate motion during drilling [7]. To reduce plate deflection during drilling, the suction cups adjust the position of the plate in a real-time control loop as pictured in Fig. 1.

The second innovation in the smart clamp demonstrator is a method for detecting tool wear using an optical one-dimensional sensor. This sensor measures the wear of the drill bit directly by measuring the dimensions of the drill to test against the original bit, allowing for replacement only when necessary to maintain performance. Before the drill

---

[1] https://www.flandersmake.be/en.

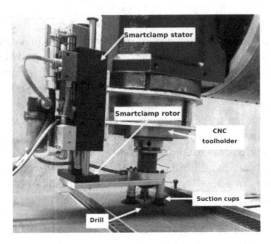

Fig. 1. A labelled photo of the drilling machine with "smart clamp" suction cups to secure the plate during drilling [4].

bit has degraded enough to impact the quality of the hole, the user can decide that a bit change is required. This ensures hole quality while avoiding unnecessary replacement of the drill bit.

Second Project Phase: Reporting on Quality Metrics. Following the initial successes on the smart clamp, other projects at Flanders Make have used the smart clamp as a test-bed platform for further innovations. For example, the smart clamp platform has been extended with an Internet of Things (IoT) architecture to enable the reporting and storage of drill and hole quality metrics.

Specifically, the storage and retrieval of historical data was implemented such that the control algorithm could be improved and further correlations detected. Metrics of the drilling process are processed and sent to a visualisation dashboard for the user. This includes the thickness of the plate, the hole location, a picture of the drilled hole, and the results from a vision algorithm for detecting plate deflection during drilling.

3   Digital Twin Description Framework

This section expands on the description framework from our earlier work [28] which aims to precisely describe digital twins (DTs), their system-under-study (SUS), and the nature of their relation. We focus on presenting DTs as a *constellation* of supporting components to support a *usage* for that DT, with the constellation evolving over time to support further usages. These characteristics encourage authors of experience reports to report the capabilities of their DTs in appropriate details, so that they can be correctly understood and classified.

3.1   Summary of Characteristics

This section summarises the "smart clamp" drilling machine DT discussed in Sect. 2 with the fourteen characteristics we have selected for our description framework, as labelled from *C1* to *C14*. The descriptions here are intentionally brief and further information can be found throughout Sect. 2 and Sect. 3. However, we hope that these brief lines, along with Fig. 2 illustrating the relationships, can allow readers to understand the purpose and utility of the smart clamp DT.

Note that the smart clamp system is actually a *Digital Shadow* by the classification of Kritzinger *et al.* [14]. This is due to the lack of automatic control from the DT on the drilling machine as reported by the *C6: Insights and Actions characteristic*. This lack of automatic control is a deliberate one as it common in industrial requirements to always have the machine operator in the loop. Thus, information is provided to the operator but no automatic actions are directly performed by the DT.

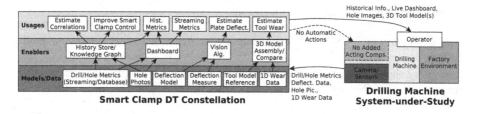

Fig. 2. The smart clamp DT represented in our description framework.

C1: System-Under-Study. - Sect. 3.2.1 - *The scope of the SUS.*
   System: Drilling machine with smart clamps and plates.
   Environment: Surroundings including temp. and humidity.
   Agent: Drilling machine operator.

C2: Acting Components. - Sect. 3.2.2 - *Additions and modifications to the SUS enabling DT actions and insights.*
   Hardware to store and display dashboard metrics.

C3: Sensing Components. - Sect. 3.2.2 - *Additions and modifications to the SUS enabling DT data collection.*
   Camera to capture hole photos, infrastructure to send data to history store and dashboard.

C4: Multiplicities. - Sect. 3.2.3 - *How many DTs and SUS entities are involved in the solution, and their relationship.*
   One drilling machine connected to DT instances for each usage.

C5: Data Transmitted. - Sect. 3.3.1 - *Info. from SUS to DT.*
   Manual: None. *Automatic:* Metrics on motor load, deflection reading, hole metrics and picture, tool dimensions.

C6: Insights/Actions. - Sect. 3.3.1 - *Info./control from DT to SUS.*
   Insights: Drill performance correlations, tool wear, machine/hole metrics.
   Manual Actions: Adjustment of drilling parameters, changing tool bit.
   Automatic Actions: None.

C7: Usages. - Sect. 3.4.1 - *The activities the DT is used for.*

Estimate correlations, improve the smart clamp control, historical and streaming metrics for drill and holes, estimate plate deflection, and estimate tool wear.

C8: Enablers. - Sect. 3.4.2 - *The DT components which use models and data to support usages.*

A historical store (or *knowledge graph*), a dashboard for the operator, vision algorithm, and three-dimensional model comparison.

C9: Models and Data. - Sect. 3.4.3 - *Input/output for enablers.*

Streaming and historical metrics for the drill and holes, photos of the holes, a model for calculating deflection and the incoming measurement, a reference model for the current tool and the incoming tool dimensions.

C10: Constellation. - Sect. 3.4.4 - *Relationships between usages, enablers, models/data.*

Figure 2 shows the constellation of the smart clamp DT, with relationships between components shown by arrows.

C11: Time-scale. - Sect. 3.5.1 - *The time-scale of the data, insights, actions, and simulations used.*

Slower-than-real-time: Find correlations, improve smart clamp control.
Real-time: Dashboard updates to operator, storage in historical store.
Faster-than-real-time: None.

C12: Fidelity Considerations. - Sect. 3.5.2 - *Explanations of fidelity of DT to SUS with respect to each DT usage.*

Moderate demands due to noisy data from manufacturing environment and resolution of sensors. Tool wear reasoning is more tolerant due to gradual decline and compensation for sensor contamination.

C13: Life-cycle Stages. - Sect. 3.5.4 - *Life-cycle stages the DT is utilized for, usages for each, and (if varying) the scope of the SUS.*

Design: Estimate correlations, improve smart clamp control, historical metrics.
Operation: Improve smart clamp control, stream metrics, estimate plate deflection, and estimate tool wear.

C14: Evolution. - Sect. 3.5.5 - *How the DT evolves during development.*

Correlations found, smart clamp built and programmed, deflection and tool wear sensors developed, then dashboard built.

3.2   Relating Digital Twin(s) and System-Under-Study

The relationship between the DT and the SUS is at the core of the DT concept. This is due to the "twinning" of the information of the SUS within the DT, as well as the communication from the DT back to the SUS. In Fig. 3, this relationship is pictured with the DT as a black-box system which is examined further in Sect. 3.4.

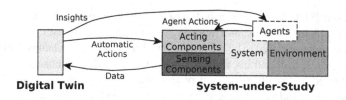

Fig. 3. Digital Twin and the System-Under-Study (replicated from [28]).

3.2.1 C1: System-Under-Study

Within the theory of modelling and simulation, the SUS takes prime importance for a practitioner to reason about [44]. This is due to the critical requirement for a practitioner to understand the bounds, influences, and properties of the SUS. This is a highly non-trivial task to clearly define the boundaries of a system, and an author of an experience report must take care to precisely identify the relevant components of their study.

Our framework takes the SUS to include the primary interacting entities (the *system*), as well as the context (or *environment*) surrounding and interacting with those entities. In the drilling machine example, the actual system is the machine with its software, signals, mechanical components, and the composite plate, while the environment includes the surrounding air pressure, temperature, humidity, ground vibrations, etc.

It is also important to denote the *agents* interacting with the SUS. In Fig. 3, these agents are represented by a dashed extension box, as they may be considered part of the SUS, or an external force acting on the SUS. An example of such an agent would be a human operator who directly manipulates the drilling machine in our running example, or healthcare agents as part of a healthcare system [18]. However, our DT description framework also allows for artificial intelligence (AI) agents to be considered a part of the SUS. This is relevant for other DTs found in the literature such as the AI agents described in [43].

Finally, Fig. 3 conceptually separates the DT and the SUS into two distinct components for understandability. However, in the systems involved there may not be such a clean physical separation. For example, sensing, processing, or acting components required for the operation of the DT may be physically present on or within the SUS. These components can directly influence the system through logical effects (competing for processing/memory/communication resources), or physical effects (temperature, vibration). Therefore, our description framework is only a starting point for an author of an experience report to more precisely define what they believe to be the SUS and what is the DT.

Smart Clamp DT. For the smart clamp example, a crucial question is whether the smart clamp controller is considered part of the underlying drilling system, or part of the DT. For the purposes of this report, the smart clamp functionality focusing on sensing the drilling procedure and controlling of the clamping system is considered part of the drilling machine (the SUS). This decision was made based on the fact that the smart clamp controller does not store any history of the drilling machine, but only reacts based on incoming information. Thus, the part of the smart clamp system which is included in our DT example primarily focuses on the communication to the user, such as dashboards, history storage, and reporting on tool and hole metrics.

The *system* is considered to be the drilling machine with smart clamps. This includes the material plates, drill and bit, drilling forces, the clamping mechanism, clamp controller, drill (CNC) controller and control algorithm. The *environment* for the drilling machine is the surroundings of the drilling machine, including any influence from ambient temperature and vibration. Finally, the *agent* in the SUS is the machine operator, who externally manipulates the SUS but is not otherwise modelled.

3.2.2 C2 and C3: Acting and Sensing Components

As practitioners develop DTs for their SUS, it may become necessary to add or modify components on the SUS to support uni- or bi- directional communication between the DT and the SUS [6,17]. A common example is the addition of Internet of Things (IoT) sensors or communication hardware to transfer data. We propose that understanding this SUS modification process is crucial to reason about the cost and effort for building DTs of a SUS. Thus, we ask that authors report the (interesting) modifications of either *acting* or *sensing* SUS components.

Acting components are those that permit *actions* on the SUS by the DT. That is, actions are received from the DT or by agents, and some state change is effected on the SUS. This may be a physical actuator to operate a switch on the SUS, or a component such as a Programmable Logic Controller able to modify software parameters.

Sensing components are those which collect and transmit information from the SUS to the DT. Typically, these are IoT components, such as a motor load sensor in the smart clamp SUS. Experience report authors may also wish to include larger components such as the addition of a Product Life-cycle Management system and related hardware to store product data in this category [35]. However, these systems and components are more likely part of the DT, outside of the scope of the SUS. Thus, they could be mentioned in a supporting technology discussion, which we do not consider in our list of fourteen characteristics.

The *acting* and *sensing* components described here are left intentionally underspecified for the authors of an experience report to adapt them to their DT example. We encourage authors to answer the following questions with these characteristics, *what was added to the SUS to enable communication with the DT*, and *what was added to the SUS to enable control by the DT*. Answering these questions will allow practitioners and researchers to better understand and categorize the development of DTs.

Smart Clamp DT. For the smart clamp system, nothing was added to the SUS to enable control by the DT, due to no desire for automatic control. For enabling insights, hardware has been added nearby the SUS to display a dashboard to the operator. A multitude of sensing components have been added, however. These include a camera to capture photos of the drilled hole quality, and the infrastructure to communicate this image and other hole metrics back to digital storage and the dashboard.

3.2.3 C4: Multiplicity

An assumption a reader may have while reading a DT experience report is that there is a one-to-one relationship of a DT to a SUS. However, this may not be true. We consider in our description framework that one SUS may be connected to multiple DTs (see Sect. 3.4.4). Each one of these DTs (called a *DT instance*) then handles one particular *usage*, by receiving and/or sending *data, insights*, and *actions* (see Sect. 3.3.1) to and from the SUS.

The SUS itself may also be composed of multiple entities. For example, consider a manufacturing factory with an array of machines. A DT instance could be constructed for each individual machine to receive data from that machine and provide insights and actions for that particular machine. This group of DTs each connected to one particular machine is then termed as a *DT Aggregate* by [10]. An alternative is to construct a DT for the factory itself which receives data for each machine (or statistical measures for the group) and insights or actions are sent for the conceptual collective. The decision about which architecture to implement is based on the system design implemented by the practitioner, as well as any technical restrictions on distributed computing.

It may not be obvious how many DTs are communicating with one particular SUS, and what the organization of entities is within the SUS. Our description framework therefore suggests that an experience report explicitly describe the *multiplicity* of the SUS and the DTs and discuss the pattern of communication within the SUS and to each DT.

Smart Clamp DT. In the running example, there is one solitary drilling machine as the SUS, with one motor, drill, drill bit, and a single plate during each drilling operation. Of course, there are multiple holes drilled during the drilling process. Connected to this one SUS are DT instances (see Sect. 3.4.4) to provide insights on the hole quality, and tool wear. That is, a conceptual DT instance is used for insights on hole quality, and another one for tool wear.

3.3 Information Connection

The backbone of the *digital twinning* activity is the information connection between the SUS and the DT [10], where the circular and continuous flow of information allows the DT to mirror the SUS [42]. As shown in Fig. 3, changes in the SUS are propagated to the DT to be reflected, and actions and insights flow from the DT back towards the SUS.

We also recall here for the reader the useful classification of Kritzinger *et al.* [14], which separates *digital representations* into *digital models, digital shadows*, and *digital twins*. This classification depends on the automatic nature of this connection. That is, a lack of automatic information flow from the SUS towards the digital representation means that it is a *digital model*. If there is no automatic information flow (automatic actions) from the digital representation to the SUS, then the digital representation is a *digital shadow*, also called a *tracking simulator*. It is only with an automatic connection in both directions that the digital representation is denoted as a *digital twin*. Again, the smart clamp DT does not have automatic control on the SUS, thus it is a *digital shadow*.

3.3.1 C5 and C6: Data, Insights, and Actions

One of the most crucial questions to be asked about a DT is *what does it do?*. In our description framework for reporting on DTs, we break this down into three broad categories: *data, insights*, and *actions*. These categories specify what information is passed back and forth between the SUS and the DT, and are extremely useful for understanding their relationship.

Data is specified as any information which flows from the SUS to the DT for processing or storage. As mentioned above, this flow may be manual (for a *digital model*) or automatic (for a *digital shadow/twin*).

Insights are actionable pieces of information travelling from the DT towards the SUS. However, insights do not provoke a change in the SUS directly. Instead, they are transmitted to the agents surrounding the SUS, who may then decide to modify the SUS. Examples in this category include dashboards on the SUS's performance, alerts about unexpected behaviour, or reports indicating a potential for improvement. For instance, Zhuang *et al.* implemented a DT which simulated a factory's geometry and the behaviour of the workers to provide insights on improved layout possibilities [46].

Actions are divided into two categories: *automatic actions* and *agent actions*. *Automatic actions* are those commands transmitted by the DT to the SUS, which directly provoke a change in the SUS. An example of an automatic action is a control signal from the DT to adjust parameters in the SUS [19,24]. In contrast, *agent actions* are the actions which agents can modify the system, either as a physical or digital action. According to the classification of Kritzinger *et al.* [14], there must be *automatic actions* for a digital representation to be classified as a *digital twin*.

Smart Clamp DT. For the smart clamp, a number of metrics need to be communicated as *data* to the DT for displaying to the operator and storage in a historical database. These include a measure of motor load on the drill, a sensor reading to calculate deflection of the plate during drilling, various metrics of the drilled hole, and a picture of the hole. The tool wear also creates a three-dimensional model of the drill bit for inspection by the operator who decides on replacing the bit [4].

A number of insights are provided to the machine operator for their consideration through both a dashboard for *reporting machine metrics and performance*. As discussed in Sect. 3.4.1, this allows for the detecting of correlations defining drill performance and improving of the smart clamp control algorithm. Monitoring of the hole and drill behaviour is also provided through images of the hole and the three-dimensional reconstruction of the drill bit for inspection.

For *agent actions*, the operator may modify or begin operation of the smart clamp drilling machine. Here, we consider only those actions relevant to the information provided by the drilling machine. This includes changing of the drill bit based on the wear information, adjusting the speed of the drill or the motor pressing the drill down, or adjusting of the control algorithm for the smart clamping system.

As mentioned in Sect. 3.1, there are no *automatic actions* performed by the DT on the SUS. This was a conscious design choice to leave the operator in the loop. However, there are no significant technological barriers to automating some of the agent actions described here. An example of such an automation could be the automatic categorization of tool wear, and the adjustment of the drilling speed and force to account for this. This would then complete the automation loop such that the DT directly controls the SUS.

3.4 Digital Twin Layers

In this section, we will break apart the black box presented in Fig. 3 representing the DT. As reported in many experience reports, each DT has multiple *usages*, which are the reasoning activities the DT provides. In our DT description framework, we wish to break these usages apart into modular components and provide an organization such that authors can precisely report the information flow from the SUS, through the DT, and back to the SUS.

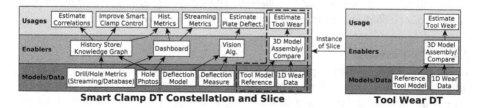

Fig. 4. A layered approach to describe the smart clamp DT, and with a "slice" defining a DT instance.

Thus, we envision three broad layers as pictured horizontally in Fig. 4: a) the *usages* of a DT, b) the *enabling components* which enable that usage of the DT, and c) a catch-all category for the *models and data* used by the enablers. The intention with this layering is that it represents information "flowing upwards" through the DT gaining context and transforming from raw data into actionable insights and actions, as in the *data-information-knowledge-wisdom* hierarchy [31].

Authors of an experience report may of course wish to present a different configuration of their DT. As with other characteristics we define, this representation is coarse to offer a starting point for reporting the characteristics of a DT. These three levels were chosen to emphasize how the DT can be thought of as a collection of modular components, which we define as a *DT constellation*.

3.4.1 C7: Usages

One of the most crucial characteristics to understand about a DT is its *usages*. That is, what activities is the DT involved in, and what direct or indirect benefits are brought to the SUS? For example, the DT may be involved in direct *control and optimisation* of the processes of the SUS. Another usage could be the *visualisation* of the state of the SUS, such as for design purposes, training maintenance workers, or on a dashboard. A third usage could be *anomaly detection* to track the performance of the SUS and raise an error or automatically perform safety actions when the system strays outside of the safe operation range. Interested readers will find further usages in [30] and usages specifically for product design in [35]. In work by Govindasamy *et al.*, these usages are termed the *applications* of the DT [9].

As part of our research into DTs, we have also found an interesting classification of a DT's usage as either *historical* or *streaming/live* [27]. Briefly, a *historical* usage is one that focuses on the past data of a SUS, while the *streaming* or *live* usage is one that focuses on the incoming information from a SUS. A historical usage focuses on the past information available about a SUS, such as the past behaviour or the organization's knowledge. This information is useful for usages such as detecting correlations, improving control algorithms, or referencing design iterations. In contrast, a streaming usage uses the incoming (semi-)real-time data from the SUS to provide insights or actions such as displaying a dashboard or performing command and control.

Smart Clamp DT. The smart clamp DT has a few usages as described in Sect. 2. The historical usages include *estimate correlations, improve the smart clamp control algorithm,* and *provide past drill and hole metrics.* The streaming usages include *monitor of hole metrics (including a picture), detect plate deflection,* and *estimate tool wear.*

3.4.2   C8: Enablers

In our conceptual layered approach visualised in Fig. 4, the *enablers* rest on a layer directly below the usages. This is because the enablers are those components which take in the models and data, and in some way enable a usage. This definition for an enabler is intentionally very broad, as different domains and usages require various types of enablers.

A concrete enabler example is a state predictor and simulator which utilises machine metrics to support a predictive maintenance usage [41]. Another example would be video game engines such as Unity or Godot[2] which can be used to create interactive visualisations, such as for personal health metrics [25] and for training of machine operation [13].

Smart Clamp DT. A number of the smart clamp usages require the storage of historical information. This then indicates the presence of a *history store* or *knowledge graph* enabler storing the past metrics of the drill and the drilled holes [16]. Other enablers include a *dashboard* for reporting metrics, a *vision algorithm* for detecting plate deflection from camera input, and a *tool wear estimator* to transform the one-dimensional tool dimensions into a full three-dimensional model [4].

3.4.3   C9: Models and Data

Finally, the lowest layer of Fig. 4 groups together a broad category of *models and data.* This is a catch-all category for the authors of an experience report to explain which models and data are used by the DT and in particular the information flow from the SUS towards the enablers in the DT. In complex DTs, this layer may indeed be separated into different categories, such as models and data that exist in the cloud versus local storage. The relationships between the models and data layer and the enabler layer may also be bi-directional. An example is a machine learning trainer (as an enabler) which takes input data to then produce a neural net (as a model) [24].

Smart Clamp DT. The data for the smart clamp example includes everything specified in Sect. 3.3.1, such as drill and hole metrics, a measure of plate deflection, and a picture of the hole itself. The database for previous drill and hole metrics would also exist on this layer. Then, models required include a model for the vision algorithm to determine plate deflection, and tool bit reference model(s) to determine tool wear.

---

[2] https://unity.com, https://godotengine.org/.

3.4.4 C10: Constellations and Slices

One of the most powerful aspects of DTs is that they can perform various types of reasoning about the SUS, and that DTs grow over time to support further usages as they gain enablers, models, and data [38]. In our description framework, we wish to emphasize this notion of a growing DT by defining a *DT constellation* as an agglomeration of related usages, enablers, models, and data for a particular SUS. This is represented visually in Fig. 4 on the left-hand side, which contains multiple usages, enablers, and models/data components for the smart clamp running example.

In our view of DTs as a constellation, a myriad of connections exist between usages, enablers, models and data. That is, one usage may be supported by multiple enablers, or an enabler could use multiple models. In figures such as Fig. 4, information flowing between DT components is represented with arrows. For example, usages *Historical Metrics* and *Streaming Metrics* are supported by the enabler *Dashboard*, which takes *Streaming/Database of Drill Hole Metrics* and *Hole Photos* as input.

A DT *slice* is then a selection of components out of a DT constellation to support a particular usage. Figure 4 shows one out of a possible six slices as represented by the dashed lines around the components which support usage *Estimate Tool Wear*. This slice can then be implemented by any number of *DT instances*, as represented in the right-hand side of Fig. 4. These slices therefore reinforce the modular and evolving nature of DTs, where the enablers and models and data are reused for multiple usages within a DT constellation and across DT projects.

Note that this representation of DT constellations and slices are conceptual objects purely for descriptive purposes. They likely are not implemented in exactly that architecture in a practitioner's DT. However, this notion of "slicing" out a DT instance supporting one usage assists in scoping the description of that usage's characteristics, such as insights and actions, time-scale, etc. This granularity thus allows researchers and practitioners to better understand the considerations for each DT usage.

Smart Clamp DT. On the left-hand side Fig. 4, we have reconstructed an explanatory DT constellation for the smart clamp. Across the top are the six usages described earlier, supported by the enablers and models/data described previously.

On the right-hand side of Fig. 4, we have sliced out the DT instance representing the *Estimate Tool Wear* usage. This DT instance would then be receiving the *one-dimensional tool wear* data, and return the insights consisting of the *3D tool model comparison* to the reference model.

3.5 Time-scale and Fidelity Characteristics

This section discusses important characteristics of the DT/SUS relationship: the *time-scales* involved and any *fidelity considerations*.

3.5.1 C11: Time-scales

The components of a DT are likely processing at different *time-scales*. As in, data acquisition, insights, and actions can all be transmitted as *slower-than-real-time* or *real-time* speeds. Enablers and the usages themselves could be considered as reasoning at *slower-than-real-time*, *real-time*, or even *faster-than-real-time* (predictive) speeds. These broad categories provide authors with the language to describe how fast their DT components are transmitting or processing.

A *slower-than-real-time* scale is where communication between the SUS and the DT does not correspond to a "live" connection. That is, the DT periodically receives its data from the SUS, or issues insights or actions for some future time. Werner *et al.* [41] provide an example for this case where data from a sensor is obtained in real-time, but the predictive maintenance insights modify worker schedules at a later time. This time-scale may also be relevant for *historical* usages as described in Sect. 3.4.1. These usages look at the SUS's past behaviour, as compared to the *streaming* or "real-time" usages.

In a *real-time* time-scale, data acquisition or insight/action communication is performed in a highly reactive manner, often within sub-second time differences. The intention with this time-scale category is to indicate the communication and processing which is happening in the DT/SUS relationship in a "live" manner, whether it is "soft" or "hard" real-time. An example of the *real-time* time-scale is where the DT is directly controlling the SUS, such as real-time feedback and control in a production plant [46]. In such a scenario, data is gathered from the SUS, processed within the DT, and insights/actions are issued within a short amount of time, which we have referred to in earlier work as a *streaming* DT [27].

Finally, DTs may employ predictive simulation to optimize the behaviour of the SUS in the (near-)future. Thus we define the time-scale of *faster-than-real-time*, where enablers for a usage may predict the future trajectories of the SUS. These predictions enable either (slower-than-real-time) insights or actions like workstation layout modifications [22], or real-time control actions like crane trajectory optimisations [45].

As reported in our earlier work [28], DTs commonly involve communication and processing components at all three time-scales. The intention of introducing this characteristic is to break down how each component in the DT relates to the SUS. In particular, some domain practitioners may have the belief that "true" DTs are only for "hard real-time" control usages. That is, where the DT immediately reacts to the SUS and modifies its behaviour for optimization. Our list of characteristics is therefore designed to provide guidance for authors to discuss their visions in their experience reports. Hopefully, future research can then illustrate what the term "digital twin" means for each practitioner domain.

Smart Clamp DT. Most components in the smart clamp running example are soft *real-time*. That is, when the drilling machine is operating, data is stored (either locally or in the cloud) and the operator sees an updated dashboard within a second or two. The exceptions to this are the usages which rely on the historical store (see Fig. 4), as finding behaviour correlations in the data and improving the smart clamp control algorithm rely on the historical data and can only be performed periodically. Therefore, these usages and components are *slower-than-real-time*.

3.5.2   C12: Fidelity Considerations

Worden *et al.* discuss a DT as a "mirror" of a SUS [42] such that the DT reflects the true state and behaviour of the SUS. That is, the *fidelity* between the DT and the SUS cannot be summarized as "high" or "low", but instead depends on the *properties of interest* and can involve trade-offs. For example, Zhidchenko *et al.* developed a DT with a simplified model to predict (in real-time) the trajectory of a mobile crane [45]. In this case the performance characteristics of the model had to be balanced against the approximation of the complex crane behaviour.

Therefore in our DT description framework we specify that authors should discuss any interesting trade-offs with respect to the fidelity of their DTs as it relates to each usage of the DT. For example, a DT usage may be visualisation for training purposes, where only coarse visual attributes such as geometry and appearance of machines are required, instead of specific details such as the surface temperature. We thus emphasize here that *fidelity* refers to the DT adequately reflecting the state and behaviour of the SUS for properties relevant to each of the DTs usage. Of course, the requirements and modelling of these properties must be defined by the practitioner for their system using established modelling and engineering principles [37,44].

The addition of this *fidelity* characteristic to our description framework is intended to steer practitioners away from defining a complex model as *high-fidelity* and therefore a "digital twin" of the SUS. First, what may be meant by these practitioners is that they have a *digital model* as classified by Kritzinger *et al.* [14]. Second, it is only with respect to certain properties that a model can represent a SUS, as not every detail of a SUS can be reflected perfectly. Therefore, those properties of interest should be explicitly stated when a "digital twin" is created.

Smart Clamp DT. The smart clamp running example contains usages with moderate demands on fidelity. As with any manufacturing system, noise exists in the values coming from sensors. This means that the drill and hole metric values stored as history and reported on the dashboard are accurate only within some bounds. The tool wear usage is more tolerant to low fidelity insights, as tool usage degrades naturally with wear and compensation can be made for debris or containments on the monitoring system [4].

3.5.3 Digital Twin and System-Under-Study Development

These final characteristics discuss the *life-cycle* of the SUS that the DT reasons about, and how the DT *evolves* over the course of the project.

3.5.4 C13: Life-Cycle Stages

A SUS may have many *life-cycle stages* over its existence, which may be labelled by domain-specific terms depending on whether the SUS is a manufactured product or not. For example, stages may include *design*, *pre-production*, and *production* [34], or *ideation*, *realisation*, and *utilisation* [15]. Another emerging stage is reasoning about a product's *reclamation* to ease disassembly and material re-use as part of "reverse logistics" [29].

During each of these life-cycle stages, the SUS may change scope and the DTs interacting with that SUS may offer different usages. For example, during the *design* stage, a DT (acting as a *digital model*) may offer usages for visualising and optimising a product [36]. During the *production* stage, the usages may involve each manufactured product in the manufacturing plant, such as optimising worker routines or machine settings to minimise product defects [34]. This could be considered an expanded SUS, or an entirely new SUS as the author prefers.

Our list of characteristics thus suggests that an author explicitly detail two aspects of their DT: a) the usages of the DT for each life-cycle stage of the SUS, and b) if the scope or structure of the SUS changes significantly throughout the stages. This assists both researchers and practitioners in understanding how the components of DTs can be utilised and re-used for each life-cycle stage. For example, enablers focusing on logistics solutions may be useful for both assembly and disassembly usages for a product.

Smart Clamp DT. For the smart clamp running example, we define two life-cycle stages: *design* and *operation*.

In the *design* stage, the smart clamps are built and set-up. For this, the *estimate correlations* usage provides the data to build and calibrate the smart clamp control algorithm. The *improve smart clamp control* and *historical metrics* usages are also included here, as successive versions of the smart clamp will rely on these usages to develop improved versions.

Throughout the *operation* of the smart clamp drilling system, the other usages provide information to the operator. Again, the *improve smart clamp control* usage could be utilised as the operator makes changes to the control algorithm. However, in the second-to-second operation of the drill, the other usages are more relevant: *stream metrics*, *estimate plate deflection*, and *estimate tool wear*. These are the usages that the operator relies on to control the drilling process.

3.5.5   C14: Evolution

The final characteristic of our list is the *evolution* of the DT throughout its development. That is, as the DT is built, connected to the SUS, and iterated upon, practitioners will encounter challenges and new requirements for the DT. As new technologies and tools are brought online to support these further usages, the DT constellation (Sect. 3.4.4) will expand to reason about more life-cycle stages or the next version of the product. For example, Soederberg *et al.* report seven usages of the DT across three phases of the product life-cycle[34], but do not list the order in which these usages were built.

Thus the *evolution* characteristic of DTs is about providing a narrative about the development of the DT as it grows and is modified throughout its development. This serves two purposes: a) connecting the usages of the DT together into a consistent story to explain the growth of the DT and the value it provides, and b) enabling further classification and research insights into this development process.

For example, it would be interesting to discover in which cases the DT project begins as a *digital model* [14] in a design stage, and passes through a *digital shadow* stage before becoming a *digital twin*. Another research question is how to organize the implementation of the DT components for a product's design-stage in parallel with the components for the product's pre-production and production stages. Finally, a third research direction is how to transfer DT components between iterations of the same product versus another product in the same family.

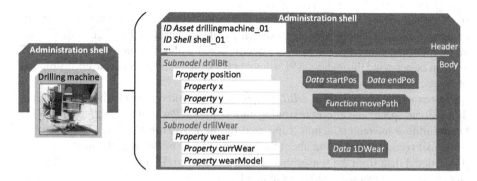

Fig. 5. AAS of the drilling machine example. (Adapted from [2].)

Smart Clamp DT. A short narrative of the development of the smart clamp and the accompanying DT has been provided in Sect. 2. Briefly, data from the drilling machine was studied for correlations to build the smart clamp device, controlled using an algorithm built with historical data. Then, a sensor was created to detect the deflection of the plate during drilling, as well as a process for measuring the wear of the tool bit. Finally, the dashboard aspect of the project was conducted to show the operator the real-time metrics of the drilling machine.

4   Mapping to the Asset Administration Shell

Systems subject to digital twinning are used in increasingly complex architectures, often scaling across companies, designed to allow rich semantic information to flow and to be reasoned about [11]. Such systems encompass physical components, processes, materials, software, and other *assets* that represent value to the organization [2]. With this increased complexity, implementing the digital twin (DT) of the system becomes a significant challenge. To alleviate this issue, the Asset Administration Shell (AAS) has been developed by the German Electrical and Electronic Manufacturers' Association[3] for the standardized digital representation of assets of the Reference Architecture Model Industrie 4.0 (RAMI4.0) [1]. The AAS provides a machine-readable, device-independent, hierarchical standard language (metamodel) for describing the properties of assets [3]. However, the AAS standard does not provide the means to describe the high-level capabilities of the DT. Here, we show how the AAS can be combined with our DT description framework by providing a mapping between AAS and our framework characteristics.

4.1   Structure of the AAS

Figure 5 shows the (partial) structure of a possible AAS for the smart clamp drilling machine running example. The *Header* contains identifying information about the assets and the shell itself. The *Body* is organized into *submodels* describing the asset

---

[3] https://www.zvei.org.

from various views. Submodels contain a hierarchy of *Properties* that are used for calculating *Data*, and supporting *Functions* which allow control of the asset. During operation, real-time data from the asset is directly stored within the submodels of the AAS and can be accessed through its API, allowing for structured and reusable encapsulation of assets.

For example, the submodel *drillBit* captures the position of the drilling bit in a three-dimensional space; and allows reasoning about the *startPosition* and *endPosition* of the head during a movement action, supported by the *movePath* function. The *drillWear* submodel records information about the wearing of this bit, such as the incoming one-dimensional data from the sensor that is stored in the *currWear* property as well as the stored three-dimensional reference model [4].

4.2   Mapping Characteristics onto the AAS

Table 1 shows how the characteristics of our DT description framework are supported (or not) by the AAS. Four out of the fourteen characteristics are explicitly supported by the AAS. That is, the AAS provides means to express and reason about these characteristics. Four characteristics are partially supported. Four characteristics are implicitly supported, i.e., while the structure of AAS would allow for reasoning about the characteristic, no means are provided to do so. Finally, two characteristics are not supported.

Table 1. Support for the characteristics by the AAS.

Characteristic	Support by the AAS
C01. System-under-study	●
C04. Multiplicities	●
C09. Models and Data	●
C10. Constellation	●
C05. Data Communicated	◖
C06. Insights and Actions	◖
C13. Life-cycle Stages	◖
C14. Evolution	◖
C02. Acting Components	◑
C03. Sensing Components	◑
C07. Usages	◑
C08. Enablers	◑
C11. Time-Scale	○
C12. Fidelity Considerations	○

● Explicit support   ◖ Partial support   ◑ Implicit   ○ No support

4.2.1 Explicitly Supported Characteristics

C1. System-Under-Study and C4. Multiplicities. Practitioners can use AAS to explicitly document and scope the asset, e.g., adding text documents or representing relationships between assets and other entities. A complex asset can also be composed of other assets to explicitly represent the System-under-Study (SUS) in a hierarchical manner. For multiplicities, an AAS maps to exactly one asset, but with a complex asset the SUS can be split into multiple entities.

C9. Models and Data. Models and data themselves are represented or stored within submodels in AAS. These can be modified by incoming information from the SUS, through the AAS API, or through the functions defined on each submodel.

C10. Constellation. In the AAS framework, the notion of slices where models and data flow into enablers and then usages is addressed in two ways. The first is the explicit *References* between submodels and their properties. Second, *Views* can provide a projection of an asset, such as showing only those AAS components relevant to a safety engineer. Above the AAS framework, slices may also be represented as the workflows in the *business layer* of the RAMI 4.0 operating on the AAS components.

4.2.2 Partially Supported Characteristics

C5. Data Communicated. As mentioned, AAS employs OPC-UA for communication between assets and from the physical device. However, a high-level view of what the data represents is only partially provided by typing and descriptions of the data fields. Note that AAS also specifies that multiple formats (XML, JSON, etc.) can be serialised from the AAS.

C6. Insights and Actions. The AAS framework does not define the high-level insights and actions available from an asset. Instead, it mainly specifies an API to be queried by an application. For example, Iñigo *et al.* build a visualisation dashboard upon the data provided by their AAS of a robotic arm [11]. However, low-level *Events* can be defined for an AAS or a submodel, representing a change of state, such as value changes.

C13. Life-Cycle Stages. In the RAMI 4.0, life-cycles are broken into four stages: *asset type development*, *asset type usage/maintenance*, *asset instance production*, and *asset instance usage/maintenance*. Relationships between these kinds of assets offers traceability in production and across product versions. However, the notion of usages of the DT is not explicitly connected to these life-cycle stages.

C14. Evolution. Evolution of assets is performed at a low-level as asset components are versioned, and there exists a *derivedFrom* relationship between AASes. This allows for tracking changes in the structure of assets. However, this does not offer the high-level narrative of the DT project as provided in Sect. 2 for the smart clamp DT.

4.2.3   Implicit Characteristics

C2. Acting Components and C3. Sensing Components. In AAS, the acting and sensing components for an asset will be modelled as submodels. Communication with the physical devices is then performed using OPC-UA[4]. However, these components are not explicitly marked and AAS does not specify whether the components were added or modified for the operation of the DT.

C7. Usages. AAS provides a mechanism for defining the *capabilities* of assets [2]. This could be interpreted to provide a tagging system for usages denoting what reasoning an asset can provide. Alternatively, Iñigo *et al.* define a *Condition Monitoring* submodel for their robot arm providing relevant data for visualisation [11].

C8. Enablers. Submodels provide *operations* to provide semantics. These submodels can then represent enablers taking in models and data, and providing values to the usage submodels.

4.2.4   Not Supported Characteristics

C11. Time-scale. The notion of *slower-than-real-time*, *real-time*, or *faster-than-real-time* is not considered in the AAS framework. Some aspects of time-scale may be handled by the OPC-UA communication layer.

C12. Fidelity Considerations. The precision of data values or submodels does not seem to be considered in the AAS framework.

4.3   Discussion

The similarity between the structures of the AAS and our framework results in a considerable overlap in concerns. However, our framework is intended for explaining the structure and capabilities of DT in a narrative-based and rather informal way. In contrast, the structure of the AAS is explicitly defined such that technical implementations can be built for communication and control between assets. For example, our list of characteristics does not explicitly touch on technical details such as communication protocols or access control. While these are certainly crucial for DT, we leave it up to each practitioner whether to describe such mechanisms in their reports. Due to the formal nature of the AAS, however, extending it to domains other than production and manufacturing, such as natural environment [5], might be difficult. As demonstrated in our previous work [28], our DT description framework can be applied across multiple domains.

Characteristics such as *time-scale* and *fidelity considerations* are also not explicitly represented in the AAS framework, while it may be relevant to include these explicitly within a implementation framework such as AAS. Much like extensions to ontologically reason about capabilities of assets [2] and combining AAS with cyber-physical

---

[4] https://opcfoundation.org/about/opc-technologies/opc-ua/.

systems (CPS) [21], perhaps these other characteristics can be added through an extension to the AAS framework. The explicit notion of properties in the AAS, along with the formulaic qualifiers aligns well with the notion of *validity frames* for models, ensuring that models are used within their range of validity [39]. This improves integration efforts and can aid in selection of appropriate models for a task [40].

5 Conclusion

Understanding and classifying the Digital Twins (DT) described in experience reports of practitioners is essential to furthering DT research. In particular, readers should be able to easily understand the essential characteristics and capabilities of the DT at hand. The framework presented in this paper aims to improve reporting practices on DTs by defining fourteen complementary characteristics. As an example of DT description guided by these characteristics, we describe the "smart clamp" drilling machine DT from Sect. 2 throughout Sect. 3. This example shows the utility of our description framework to provide clarity on both the capabilities and structure of the drilling machine DT.

Our previous report has shown that the characteristics of our description framework are relatively domain-agnostic [28]. We hope that this assists researchers and practitioners in mapping, analysing, and comparing digital twinning practices of distant domains that would otherwise not be comparable. This DT description framework can therefore lower the barrier for knowledge- and technology- transfer across domains and aid in DT research and utilisation.

Current standardization efforts such as the Asset Administration Shell (AAS) focus on representing digital assets at technical, implementation-based level. Our DT description framework is complementary to such approaches, as it focuses on the high level capabilities of digital assets. To assess the feasibility of future integration between the two approaches, we have provided a mapping to AAS which shows a substantial overlap in structure despite the differing level of abstraction.

Future work will focus on deep integration of our framework with AAS and other frameworks, such as the Reference Architectural Model Industrie 4.0 (RAMI4.0) [1], or that of [21]. Such integrated approaches are sought after in advanced engineering settings, such as the Digital Thread [33], e.g., for the automated extraction of a textual or visual description of the DT based on the AAS implementation, and suggesting AAS implementations based on an informal description.

Acknowledgements. This research was supported by Flanders Make, the strategic research centre for the manufacturing industry, and was partially funded by the DTDesign ICON (Flanders Innovation & Entrepreneurship FM/ICON :: HBC.2019.0079) project.

References

1. Adolphs, P., Bedenbender, H., et al.: Reference Architecture Model Industrie 4.0 (RAMI4.0). ZVEI and VDI, Status report (2015)
2. Bayha, A., Bock, J., et al.: Describing capabilities of Industrie 4.0 components. German Electrical and Electronics Manufacturers Association, Frankfurt am Main, Germany (2020)

3. Bedenbender, H., Billmann, M., et al.: Examples of the Asset Administration Shell for Industrie 4.0 components-basic part. ZVEI white paper (2017)
4. Bey-Temsamani, A., Ooijevaar, T., Depraetere, B.: An assessment of two technologies for high performance composite machining; adaptive fixturing and in process tool profile monitoring. Procedia CIRP **85**, 201–206 (2019)
5. Blair, G.S.: Digital twins of the natural environment. Patterns **2**(10), 100359 (2021)
6. Chhetri, S.R., Faezi, S., et al.: QUILT: quality inference from living digital twins in IoT-enabled manufacturing systems. In: Proceedings of International Conference on Internet of Things Design and Implementation, pp. 237–248. ACM, April 2019. https://doi.org/10.1145/3302505.3310085
7. Flanders Make: Smart clamping mechanism. Patent application 2020554, Octrooicentrum Nederland, March 2018
8. Fuller, A., Fan, Z., et al.: Digital twin: enabling technologies, challenges and open research. IEEE Access **8**, 108952–108971 (2020)
9. Govindasamy, H.S., Ramya, J., et al.: Air quality management: an exemplar for model-driven digital twin engineering. In: First International Workshop on Model-Driven Engineering for Digital Twins, ModDiT 2021 co-located with MODELS 2021 (2021)
10. Grieves, M., Vickers, J.: Digital twin: mitigating unpredictable, undesirable emergent behavior in complex systems. In: Kahlen, F.-J., Flumerfelt, S., Alves, A. (eds.) Transdisciplinary Perspectives on Complex Systems, pp. 85–113. Springer, Cham (2017). https://doi.org/10.1007/978-3-319-38756-7_4
11. Iñigo, M.A., Porto, A., et al.: Towards an Asset Administration Shell scenario: a use case for interoperability and standardization in Industry 4.0. In: NOMS 2020–2020 IEEE/IFIP Network Operations and Management Symposium, pp. 1–6. IEEE (2020)
12. Jones, D., Snider, C., et al.: Characterising the digital twin: a systematic literature review. CIRP J. Manuf. Sci. Technol. **29**, 36–52 (2020). https://doi.org/10.1016/j.cirpj.2020.02.002
13. Karadeniz, A.M., Arif, I., et al.: Digital twin of eGastronomic things: a case study for ice cream machines. In: IEEE International Symposium on Circuits and Systems, pp. 1–4, May 2019. https://doi.org/10.1109/iscas.2019.8702679
14. Kritzinger, W., Karner, M., et al.: Digital twin in manufacturing: a categorical literature review and classification. IFAC-PapersOnLine **51**(11), 1016–1022 (2018). https://doi.org/10.1016/j.ifacol.2018.08.474
15. Leinen, R.: Driving the digital enterprise in product development and manufacturing. In: Presented at 6th CSIR conference, October 2017
16. Lietaert, P., Meyers, B., Van Noten, J., Sips, J., Gadeyne, K.: Knowledge graphs in digital twins for AI in production. In: Dolgui, A., Bernard, A., Lemoine, D., von Cieminski, G., Romero, D. (eds.) APMS 2021. IAICT, vol. 630, pp. 249–257. Springer, Cham (2021). https://doi.org/10.1007/978-3-030-85874-2_26
17. Lindström, J., Larsson, H., et al.: Towards intelligent and sustainable production: combining and integrating online predictive maintenance and continuous quality control. Procedia CIRP **63**, 443–448 (2017). https://doi.org/10.1016/j.procir.2017.03.099
18. Liu, Y., Zhang, L., et al.: A novel cloud-based framework for the elderly healthcare services using digital twin. IEEE Access **7**, 49088–49101 (2019). https://doi.org/10.1109/access.2019.2909828
19. Ludvigsen, K.B., Jamt, L.K., et al.: Digital twins for design, testing and verification throughout a vessel's life cycle. In: Proceedings 15th International Conference on Computer and IT Applications in the Maritime Industries, pp. 448–456 (2016). http://data.hiper-conf.info/compit2016_lecce.pdf
20. Madni, A.M., Madni, C.C., Lucero, S.D.: Leveraging digital twin technology in model-based systems engineering. Systems **7**(1), 7 (2019). https://doi.org/10.3390/systems7010007

21. Malakuti, S., Juhlin, P., et al.: An architecture and information meta-model for back-end data access via digital twins. In: IEEE 26th International Conference on Emerging Technologies and Factory Automation, September 2021
22. Malik, A.A., Bilberg, A.: Digital twins of human robot collaboration in a production setting. Procedia Manuf. **17**, 278–285 (2018). https://doi.org/10.1016/j.promfg.2018.10.047
23. Miller, A.M., Alvarez, R., Hartman, N.: Towards an extended model-based definition for the digital twin. Comput.-Aided Des. Appl. **15**(6), 880–891 (2018). https://doi.org/10.1080/16864360.2018.1462569
24. Min, Q., Lu, Y., et al.: Machine learning based digital twin framework for production optimization in petrochemical industry. Int. J. Inf. Manage. **49**, 502–519 (2019)
25. Mohammadi, N., Taylor, J.: Knowledge discovery in smart city digital twins. In: Proceedings of the 53rd Hawaii International Conference on System Sciences, pp. 1656–1664 (2020). https://doi.org/10.24251/hicss.2020.204
26. Oakes, B., Parsai, A., et al.: Digital Twin experience report analysis (2020). https://msdl.uantwerpen.be/git/bentley/2020.MODELSWARD.DT
27. Oakes, B.J., Meyers, B., et al.: Structuring and accessing knowledge for historical and streaming digital twins. In: Proceedings First Workshop on Ontology-Driven Conceptual Modeling of Digital Twins (2021)
28. Oakes, B.J., Parsai., A., et al.: Improving digital twin experience reports. In: Proceedings of the 9th International Conference on Model-Driven Engineering and Software Development - Volume 1: MODELSWARD, pp. 179–190. INSTICC, SciTePress (2021). https://doi.org/10.5220/0010236101790190
29. Pokharel, S., Mutha, A.: Perspectives in reverse logistics: a review. Resour. Conserv. Recycl. **53**(4), 175–182 (2009). https://doi.org/10.1016/j.resconrec.2008.11.006
30. Rasheed, A., San, O., Kvamsdal, T.: Digital twin: values, challenges and enablers from a modeling perspective. IEEE Access **8**, 21980–22012 (2020). https://doi.org/10.1109/access.2020.2970143
31. Rowley, J.: The wisdom hierarchy: representations of the DIKW hierarchy. J. Inf. Sci. **33**(2), 163–180 (2007)
32. Ruohomäki, T., Airaksinen, E., et al.: Smart city platform enabling digital twin. In: 2018 International Conference on Intelligent Systems (IS), pp. 155–161. IEEE, September 2018. https://doi.org/10.1109/is.2018.8710517
33. Singh, V., Willcox, K.E.: Engineering design with digital thread. AIAA J. **56**(11), 4515–4528 (2018)
34. Söderberg, R., Wärmefjord, K., et al.: Toward a digital twin for real-time geometry assurance in individualized production. CIRP Ann. **66**(1), 137–140 (2017). https://doi.org/10.1016/j.cirp.2017.04.038
35. Tao, F., Cheng, J., et al.: Digital twin-driven product design, manufacturing and service with big data. Int. J. Adv. Manuf. Technol. **94**(9–12), 3563–3576 (2018). https://doi.org/10.1007/s00170-017-0233-1
36. Tao, F., Sui, F., et al.: Digital twin-driven product design framework. Int. J. Prod. Res. **57**(12), 3935–3953 (2019). https://doi.org/10.1080/00207543.2018.1443229
37. Traoré, M.K., Muzy, A.: Capturing the dual relationship between simulation models and their context. Simul. Model. Pract. Theory **14**(2), 126–142 (2006). https://doi.org/10.1016/j.simpat.2005.03.002
38. Uhlemann, T.H.J., Lehmann, C., Steinhilper, R.: The digital twin: realizing the cyber-physical production system for Industry 4.0. Procedia CIRP **61**, 335–340 (2017). https://doi.org/10.1016/j.procir.2016.11.152
39. Van Acker, B., Mertens, J., De Meulenaere, P., Denil, J.: Validity frame supported digital twin design of complex cyber-physical systems. In: 2021 Annual Modeling and Simulation Conference (ANNSIM), pp. 1–12. IEEE (2021)

40. Van Mierlo, S., Oakes, B.J., Van Acker, B., Eslampanah, R., Denil, J., Vangheluwe, H.: Exploring validity frames in practice. In: Babur, Ö., Denil, J., Vogel-Heuser, B. (eds.) ICSMM 2020. CCIS, vol. 1262, pp. 131–148. Springer, Cham (2020). https://doi.org/10.1007/978-3-030-58167-1_10

41. Werner, A., Zimmermann, N., Lentes, J.: Approach for a holistic predictive maintenance strategy by incorporating a digital twin. Procedia Manuf. **39**, 1743–1751 (2019). https://doi.org/10.1016/j.promfg.2020.01.265

42. Worden, K., Cross, E.J., Gardner, P., Barthorpe, R.J., Wagg, D.J.: On digital twins, mirrors and virtualisations. In: Barthorpe, R. (ed.) Model Validation and Uncertainty Quantification, Volume 3. CPSEMS, pp. 285–295. Springer, Cham (2020). https://doi.org/10.1007/978-3-030-12075-7_34

43. Wuest, T., Hribernik, K., Thoben, K.D.: Accessing servitisation potential of PLM data by applying the product avatar concept. Prod. Plann. Control **26**(14–15), 1198–1218 (2015). https://doi.org/10.1080/09537287.2015.1033494

44. Zeigler, B.P., Kim, T.G., Praehofer, H.: Theory of modeling and simulation: integrating discrete event and continuous complex dynamic systems. Academic press, San Diego (2000). https://www.elsevier.com/books/theory-of-modeling-and-simulation/zeigler/978-0-08-051909-8

45. Zhidchenko, V., Malysheva, I., et al.: Faster than real-time simulation of mobile crane dynamics using digital twin concept. J. Phys. Conf. Ser. **1096**, 012071 (2018). https://doi.org/10.1088/1742-6596/1096/1/012071

46. Zhuang, C., Liu, J., Xiong, H.: Digital twin-based smart production management and control framework for the complex product assembly shop-floor. Int. J. Adv. Manuf. Technol. **96**(1–4), 1149–1163 (2018). https://doi.org/10.1007/s00170-018-1617-6

Acknowledging Implementation Trade-Offs When Developing with Units of Measurement

Steve McKeever$^{(\boxtimes)}$ ⓘ

Department of Informatics and Media, Uppsala University, Uppsala, Sweden
`steve.mckeever@im.uu.se`

Abstract. Physical quantities expressed as units of measurement (UoM) are used regularly in scientific and engineering applications. The loss of the Mars climate orbiter, attributed to a confusion between the metric and imperial unit systems, popularised the disastrous consequences of incorrectly handling measurement values. We aim to classify the many solutions that have been proposed by looking at their capabilities and computational overheads. We assume an overall view, starting with a quantity aware Software Model, and then looking at the various approaches which allow these annotations to be transferred into code. Through a formal definition of both dimension checking and UoM conversion we are able to categorise the various options with regards to the stage at which they can be undertaken, their useability, and their coverage of potential errors.

Keywords: Dimension checking · Unit of measurement conversion · Quantity pattern · Libraries · Component based checking · Testing

1 Introduction

Engineering applications manipulate values that represent physical quantities. Popular programming languages allow developers to describe numeric expressions that need to be evaluated but not how to detect inappropriate actions on quantities. Notorious examples such as the Mars Climate Orbiter [52] or the Gimli Glider incident [55] substantiate this. With ubiquitous digitalisation and greater automated decision making, the need to ensure robustness with regards to the manipulation of quantities in physical systems is ever increasing. There are a multitude of verification and validation techniques that allow the designer or programmer to perform some kind of quantity checking, either at compile-time or run-time. Not only is there a lack of awareness of these solutions but it is not always clear which approach is appropriate for a given problem. This means that implementers often reinvent existing solutions or forgo any kind of checking.

Extending conventional programming languages with UoM checking goes back to the 1970s [29] and early 80s with proposals to extend Fortran [19] and then Pascal [14]. These efforts were mostly syntax based and required extensions to the underlying language, along with dedicated compilers. The net effect was to reduce backwards compatibility and thus uptake. The 80s saw the adoption of more modular and generic programming language features. Hilfinger [24] demonstrated how to exploit Ada's abstraction facilities, namely operator overloading and type parametrization, to assign attributes for UoM to variables and values. The arrival of object oriented programming languages

ⓒ Springer Nature Switzerland AG 2023
L. F. Pires et al. (Eds.): MODELSWARD 2021/2022, CCIS 1708, pp. 25–47, 2023.
https://doi.org/10.1007/978-3-031-38821-7_2

allowed developers to implement UoM either through a class hierarchy of units and their derived forms, or through the Quantity pattern [17]. There are a large number of libraries for all popular object oriented programming languages that support this approach [39].

It is not uncommon for software development to begin with a less detailed form than a programming language through diagrams and rules that focus on the conceptual model that is to be implemented. By extending the Unified Modeling Language (UML), quantities can be introduced into an object-oriented modeling platform. Unit checking and conversion can be undertaken before code is generated, either through a compilation workflow that leverages Object Constraint Language (OCL) expressions [35] or staged computation [2]. The Event-B modelling language [20] provides UoM and leverages the Rodin theorem prover to detect inconsistencies before compiling to Java. Similar ideas have been presented for the formal specification language Z [23] and Maude [10]. More specialized UML based systems modeling languages such as MARTE[1] and SysML[2] also have UoM support [8]. All of these abstractions lift the definition of quantities into Software Models. Once the code has been generated however, UoM information might very well be lost unless the workflow has been tailored explicitly. This is the research question that we address, namely *what is the most appropriate approach to transferring UoM information into software.* We consider aspects such as ease of use, execution speed, numeric accuracy, ease of integration and coverage of unit error detection capabilities. These aspects reflect our study of UoM libraries, survey of practitioners and preliminary design suggestions summarised in [38].

We develop a simple programming language with both explicit dimensions and units of measurement in order to illustrate and gauge the four main implementation methods that support unit checking. From a correctness perspective, the optimal solution would be to natively support UoM as this allows for efficient unit conversion and static checking, in-line with a software model. However none of the mainstream languages provide such support, nor is that level of rigour always required. Libraries might seem compelling, and all popular programming languages have a multitude of alternatives, but they're cumbersome in practice and have specific performance costs. Libraries are best suited to applications in which UoM checking is desirable at run-time in order to ensure systems are robust. Lightweight methods, such as component based checking or black-box testing, provide many benefits of UoM libraries with minimal overheads but sacrifice completeness of the checking procedure. Different stakeholders will have different robustness concerns and willingness to compromise on the proportion of unit annotations required.

Apart from the well known catastrophic errors, it is unclear how often unit inconsistencies occur in development and their cost of detection or repair. The literature is not very comprehensive on this matter but it is clearly significant. When applied to a repository of CellML models, a validation tool [11] found that 60% of the descriptions that were invalid had dimensionally inconsistent units. A spreadsheet checker [3] was applied to 22 published scientific spreadsheets and detected 3, nearly 14%, with errors. Ore [45] applied his lightweight C++ unit inconsistency tool to 213 open-source

---

[1] https://www.omg.org/omgmarte/.

[2] https://sysml.org.

systems, finding inconsistencies in 11% of them. A further study [47] using a corpus of robot software with 5.9M lines of code, found dimensional inconsistencies in 6% of repositories. It must be noted that these figures are gleaned from post development studies and are not representative of a quantity adhering software discipline. One must assume that during the development and testing phases many more UoM inconsistencies were uncovered. It is therefore important to ensure UoM information existing in Software Models is supported in derived implementations.

This paper is an extended version of [36], in which Sect. 3 provides a formal description of a simple programming language supporting both dimension checking and unit conversion. Thereby enabling a rigorous presentation of a native language based solution versus popular library based implementations that cannot leverage compile-time optimisation. Moreover we can precisely characterise component-based solutions which are useful for allowing disparate research groups to collaborate without the burden of ensuring all entities are annotated The rest of this paper is structured as follows. In Sect. 2 we provide a brief background to UoM and the Quantity pattern. In Sect. 4 we describe the four means of supporting UoM information in implementations and in Sect. 5 we summarise the results of our comparative study, providing suggestions for developers as to which method to choose depending on their requirements.

2 Background

Humans have used local units of measurement since the days of early trade, enhanced over time to fulfil the accuracy and interoperable needs of science and technology. The technical definition of a physical quantity is a *"property of a phenomenon, body, or substance, where the property has a magnitude that can be expressed as a number and a reference"* [27]. Dimensions are physical quantities that can be measured, while units are arbitrary labels that correspond to a given dimension to make it relative. Each dimension is declared as a number (the magnitude of the quantity) with an associated unit [7].

One can assert the physical dimension of length with the unit metre and the magnitude 10 (10m). However, the same length can also be expressed using other units such as centimetres or kilometres, at the same time changing the magnitude (1000cm or 0.01km). Although these examples are all based on the International System of Units (SI), which is the most used and well known unit system, there exists several other systems, such as the *Imperial system*. On this basis a very simple object oriented design would entail a superclass for each dimension, such as Length, and then specific subclasses for the various units, each of which would contain overloaded operators to ensure unit based arithmetic could be performed correctly:

```
Length l1 = new LengthMetre (5.0);
Length l2 = new LengthYard (4.0);
Length l3 = l1.addlength (l2);
```

The addlength command would convert l2 into metres and perform the addition.

Units can be defined in the most generic form as either *base quantities* or *derived quantities*. The base quantities are the basic building blocks, and the derived quantities are built from these. The base quantities and derived quantities together form a way of describing any part of the physical world [51]. For example length (metre) is a base quantity, and so is time (second). If these two base quantities are combined they express velocity (metre/second or metre $\times$ second^{-1}) which is a derived quantity. The International System of Units (SI) defines seven base quantities (length, mass, time, electric current, thermodynamic temperature, amount of substance, and luminous intensity) as well as a corresponding unit for each quantity [44]. We could extend our object oriented design to create a class hierarchy for each base type and use a tree structure to construct derived types. However this would result in hundreds of units and thousands of conversions. Also showing two unit definitions to be equivalent would be non-trivial.

Conveniently, a canonical form exists which makes storage and comparison a lot easier. Any system of units can be derived from the base units as a product of powers of those base units: $base^{e_1} \times base^{e_2} \times \ldots base^{e_n}$, where the exponents $e_1, \ldots, e_n$ are rational numbers. Thus an SI unit can be represented as a 7-tuple $\langle e_1, \ldots, e_7 \rangle$ where e_i denotes the i-th base unit; or in our case e_1 denotes the base unit for length, e_2 mass, e_3 time and so on. In Java this would be represented as:

```
class Unit {
    private int [7] dimension;
    private float [7] conversionFactor;
    private int [7] offset;
    ...
    boolean isCompatibleWith (Unit u);
    boolean equals (Unit u);
    Unit multiplyUnits (Unit u);
    Unit divideUnits (Unit u);
}
```

The dimension array contains the 7-tuple of base unit exponentials. The attributes conversionFactor and offset enable conversions from this unit system to the SI units. The class Unit also defines operations to compare and combine units. The method isCompatibleWith checks whether two units are compatible for being combined, such as miles and centimetres. While equals returns true if the units are exactly the same, which is used when adding or subtracting quantities. When two quantities are multiplied then multiplyUnits adds the two dimension arrays. Correspondingly, divideUnits subtracts each of the elements of the dimension array.

Using this representation for a unit we can construct what is known as the Quantity pattern [17]:

```
class Quantity {
    private float value;
    private Unit unit;
    ....
}
```

We can include arithmetic operations to the Quantity class that ensures addition and subtraction only succeed when their units are equivalent, or multiplication and division generate a new unit that represents the derived value correctly. This pattern is the basis for many UoM Libraries [39] but can also be described in UML.

The Quantity pattern provides a method for annotating variable declarations and method signatures with behavioural UoM specifications. However, two values that share the same UoM might not represent the same *kinds of quantities* (KOQ) [15, 16, 21] such as torque and work. Torque is a rotational force which causes an object to rotate about an axis while work is the result of a force acting over some distance. We have recently developed a simple set of rules for arithmetic and function calls that allow quantities to be named and handled *safely* [37].

A further complication that impedes adoption is that of the annotation burden, Ore [48] found subjects choose a correct UoM annotation only 51% of the time and take an average of 136 s to make a single correct annotation. In a Software Model, entities annotated in this manner are merely decorative. Tools can be written to ensure that the models use quantity information correctly, but they need to be rendered into the codebase to ensure implementations are robust with regards to UoM. In the next Section we explore what it means algorithmically to perform dimension checking and unit conversion before we detail the various options for transferring UoM information into real codebases.

3 Dimension Checking and Unit Conversion

Computations can often be divided into stages, contingent on the availability of data [28]. If the dimensions of variables are known prior to compilation then checking a design or an implementation early will catch errors before a system is put in place and reduce the amount of run-time computation.

3.1 A Simple Programming Language

Performing calculations in relation to quantities, dimensions and units is often complex and can easily lead to mistakes. A dimensional analysis needs to check that (1) two physical quantities can only be equated if they have the same dimensions, known as *dimensional homogeneity*; (2) two physical quantities can only be added if they have the same dimensions; (3) the dimensions of the multiplication of two quantities is given by the addition of the dimensions of the two quantities. In order to demonstrate how this staging for both dimensions and units can occur we shall begin with a standard imperative programming language, defined below, that allows computations on real numbers, r and general purpose variables v. Statements include assignments, conditionals, and while loops.

$$prog \ ::= \texttt{begin} \ decs \ ; \ stmts \ \texttt{end}$$
$$decs \ ::= dec_1; \ \ldots; \ dec_n$$
$$stmts \ ::= stmt_1; \ \ldots; \ stmt_m$$
$$dec \ ::= v : type$$
$$type \ ::= \texttt{int} \mid \texttt{bool} \mid \texttt{char} \mid \texttt{string} \mid \texttt{real}$$
$$stmt \ ::= v := exp \mid \texttt{if} \ bexp \ \texttt{then} \ stmts \ \texttt{else} \ stmts \mid \texttt{while} \ bexp \ \texttt{do} \ stmts$$
$$exp \ ::= r \mid v \mid exp_1 + exp_2 \mid exp_1 - exp_2 \mid exp_1 * exp_2 \mid exp_1 \ / \ exp_2$$
$$bexp \ ::= \texttt{true} \mid \texttt{false} \mid bexp_1 \ \texttt{and} \ bexp_2 \mid bexp_1 \ \texttt{or} \ bexp_2 \mid \texttt{not} \ bexp \mid exp_1 \ rop \ exp_2$$
$$rop \ ::= > \mid >= \mid <= \mid < \mid = \mid =/=$$

3.2 Dimension Checking

Without any means of annotating variables denoting quantities, programmers need to be very careful to ensure their models are faithfully converted into code. As every line of code can be subjected to a large range of values and dependencies, unit errors are bound to arise.

This can be alleviated by introducing dimension annotations. We extend our imperative language to include unit declarations, *udec*, that allow dimension variables, *dim*, to be declared. We shall consider the three common base dimensions of length, mass and time.

Using the Quantity pattern representation velocity, namely length $\times$ time^{-1}, becomes $(1, 0, -1)$ and this is how we define dimension variables *dim*.

$$decs ::= \ldots \mid udec_1; \ \ldots; \ udec_m$$
$$udec ::= uv : \texttt{real of } dim$$
$$dim ::= (int, int, int)$$

Embedding quantity expressions within the existing syntax produces compromises that are problematic. What does it mean for a number to be added to a quantity? Should one assume the number can have the same unit as the quantity or should we raise an error? We extend our language to include explicit unit expressions, *uexp*, and variables, *uv*. Consequently we extend statements, to support quantity variable assignments. Boolean expressions are also extended to support relative boolean expressions including units. Unit arithmetic expressions, *uexp*, impose syntactic restrictions so that their soundness can be inferred using the algebra of quantities.

$$stmt ::= \ldots \mid uv \ := \ uexp$$
$$uexp ::= uv \mid uexp_1 + uexp_2 \mid r \star uexp \mid uexp \star r \mid uexp_1 \star uexp_2 \ \ldots$$
$$bexp ::= \ldots \mid uexp_1 \ rop \ uexp_2$$

In Fig. 1 we present the essential quantity rules for declarations, assignments and expressions. The rules for declarations build an environment, ϱ, mapping variables to their dimension, *dim*. The environment will not change throughout the lifetime of the block. Thus, once a variable has been defined to be of a given quantity, then it will remain as such. Many library based systems allow programmers to change the dimension of unit variables as they are objects of type Quantity, namely a mutable array. The rules for statements return either DimValid or DimFail depending on whether their use of quantities is correct or not. An assignment statement is valid only if the quantity of the unit expression is dimensionally homogeneous with the unit variable that it is being assigned to. For constructs that embed statements such as conditionals, while loops and statement sequences; each embedded statement must be valid for the whole statement to be considered valid. The rule for unit variables is just a lookup on the quantity environment ϱ. The rule for addition and comparison ensures that both the left hand and right hand side subexpressions have the same quantities. The rules for multiplication allow constants to be applied and multiplying two unit expressions will create a combined quantity, where each dimension is added.

$$\langle uv \,:\, \texttt{real of } d,\, \varrho \rangle \rightarrow_{udec} \varrho \oplus \{uv \mapsto d\} \qquad\qquad \text{[Dim Var Decl]}$$

$$\frac{\langle udec_1,\, \varrho \rangle \rightarrow_{udec} \varrho_1 \quad\cdots\quad \langle udec_m,\, \varrho_{m-1} \rangle \rightarrow_{udec} \varrho_m}{\langle udec_1;\, \ldots;\, udec_m,\, \varrho \rangle \rightarrow_{udecs} \varrho_m} \qquad \text{[Dim Var Decls]}$$

$$\frac{\varrho \vdash uexp \rightarrow_{uexp} (l, m, t) \qquad\qquad \varrho\; uv = (l, m, t)}{\varrho \vdash uv \,:= \,uexp \rightarrow_{stmt} \mathsf{DimValid}} \qquad \text{[Valid Asgn Stmt]}$$

$$\frac{\varrho \vdash uexp \rightarrow_{uexp} (l, m, t) \qquad\qquad \varrho\; uv \neq (l, m, t)}{\varrho \vdash uv \,:= \,uexp \rightarrow_{stmt} \mathsf{DimFail}} \qquad \text{[Fail Asgn Stmt]}$$

$$\varrho \vdash uv \rightarrow_{uexp} \varrho\; uv \qquad\qquad\qquad \text{[Dim Var Expr]}$$

$$\frac{\varrho \vdash uexp_1 \rightarrow_{uexp} (l, m, t) \qquad \varrho \vdash uexp_2 \rightarrow_{uexp} (l, m, t)}{\varrho \vdash uexp_1 + uexp_2 \rightarrow_{uexp} (l, m, t)} \qquad \text{[Dim Add Expr]}$$

$$\frac{\varrho \vdash uexp \rightarrow_{uexp} (l, m, t)}{\varrho \vdash r \star uexp \rightarrow_{uexp} (l, m, t)} \qquad \text{[Dim Mult Expr]}$$

$$\frac{\varrho \vdash uexp \rightarrow_{uexp} (l, m, t)}{\varrho \vdash uexp \star r \rightarrow_{uexp} (l, m, t)} \qquad \text{[Dim Mult Expr]}$$

$$\frac{\varrho \vdash uexp_1 \rightarrow_{uexp} (l_1, m_1, t_1) \qquad \varrho \vdash uexp_2 \rightarrow_{uexp} (l_2, m_2, t_2)}{\varrho \vdash uexp_1 \star uexp_2 \rightarrow_{uexp} (l_1 + l_2, m_1 + m_2, t_1 + t_2)} \qquad \text{[Dim Mult Expr]}$$

Fig. 1. Quantity Checking rules for declarations, assignments and expressions.

A native language that supports quantities will implement similar rules as part of their static analysis. Checking that all annotated entities behave according to these rules ensures both *completeness* and thus *correctness* with respect to the quantities of the model or programme. Aiming to reduce the annotation burden, some native systems such as F# [31,32] allow unit type variables. Much like polymorphic type variables in functional languages, the static analysis phase will try to resolve them using a solver. If all quantities are inferred for type variables then quantity correctness is achieved.

3.3 Compile-Time Unit Conversion

Dimension analysis would be sufficient if only one unit system, such as the SI system, was required. In such cases the base units of `Metre`, `Gram` and `Second` could be implicit in implementations. Unit expressions would be evaluated in much the same way as normal arithmetic expressions, as shown in OCaml below. Note the environment, env, binds variables to their values, and has type (`string * float`) `list`:

```
type uexp = Var of string | Num of float
          | Add of uexp * uexp | Mul of uexp * uexp

let rec eval uexp env =
  match uexp with
```

```
   (Var v)              -> lookup v env
 | (Add (ue1,ue2))      -> (eval ue1 env) +. (eval ue2 env)
 | (Mul (Num n,ue2))    -> n *. (eval ue2 env)
 | (Mul (ue1,Num n))    -> (eval ue1 env) *. n
 | (Mul (ue1,ue2))      -> (eval ue1 env) *. (eval ue2 env)
```

As this is rarely the case in scientific applications where a myriad of unit systems and magnitudes are used, a second stage is required to perform unit conversions either prior to evaluating unit expressions or during. Conversions can occur within a given unit system, such as Metres to Kilometres, or between unit systems, such as Kilometres to Miles. For our three base units we would need OCaml conversion functions such as the following:

```
type lengthunit = Metre | Kilometre | Mile ...
let con_length (l1,l2) =
  match (l1,l2) with
     (Metre,Kilometre)     -> 0.001
   | (Kilometre,Metre)     -> 1000.0
   | (Mile,Kilometre)      -> 1.609
   ...
   | _                     -> 1.0

type massunit = Gram | Kilogram
let con_mass (m1,m2) =
  match (m1,m2) with
     (Gram,Kilogram)       -> 0.001
   | (Kilogram,Gram)       -> 1000.0
   | _                     -> 1.0

type timeunit = Minute | Second
let con_time (t1,t2) =
  match (t1,t2) with
     (Minute,Second)       -> 60.0
   | (Second,Minute)       -> 0.016667
   | _                     -> 1.0
```

The final wildcard patterns are there to catch cases where conversions are not needed. We can use the conversion functions to convert from Metre to Kilometre for instance but we also need to take the exponent into account when we move between units and systems. For example, the density of iron is $7.86\,g/cm^3$, and can be converted into kg/m^3 as follows:

$$7.86 * (\text{con\_mass (Gram,Kilogram)}) * (\text{con\_length (Centimetre,Metre)})^{-3}$$
$$= 7.86 * 0.001 * 0.01^{-3}$$
$$= 7860\ kg/m^3$$

Although converting values to ensure compatibility can create round-off errors. Unit variables will be defined as their value, along with a tuple containing their units and associated exponents. The environment uenv maps unit variables to their values and units, (string * (float * unit_exponents)) list:

```
type units_exponents = ( (lengthunit * int)
                       * (massunit * int)
                       * (timeunit * int))
```

The function coneval below converts the right hand side subexpression to the left hand side's units and performs the required calculation, returning both the value and its units_exponents.

```
let rec coneval uexp uenv =
  match uexp with
      (Var v)              -> lookup v uenv
    | (Add (ue1,ue2))     ->
        let (v1, ((lu1,xl1),(mu1,xm1),(tu1,xt1))) = (coneval ue1 uenv) in
        let (v2, ((lu2,xl2),(mu2,xm2),(tu2,xt2))) = (coneval ue2 uenv) in
        let v2' = v2 *.
                  (con_length (lu2,lu1) ** (float_of_int xl2)) *.
                  (con_mass (mu2,mu1) ** (float_of_int xm2)) *.
                  (con_time (tu2,tu1) ** (float_of_int xt2))
        in (v1+.v2',((lu1,el1),(mu1,xm1),(tu1,xt1)))
    | (Mul (Num n,ue2)) ->
        let (v2, ((lu2,xl2),(mu2,xm2),(tu2,xt2))) = (coneval ue2 uenv)
        in (n*.v2, ((lu2,xl2),(mu2,xm2),(tu2,xt2)))
    | (Mul (ue1,Num n)) ->
        let (v1, ((lu1,xl1),(mu1,xm1),(tu1,xt1))) = (coneval ue1 uenv)
        in (v1*.n, ((lu1,xl1),(mu1,xm1),(tu1,xt1)))
    | (Mul (ue1,ue2))     ->
        let (v1, ((lu1,xl1),(mu1,xm1),(tu1,xt1))) = (coneval ue1 uenv) in
        let (v2, ((lu2,xl2),(mu2,xm2),(tu2,xt2))) = (coneval ue2 uenv) in
        let v2' = v2 *.
                  (con_length (lu2,lu1) ** (float_of_int xl2)) *.
                  (con_mass (mu2,mu1) ** (float_of_int xm2)) *.
                  (con_time (tu2,tu1) ** (float_of_int xt2))
        in (v1*.v2',((lu1,xl1+xl2),(mu1,xm1+xm2),(tu1,xt1+xt2)))
```

The function coneval performs both unit conversion and arithmetic evaluation in one stage. It is therefore a *dynamic* activity as the actual values will not be known until the programme begins executing. If the units are declared at *compile-time* as part of the unit variable declarations then we can perform the conversions prior to compiling arithmetic expressions. The conversion factor can be expressed as a multiplication of a number in the uexp datatype. The function con performs the initial stage and inserts the conversion into the returned expression. It uses the environment up that maps variables to their units_exponents.

```
let rec con uexp up =
  match uexp with
      (Var v)              -> (Var v, lookup v up)
    | (Add (ue1,ue2))     ->
        let (e1, ((lu1,xl1),(mu1,xm1),(tu1,xt1))) = (con ue1 up) in
        let (e2, ((lu2,xl2),(mu2,xm2),(tu2,xt2))) = (con ue2 up) in
        let e2' = Mul (e2, Num ((con_length (lu2,lu1) ** (float_of_int xl2)) *.
                                (con_mass (mu2,mu1) ** (float_of_int xm2)) *.
                                (con_time (tu2,tu1) ** (float_of_int xt2))))
        in (Add (e1,e2'),((lu1,el1),(tu1,xt1),(mu1,xm1)))
    ...
```

Theorem 1. *Assuming for a given set of unit declarations,* v, *the following equivalence holds on environments* uenv, env *and* up:

```
lookup v uenv = (lookup v env, lookup v up)
```

Then for any valid unit expression in uexp *the following holds:*

```
coneval ue uenv =  let (ue',units) = con ue up
                   in (eval ue' env, units)
```

Namely, that performing the conversion before evaluation will yield the same result as performing both together. As con *is a straightforward recursive-descent of the expression tree, it is bound to terminate.*

Proof. By structural induction on valid unit expressions. We show the cases for variables and addition in Appendix A.

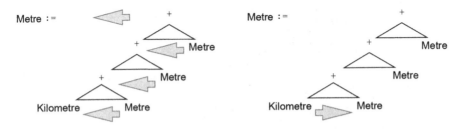

Fig. 2. Simple unit conversion algorithm versus one that seeks to limit the number of conversions.

The unit conversion algorithm always converts the right hand side's units to the left hand side's which is rarely the most efficient. In Fig. 2 we show a worst-case example of what this may entail when an alternative strategy would yield far fewer conversions. The naive algorithm will generate four conversions for the given assignment while a more refined version will generate only one. Our algorithm can be improved to choose the least number of conversions by generating all possible valid unit conversions from a given expression, and selecting the one with the fewest conversions. This technique is similar to that described by Cooper [11].

3.4 Dimension Checking Functions

Most programming languages support the creation of named expressions, *funs*. A function is an abstraction of an expression. Quantity functions, *ufun*, differ from normal functions in that they can take a number of arguments, some of which are quantities, and return a quantity. Both a definition mechanism and an invocation mechanism are necessary for quantity functions.

$prog$ ::= begin *funs; decs; stmts* end
$funs$ ::= $fun_1; \dots; fun_j; ufun_1; \dots; ufun_k$
$ufun$ ::= fun $ufnm$ ($v_1 : type_1, \dots, v_n : type_n, uv_1 : dim_1, \dots, uv_m : dim_m$) : dim_{out}
      is *uexp*
$uexp$ ::= $\dots$ | $ufnm$ ($exp_1, \dots, exp_n, uexp_1, \dots, uexp_m$)

We require a second environment, σ, to store the relevant quantity information belonging to each quantity function. In order to guarantee quantity functions are handled correctly by the main programme we need to ensure two criteria: that each invocation's quantity arguments have the same dimension as those in the function definition, and that the function body has the specified return quantity as shown in Fig. 3. Assuming UoM are known at compile-time, a compiler can perform unit conversions on function calls. This means that a useful mathematical function, written using a set of units from a given unit system, can be *correctly* called from many different parts of the programme, each with their own units and unit systems, so long as the signature quantities are compatible and conversion functions exist to translate values from one system to another.

$$\texttt{def } \mathit{ufnm} \, (\ldots, uv_1 : dim_1, \ldots, uv_m : dim_m) : dim_{out} \texttt{ is } uexp, \, \sigma \rangle$$
$$\rightarrow_{ufun} \sigma \oplus \{\mathit{ufnm} \mapsto ((uv_1, dim_1), \ldots, (uv_m, dim_m), uexp, dim_{out})\} \quad [\text{Dim FDef}]$$

$$\cfrac{\sigma \, \mathit{ufnm} = ((uv_1, dim_1), \ldots, (uv_m, dim_m), uexp, dim_{out}) \\ \sigma, \varrho \vdash uexp_1 \rightarrow_{uexp} dim_1 \; \cdots \; \sigma, \varrho \vdash uexp_m \rightarrow_{uexp} dim_m \\ \sigma, \{uv_1 \mapsto dim_1, \ldots, uv_m \mapsto dim_m\} \vdash uexp \rightarrow_{uexp} dim_{out}}{\sigma, \varrho \vdash \mathit{ufnm} \, (exp_1, \ldots, exp_n, uexp_1, \ldots, uexp_m) \rightarrow_{uexp} dim_{out}} \quad [\text{Dim FCall}]$$

Fig. 3. Quantity Checking rules for Function Declarations and Invocation.

3.5 Dimension Checking Components

A Component is a collection of function signatures; consisting of their method names, parameter lists and return types. A component based approach seeks to add UoM information to only the signatures of quantity functions in order to enforce unit consistency when calling or composing functions. Thereby reducing the annotation burden at the expense of quantity checking coverage. In Fig. 4 we present the rules for function definitions and calls. The only difference between these and the ones in Fig. 3 is that we do not check the body of the function call, just its signature.

$$\langle \texttt{def } \mathit{ufnm} \, (\ldots, uv_1 : dim_1, \ldots, uv_m : dim_m) : dim_{out} \texttt{ is } uexp, \, \sigma \rangle$$
$$\rightarrow_{ufun} \sigma \oplus \{\mathit{ufnm} \mapsto (dim_1, \ldots, dim_m, dim_{out})\} \quad [\text{Comp FDef}]$$

$$\cfrac{\sigma \, \mathit{ufnm} = (dim_1, \ldots, dim_m, dim_{out}) \\ \sigma, \varrho \vdash uexp_1 \rightarrow_{uexp} dim_1 \; \cdots \; \sigma, \varrho \vdash uexp_m \rightarrow_{uexp} dim_m}{\sigma, \varrho \vdash \mathit{ufnm} \, (exp_1, \ldots, exp_n, uexp_1, \ldots, uexp_m) \rightarrow_{uexp} dim_{out}} \quad [\text{Comp FCall}]$$

Fig. 4. Component Checking rules for Function Declarations and Invocation.

3.6 Summary of Quantity Checking

Through the use of an illustrative programming language we have shown how to ensure programs correctly manipulate both the dimensions and UoM of quantities. In doing so we have raised two important issues relating to the implementation of quantities: at what point checking and conversions can occur, and how extensive the coverage will be. If all unit variables are annotated, or their annotations inferred, then both dimension checking and unit conversions can be undertaken by the compiler. This means that programs with UoM errors will be detected early, before the system is put in place, creating a strongly UoM typed language. Moreover, the code can be optimised so as to reduce rounding errors, increasing the accuracy of its calculations. The technique can be extended to include assertions on allowable unit conversions. If UoM are only known at run-time, or their design is embedded within the host language, then dimension checking and unit conversions will be undertaken at run-time. Programmes will still manipulate UoM robustly but with a performance penalty and errors will only be detected once the programme is running. As annotating all unit variables is often undesirable and impractical, component based solutions allow checking and conversions to only occur at the point when functions are called. It is assumed that the body of the function will behave correctly. Thus only the interface between two components is verified, either at compile-time or run-time, and with substantially less code coverage the checking will be incomplete. The onus is very much on the component developers to ensure that their codes behave correctly with respect to dimensions and UoM.

4   Implementation Options

Certain aspects of a Software Model can be translated directly into a programming language. For instance, a UML class diagram can be used to build the class structure of an object oriented implementation. UoM annotations cannot be handled in the same way as traditional types, namely symbolically. As described in Sect. 3, they require an equational checker to ensure assignments and method calls are handled soundly by the compiler.

In this Section we shall inspect four practical methods that support unit checking of code basis. However we must be cognisant of the wider context of unit of measurement checking, as all implementation options are affected by the following three concerns [38]:

Lack of Awareness: many developers are totally unaware of software solutions that deal with UoM. Inertia from developers stem from factors like tradition, fear of change and effort of learning something new.

Technical Internal Factors: many solutions are awkward and imprecise, introducing a loss of precision and struggling at times with dimensional consistencies.

External Factors: modern systems are not built in a vacuum but form part of an ecosystem [34]. Adding quantity annotations to code bases will have minimal impact if values pass through numerous generic components that do not support them, such as legacy systems, databases, spreadsheets, graphics tools and many other components that are unlikely to support UoM without costly updates.

The rest of this section will focus on the technical factors of each approach before we summarise their strengths and weaknesses.

4.1 Native Language Support

Augmenting existing imperative, object-oriented and functional languages to support UoM checking requires extending the algorithmic scope of their type checkers. The pioneering foundational work [54] showed how to add dimensions to the simply-typed lambda calculus, such that polymorphic dimensions can be inferred in a way that is a natural extension of Milner's polymorphic type inference algorithm [41]. The intrinsic nature of dimensional analysis is that it cannot be solved symbolically but equationally using the theory of Abelian groups [31]. Providing UoM syntax, an equational checker and unit conversion functions is what distinguishes a language with native support. UoM metadata is checked at compile-time and can be removed from the generated run-time code. Moreover unit conversions can be minimised in order to reduce round-off errors as discussed in Sect. 3.3.

Apple's Swift language [4] is the only one in the 20 most popular programming languages [53] that supports units of measurement. Another well-known language which supports UoM is F# [40]. It has the added quality of allowing unit variables, namely undefined unit types, that the compile-time checker will attempt to resolve. If there is insufficient information then the program will be declined. This feature allows a small degree of incompleteness in language definitions so the burden of annotation is mitigated somewhat, but the static checker will derive the missing UoM information so correctness is ensured. Even so, neither Swift nor F# are common in large software engineering projects.

C++ Boost Library: For efficiency reasons, C++ has great traction within the scientific community, and is still in the top five most popular [53] programming languages. It has a de facto UoM library that exploits the template meta-programming feature[3]. Consequently BoostUnits is more than just a library as it supports a staged computation model, similar to MixGen [2], that is more akin to a language extension and supports backwards compatibility. This flexible compilation strategy is unique amongst prominent programming languages. A staged approach offers many of the expressive features of native language support and, with appropriate compiler optimisation, no run-time execution cost is introduced. C++ with the BoostUnits library supports UoM checking in performance-critical code. In practice, however, the survey [49] found both accuracy and usability issues with the use of this extension.

Unit of Measurement Validators: Developing a new compiler feature for an existing language is contentious as there are standards to ensure languages stay constant. The actual implementation of UoM would be non-trivial and likely to become outmoded if not supported by the language development team. An alternative compile-time approach is to define UoM through comments or attributes and to build a tool that attempts to perform as much scrutiny as possible. This kind of validator checks at compile-time for unit violations without adding new syntax or changing the run-time behaviour of the code. Figure 5 shows an example of the Unit of Measurement Validator for C# [13]. The

---

[3] http://github.com/boostorg/units.

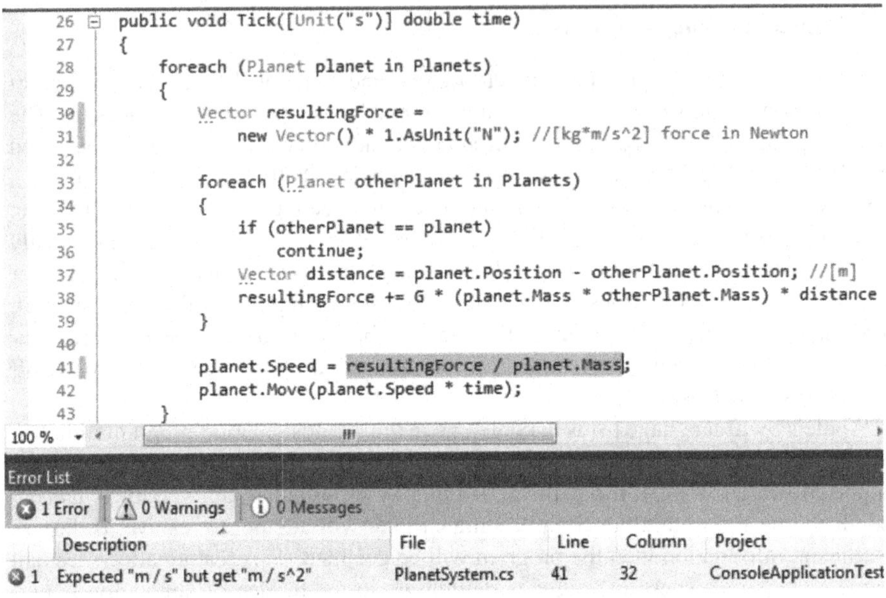

```
26 ⊟   public void Tick([Unit("s")] double time)
27     {
28         foreach (Planet planet in Planets)
29         {
30             Vector resultingForce =
31                 new Vector() * 1.AsUnit("N"); //[kg*m/s^2] force in Newton
32
33             foreach (Planet otherPlanet in Planets)
34             {
35                 if (otherPlanet == planet)
36                     continue;
37                 Vector distance = planet.Position - otherPlanet.Position; //[m]
38                 resultingForce += G * (planet.Mass * otherPlanet.Mass) * distance
39             }
40
41             planet.Speed = resultingForce / planet.Mass;
42             planet.Move(planet.Speed * time);
43         }
```

100 % ▾ ◂   III   ▸

Error List

❸ 1 Error   ⚠ 0 Warnings   ⓘ 0 Messages

	Description	File	Line	Column	Project
❸ 1	Expected "m / s" but get "m / s^2"	PlanetSystem.cs	41	32	ConsoleApplicationTest

Fig. 5. Example of Unit of Measurement Validator for C#.

Osprey [26] system is a C front end that automatically checks for all potential quantity errors. UoM are annotated with a $ and are modelled as types, reducing dimensional analysis to type checking, with Gaussian elimination to resolve unspecified UoM variable exponents. Simiarly [25] allows one to express relationships between the units of function parameters and return values, ensuring the validity of unit conversions can be specified. PUnits [56] is a Java front end, or pluggable type system, that has many additional features. It can be used in three ways: checking the correctness of a program, solving UoM type variables, and subsequently annotating a program with units for inspection. These approaches are lightweight and scalable but they need to be maintained as the host language evolves.

Domain-Specific Languages (DSLs) with Quantities: DSLs are languages specialized to a particular application domain. They are often written in a mark-up language such as XML or JSON which facilitates their use with general purpose languages as they can be easily parsed. They might have originally been designed for the purpose of curation, such as CellML and SMBL where the intention was to build biological repositories of computational models. A model will include the constants, variables and equations denoting a particular biological system. Thus, translating them into a programming language with the aid of a differential equation solver means that they can be readily simulated [18]. If the DSL contains UoM declarations then separately analysing source files can be undertaken before they are uploaded to a repository and translated into the run-time system [11]. Naturally this means that quantity checking coverage will be restricted to the DSL files and not the supporting program, but the case can be made that manipulating quantities with the files is where the vulnerabilities would be.

4.2   Static or Dynamic Library Support

A second technique for supporting units of measurement is through the use or development of a UoM library. Advanced abstraction methods such as classes and generics allow libraries to be created that work well with existing code bases. As a result there are many libraries for all contemporary languages [6]. The core issue that these libraries aim to solve is something that is relatively easy to understand and familiar. Nevertheless, Bekolay argues *"making a physical quantity library is easy but making a good one is hard"* [5]. Trying to make a more complete library, including more units, more operators, effective conversions, good error messages, efficient and accurate is far more demanding than a robust implementation of the Quantity pattern [17, 33].

In practice there are many problems with their use. They require too much boilerplate code, they're rarely idiomatic to their host language, provide poor error messages, lack support for user defined types and restrict underlying storage to a single floating point representation. Certain languages, like Ruby, are less affective by these shortfalls as they encourage duck typing and a flexible syntax that facilitates domain specific language creation. Nonetheless [38], concludes that UoM types need to be as straightforward to use as arithmetic types or at least as close as possible for adoption to occur.

A strong point of libraries is that they can support both compile-time and run-time error detection. Compile-time checking can be achieved through static overloading, or Java generic instantiations. While run-time checking is achieved through overriding. An example of both styles is shown in [38]. Combining the two semantics, even with the compact Quantity Pattern representation, would double the amount of syntax required and further complicate usage. Dynamically typed languages, such as Ruby or Python, will by definition perform quantity checking at run-time. Run-time support is a key requirement for certain projects: *"In our product line, our users may very well have one file whose units are "$kg \cdot m^3$", another whose units are "g_cc" and a third whose units are "degrees Celsius". We therefore need to be able to operate on units at run-time, not compile-time"* [49].

A weakness of libraries compared to native language support is that variables of a Quantity class can be reassigned at run-time, due to their semantics being embedded within the `dimension` array, so that a metre could become a kilogram. Unit mismatch and conversion errors can be detected by UoM libraries but avoiding programming style errors requires further discipline that a conventional static checker provides. Such errors are caused by violations of standard type systems, such as when an intermediate variable is used with different units. These were found to account for 75% of inconsistencies in the study of 5.9M lines of code [47].

Their core disadvantage, however, is that their implementation requires boxed values rather than the standard primitive entities. When units are not part of the language then there is a cost at both compile-time and run-time. For applications that carry out lots of calculations (such as matrix multiplications), their performance tends to matter more and boxed values with types would have unnecessary performance overheads. At first glance, a UoM library might seem easy to use and include in a software project, but the inner workings of the UoM library often increase the complexity of a project.

4.3   Component or Interface Description Support

Encapsulating implementation details, components are a collection of the externally visible entities and function signatures. They are used by the compiler to ensure access is handled correctly. Component based approaches are lightweight and aim to liberate the scientific programmer from the need to annotate every variable. In Sect. 3 we described the difference between dimensional analysis of functions and components. The former requiring all declarations to be checked, such as is undertaken for native language support and libraries, versus a component based approach that only checks signatures.

Consequently, a component based approach seeks to add UoM information to the interface in order to enforce unit consistency when composing components and thereby reduce dimensional mismatch errors as described in Sect. 3.5. In [12], it is argued that units of measurement should be inserted in software component interfaces. There is some anecdotal evidence in the many quotes of [49] to support this approach. Damevski postulates that unit libraries are too constraining and incur an annotation or migration burden. His algorithm attempts to resolve UoM at run-time so that if the types of the called method's parameters are compatible with the arguments then unit conversions occur. Consider the C++ class Earth [12]:

```
class Earth {
  void setCircumference(in Metre circumference);
  Metre getCircumference();
}
```

It assigns and queries the earth's circumference using `metre` internally but can be called with `kilometre` and the return value bound to a variable of, say, type `mile`. Unlike libraries, within the class `Earth` no further annotations are required, nor will it ever be checked. The variable `circumference` will be assigned to a `double`. This is a dynamic component based approach, units are converted at run-time.

Another lightweight methodology was presented by Ore [45] that uses an initial pass to build a mapping from attributes in C++ shared libraries to units. The shared libraries contain UoM specifications so this mapping is used to propagate into a source program and detect inconsistencies at compile-time. Their algorithm leverages dimensional analysis rules for arithmetic operators to great effect [46]. This is an example of a static component based approach.

A component based discipline means that the consequences of local unit mistakes are underestimated. On the other hand, it allows diverse teams to collaborate even if their domain specific environments or choice of quantity systems were, to some extent, dissimilar. More importantly, either a static or dynamic component implementation would have been sufficient to have corrected the Mars Climate Orbiter error.

4.4   Black-Box Testing

The last method of performing UoM validation is through automated testing. Black box testing mainly focuses on input and output of software applications and it is entirely based on software requirements and specifications. It seeks to spot incorrect or missing

```
class Distance {
 public double add_km(boolean t,
              double a, double b) {
   return ((t)? a+b : a+(b*1.609));}}
 ...
 public class DistanceTest {
  public void test_add_km() {
    Distance d = new Distance();
    assert(d.add_km(true,10.0,10.0)==20.0);
    assert(d.add_km(false,10.0,10.0)==26.09);}}
```

Fig. 6. Java code and JUnit test case for simple addition of two kilometres, or kilometre and mile distances [36].

functions, interface errors, initialisation errors and errors in data structures. Creating black box unit tests from Software Models is another lightweight approach. The testing will not be exhaustive, as the focus would be on the initialisation of variables, the correctness of assignments and method calls. There have been many efforts to automatically generate unit tests from UML descriptions [1,9,22,43]. However these techniques are seen to be costly and non-trivial in practice [30]. Moreover, they have not been applied to quantity checking.

Nonetheless, it is fairly common nowadays to manually develop tests alongside models, not only for the purpose of test driven development but also to ensure maintainability through refactoring. Including UoM tests requires no extra tool support and will not affect the eco-system as shown in Fig. 6, where we show the testing required for a simple UoM based addition function. Spending time writing unit tests would equate to adding unit annotations without the introduction of a library: *"I could use the same time to write tests and that would really find and prevent errors and at the same time not introduce a crazy complicated library every other developer in my team would have to deal with."* [49]. However, the UoM knowledge will be localised to each particular unit so the slight implementation cost comes at the expense of potentially average checking.

Table 1. Contrasting alternative methods of Implementing Units of Measurement in Software Projects, extended from [36].

Technique	Programming Ease of Use	Execution Speed	Numeric Accuracy	Ease of Integration	Unit Error Detection
Native Support	High	Very High	Excellent	Low	Very High
Validator	High	High	Very Good	Average	Average
DSL	Low	High	Very Good	Low	Average
Static Library	Low	Average	Good	Low	High
Dynamic Library	Average	Low	Good	Low	High
Static Component Based	High	High	Very Good	High	Average
Dynamic Component Based	High	Average	Good	High	Low
Black Box Testing	Average	High	Very Good	Very High	Average

5 Conclusion

The software engineering benefits of adopting dimension checking and automatic unit conversion support is indisputable. Many solutions have been proposed but understanding their nuances, their capabilities and computational overheads, with regards to alternative methods, has never been critically assessed. We have attempted to take a broader perspective, beginning with a quantity aware Software Model, and then looking at the various approaches which allow UoM annotations to be transferred into code. With greater interoperability, industrial use of computational simulations and penetration of digitalisation through cyber-physical systems; it seems pertinent to faithfully represent key properties of physical systems [50]. We have also presented the formal aspects of how to perform dimensional analysis and unit conversion. We have shown, through a simple programming language, how both the analysis and conversion can be undertaken before a program is run. Compile-time techniques provide correctness assurances with regards to UoM, while run-time methods provide robustness, namely the ability of a computer system to handle errors during execution and cope with erroneous input. However ensuring legacy databases, medical software and other custom formats support quantity annotations is a very challenging task.

A key feature of programming languages is that they remain broadly constant. Even subtle changes can have dramatic effects on backwards compatibility and legacy code. All of the mainstream languages were developed before the ubiquitous and hyperconnected digitalisation of modern computing. Thus, native language support for quantities in these popular programming languages is unlikely to occur as it would require new language definitions and expensive compiler rewrites. Validators solve some of these issues but require assurances that tool support will be maintained. DSL checkers are very effective for their given domain but lack generality and interoperability. It is clear that even the best libraries currently cause significant performance issues while not being relevant for most developers. However some of the dynamic libraries include a lightweight syntax that makes UoM definitions easier. Component based techniques can be undertaken at both compile-time and run-time. They forgo completeness and thus correctness to ensure ease of adoption. Compile-time component based approaches can project UoM annotations into non annotated code segments. Thereby expanding quantity checking coverage. Black box testing based approaches are currently undertaken manually but offer many of the advantages of compile-time component based techniques without additional syntax. However, UoM information will then be embedded within the unit tests and not part of the code base. Foregoing this coupling is not advisable from a software engineering perspective.

UoM annotations are initially costly for the developer but relatively stable to program reorganisation. Refactoring does not change the external behaviour of the software, it will rarely require UoM annotation changes unless the underlying data structures are also modified, thus ensuring maintainability and scalability within potentially safety-critical code. Approaches that leverage the compiler to optimise unit conversions without boxed values, such as native support or static lightweight solutions, will ensure greater numeric accuracy.

We have summarised the pros and cons of each approach in Table 1 using some of the essential characteristics that we have focused on. These represent best case scenarios. As such, it becomes evident that static UoM libraries offer few compelling advantages over component or black box based testing if robustness is the main concern. Native languages that provide integral UoM support excel where correctness is a necessary condition, ease of integration is low and efficiency is high. Although, complex modern software tends to favor more lightweight solutions that integrate seamlessly into existing software systems. Choosing an approach that supports UoM information also requires taking the software eco-system into account. Stand-alone safety critical applications, where all unit information will be known and supported at compile-time, are very different to the needs of a rapidly evolving on-line application that expects to deal with varying UoM input at run-time. Nonetheless software-intensive systems are prevalent in our daily lives, with complex functionality and strong interconnection. The need to ensure UoM values behave correctly are greater than ever before.

A   Staging Unit Conversions Proof

- Case for variables:

```
coneval (Var v) uenv
    = lookup v uenv
        {environment assumption}
    = (lookup v env, lookup v up)
        {fold on eval}
    = (eval (Var v) env, lookup v up)
        {let introduction and fold on con}
    = let(Var v,units= con(Var v) up in (eval(Var v)env,units)
```

- Case for addition:

```
coneval (Add (ue1,ue2)) uenv
    = let (v1,((lu1,x11),(mu1,xm1),(tu1,xt1)))=(coneval ue1 uenv) in
      let (v2,((lu2,x12),(mu2,xm2),(tu2,xt2)))=(coneval ue2 uenv) in
      let v2' = v2 *.
            (con_length (lu2,lu1) ** (float_of_int x12)) *.
            (con_mass (mu2,mu1) ** (float_of_int xm2)) *.
            (con_time (tu2,tu1) ** (float_of_int xt2))
      in (v1+.v2',((lu1,el1),(mu1,xm1),(tu1,xt1)))

      {inductive hypothesis on both subexpressions}
    = let (v1, ((lu1,x11),(mu1,xm1),(tu1,xt1))) =
            (let (ued1,units1) = con ue1 up in (eval ued1 env, units1)) in
      let (v2, ((lu2,x12),(mu2,xm2),(tu2,xt2))) =
            (let (ued2,units2) = con ue2 up in (eval ued2 env, units2)) in
      let v2' = v2 *.
            (con_length (lu2,lu1) ** (float_of_int x12)) *.
            (con_mass (mu2,mu1) ** (float_of_int xm2)) *.
            (con_time (tu2,tu1) ** (float_of_int xt2))
      in (v1+.v2',((lu1,el1),(mu1,xm1),(tu1,xt1)))

      {rearrange let expressions}
    = let (ued1,((lu1,x11),(mu1,xm1),(tu1,xt1))) = con ue1 up in
      let (ued2,((lu2,x12),(mu2,xm2),(tu2,xt2))) = con ue2 up in
      let v1 = eval ued1 env in
      let v2 = eval ued2 env in
      let c = (con_length (lu2,lu1) ** (float_of_int x12)) *.
              (con_mass (mu2,mu1) ** (float_of_int xm2)) *.
              (con_time (tu2,tu1) ** (float_of_int xt2)) in
      let v2' = v2 *. c
      in (v1+.v2',((lu1,el1),(mu1,xm1),(tu1,xt1)))
```

```
       {inline v1 and v2 bindings}
   =   let (ued1,((lu1,xl1),(mu1,xm1),(tu1,xt1))) = con ue1 up in
       let (ued2,((lu2,xl2),(mu2,xm2),(tu2,xt2))) = con ue2 up in
       let c = (con_length (lu2,lu1) ** (float_of_int xl2)) *.
               (con_mass (mu2,mu1) ** (float_of_int xm2)) *.
               (con_time (tu2,tu1) ** (float_of_int xt2)) in
       let v2' = (eval ued2 env) *. c
       in ((eval ued1 env) +.v2',
                       ((lu1,el1),(mu1,xm1),(tu1,xt1)))

       {fold on eval to perform addition and multiplication}
   =   let (ued1,((lu1,xl1),(mu1,xm1),(tu1,xt1))) = con ue1 up in
       let (ued2,((lu2,xl2),(mu2,xm2),(tu2,xt2))) = con ue2 up in
       let e2' = Mul (ued2, Num (
               (con_length (lu2,lu1) ** (float_of_int xl2)) *.
               (con_mass (mu2,mu1) ** (float_of_int xm2)) *.
               (con_time (tu2,tu1) ** (float_of_int xt2))))
       in ((eval (Add (ued1, e2')) env),
                       ((lu1,el1),(mu1,xm1),(tu1,xt1)))

       {create a nested block to perform conversion}
   = let (ue', units) =
         (let (ued1,((lu1,xl1),(mu1,xm1),(tu1,xt1))) = con ue1 up in
          let (ued2,((lu2,xl2),(mu2,xm2),(tu2,xt2))) = con ue2 up in
          let e2' = Mul (ued2, Num (
               (con_length (lu2,lu1) ** (float_of_int xl2)) *.
               (con_mass (mu2,mu1) ** (float_of_int xm2)) *.
               (con_time (tu2,tu1) ** (float_of_int xt2))))
          in (Add (ued1, e2'), ((lu1,el1),(mu1,xm1),(tu1,xt1))) )
       in (eval ue' env, units)

       {fold on con}
   = let (ue', units) = con (Add (ue1,ue2)) up
       in (eval ue' env, units)
```

The cases for the remaining multiplication rules are similar to that for addition.

References

1. Ali, S., Hemmati, H., Holt, N.E., Arisholm, E., Briand, L.C.: Model transformations as a strategy to automate model-based testing-a tool and industrial case studies. Simul. Res. Lab. Tech. Rep. **2010–01**, 1–28 (2010)
2. Allen, E., Chase, D., Luchangco, V., Maessen, J.-W., Steele, G.L.: Object-oriented units of measurement. In: Proceedings of Object-oriented Programming, Systems, Languages, and Applications, OOPSLA 2004, pp. 384–403, NY, USA. ACM (2004)
3. Antoniu, T., Steckler, P.A., Krishnamurthi, S., Neuwirth, E., Felleisen, M.: Validating the unit correctness of spreadsheet programs. In: Proceedings of Software Engineering, ICSE 2004, pp. 439–448, Washington, DC, USA. IEEE Computer Society (2004)
4. Apple. Swift open source. Online https://swift.org (2020). Accessed 15 Apr 2020
5. Bekolay, T.: A comprehensive look at representing physical quantities in python. In: Scientific Computing with Python (2013)
6. Bennich-Björkman, O., McKeever., S.: The next 700 unit of measurement checkers. In: Proceedings of Software Language Engineering, SLE 2018, pp. 121–132, NY, USA. Association for Computing Machinery (2018)
7. Bureau International des Poids et Mesures. SI Brochure: the international system of units (SI), 9th Edition, Dimensions of Quantities. Online https://www.bipm.org (2019). Accessed 15 Apr (2020)

8. Burgueño, L., Mayerhofer, T., Wimmer, M., Vallecillo, A.: Specifying quantities in software models. Inf. Softw. Technol. **113**, 82–97 (2019)
9. Cavarra, A., Crichton, C., Davies, J., Hartman, A., Jeron, T., Mounier, L.: Using UML for automatic test generation. In: Proceedings of ISSTA, 01 (2002)
10. Chen, F., Rosu, G., Prasad Venkatesan, R.: Rule-based analysis of dimensional safety, In: RTA (2003)
11. Cooper, J., McKeever, S.: A model-driven approach to automatic conversion of physical units. Softw. Pract. Exper. **38**(4), 337–359 (2008)
12. Damevski, K.: Expressing measurement units in interfaces for scientific component software. In: Proceedings of Component-Based High Performance Computing, CBHPC 2009, pp. 13:1–13:8, NY, USA. ACM (2009)
13. Henning, D.: Units of measurement validator for C#. Online https://www.codeproject.com/Articles/413750/Units-of-Measure-Validator-for-Csharp (2021). Accessed 25 Oct 2021
14. Dreiheller, A., Mohr, B., Moerschbacher, M.: Programming pascal with physical units. SIGPLAN Notes **21**(12), 114–123 (1986)
15. Marcus Foster and Sean Tregeagle. Physical-type correctness in scientific python (2018)
16. Foster, M.P.: Quantities, units and computing. Comput. Stand. Interfaces **35**, 529–535 (2013)
17. Fowler, M.: Analysis Patterns: Reusable Objects Models. Addison-Wesley Longman Publishing Co. Inc., Boston, MA, USA (1997)
18. Garny, A., et al.: CellML and associated tools and techniques. Philosophical Transactions of the Royal Society, A: Mathematical, Physical and Engineering Sciences, 366 (2008)
19. Gehani, N.: Units of measure as a data attribute. Comput. Lang. **2**(3), 93–111 (1977)
20. Gibson, J.P., Méry, D.: Explicit modelling of physical measures: from Event-B to Java. In: International Workshop on Handling IMPlicit and EXplicit knowledge in formal system development (2017)
21. Hall, B.D.: Software for calculation with physical quantities. In: 2020 IEEE International Workshop on Metrology for Industry 4.0 IoT, pp. 458–463 (2020)
22. Hartmann, J., Vieira, M., Foster, H., Ruder, A.: A UML-based approach to system testing. Innov. Syst. Softw. Eng. **1**, 12–24 (2005)
23. Hayes, I.J., Mahony, B.P.: Using units of measurement in formal specifications. Formal Aspects Comput. **7**(3), 329–347 (1995)
24. Hilfinger, P.N.: An ada package for dimensional analysis. ACM Trans. Program. Lang. Syst. **10**(2), 189–203 (1988)
25. Hills, M., Feng, C., Grigorem, R.: A rewriting logic approach to static checking of units of measurement in C. Electron. Notes Theor. Comput. Sci. **290**, 51–67 (2012)
26. Jiang, L., Su, Z.: Osprey: a practical type system for validating dimensional unit correctness of C programs. In: Proceedings of the 28th International Conference on Software Engineering, ICSE 2006, pp. 262–271, New York, NY, USA. ACM (2006)
27. Joint Committee for Guides in Metrology (JCGM). International Vocabulary of Metrology, Basic and General Concepts and Associated Terms (VIM). Online https://www.bipm.org/en/about-us/ (2012). Accessed 15 Apr 2020
28. Jørring, U., Scherlis, W.L.: Compilers and staging transformations. In: Proceedings of the 13th ACM SIGACT-SIGPLAN Symposium on Principles of Programming Languages, POPL 1986, pp. 86–96, New York, NY, USA. Association for Computing Machinery (1986)
29. Karr, M., Loveman, D.B.: Incorporation of units into programming languages. Commun. ACM **21**(5), 385–391 (1978)
30. Kasurinen, J., Taipale, O., Smolander, K.: Software test automation in practice: empirical observations. Adv. Softw. Eng. **2010**, 01 (2010)
31. Kennedy, A.: Dimension types. In: Sannella, D. (ed.) ESOP 1994. LNCS, vol. 788, pp. 348–362. Springer, Heidelberg (1994). https://doi.org/10.1007/3-540-57880-3_23

32. Kennedy, A.: Types for units-of-measure: theory and practice. In: Central European Functional Programming School - Third Summer School, CEFP 2009, Budapest, Hungary, May 21–23, 2009 and Komárno, Slovakia, May 25–30, 2009, Revised Selected Lectures, pp. 268–305 (2009)

33. Krisper, M., Iber, J., Rauter, T., Kreiner, C.: Physical quantity: towards a pattern language for quantities and units in physical calculations. In: Proceedings of Pattern Languages of Programs, EuroPLoP 2017, pp. 9:1–9:20, NY, USA. ACM (2017)

34. Lungu, M.: Towards reverse engineering software ecosystems. In: 2008 IEEE International Conference on Software Maintenance, pp. 428–431 (2008)

35. Mayerhofer, T., Wimmer, M., Vallecillo, A.: Adding uncertainty and units to quantity types in software models. In Software Language Engineering, SLE 2016, pp. 118–131, NY, USA. ACM (2016)

36. McKeever, S.: From quantities in software models to implementation. In: Proceedings of the 9th International Conference on Model-Driven Engineering and Software Development - MODELSWARD, pp. 199–206. INSTICC, SciTePress (2021)

37. McKeever, S.: Discerning quantities from units of measurement. In: Proceedings of the 10th International Conference on Model-Driven Engineering and Software Development - MODELSWARD, pp. 105–115, Portugal. INSTICC, SciTePress (2022)

38. McKeever, S., Bennich-Björkman, O., Salah, O.-A.: Unit of measurement libraries, their popularity and suitability. Practice and Experience, Software (2020)

39. McKeever, S., Paçaci, G., Bennich-Björkman, O.: Quantity checking through unit of measurement libraries. Current status and future directions. In: Model-Driven Engineering and Software Development, MODELSWARD (2019)

40. Microsoft. F# software foundation. Online https://fsharp.org (2020). Accessed 15 Apr (2020)

41. Milner, R.: A theory of type polymorphism in programming. J. Comput. Syst. Sci. **17**, 348–375 (1978)

42. Modelica. The Modelica Association. Online https://www.modelica.org (2020). Accessed 15 Apr 2020

43. Mussa, M., Ouchani, S., Sammane, W., Hamou-Lhadj, A.: A survey of model-driven testing techniques. In: Proceedings - International Conference on Quality Software, pp. 167–172, 08 (2009)

44. NIST. International System of Units (SI): base and derived. Online https://physics.nist.gov/cuu/Units/units.html (2015). Accessed 02 Oct 2019

45. Ore, J.-P., Detweiler, C., Elbaum, S.: Lightweight detection of physical unit inconsistencies without program annotations. In: Proceedings of International Symposium on Software Testing and Analysis, ISSTA 2017, pp. 341–351, NY, USA. ACM (2017)

46. Ore, J.-P., Detweiler, C., Elbaum, S.: Phriky-Units: a lightweight, annotation-free physical unit inconsistency detection tool. In: Software Testing and Analysis, ISSTA 2017, pp. 352–355, NY, USA. Association for Computing Machinery (2017)

47. Ore, J.-P., Elbaum, S., Detweiler, C.: Dimensional inconsistencies in code and ROS messages: a study of 5.9 m lines of code. In: Intelligent Robots and Systems, IROS, pp. 712–718. IEEE (2017)

48. Ore, J.-P., Elbaum, S., Detweiler, C., Karkazis, L.: Assessing the type annotation burden. In: Automated Software Engineering, ASE 2018, pp. 190–201, NY, USA. ACM (2018)

49. Salah, O.-A., McKeever, S.: Lack of adoption of units of measurement libraries: survey and anecdotes. In: Proceedings of Software Engineering in Practice, ICSE-SEIP 2020. ACM, May (2020)

50. Selic, B.: Beyond mere logic: A vision of modeling languages for the 21st century. In: Pervasive and Embedded Computing and Communication Systems (PECCS), pp. IS-9-IS-9 (2015)

51. Sonin, A.A.: The physical basis of dimensional analysis, Technical report. Massachusetts Institute of Technology (2001)

52. Stephenson, A., et al.: Mars climate orbiter mishap investigation board phase 1 report (1999). Accessed 01 Oct 2019
53. TIOBE. The importance of being earnest index. Online https://www.tiobe.com/tiobe-index/, 2022. Last Accessed on 2nd of October
54. Wand, M., O'Keefe, P.: Automatic dimensional inference. In: Computational Logic - Essays in Honor of Alan Robinson, pp. 479–483 (1991)
55. Witkin, R.: Jet's fuel ran out after metric conversion errors. The New York Times, July (1983)
56. Xiang, T., Luo, J.Y., Dietl, W.: Precise inference of expressive units of measurement types. Proc. ACM Program. Lang., 4(OOPSLA), November (2020)

HERO vs Zombie: Destroying Zombie Guests in Virtual Machine Environments

Nezer Jacob Zaidenberg[1,2,3(⊠)], Michael Kiperberg[1,2,3], Yael Elinav[1,2,3], Alex Moshinky[1,2,3], and Lior Siag[1,2,3]

[1] Ariel University, Ariel, Israel
michael@trulyprotect.com
[2] Shamoon College of Engineering, Beer-Sheva, Israel
scipio@scipio.org
[3] University of Jyväskylä, Jyväskylä, Finland

Abstract. Virtual servers are now standard in data centres. Multiple virtual machines (guests) are consolidated on much fewer hosts on-site or on "the cloud", Thus saving most of the hosting costs. Virtual servers serve most of our computational needs. However, virtual machines consume no physical space. Thus abandoned servers are often unnoticed. The system administrators do not delete the servers. Sometimes the administrators do not know the servers are not in use. (Some servers often "become" unused as business processes changes, and the System administrators are not informed when the last user no longer uses the server) These servers are known as "zombie" machines. "Zombie" machines waste resources and (as they are left unattended and unpatched) pose a cyber security risk. We present HERO (Host Environment Resource Optimization). HERO is a novel tool to optimize resource use and security. HERO uses multiple tests and machine learning approaches to assist system administrators in identifying and removing "zombie" machines.

Keywords: Virtualization sprawling · Inactive virtual machines · Virtual machines · Remote management · System administration · Green computing

1 Introduction

Virtualization systems are a crucial part of modern enterprises computing needs. Virtualization systems allow for higher availability and reliability, improved flexibility in scalability (both scale-out and scale-in) as well as reduced costs when compared with traditional (physical) servers [36]. Virtualization also improves server security by facilitating patch management through the virtualization software [33]. Virtualization and related technologies such as AMD's SEV intel's SGX and TME and ARM's Trust-Zone [38] are key factors in industry 4.0 security. However, the ease of adding new virtual machines using nothing but a mouse click introduces new problems. Virtualization sprawling [37] is a phenomenon that occurs when the virtual environment grows to a scale too large to be managed effectively by the system administrator. Growth in the virtual environment introduces virtualization sprawling. Sprawling causes security

---

N. J. Zaidenberg—This chapter is an extended version of a conference paper [11].

© Springer Nature Switzerland AG 2023
L. F. Pires et al. (Eds.): MODELSWARD 2021/2022, CCIS 1708, pp. 48–59, 2023.
https://doi.org/10.1007/978-3-031-38821-7_3

risks [26] and administration overhead [6], and also wastes valuable system resources due to cores, storage and RAM allocation, increased electricity use, and CO_2 emissions [2]. Furthermore, some spawned virtual machines are not in use at all (or were used in the past, but are no longer in service). Such "Zombie" virtual machines, or comatose virtual machines [24], cause this phenomenon. A "zombie" virtual machine is a virtual machine that was created once and is no longer needed. However, "zombie" virtual machines are still active and consuming resources. A server can turn into a "zombie" for many reasons. For instance, a system administrator may forget to eliminate an experimental virtual machine. In another example, whenever a new system replaces an outdated virtual machine, The admins can delete and discard the old virtual machine. However, the system team often keeps the older system intact to ensure fast rollback should a problem with the new system occurs [9]. As a result, the system team may forget to delete these older systems long after the newer ones are considered as stable as the old ones. Another cause for unattended virtual machines is the natural swapping of employees and workplaces. Sometimes, virtual machines that belonged to former employees are left unattended as current system staff forget about their existence or purpose. Even if the team finds the system, the team may be too concerned to turn it off as the system team does not want to risk compromising the enterprise operations. The number of "zombies" varies from company to company and can comprise up to 30% of virtual machines in a given cloud environment [28]. Removing the "Zombies" can improve resource allocation at no additional cost and save money due to reduced licensing fees and cloud costs. Furthermore, "zombies" incur considerable monthly costs through increased server and air conditioning power consumption. Last, "zombie" servers constitute a security risk as they have no owner, and thus these systems are never updated or patched as discussed in [34] and other sources.

This chapter suggests a solution to address the growing problem of virtualization sprawling.

The primary purpose of our system is to discover "zombie" virtual machines using accurate, efficient, and reliable tools. Our goals are to separate and distinguish between hardly used and low-load servers that should remain intact and unused "zombies" that should be removed. HERO(Host Environment Resource Optimization), the software we introduce, runs on the host hypervisors and tests the guest virtual machines. HERO performs multiple tests to determine with high probability which virtual machines are "zombie" virtual machines. In this chapter, we describe these tests and the weight mechanism that adjusts the test result to the unique characteristics of the data center in which HERO runs.

Here we extend the work of Elinav [11] in the following aspects:

- We have developed pass-though drivers for the keyboard and the mouse to facilitate the development of usage-oriented tests.
- We have introduced a usage test based on the aforementioned drivers.
- We have introduced a extended test of software versions that considers also the versions of software components that execute in kernel-mode.
- We have extended the definition of the name test.
- We have introduced a new test based on performance counters.

- We have ported our system to another virtualized environment and to the Windows operating system, in order to demonstrate its applicability to different execution environments.
- We have extended the "Related Work" section.

2   Hero System Overview

We built HERO using Python 3.8, collecting and parsing the data using Python and shell scripts. We developed HERO for the KVM (kernel virtual machine [17] hypervisor running on CentOS Linux 7.6. KVM is an open-source virtualization technology, and HERO can support multiple KVM servers from one instance. All the virtual machines that write the program use the Ubuntu operating system and run Prometheus [29] to publish raw data via HTTP. In addition to KVM, we used VMWare VSphere 7.0 hypervisor to reach similar results. We believe HERO can be ported to other hypervisors and guest operating systems, but we tested only on VMWare and KVM with Linux and Windows guests.

HERO needs to operate from a server with access to the virtual machines in the KVM environment and a user to run KVM "virsh" [25] commands. HERO can run on a virtual machine inside the KVM hosts. On VMWare, HERO requires the NSX API and can run on any hosts that can send NSX commands to the host server. The HERO program contains four key modules:

Discovery. This module is responsible for the discovery of virtual machines and gathering information about virtual machines. An additional program, Prometheus, is used to make the information available for further processing by the other modules. We implemented the module according to Prometheus methodology [30]. On VMWare, vSphere NSX API should be installed and accessible.
Inspection. This module is responsible for all the tests that run on the virtual machines themselves. The module also collects the results data. HERO uses this data to determine what virtual machines might be "zombies".
Action. This module is responsible for the activities that HERO performs on suspected "zombies". These activities are listed online for the system administrator.
Training. This module is responsible for gathering and analyzing the data obtained from virtual machines and confirmed as "zombies" by the system administrator. In addition, we support re-adjusting the weight of each test to reflect the characteristics of the "zombies" remaining in the cloud environment.

2.1   Discovery Module

We used Node export [16] and wrote custom scripts for those metrics. The scripts periodically read and parse the data published by the node-exporter to allow virtual machine testing. The files containing the parsed data are continuously updated and limited by size. Therefore, the files usually contain data from approximately the last two weeks of operation to ensure relevance.

2.2   Inspection Module

HERO executes several tests on every virtual machine. These tests return a confidence score representing the level of confidence that the machine is indeed a "zombie". This grade will produce a weighted average with all other tests to produce a single "zombie confidence score". The weights represent how significant the test is (e.g., the "name test" is less valuable than the "CPU test"). We also support giving weighted averages to a combination of tests (for example, CPU and RAM changes test together.) The "zombie confidence score" is the confidence score HERO gives to the assumption that the machine is indeed a "zombie". "Zombie" virtual machines can act in different ways. For example, these machines still run some OS and other services (for example, an out-of-date anti-virus) and may have some CPU consumption. Furthermore, operational virtual machines that are rarely used (but are still in use) may have several "zombie" characteristics. Therefore, we chose to conduct many tests and give these tests a weighted average for significance.

2.3   Tests

Usually, it is easy to ensure that a server is not a "zombie". For example, port TCP-22 (ssh) traffic indicates someone logged in to the server. In addition, changing CPU and network usage levels usually indicates that a virtual machine is in use and operational. No network traffic or close to zero CPU usage for a long time often (but not always) indicates that a virtual machine is indeed a "zombie".

Note that in some cases, license servers are "servers in use", and these servers have very low CPU and network usage, so this is not a distinct separator (Fig. 1).

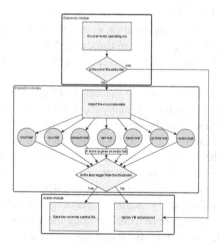

Fig. 1. HERO architecture. Graphics taken from [11].

A server that does not communicate with external sources for long periods or reboots frequently and fails to demonstrate the stability expected from production servers is likely to be a "zombie" server. However, such servers may simply be temporarily off-duty (for example, during off-peak periods) or backup servers (that will be used only if the main site has failed). HERO will attempt to confirm which servers are "zombies" and which are legitimate virtual machines that are temporarily idle.

CPU Test. HERO checks the CPU usage of the virtual machine. A server that is mostly idle is not likely to be an operational server and thus is a potential "zombie". However, even on a "zombie" virtual machine, some OS services (e.g., the scheduler) and some services are still running, so the load will not be zero. (for example, an anti-virus may run periodically) CPU usage varies when the virtual machine only runs default services compared to servers that also start programs. The test checks the 15-minute average CPU load against a configured threshold and returns the percentage of those occurrences. [4] used similar tests to detect idle systems.

High CPU load multiple times per day (So not likely to be a result of scheduled processes such as anti-virus tests) is an indication that the server is not a zombie. Very low CPU usage is an indication of a zombie server.

RAM Test. We have two RAM tests. In the first test, HERO checks how often the virtual machine allocates RAM. An idle server is likely not operational, and its RAM usage varies when the virtual machine only runs default services versus initiated programs. This test works similarly to the CPU test. The RAM can be checked and compared to the previous running of HERO using hashes. A similar method was used in [4]. The RAM and swap can also be analyzed for running processes and changes.

In the second RAM test, the virtual memory of the virtual machine can be obtained [3,22] and analyzed using volatility [7] and similar tools. We scan the process list and examine for new processes spawned. If there is no process spawn, possibly, the server is not used, at least during the test. If a new process spawns, then the server usually is not a "zombie". Again this is not a distinct separation. There are backup servers that are critical for the organization's business continuity (though they spawn no new process and are not currently in use), and there are "cron" jobs that spawn processes automatically on "zombie" servers. Again, this is not a distinct separator but a strong indication.

Very few memory changes between the execution of HERO strongly indicate that the server is a zombie server. In contrast, many memory changes between the execution of HERO strongly indicate that the server is not a zombie server. No or very few new processes between executions of HERO is a weak indication of a zombie server.

Network Test. HERO checks the communication with the virtual machine. As all virtual machines are likely to generate network traffic, even "zombie" virtual machines, (Traffic such as ARP, broadcast responses, and DHCP will appear on all systems.) [14]. This test checks if the daily incoming and outgoing network traffic exceeds a certain threshold. The test score reflects how long the virtual machine has not communicated with another device (transmit or receive). Some virtual machines may not even have a network adapter and are inaccessible by the network. Unlike physical servers (That may run offline processes), virtual machines without network adapters are highly likely to be "zombies". (as it is highly unusual to have a virtual machine without network access)

We treat a high network load as indicating that the machine is not a zombie. We treat low network load as a weak indication that the machine is a zombie.

Uptime Test A server that has a very long uptime means that the server has gone through no significant upgrades. Also, periodic maintenance shutdowns were not performed on the server [10].

Frequent Booting Test. Frequent rebooting is an abnormal behaviour that will be quickly noticed and fixed in a non- "zombie" virtual machine. This test will determine the number of times the virtual machine has rebooted in the documented period [13]. Thus, very high uptime (which indicates lack of maintenance and upgrade) and very low values (which indicates instability are both indicators for "zombie" virtual machines.

Name Test. Suspicious names (Such as "test," "check," "ABC," "try," and "temp") usually indicate that a virtual machine is temporary. However, production virtual machines most likely have a more meaningful name. Thus any of the names above will indicate a "zombie" virtual machine. Furthermore, we discovered that some servers who are not zombies are acting as license servers for software that is seldom used. For example, memory checking and profiling software that is used only once a product is released. These license servers may appear as zombies (receiving and sending no data for long periods) only to be used eventually. Thus we removed names that included "license" from the zombie check.

Software Version Test. The HERO software check if the virtual machine's software version exists in the "approved versions" list. HERO performs the software version test using agents, or by examining the RAM of the inspected system using LibVMI [31], NSX [32], or similar systems. A virtual machine with an old version will indicate an unmaintained and rarely upgraded virtual machine. The software version test is very important because virtual machines with older operating system versions are unlikely to have recent security patches, meaning they can also be a cybersecurity threat. (and thus pose a cybersecurity threat in addition to wasting resources)

Physical Usage Test. The HERO software creates virtual mouse and keyboard drivers that serve almost like "pass-through" drivers. The only difference between the HERO driver and the standard driver is that HERO records keyboard usage and mouse usage in the log (but HERO does not create a keylogger!).

While some minimal usage may exist in zombies (for example logging in and finding out it is the wrong server), we believe that usage of over 1 min in a month indicates that the server is not a zombie. (If the login was incidental, the system will mark the system for removal on the next check.)

Operating system updates test This test is similar to the software version tests but checks the operating system itself. The HERO software scans the memory using volatility or NSX. First, HERO detects the OS version running on the guests. Then, using hashes (This method is similar to H-KPP [23]), We detect changes, mark the time since the last OS upgrade. We also check for missed critical security updates. A server missing several critical security updates is likely to be a zombie.

The operating system updates test is not a strong factor as sometimes production servers are behind corporate firewalls and are not a security risk. Furthermore, as updates may require downtime and cause software problems, production servers' operating systems not exposed to external users are not updated. On the other hand, sometimes all servers (including zombies) are updated in an automatic process. However lack of updates is another indication for a zombie server. Therefore, we treat missing updates for over one year a weak indication and missing updates for two years strong indication.

Performance Counters Test. Architectural performance counters are usually used for software profiling. However, some performance counters can be used to indicate that a particular server is a zombie. During the "Performance counters test" we periodically obtain the values of certain performance counters and check whether they increase significantly. In particular, we have selected the following performance counters for this test: (a) ARITH — counts the number of arithmetic divisions and multiplications, (b) HW_INT — counts the number of hardware interrupts, (c) IO_TRANSACTIONS — counts the number of IO transactions, (d) DTLB_LOAD_MISSES — counts the number of TLB misses of different kinds.

3   Results

We tested HERO in a lab environment, Using KVM hosts and VMWare hosts.

3.1   Using KVM Hosts

We also run simulated tests. Our hosts hosted 8 "zombie" virtual machines and 25 working virtual machines. We simulated the workload by scripts that initiated random network communication and used CPU and RAM for long periods.

At the first execution of HERO, with the weights we chose, the following results were obtained: True Positive Rate (TPR) = 0.363 and True Negative Rate (TNR) = 0.818, with balanced accuracy of 0.590. After training HERO once, we obtained the following results using our training code: TPR = 0.454 and TNR = 0.863, with a balanced accuracy of 0.658. Then, we executed the training code several more times and reached TPR = 0.521 and TNR = 0.912 with balanced accuracy of 0.717 The results show that HERO was able to learn and adjust the weights according to our test lab environment.

On data taken from real world site, The site included 19 VMs both Linux and Windows. We detected 3 machines that were true zombie. We also had one false positive detection (The license server that led us to update the name test). The rest of the 15 machines were true negatives.

3.2   Using VMWare Hosts

We run HERO on VMWare 7 WebSphere hosting 8 "zombie" virtual machines and 25 working virtual machines. We created workload using the same scripts as above.

At the first execution of HERO, with the weights we chose, the following results were obtained: True Positive Rate (TPR) = 0.343 and True Negative Rate (TNR) = 0.825, with balanced accuracy of 0.584. After training HERO, the following results were obtained: TPR = 0.462 and TNR = 0.853, with a balanced accuracy of 0.658. Additional runs managed to increase the TPR=0.531, TNR =0.899 and balanced accuracy of 0.715.

4   Related Work

There are several virtual machine management and monitoring tools. However, few of these tools inspect virtual environments and address the "zombie" virtual machine problem. We describe some of them, their merits, and why they do not completely solve the "zombie" virtual machine problem. One such similar solution is ICSI. ICSI [21] is a garbage collector based on the resource utilization decision model. ICSI first identifies the purpose of each virtual machine, as differently purposed virtual machines have different utilization patterns and thus different ways to determine inactivity. It then searches for active virtual machines, as they have a stronger affinity towards those patterns. Finally, it performs network affinity analysis for the virtual machines marked as inactive in order to reduce the number of virtual machines wrongly marked as inactive. Another utilization-based model [12] adds client-virtual machine network activity and screen changes into consideration. This approach says that a user interacts with the system if there are many changes to the screen. Likewise, if many packets transmit between the client and the virtual machine, likely, the virtual machine is currently in use. If both do not indicate activity, it refers to CPU, memory, and network usage to determine the activity level. Garbo [8] creates a directed graph with edges representing dependency between resources. The user inputs a set of core resources used with non-cloud dependencies. Garbo uses these resources as the roots of a Mark & Sweep process. This approach fails to consider stand-alone virtual machines, which can be active, just not connected to other resources. Pleco [35] is another example for the graph-based approach. It creates a dependency graph between applications and resources, assigns weight for each reference which represents how much the connection indicates activity, and calculates the confidence level for the virtual machines marked as inactive. [20] Attempts to identify inactive virtual machines by checking different parameters. First, they establish that most virtual machines have low resource utilization. They added a login history check into their parameters testing. Finally, they established that different virtual machines have different purposes and, thus, different resource usage patterns. Therefore, each group require different evaluation. We could not perform such evaluation without access to real world data from multiple sources but we believe multiple evaluations may also improve HERO.

They trained their model to find active virtual machines from the virtual machines after filtering the obvious inactive ones. They did that because active virtual machines show stronger features to determine whether there are active than inactive virtual machines to determine they are inactive. So the group that is left is then the inactive one. Thus it is a competing approach to HERO. [1] is an implementation of a similar system. This one simply has a mechanism that deletes virtual Machines nobody has accessed for a long time. It does not consider other parameters. Thus it is another example of inactive virtual Machine detection and garbage collection, but it is much simpler than HERO.

SolarWinds Virtualization Manager [19] provides high-quality and reliable virtual machine management and monitoring, performance management, capacity planning, and cluster optimization. SolarWinds can control virtual machine sprawl and resource inefficiencies by powering off idle virtual machines or deleting virtual machines that are no longer in use. This can help reclaim resources that the host hypervisor and other virtual machines can use. SolarWinds Virtualization Manager can find some "zombie" virtual machines. However, SolarWinds Virtualization Manager works only on VMWare and Hyper-V. It does not work with KVM. SolarWinds Virtualization Manager is proprietary software and requires an expensive license.

RVTools [27] is a Windows application that can display information about virtual environments. RVTools is able to list information about running virtual machines. RVTools present CPU, memory, disks, partitions, networks, and other resources that each virtual machine use. RVTools can find some "zombie" virtual machines, but RVTools works only with VMWare ESXi virtualization servers. RVTools does not work with KVM.

Prometheus [29] is an open-source system monitoring and alerting toolkit originally built at SoundCloud. Prometheus is a full monitoring system with built-in active scraping, storing, and other features. Prometheus knows the virtualization data center's contents (which endpoints should exist and what time series patterns mean trouble) and actively tries to find faults. Thus Prometheus can detect "zombies". Though Prometheus is an extensive virtual machine monitoring tool, Prometheus does not have a specific "zombie" machine finder.

WhatsUp Gold [18] is an end-to-end monitoring, performance and availability reporting tool. WhatsUp Gold displays information about hosts and guests, host/guest relationships, clusters, and real-time status. WhatsUp Gold also monitors hosts' and guests' performance and resource consumption, including CPU, memory, disk, and more. Unfortunately, WhatsUp Gold does not have a specific "zombie" machine finder and only works in VMWare and Hyper-V environments.

Veeam One [15] provides historical data regarding virtual machine resource usage. In addition, Veeam One provides forecasts about resource usage, assists in planning for capacity changes, and can model usage trends and predict costs for storage, compute power, and backup. Veeam One can find possible infrastructure weaknesses or vulnerabilities, but it does not have a specific "zombie" machine finder. Veeam One only works in VMWare and Hyper-V environments. SolarWinds is one of the strongest monitoring tools in the market and advertises its virtual machine utilization as one of its most important features. As shown above, most of the monitoring tools available today work only with VMWare and Hyper-V, some do not look for "zombie" virtual machines, and most of them charge licensing fees. These factors emphasize the need for a project such as ours. Another way to detect "zombies" is by using an introspection solution, such as libvmi [31] or NSX [32], or software inside the virtual machine [22]. The memory can later be analyzed using tools such as rekall [5], or volatility [7] While these systems may provide all the required components to detect "zombies", These systems do not include a unique "zombie"-finding tool and some hacking may be required. In addition, the performance cost of using these tools is quite high.

5   Conclusions

We designed and developed HERO, a system to locate and identify "zombie" virtual machines. We found that HERO could successfully locate "zombie" virtual machines by deploying HERO in a virtual server environment. Thus hero can improve the cost of ownership for such a cluster and eliminate cybersecurity risks.

We have used HERO on KVM and VMWare environments. However, Other hypervisors provide all the required capabilities for the system to be easily ported.

The work can improved further by accessing real live data from a data center. We had to estimate the common "zombie" characteristics based on our knowledge and experience. Because HERO cannot definitively verify which virtual machines are "zombies", system administrators must still confirm which virtual machines to deactivate. However, with further development and additional tests and accuracy improvements, HERO could be an invaluable tool for system administrators, empowering them to quickly and accurately track down "zombie" machines.

References

1. wook Baek, H., Srivastava, A., Van der Merwe, J.: Cloudvmi: virtual machine introspection as a cloud service. In: 2014 IEEE International Conference on Cloud Engineering, pp. 153–158. IEEE (2014)
2. Belanger, S., Casemore, B.: "Exploring the impact of infrastructure virtualization on digital transformation strategies and carbon emissions'" an idc white paper, sponsored by vmware
3. Ben Yehuda, R., Shlingbaum, E., Gershfeld, Y., Tayouri, S., Zaidenberg, N.J.: Hypervisor memory acquisition for arm. Forensic Sci. Int. Dig. Invest. **37**, 301106 (2021)
4. Bila, N., de Lara, E., Joshi, K., Lagar-Cavilla, H.A., Hiltunen, M., Satyanarayanan, M.: Jettison: Efficient idle desktop consolidation with partial VM migration. In: Proceedings of the 7th ACM European Conference on Computer Systems, pp. 211–224 (2012)
5. Block, F., Dewald, A.: Linux memory forensics: dissecting the user space process heap. Digit. Invest. **22**, S66–S75 (2017)
6. Carroll, M., Kotzé, P., Van der Merwe, A.: Secure virtualization: benefits, risks and constraints (2011)
7. Case, A., Richard, G.G., III.: Memory forensics: the path forward. Digit. Invest. **20**, 23–33 (2017)
8. Cohen, N., Bremler-Barr, A.: Graph-based cloud resource cleanup
9. Colman-Meixner, C., Develder, C., Tornatore, M., Mukherjee, B.: A survey on resiliency techniques in cloud computing infrastructures and applications. IEEE Commun. Surv. Tutor. **18**(3), 2244–2281 (2016)
10. Colman-Meixner, C., Develder, C., Tornatore, M., Mukherjee, B.: A survey on resiliency techniques in cloud computing infrastructures and applications. IEEE Commun. Surv. Tutor. **18**(3), 2244–2281 (2016). https://doi.org/10.1109/COMST.2016.2531104
11. Elinav, Y., Moshinky, A., Siag, L., Zaidenberg, N.J.: Hero vs. zombie: identifying zombie guests in a virtual machine environment. In: MODELSWARD. INSTICC (2021)
12. Fesl, J., Gokhale, V., Feslová, M.: Efficient virtual machine consolidation approach based on user inactivity detection. Cloud Comput. **2019**, 115 (2019)
13. Galante, G., de Bona, L.C.E.: A survey on cloud computing elasticity. In: 2012 IEEE Fifth International Conference on Utility and Cloud Computing, pp. 263–270. IEEE (2012)
14. Georgiou, S., Tsakalozos, K., Delis, A.: Exploiting network-topology awareness for VM placement in IAAS clouds. In: 2013 International Conference on Cloud and Green Computing, pp. 151–158. IEEE (2013)
15. Graziano, M., Lanzi, A., Balzarotti, D.: Hypervisor memory forensics. In: Stolfo, S.J., Stavrou, A., Wright, C.V. (eds.) RAID 2013. LNCS, vol. 8145, pp. 21–40. Springer, Heidelberg (2013). https://doi.org/10.1007/978-3-642-41284-4_2

16. Großmann, M., Schenk, C.: A comparison of monitoring approaches for virtualized services at the network edge. In: 2018 International Conference on Internet of Things, Embedded Systems and Communications (IINTEC), pp. 85–90. IEEE (2018)

17. Habib, I.: Virtualization with KVM. Linux J. **2008**(166), 8 (2008)

18. Hernantes, J., Gallardo, G., Serrano, N.: It infrastructure-monitoring tools. IEEE Softw. **32**(4), 88–93 (2015)

19. Kedia, P., Nagpal, R., Singh, T.P.: A survey on virtualization service providers, security issues, tools and future trends. Int. J. Comput. Appl. **69**(24) (2013)

20. Kim, I.K., Zeng, S., Young, C., Hwang, J., Humphrey, M.: A supervised learning model for identifying inactive VMS in private cloud data centers. In: Proceedings of the Industrial Track of the 17th International Middleware Conference, pp. 1–7 (2016)

21. Kim, I.K., Zeng, S., Young, C., Hwang, J., Humphrey, M.: ICSI: a cloud garbage VM collector for addressing inactive VMs with machine learning. In: 2017 IEEE International Conference on Cloud Engineering (IC2E), pp. 17–28. IEEE (2017)

22. Kiperberg, M., Leon, R., Resh, A., Algawi, A., Zaidenberg, N.: Hypervisor-assisted atomic memory acquisition in modern systems. In: International Conference on Information Systems Security and Privacy. SCITEPRESS Science And Technology Publications (2019)

23. Kiperberg, M., Zaidenberg, N.J.: H-kpp: Hypervisor-assisted kernel patch protection. Applied Sciences 12(10) (2022). https://doi.org/10.3390/app12105076, https://www.mdpi.com/2076-3417/12/10/5076

24. Koomey, J., Taylor, J.: Zombie/comatose servers redux. Report by Koomey Analytics and Anthesis. Recuperado de http://anthesisgroup. com/zombie-servers-redux (2017)

25. Kovari, A., Dukan, P.: KVM & openvz virtualization based IAAS open source cloud virtualization platforms: opennode, proxmox ve. In: 2012 IEEE 10th Jubilee International Symposium on Intelligent Systems and Informatics, pp. 335–339. IEEE (2012)

26. Luo, S., Lin, Z., Chen, X., Yang, Z., Chen, J.: Virtualization security for cloud computing service. In: 2011 International Conference on Cloud and Service Computing, pp. 174–179. IEEE (2011)

27. Mauro, A., Valsecchi, P., Novak, K.: Mastering VMware vSphere 6.5: leverage the power of vSphere for effective virtualization, administration, management and monitoring of data centers. Packt Publishing Ltd. (2017)

28. Mazumdar, S., Pranzo, M.: Power efficient server consolidation for cloud data center. Futur. Gener. Comput. Syst. **70**, 4–16 (2017)

29. Padgham, L., Winikoff, M.: Prometheus: a methodology for developing intelligent agents. In: Giunchiglia, F., Odell, J., Weiß, G. (eds.) AOSE 2002. LNCS, vol. 2585, pp. 174–185. Springer, Heidelberg (2003). https://doi.org/10.1007/3-540-36540-0_14

30. Padgham, L., Winikoff, M.: Prometheus: a practical agent-oriented methodology. In: Agent-Oriented Methodologies, pp. 107–135. IGI Global (2005)

31. Payne, B.D.: Simplifying virtual machine introspection using LIBVMI. Sandia report, pp. 43–44 (2012)

32. Pettit, J., Pfaff, B., Stringer, J., Tu, C.C., Blanco, B., Tessmer, A.: Bringing platform harmony to vmware nsx (2018)

33. Ray, E., Schultz, E.: Virtualization security. In: Proceedings of the 5th Annual Workshop on Cyber Security and Information Intelligence Research: Cyber Security and Information Intelligence Challenges and Strategies, pp. 1–5 (2009)

34. Sapp, K.L.: Managing Virtual Infrastructure with Veeam® ONE™. Packt Publishing Ltd (2014)

35. Shen, Z., Young, C.C., Zeng, S., Murthy, K., Bai, K.: Identifying resources for cloud garbage collection. In: 2016 12th International Conference on Network and Service Management (CNSM), pp. 248–252. IEEE (2016)

36. Steinder, M., Whalley, I., Carrera, D., Gaweda, I., Chess, D.: Server virtualization in auto-
    nomic management of heterogeneous workloads. In: 2007 10th IFIP/IEEE International
    Symposium on Integrated Network Management, pp. 139–148. IEEE (2007)
37. Suchithra, R., Rajkumar, N.: Efficient migration-a leading solution for server consolidation.
    Int. J. Comput. Appl. **60**(18) (2012)
38. Zaidenberg, N.J.: Hardware rooted security in industry 4.0 systems. In: Cyber Defence in
    Industry 4.0 Systems and Related Logistics and IT Infrastructures, vol. 51, pp. 135–151
    (2018)

Multi-view FMEA Re-validation: Efficient Risk and Engineering Knowledge Integration in Agile Production Systems Engineering

Felix Rinker[1,2(✉)], Sebastian Kropatschek[3], Thorsten Steuer[3], Elmar Kiesling[4], Kristof Meixner[1,2], Laura Waltersdorfer[2], Patrik Sommer[5], Arndt Lüder[6], Dietmar Winkler[1,2], and Stefan Biffl[2,3]

[1] CDL for Security and Quality Improvement in the Production System Lifecycle, TU Wien, Vienna, Austria
{felix.rinker,kristof.meixner,dietmar.winkler}@tuwien.ac.at
[2] Institute of Information Systems Engineering, Technische Universität Wien, Vienna, Austria
{laura.waltersdorfer,stefan.biffl}@tuwien.ac.at
[3] Center for Digital Production, Vienna, Austria
{sebastian.kropatschek,thorsten.steuer,stefan.biffl}@acdp.at
[4] Institute of Data, Process, and Knowledge Engineering, WU Wien, Vienna, Austria
elmar.kiesling@wu.ac.at
[5] Neuman Aluminium, CAG Holding GmbH, Lilienfeld, Austria
patrik.sommer@neuman.at
[6] IAF at FMB, Otto-v.Guericke University, Magdeburg, Germany
arndt.lueder@ovgu.de

Abstract. In agile Production Systems Engineering (PSE), multi-disciplinary teams work concurrently on various PSE artifacts in an iterative process that can be supported by common concept and Product-Process-Resource (PPR) modeling. However, keeping track of the interactions and effects of changes across engineering disciplines and their implications for risk assessment is exceedingly difficult in such settings. To tackle this challenge and systematically co-evolve Failure Mode and Effects Analysis (FMEA) and PPR models during PSE, it is necessary to propagate and validate changes across engineering artifacts. To this end, we design and evaluate a *FMEA-linked-to-PPR assets (FMEA+PPR) meta model* to represent relationships between FMEA elements and PSE assets and trace their change states and dependencies in the design and validation lifecycle. Furthermore, we design and evaluate the FMEA+PPR method to efficiently re-validate FMEA models upon changes in multi-view PSE models. We evaluate the model and method in a feasibility study on the quality of a joining process automated by a robot cell in automotive PSE. The study results indicate that the FMEA+PPR method is feasible and addresses requirements for FMEA re-validation better than alternative traditional approaches. Thereby, the FMEA+PPR approach facilitates a paradigm shift from traditional, isolated PSE and FMEA activities towards an integrated agile PSE method.

Keywords: Agile production systems engineering · FMEA · Model-driven engineering · Multi-view modeling · Multi-disciplinary engineering · Change impact analysis

© Springer Nature Switzerland AG 2023
L. F. Pires et al. (Eds.): MODELSWARD 2021/2022, CCIS 1708, pp. 60–83, 2023.
https://doi.org/10.1007/978-3-031-38821-7_4

1   Introduction

In recent years, a technological revolution in industrial systems has been discussed under various labels – in Europe, most notably under the term Industry 4.0 (I4.0) [14]. Key goals of I4.0 include, among others, IT-enabled mass customization of manufactured products and automatic and flexible adaptation of the production chain [35,36]. These goals require a flexible approach towards the engineering of industrial systems and a shortening of development cycles. Consequently, Production Systems Engineering (PSE) has become agile as engineers from several disciplines work iteratively and in parallel to develop Product-Process-Resource (PPR) assets, such as product designs, production process models, and production resource plans, using PPR modeling approaches [1,32].

In agile engineering processes, engineers update their PPR design assumptions multiple times throughout a project [5]. Reasons for such revised assumptions include changed requirements from product design updates, changes in process design, or a better understanding of system characteristics resulting from collaborative design, simulation, and testing. Stakeholders across engineering disciplines make design changes frequently and routinely. Consequently, these changes make it exceedingly difficult to assess potential quality implications and risk factors as PSE artifacts evolve. Hence, managing risks efficiently and effectively has become a significant challenge in multidisciplinary, agile PSE [13].

In this context, the Failure Mode and Effects Analysis (FMEA) is an established method for evaluating the effects of potential failures of system components, assessing risk factors, and detecting and isolating faults [47]. FMEA reports are typically required to demonstrate compliance with safety and quality requirements, such as ISO 9001, QS 9000 and ISO/TS 16949 [22]. However, document-driven or paper-based FMEA hinders the efficient identification of potential design flaws and the mitigation of risks in the early stages of system design. Furthermore, in late project phases, i.e., after requirements analysis, design, and development, the re-validation of FMEA results is often limited; late changes in the design documentation are often not considered. Therefore, error-prone and laborious reconstruction of knowledge from design documentation is often necessary [34] to maintain the FMEA.

This paper aims to facilitate FMEA re-validation as an integral part of the PSE process. To this end, it is necessary to implement FMEA re-validation into engineering workflows to maintain the FMEA, track the validity of its elements, and foster the continuous reflection of changes to engineering assets. In the following, we present challenges that hinder the efficient re-validation of FMEA in multi-disciplinary PSE settings [5].

Challenge 1. *Scattered and Implicit Domain Expert Knowledge.* Typically, there are semantic gaps between concepts used by stakeholders who conduct FMEA analyses and other domain experts in PSE projects. Bridging that gap requires domain knowledge, which is often not explicitly documented or scattered across heterogeneous artifacts. This makes the process of comparing and aligning FMEA models and PSE artifacts inefficient and error-prone.

Challenge 2. *Inefficient analysis of changes.* The FMEA shall reuse concepts from PPR models to use shared knowledge. However, it remains unclear how map FMEA to

PPR models to efficiently re-validate elements after PSE artifact changes. Therefore, it is necessary to provide and automate the following capabilities *(i)* a multi-view PPR model that integrates and preserves the PSE knowledge and stakeholder perspectives; *(ii)* identify and manage changes in and between PPR assets and FMEA model elements; *(iii)* a data integration process that enables agile engineering workflows such as the update propagation between PPR assets and FMEA model elements property values; and *(iv)* analyzing which FMEA model elements require re-validation due to PPR asset changes.

This paper tackles these challenges by exploring how a PPR Asset Network (PAN)-based coordination [8] can facilitate the efficient integration of multi-view PPR and FMEA models. As an illustrative use case, we show a *torque value* change in several engineering views (quality, mechanics, engineering, automation) and its effect for FMEA re-validation w.r.t. *joining quality* (cf. Sect. 4).

This work builds on and extends our previous work on multi-view model risk assessment and engineering knowledge integration in agile PSE [6,28,30] and consists of *(i)* a more detailed use case and domain analysis description, resulting in requirements for risk and engineering knowledge integration to enable an efficient FMEA-linked-to-PPR assets (FMEA+PPR) re-validation approach, *(ii)* the *FMEA+PPR meta model* to represent relationships between FMEA elements and PPR assets and trace their change states and dependencies in the design and validation lifecycle, refined by a PAN-based coordination of asset property value changes, *(iii)* the *FMEA+PPR method* is described in more detail to provide capabilities for change analysis with FMEA concepts and constraints in agile PSE, *(iv)* the *FMEA+PPR system architecture* is newly introduced to automate the multi-view risk and engineering knowledge integration capabilities. We evaluate the FMEA+PPR model and method in a feasibility study on the quality of a joining process automated by a robot cell in an automotive PSE context. Additionally, we report on previously conducted evaluation result of this method in comparison to alternative approaches [28].

The main contributions of this paper are: *(i)* The provision of *insights* to Model-based Systems Engineering (MBSE) researchers on PSE domain concepts and issues. *(ii)* The *FMEA+PPR meta model* to represent the concepts required for FMEA re-validation after updates to PSE artifacts. *(iii)* The *FMEA+PPR method* to define multi-view model integration as a basis for efficient FMEA re-validation after updates to PSE artifacts. *(iv)* Results of a *feasibility study* on the FMEA+PPR approach by providing a FMEA+PPR model instance for a use case derived from real-world data in comparison to two traditional approaches.

The remainder of this paper is structured as follows. Section 2 summarizes related work on Knowledge Management in PSE and FMEA. Section 3 motivates the research question and describes the research method. Section 4 introduces an illustrative use case for evaluation and requirements for efficient FMEA re-validation in PSE. Section 5 outlines the FMEA+PPR meta model and process for the representation of knowledge and the steps for efficient FMEA re-validation after changes to PSE artifacts. Section 6 reports on a feasibility study with a FMEA+PPR model instance based on real-world industry data to validate the research results. Section 7 discusses the research results and limitations. Section 8 concludes and delineates future work.

2   Related Work

This section summarizes related work on Knowledge Management in PSE and the FMEA method.

2.1   Traceable Knowledge Management in PSE

In PSE, engineers collaborate in a Multi-Disciplinary Engineering Environment (MDEE) to design a production system [2]. This requires an iterative, consistent, and highly qualitative design, construction, and validation process [5]. The challenge is to integrate the discipline-specific engineering views, concepts and artifacts into a holistic data view. This requires effective and efficient collection, selection, and transformation of scattered and heterogeneous information.

System Modeling in PSE. Typically, the engineering information in PSE projects is encapsulated in discipline- and tool-specific artifacts [42]. Discipline-specific artifacts and processes hinder a seamless and traceable information exchange across disciplines and stakeholders [44], which is needed to support the Industry 4.0 transformation in PSE. Domain-specific modeling languages and model-driven engineering can facilitate complex data-driven use cases in the Industry 4.0 context [46]. Reference Architecture Model for Industry 4.0 (RAMI40) is a main building block of the Industry 4.0 initiative and is supported by established standards and technologies, like AutomationML (AML), Systems Modeling Language (SysML), Data Exchange in the Process Industry (DEXPI) and OPC Unified Architecture (OPCUA), which aim at alleviating these limitations [15]. Blockchain technologies can also increase the traceability across the lifecycle of Industry 4.0 systems [19].

Multi-view Modeling and Common Concepts in PSE. Multi-view modeling [4] supports collaboration and knowledge integration in Multi-Disciplinary Engineering Environment (MDEE): Achieving multi-view models in PSE projects, requires to identify relevant information across domain-specific concepts and models, defined as boundary objects [41]. Common views on assets [29] seem promising to describe Industry 4.0 components [20,26]. Schleipen *et al.* [33] describe PPR modeling, detailing requirements and an integrated model in PSE. PPR modeling incorporates the three main aspects of a production system: (1) *products* with their properties, (2) *processes* that produce products, and (3) *resources* that execute production processes. Meixner *et al.* [24] introduced the PPR Domain Specific Language (DSL), a machine-readable and technology-agnostic DSL for PSE modeling. A PPR Asset Network (PAN) [8] is an integrated multi-view engineering model that consists of these common concepts, their properties, and multi-disciplinary interfaces [23].

Multi-view Model Integration in PSE. Adequate multi-view process and framework support is a major concern to support interdisciplinary PSE [4,44]. Tunjic *et al.* [43] introduce a Single Underlying Model (SUM), a common unified model, to enable multi-view modeling environments. To populate a SUM, previously defined mappings between the common and the single views, are used. Biffl *et al.* [7] define *Engineering Data Logistics* as a socio-technical system ensuring that engineers receive the required data at the right amount, quality, and point in time using an integrated model. Several framework architectures [16,21] propose AML for modeling such a integrated model in the PSE context. Rinker *et al.* [30] propose a Multi-view Model Transformation (MvMT) architecture, which uses AML to enable and automate an multi-disciplinary and view-specific data integration pipeline.

2.2   Failure Mode and Effects Analysis (FMEA)

Quality assurance is crucial part in the engineering of technical systems [17]. It involves many disciplines and related engineering roles, but is mainly centered around quality engineering that uses appropriate quality models [13]. The FMEA is an engineering and quality assurance method to identify and mitigate risks and potential production failures before a customer can be effected by poor product performance [40,47]. A typical FMEA identifies known and potential failure modes along with their corresponding causes and effects, prioritizes them, and defines corrective actions. Several FMEA types have been reported [40]. The *process FMEA* focuses on failure modes occurring during the manufacturing and/or the assembly process. The *design* and *concepts FMEA* addresses product-level or concept-level failure modes [37]. Other approaches aim at enhancing the FMEA method to identify waste modes or to monitor service quality [10, 38].

In multi-disciplinary engineering processes, the FMEA typically starts with assembling a FMEA team of experts with relevant domain knowledge [47]. This team analyses the system's architecture, functions, and characteristics. Utilizing expert meetings, (a) potential failure modes of the analyzed objects, (b) the respective impact and consequences, and (c) potential mitigation actions are identified and assessed. The evaluation is based on the criteria severity, occurrence, and detection [47], represented by the Risk Priority Number (RPN). All steps of the analysis are documented in a comprehensive FMEA report, including a priority list of failure modes and corrective actions.

Although there exists a number of tools to support the FMEA, the monitoring of artifact updates remains challenging [39]. Therefore, we explore the feasibility of representing FMEA model elements alongside with PSE model elements in a PPR Asset Network for facilitating efficient analysis and updates.

Traditional FMEA Applications. We observed the following FMEA application areas, relevant for automation system integrators:

FMEA Model Representation. FMEA knowledge can be represented in plain text, spreadsheet tables, graph modeling tools and dedicated FMEA tools. However, few FMEA representations consider the knowledge of PSE tools or databases. Established FMEA tools, such as APIS[1], focus on the textual description (in natural language) of FMEA concepts. Therefore, it is difficult to provide tool support for the efficient identification of FMEA elements that require re-validation.

Early FMEA as Living Documentation. Early FMEA can start after the initial definition of the production system, as soon as the main resources are specified. In this case, findings from FMEA can inform detail engineering to mitigate important risks early and efficient.

---

[1] APIS: http://www.apis-iq.com/.

FMEA as Documentation for Regulators. To fulfill regulatory requirements for risk management, the FMEA is created/updated before delivering the production system to the customer. If the FMEA approach is applied in this context, often no frequent updates are required/executed. Consequently, findings in late project phases can lead to expensive late design changes.

Knowledge Management for FMEA Re-validation. Two main approaches have emerged to manage knowledge in PSE for FMEA re-validation. They can be categorized based on their capabilities for knowledge representation and access as well as capabilities for data collection and process coordination.

FMEA re-validation based on Engineering Artifacts is common for FMEA models and engineering artifacts that have been developed and maintained independently [13]. Quality engineers re-validate the correctness of FMEA models based on their knowledge of the engineering project. Therefore, they manually review PSE artifacts and the semantics of the engineering objects, which typically requires support by domain experts. The re-validation results in new or revised versions of FMEA models. Feedback to the engineering team is given manually based on document exchange. Hence, the quality of the FMEA re-validation outcome hinges on the experts' knowledge and their coordination capabilities.

FMEA re-validation in Tool Suites aims at improving FMEA re-validation by exploiting tool suites that can integrate engineering artifacts into engineering objects. These engineering objects represent the data required by a selected subset of the engineering disciplines in an engineering organization [16]. Tool suites simplify the re-validation process by supporting (i) the review of engineering artifact changes to engineering objects and (ii) the interaction and coordination with domain experts. In addition, tool suites can enable the integration of FMEA models into the tool suite to provide automatic feedback to experts. However, typical PSE tool suites do not provide the required re-validation support.

In this paper, we explore the *FMEA re-validation with dependencies to a PPR* by representing dependency links between FMEA models and PPR asset concepts [8]. This facilitates the concurrent engineering of the FMEA model and PPR assets. To provide sufficient access to integrated PPR knowledge, this approach is based on engineering data logistics [9], which provides integrated information management on engineering artifacts coming from the disciplines required in an engineering project. This approach builds on handling engineering objects similar to the asset administration shell in Industry 4.0 [26]. To this end, we integrate all engineering information on these objects as stakeholder views, including FMEA-based information that forms a PPR. This is similar to the coordination artifact described in [8], but in addition integrates additional cause and effect assets. This integrated information can strongly support the quality engineer in the re-validation process by efficiently providing the relevant system knowledge required for FMEA re-validation and for efficient coordination with domain engineers [8]. However, this approach requires efficient management of dependencies between engineering objects of the different disciplines involved and tools of the engineering organization.

3   Research Questions and Approach

To tackle the identified challenges and to improve the coordination of FMEA re-validation after changes in PSE, we followed a *Design Science* approach [45].

First, we reviewed literature on PSE and multi-view model integration related to FMEA. Next, we conducted workshops with stakeholders at four engineering organizations with 9 domain experts coming from 3 domains and 6 researchers with focus on exploring PSE risks, engineering artifact exchange between work groups, required knowledge, and gaps in artifact exchange.

Building on the domain analysis at large PSE companies in automotive manufacturing [23], the guidelines for coordinating agent systems [25], and on the Industry 4.0 initiative [26], we derived the following research questions (RQs).

RQ1. Knowledge Representation for FMEA Integration into Agile Production Systems Engineering. *What model in agile PSE can represent FMEA concepts linked to PSE assets and their change/validation states to manage the efficient re-validation of FMEA model elements after updates to PPR asset property values?* To address RQ1, we built on [6, 28] meta model extended by the *PAN* [8] concepts to build the FMEA+PPR meta model, including FMEA and PPR concepts, FMEA links and change/validation states.

These foundations allow designing the FMEA+PPR with coordination states and multi-aspect change dependencies as a basis to design business processes in engineering projects. We illustrate the design with examples from the use case *FMEA Re-Validation after Changes to Engineering Artifacts* (cf. Sect. 4).

RQ2. Process for FMEA Integration into Agile Production Systems Engineering. *What process can integrate multi-view FMEA and PSE asset models as a foundation for analyzing the required re-validation scope of FMEA model elements after updates to PPR asset property values?* To address RQ2, we built on the FMEA+PPR meta model coming from RQ1 and (a) designed the FMEA+PPR process to define a FMEA+PPR model for an application scope and (b) to configure and run a multi-view data logistics for identifying FMEA elements to re-validate after changes to PSE assets.

For evaluation we conducted a feasibility study on instantiating a FMEA+PPR model from typical PSE artifacts to answer key stakeholder questions regarding the re-validation of FMEA elements. We investigated the number of the FMEA+PPR model elements and the dependencies that drive the effort for modeling, data provision/ maintenance, and the analysis for FMEA re-validation. Therefore, we considered work cells of different sizes in a typical automotive production plant with up to 300 work cells. Further, we used the FMEA+PPR model instance to evaluate the FMEA+PPR model concept regarding the identified requirements in comparison to traditional best-practice approaches in PSE.

4   Illustrative Use Case

This section introduces the use case *FMEA Re-Validation after Changes to Engineering Artifacts* to elicit requirements for improving the efficiency of FMEA re-validation in PSE with PPR asset-based coordination [8]. We report on PSE and FMEA re-validation processes abstracted from real-world use cases from system integrators of high-performance automation for car part manufacturing in Germany and Austria. The goal of this illustrative use case is to automate discrete assembly processes, such as positioning and joining of car parts, with robot work cells. A typical car production plant consists of 200 to 300 robot work cells that use 20 to 30 robot types [23]. This large number of components makes frequent and manual re-validation complex and expensive.

Engineering Process. Traditionally, PSE projects follow a sequential engineering process, including quality engineering for system design validation and risk management with FMEA. Typically, engineers work in parallel and iteratively within a phase. Therefore, engineers often need to work on PSE artifacts that belong to several phases (e.g., artifacts that evolve over different phases). These parallel engineering activities of several engineers require flexible and agile solutions. An early-stage FMEA can be conducted based on an initial PPR model that results from basic planning. However, the FMEA model has to be refined and updated as new FMEA-relevant knowledge emerges in engineering activities along the PSE project course. These activities are driven by change requests, which may be triggered by engineering needs or FMEA results and consequently require (a) changes to (validated) engineering results and (b) the re-validation of FMEA elements that depend on changes. Such changes become significantly more expensive within late phases [7].

Design and Validation Lifecycle. In PSE, assets and their properties have to be designed and validated. For the coordination of design and validation activities, these elements are usually assigned to *design* and *validation states* [8], e.g., "to design", "in design", "designed"; "to validate", "in validation", "validated", "validated with issue". Based on these states, related stakeholders can describe rules for the re-validation (and rework) of assets after changes. Traditional approaches often lack in explicitly defining and using design and validation states [8]. To address these shortcomings, we explore the FMEA+PPR approach to efficiently link FMEA concepts to PSE artifacts via a PAN. Note that the PAN holds FMEA concepts and can be efficiently derived from PSE artifacts [6].

Stakeholder Views on FMEA and PPR Assets and Artifacts. PSE stakeholders usually come from several disciplines, including mechanical, electrical, software/ automation, and simulation engineering [8,23].

Figure 1 illustrates selected stakeholder views on FMEA and PSE assets – in particular, products and processes, resources (e.g., mechanical and automation resources), and shared engineering artifacts along the progress of a typical PSE project. Each row shows a stakeholder view of assets and associated engineering artifacts that they design in *private work spaces* and share in a *team work space* (cf. Fig. 4 in Sect. 5.3). A major challenge for quality engineers is to keep the FMEA model synchronized with design changes and shared engineering assets.

The *Quality Engineer* (QE) designs an FMEA model by collecting and analyzing FMEA data to identify, prioritize, and mitigate risks related to the production system that have an impact on business performance, such as product quality, throughput, and

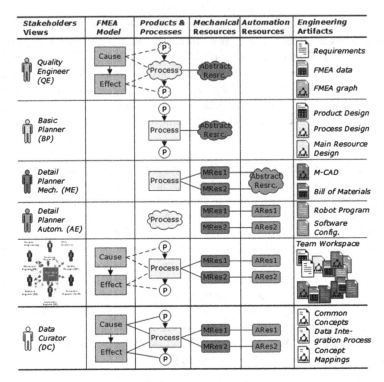

Stakeholders Views	FMEA Model	Products & Processes	Mechanical Resources	Automation Resources	Engineering Artifacts
Quality Engineer (QE)	Cause / Effect	P / Process / P	Abstract Resrc.		Requirements / FMEA data / FMEA graph
Basic Planner (BP)		P / Process / P	Abstract Resrc.		Product Design / Process Design / Main Resource Design
Detail Planner Mech. (ME)		Process	MRes1 / MRes2	Abstract Resrc.	M-CAD / Bill of Materials
Detail Planner Autom. (AE)		Process	MRes1 / MRes2	ARes1 / ARes2	Robot Program / Software Config.
	Cause / Effect	P / Process / P	MRes1 / MRes2	ARes1 / ARes2	Team Workspace
Data Curator (DC)	Cause / Effect	P / Process / P	MRes1 / MRes2	ARes1 / ARes2	Common Concepts / Data Integration Process / Concept Mappings

Fig. 1. Stakeholder concepts and artifacts for the use case *FMEA Re-Validation after Changes to Engineering Artifacts*, based on [8,23].

cost. The QE typically refers to PSE/PPR concepts but does not maintain links between FMEA and PSE models explicitly. *Basic planners* design high-level solutions for PSE assets, e.g., resources such as high-level library elements and parameters. *Detail planners* design plans for technological aspects of production system parts to automate the production processes. The *Data Curator* manages the integrated model of all stakeholder views and coordinates the definition of PSE artifacts as Common Concepts (CCs) and the semantic links between disciplines views and attributes. PSE artifact changes, can have a critical impact on dependent resource assets and on the key parameters of the production system (e.g., product quality or throughput). Thus, the QE interacts with related engineers to identify and describe candidate failure modes, e.g., breaking of a screw, and possible relationships to causes, e.g., insufficient torque regulation and a robot's position accuracy.

In Fig. 1, the fifth row shows the team work space where engineering teams share their results as human- and machine-readable artifacts. Example artifacts are spreadsheets or engineering tool data, e.g., in (AML) [3]. Depending on engineering knowledge management capabilities, the PSE assets are mostly represented as engineering data with implicit domain knowledge. Thus, the PSE asset representations may be incomplete and inconsistent and often require the interpretation of domain experts. However, the engineering artifacts should provide a consistent shared view on engineering requirements and designs.

The FMEA model for a typical work cell in automotive production (cf. Fig. 5) contains dozens to hundreds failure modes and causes that refer to several hundreds PSE assets and properties defined in many engineering artifacts, such as CAD drawings and data sheets. The heterogeneity of engineering artifacts and data often results in a semantic gap between the FMEA model and local stakeholder views. Therefore, the comparison of the FMEA model and PSE concepts and the FMEA re-validation becomes inefficient and error-prone. To overcome this gap, multi-view model integration [30] can provide a PSE asset model [8] as a foundation to explicitly model dependencies between FMEA and PSE asset concepts. In this paper, we assume the role of a *data curator* (cf. Fig. 1, bottom row), who focuses on (a) eliciting PSE concepts that are common to several stakeholders and (b) configuring data logistics for multi-view model integration to extract the common concepts from engineering artifacts.

FMEA Concerns for Efficient Re-validation. The aim of a screwing process is joining two or more components or materials with a screw, e.g., two or more objects (cf. Fig. 5). Therefore, a key characteristic focuses on the quality of the joining process and the joint itself. An important fault in this context is an incorrect or insufficient screwing process, potentially caused by an incorrect torque caused by abrasion and friction. Friction, in turn, depends on the position of the blind rivet nuts, which need to be inserted with the required precision (cf. Fig. 5, property *M.Pos.accuarcy* of the resource *Robot*). However, if the setting process does not join the rivet element properly, the friction may be insufficient to install the screw, and the desired breakaway torque might not be achieved. A setting process is only reliable if the force *M.Torque* and the position are controlled and monitored. Furthermore, the setting speed should also be adapted to the rivet element and material. A setting process that slows down towards its end ensures more precise process control and outcome but will increase the process property *Q.cycle time*. Insufficient friction may result in the failure mode *screw breakaway out of tolerance* (cf. Fig. 5) and incur high costs or result in liability claims by end customers. Hence, a change of the torque or calibration of the robot may have immediate effects on the corresponding failure mode in the FMEA. A divergence between FMEA and PSE concepts can result in too many or too few quality checks during the production process. Therefore, updates of values of related concepts in engineering views require the re-validation of FMEA model elements by involved domain experts. There may be hundreds of FMEA conditions for a machine concerning hundreds of engineering concepts in a variety of stakeholder views. Therefore, the efficient re-validation of the FMEA model requires capabilities for the prioritization of FMEA model elements related to changes in stakeholder views and the grouping of FMEA concerns to involved stakeholders to conduct focused workshops for re-validation.

Requirements. We identified the following requirements (Rx) for an efficient FMEA+PPR re-validation approach based on [28].

R1. FMEA Concept Representation. The model shall be capable to represent FMEA concepts such as failure modes and causes. Additionally, relationships and characteristics between FMEA concepts, such as severity and probability should is needed.

R2. PAN Concept Representation. The model shall represent PAN concepts [8] such as products, production processes, production resources, and their relationships and properties.

R3. FMEA-to-PPR Dependency Representation. The model shall represent links between FMEA concepts and PAN concepts e.g., PPR concepts, that are semantically similar to concepts used in the FMEA.

R4. FMEA/PPR Change Coordination Representation. The approach shall represent design and validation states for change coordination, such as model elements that changed or have to be re-validated after changes.

R5. Efficient FMEA Re-validation after PPR Changes. The process shall provide capabilities (a) for defining and instantiating an FMEA+PPR model and (b) for the efficient identification of FMEA model elements that require re-validation after changes.

5   Linking FMEA Models to Engineering Assets

This section introduces (a) the FMEA+PPR Meta Model, (b) the FMEA+PPR Process, and (c) the FMEA+PPR System Architecture that link FMEA models to engineering assets. We explore the *FMEA+PPR approach* to efficiently link FMEA concepts to PPR assets in a PAN [8].

5.1   FMEA+PPR Meta Model

To address RQ1 (cf. Sect. 3) and the requirements (cf. Sect. 4), we introduce the FMEA+PPR meta model that is based on (a) the insights and knowledge we acquired in the domain analysis [23], (b) the CPPS-RA approach [6], and (c) the coordination artifact PAN [8]. We extend the PAN meta model with FMEA concepts and elements that link them to the PAN, depicted in Fig. 2.

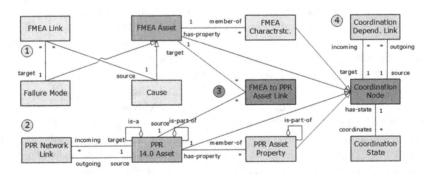

Fig. 2. FMEA+PPR Meta Model using UML notation, based on [8,23].

FMEA Concepts. To address the requirement R1 (cf. Sect. 4), the FMEA+PPR meta-model represents *FMEA Assets* (cf. Fig. 2, tag 1) with their *Characteristics* and *Links*. An *FMEA Asset* can be a *Failure Mode* (effect) or a Cause.

PAN Concepts. To address requirement R2 (cf. Sect. 4), the meta-model represents *PPR I4.0 Assets* (cf. Fig. 2, tag 2) with their *Asset Properties* and *Links*, similar to the coordination artifact PAN in [8].

Links between FMEA and PAN Concepts. To address requirement R3 (cf. Sect. 4), the meta-model includes *links between FMEA and PAN concepts* (cf. Fig. 2, tag 3), i.e., mappings between PPR concepts that are semantically similar to FMEA concepts.

Change Coordination States of and Dependencies between PPR and FMEA Assets/Concepts. To address requirement R4 and R5 (cf. Sect. 4), the meta-model represents (a) change coordination states of PPR and FMEA assets and concepts and (b) coordination dependencies between PPR and FMEA assets and concepts. (cf. Fig. 2, tag 4). These coordination states can represent states in the design and validation life cycles of a model element (cf. Sect. 4), e.g., whether a model element has changed and need to be re-validated (cf. Fig. 5, state markers in diamond shape). The coordination dependencies facilitate the representation of domain-specific dependencies, e.g. mechanical, topological, or logical links between PPR and/or FMEA elements, indicating model elements to evaluate for re-validation in case of a changes in a PPR or FMEA asset.

5.2 FMEA+PPR Process

To address RQ2 (cf. Sect. 3), we propose the FMEA+PPR process (cf. Fig. 3) including the following steps:

Step 1. Specify Scope for FMEA and PPR Models. In this step, FMEA and domain experts determine the scope of the FMEA and identify relevant PSE artifact models from use case data. Furthermore, in cooperation with domain experts, FMEA experts design an FMEA model (cf. Sect. 5.1) according to FMEA guidelines. The data curator designs an integrated multi-view model, i.e., the PAN (cf. Sect. 5.1), using the SUM approach [4] in the context of a multi-view model integration pipeline [30].

Step 2. Define FMEA-to-PPR Dependencies. In Step 2, the FMEA expert builds on the FMEA and PPR models mapping both model's concepts (cf. Sect. 5.1, links between FMEA and PAN concepts). Furthermore, this expert cooperates with domain experts to collect and explicitly model re-validation dependencies (cf. Sect. 5.1, change coordination states and dependencies).

Step 3. Configure and Run Multi-view Data Logistics. In this step, the data curator configures a multi-view data logistics with links between PSE artifacts and PPR assets [8] to extract the asset information from the artifacts. The data curator operates the data logistics to instantiate the FMEA+PPR network – e.g., in a graph database – which provides a foundation for reading or setting change and validation states and coordination dependencies. Furthermore, the data logistics propagates changes in PSE artifacts to PSE/FMEA assets. This propagation results in PPR asset model updates that facilitate their efficient analysis, e.g., by querying a graph database holding a PAN instance.

To define the FMEA+PPR network, the PPR DSL [24] is utilized to specify the Common Concepts (Common Concepts (CCs)) and links between discipline-specific concepts and views. The resulting FMEA+PPR model represents the basis for deriving a SUM to setup the multi-view model integration, using the *model generator* [30].

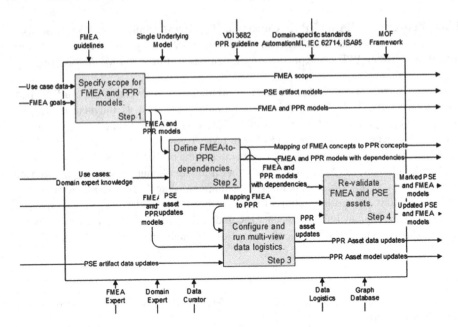

Fig. 3. FMEA+PPR process steps (in IDEF0 notation [11]).

Step 4. Re-validate FMEA and PSE Assets. In this step, the FMEA expert or the data curator analyze and mark the scope of assets in the FMEA and PPR models for re-validating, e.g., update of PPR asset property values. The FMEA expert and domain experts re-validate and improve FMEA and PPR models to reduce the risk of invalid assets in the FMEA model.

5.3 FMEA+PPR System Architecture

To automate the FMEA+PPR process, a *Engineering Data Logistics System Architecture* is designed, based on [7,27,30]. Figure 4 illustrates the system architecture consisting of three parts: (1) The **Data Integration** handles the import of engineering artifacts coming from the data providers *private work* spaces to the *team work space*. Discipline-specific *transformers* [30] are used to transform discipline-specific artifacts such as Extensible Markup Language (XML) or Comma Separated Value (CSV) files into view models. These view models are integrated using the *model integration services* [30] consisting of four operation services, such as the *converter, comparator, merger,* and the *rule engine* which handles the integration of different views and calculate changes to the SUM. (2) The **Engineering Data Logistics System** manages the *common unified model* and all semantic links between engineering views. Here, the data curator supervises multi-view model integration to import and integrate updates from several disciplines into the common view. For instance, a specific view within a Common Concept (CC) is linked to another view in the same CC (e.g. black link between green and orange or red and orange view). Also views across CCs can be linked (e.g. yellow views in drive and motor). (3) The **Data Delivery** handles data consumer requests such as the FMEA model. Data consumers can request data deliveries (a) in their domain-specific hierarchy (e.g., a simulation view for the simulation expert) or (b) as domain-agnostic networks (e.g., for analysis tasks across several views for the FMEA expert) [6]. The domain experts can specify their request themselves or the data curator must address requests by selecting and delivering required views on the common unified model. The requested data are converted to the discipline-specific hierarchy using related *transformers*.

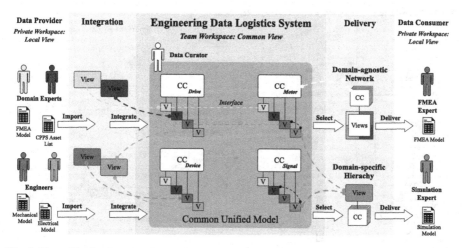

Fig. 4. Traceable *Engineering Data Logistics System* with private and team workspaces, based on [21,27]. (Color figure online)

A described, the data logistics enables the transformation of engineering data from stakeholder specific formats and to a FMEA+PPR model instance e.g. implemented in a *Neo4J*[2] database. Alternatives could be a XML database with AML [3] or *Semantic Web*[3] technologies. The *Neo4J* graph database, used for the evaluation in the next section, provided sufficient capabilities for browsing and querying the FMEA+PPR model instance.

6 Evaluation

This section demonstrates the FMEA+PPR approach's feasibility employing the illustrative use case, introduced in Sect. 4. We build on a data sample, coming from automotive manufacturing, for the FMEA of 100 production process steps with their associated production resources. In the feasibility study, we (a) instantiated the *FMEA+PPR model*, (b) analyzed and estimated the number of FMEA elements, PSE assets, and coordination dependencies in FMEA+PPR models for typical robot work cells as part of a manufacturing plant, and (c) assessed the fulfillment of FMEA+PPR requirements and the FMEA+PPR model in comparison to the traditional FMEA approach and engineering artifacts.

---

[2] Neo4J: https://neo4j.com/.
[3] SemanticWeb: www.w3.org/standards/semanticweb/.

Model Instantiation. To explore the feasibility and estimate the effort required for creating a FMEA+PPR model instance, we selected a sample of robot cells. Next, we collected typical PSE artifacts described in the FMEA, such as bills of materials, processes and their links, for several instances of the use case *FMEA Re-Validation after Changes to Engineering Artifacts* [23].

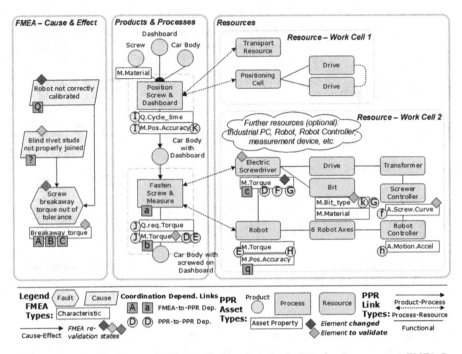

Fig. 5. FMEA model elements with coordination links to a PPR for the use case *FMEA Re-Validation after Changes to Engineering Artifacts*, based on [8].

Figure 5 illustrates the derived instance of the FMEA cause-effect diagram linked to a PAN. Column *FMEA - Cause & Effect* in this figure shows an example failure mode *Screw breakaway torque out of tolerance* linked to two potential causes, (a) *i.e., Robot not correctly calibrated* and (b) *Blind rivet studs not properly joined*. The column *Products & Processes* contains two processes, including *Fasten Screw & Measure* with the property *M.Torque*, automated by resources, including an *Electric Screwdriver* with the property *M.Torque*. The failure mode has a characteristic *Breakaway torque* that is linked to PPR assets and properties. Specifically, the property *M.Torque* of the process *Fasten Screw* and the resource *Electric Screwdriver* (FMEA+PPR links *B* and *C*).

In our example, a change to an engineering artifact related to the *Electric Screwdriver* is – via a data logistics process described in [8,30] – reflected in an update of the respective property *M.Torque*. Consequently, the coordination state of this property is set to *changed* (red diamond marker). Following a PPR re-validation policy, the affected PAN assets and properties are marked as *to validate* (yellow diamond markers).

```
MATCH (startnode)-[edge]-(endnode)
  WHERE startnode.ChangeState = "Changed"
  SET endnode.ValidationLifeCycleState="To Validate"

MATCH (startnode:FMEAAttribute)-[edge]-(endnode:FMEAAsset)
  WHERE startnode.ValidationLifeCycleState="To Validate"
  SET endnode.ValidationLifeCycleState="To Re-Validate"
```

Listing 1. Selected Cypher queries for FMEA element re-validation.

Next, based on the FMEA re-validation policy (cf. Sect. 4), *(i)* the property failure mode characteristic *Breakaway torque* gets marked as *to validate*; and *(ii)* failure mode *Screw breakaway torque out of tolerance* gets marked as *to re-validate* (orange diamond markers). FMEA cause *Robot not correctly calibrated* carries a marker *validated* (green diamond) from a recent validation task. FMEA cause *Blind rivet studs not properly joined*, by contrast, carries a marker *unclear* (grey diamond) because there is no valid FMEA+PPR link (cf. Fig. 5, FMEA+PPR link with label *?*)

The FMEA/PPR assets, properties, and links provide a basis for graph queries in *Neo4J* that answer the questions from the FMEA re-validation policy, e.g., *which FMEA assets are linked to a changed PAN node?* An instantiation of such a *Neo4J* graph is accessible online[4]. The following *Cypher*[5] query sets coordination markers to PAN and FMEA elements.

FMEA+PPR Model Size. To investigate the viability of collecting and maintaining a FMEA+PPR model for typical production processes automated by robot cells in automotive manufacturing, we built on an FMEA data sample. The analysis was conducted for 100 production steps automated by robot cells varying in size from a small cell that automates one production step to a large cell that automates 19 production steps. Figure 5 shows a typical robot work cell with a single robot with an electric screwdriver. Larger robot cells contain further resources, such as an industrial PC, robots, and measurement devices, leading to a similar structure of the PAN containing more assets and links.

Table 1. Number of FMEA/PAN graph elements and FMEA+PPR & coordination links for a typical range of robot work cells in automotive manufacturing.

FMEA Graph	#min/avg/max	FMEA+PPR & Coordinatn.	#min/avg/max	PPR Asset Network	#min/avg/max
FMEA Asset	5/70/280	FMEA+PPR Links	8/115/394	PPR Asset	12/124/198
FMEA Characteristic	3/52/134	FMEA/PPR Coord. States	40/192/518	PPR Asset Property	12/248/990
FMEA C-E Link	5/85/320	FMEA/PPR Coord. Links	6/50/220	PPR Asset Link	19/186/396
Sum	**13/207/734**	**Sum**	**54/357/1132**	**Sum**	**43/568/1584**

Table 1 summarizes a sample of FMEA/PAN graph elements and FMEA+PPR and coordination links showing the minimal, average, and maximal number of (a) FMEA graph elements, (b) FMEA+PPR and coordination elements, and (c) PAN elements.

---

[4] FMEA-PAN.NEO4J: https://github.com/tuw-qse/fmea-revalidation-resources.
[5] Cypher: www.opencypher.org/.

According to the FMEA+PPR model topology, the number of FMEA+PPR links was comparable to the *sum* of FMEA asset and characteristics. In the study, the number of FMEA/PPR coordination states was driven by the *sum* of FMEA/PPR assets and their characteristics/properties. The number of FMEA/PPR coordination links is the number of dependencies that domain experts make explicit, e.g., to define change dependencies in the PAN.

The FMEA+PPR model for a process automated by a small robot cell, consisting of 12 PPR assets, was defined by 13 FMEA assets, characteristics, and cause-effect links, and by up to 8 FMEA+PPR link candidates, 40 FMEA/PPR coordination states, and 6 FMEA/PPR coordination link candidates.

The FMEA+PPR model for 19 processes automated by a large robot cell, consisting of 198 PPR assets, was defined by 734 FMEA assets, characteristics, and cause-effect links, and by up to 394 FMEA+PPR link candidates, 518 FMEA/PPR coordination states, and 220 FMEA/PPR coordination links.

We assume the FMEA graph to be available and the PAN to be efficiently derived from engineering artifacts in a team work space (cf. Sect. 5). FMEA/PPR coordination can be determined efficiently with graph queries (cf. Listing 1), given a sufficiently complete linking of the FMEA graph and the PAN. However, the considerable number of FMEA+PPR links and FMEA/PPR coordination links will require an approach for the prioritization and/or automation. Similar structures of robot cells can typically be generalized, i.e., FMEA+PPR links and FMEA/PPR coordination links can be defined on robot cell and FMEA/PPR asset types, which allows for an efficient definition of graph queries that will be applicable to a range of similar robot cell types [31]. Furthermore, domain experts can start by modeling an initial small set of high-priority FMEA characteristics, FMEA+PPR links and FMEA/PPR coordination links.

Evaluation of Requirements for FMEA Re-validation Capabilities. For evaluation purposes, we compare the FMEA+PPR to the traditional approaches (a) FMEA+EA: *FMEA re-validation based on Engineering Artifacts* in a team work space, requiring manual mapping and co-evolution of FMEA models and PSE artifacts, and (b) FMEA+TS/EO: *FMEA re-validation in Tool Suites* that manage engineering objects in a data base as a basis for co-evolution with FMEA model versions. We used a 5-point *Likert* scale (++, +, o, −, −−), where ++/−− indicate very high/low capabilities, to evaluate the fulfillment of the requirements in comparison with alternative approaches. Table 2 summarizes the results.

Table 2. FMEA re-validation capabilities of FMEA+EA, FMEA+TS/EO, and FMEA+EA coordination approaches, based on [28].

Req. Rx/FMEA + coordination artifacts	FMEA+EA	FMEA+TS/EO	FMEA+PPR
R1. FMEA concept representation	o	+	++
R2. PPR Asset Network concept representation	−−	o	++
R3. FMEA-to-PPR dependency representation	−−	+	++
R4. FMEA/PPR change coordination representation	−−	+	++
R5. Efficient FMEA re-validation after PPR changes	−	−	+

R1. FMEA Concept Representation. For all approaches, we assume the use of a best-practice FMEA tool, such as APIS, with FMEA concepts and conditions represented in natural language, possibly with references to PSE concepts. FMEA+EA is rated average as the FMEA concepts can refer to stakeholder views in heterogeneous engineering artifacts (EAs), requiring for one FMEA concept the management of references to several stakeholder views, e.g., mechanical/electrical identifiers in M-CAD/E-CAD, software identifiers in programs and configurations, which concern an Electric Screwdriver. FMEA+TS/EO is rated high as one FMEA concept can refer to one engineering object, e.g., the Electric Screwdriver, which represents several stakeholder views in the tool suite data model. However, the tool suite data model covers only a limited set of stakeholder views and falls back to engineering artifacts for stakeholder views not covered by the tool suite. FMEA+PPR is rated very high as one FMEA concept can refer to PPR concepts and, if required, stakeholder views attached to a PPR asset. By design, the FMEA+PPR model represents the required FMEA graph concepts (cf. Fig. 2, tag 1, model elements in violet color).

R2. PPR Asset Network Concept Representation. FMEA+EA is rated very low as the approach concerns engineering artifacts that, in general, do not consider PPR assets. FMEA+TS/EO is rated average as the engineering objects may represent PPR assets and their properties, but do not consider dependencies between PPR assets. Furthermore, the tool suite covers only a limited set of PPR assets. FMEA+PPR is rated very high as it represents all relevant stakeholder views as PPR assets and their properties. Moreover, explicit dependencies between PPR concepts represent domain expert knowledge, e.g., on change dependencies (cf. Fig. 2, tag 2, model elements in blue color).

R3. FMEA-to-PPR Dependency Representation. FMEA+EA is rated very low as the approach considers dependencies to engineering artifacts, not PPR assets or properties. FMEA+TS/EO is rated high as it considers dependencies to engineering objects, but with limited stakeholder views. FMEA+PPR is rated very high as the FMEA+PPR model explicitly represents FMEA+PPR links between FMEA and PPR Asset Network concepts (cf. Fig. 2, tag 3).

R4. FMEA/PPR Change Coordination Representation. FMEA+EA is rated very low as change coordination is limited to engineering artifacts in the team work space and neither covers FMEA nor PPR concepts. FMEA+TS/EO is rated high as change coordination concerns individual engineering objects. However, there is no consideration of a network of change dependencies and the scope of stakeholder views is limited. FMEA+PPR is rated very high as the model represents the required change coordination states, e.g., markers for representing the state of change and re-validation, missing links (cf. Fig. 5, diamonds), and dependencies of PPR and FMEA assets/concepts (cf. Fig. 2, tag 4, coordination model elements in green color).

R5. Efficient FMEA Re-validation after PPR Changes. FMEA+EA is rated low as comparing FMEA concepts to changes in heterogeneous engineering artifacts involves significant manual effort from domain experts to identify FMEA concepts for re-validation after each change to an engineering artifact. FMEA+TS/EO is rated low as the automation of FMEA re-validation in the tool suite would require adding the FMEA view to the tool suite with considerable effort to design. However, once implemented, the FMEA re-validation could become very efficient in the limited scope on engineering disciplines in the tool suite. FMEA+PPR is rated high as the approach considers the relevant scope of engineering disciplines and tools in a PSE project assuming the multi-view data logistics capabilities for efficient update of PPR assets from engineering artifacts.

Overall, the FMEA+PPR approach seems well-suited to provide FMEA re-validation capabilities for integrating FMEA with agile PSE. We demonstrate this in a *Neo4J* graph instance that enables efficient queries to analyze linked FMEA and PPR knowledge, e.g., for efficient FMEA re-validation based on graph queries to select and prioritize relevant v elements for re-validation.

7   Discussion

This section discusses this work regarding the research questions and limitations.

RQ1. *What model in agile PSE can represent FMEA concepts linked to PSE assets and their change/validation states to manage the efficient re-validation of FMEA model elements after updates to PPR asset property values?*

We introduced the FMEA+PPR meta model that simplifies the coordination of FMEA re-validation in agile PSE. Introducing a FMEA+PPR model as advanced coordination artifact for the re-validation of FMEA models appears particularly beneficial in medium-to-large PSE projects. In such projects artifact-mediated coordination can be expected to be considerably less risky and more efficient than point-to-point coordination which requires manual analysis of changes that are relevant to the FMEA.

The FMEA+PPR model is a knowledge graph that explicitly represents dependencies among FMEA and PPR assets and their characteristics to provide context for the re-validation of an FMEA asset. Thus, the FMEA+PPR model is the basis for *(i)* exploring and analyzing a task-specific FMEA+PPR model instance (cf. Fig. 5), *(ii)* automating queries to FMEA and PSE assets (cf. Sect. 6), and *(iii)* coordinating processes that require expert knowledge and labor, such as identifying FMEA asset candidates for re-validation, reuse, or refactoring.

In this work, we explored the knowledge representation, represented as a graph, required for FMEA re-validation relevant for FMEA experts. However, for daily work, FMEA experts typically want to work with the coordination information in the PPR elements. This representation in the tool would require the exploration of ways to augment FMEA tool data with coordination information, e.g., by repurposing a comment data field to hold markers similar to the graph database (cf. Sect. 6), and import the coordination information into the FMEA tool for further use in search capabilities.

RQ2. *What process can integrate multi-view FMEA and PSE asset models as a foundation for analyzing the required re-validation scope of FMEA model elements after updates to PPR asset property values?*

To address RQ2, we introduced the FMEA+PPR process (cf. Sect. 5) that *(i)* defines FMEA+PPR dependencies for a particular scope of FMEA and PPR models; and *(ii)* configures and runs a multi-view data logistics that iteratively instantiates a PAN to configure the *Engineering Data Logistics System* fostering multi-view model integration [30] (cf. Sect. 5) as a foundation for *(iii)* identifying FMEA assets for re-validation that depend on changes to PSE assets.

The feasibility study (cf. Sect. 6) illustrated the definition of a FMEA+PPR model in a *Neo4J* database instance, from typical PSE artifacts (cf. Fig. 5). We use this model instance to evaluate the scaling characteristics of the approach in terms of the number of elements for work cells of different sizes (cf. Table 1). Regarding the FMEA re-validation requirements (cf. Sect. 4), the rating of the FMEA+PPR results showed clear improvements over traditional best-practice approaches (cf. Table 2). In particular regarding PAN concept representation, FMEA/PPR change coordination representation, and efficient FMEA re-validation after PPR changes. The study results indicate that the FMEA+PPR approach provides a sound foundation for PSE domain experts to identify FMEA elements for re-validation. This provides a foundation for an evaluation of the usability and scalability of the approach in a broader context, including agile PSE scenarios of different sizes and complexities.

This work focused on efficiency by automating the analysis of change impact in PSE artifact property values on FMEA elements. This consideration provides the foundation for exploring the effort in PSE environments for designing and using the FMEA+PPR approach with typical tools and domain experts in comparison to benefits from improved capabilities for FMEA re-validation.

These research results build on coordination artifact design [8,25], recent advances in I4.0 asset data integration [26], and our previous work in multi-view model integration methods and techniques [30]. The results go beyond the state of the art in the area of coordinating in multi-disciplinary PSE processes [12,18,23], in particular FMEA re-validation *(i)* by defining a sufficiently fine-grained FMEA+PPR models for coordination based on FMEA and PAN concepts and *(ii)* by demonstrating the feasibility of instantiating the FMEA+PPR model based on data from FMEA and PSE artifacts.

Limitations. The following limitations require further investigation. The *feasibility study* focused on a use case derived from projects at large PSE companies in the automotive industry. This may introduce bias due to the specific selection of FMEA re-validation challenges and approaches considered, as well as the roles or individual preferences of the domain experts. To overcome these limitations, we plan case studies in a wider variety of application contexts.

The *expressiveness* of the re-validation concepts and dependencies used in the evaluation can be considered a limitation. Industrial scenarios may also require more detailed modeling of FMEA conditions. Furthermore, whereas evaluation results with FMEA+PPR model instances with a limited set of attributes required for selected FMEA re-validation tasks were encouraging, the ability to address FMEA models that require many asset types and are linked to large PANs remains an open issue for further investigation.

Finally, our evaluation environment involved a limited number of stakeholders, and we plan to investigate the effectiveness of the approach in more detail in a setting that involves a larger number of stakeholders and roles.

8   Conclusion and Future Work

In agile PSE, multi-disciplinary stakeholders, such as mechanical, electrical, and software engineers, work on their partial PPR views in engineering artifacts, such as plans, configurations, and programs, in an iterative parallel process to address requirements towards a functional production system. In such settings, FMEA is vital to reduce the risk of PSE design errors, such as mismatches between stakeholder designs, that may be costly to resolve in late PSE stages. Therefore, there is a strong need to reuse FMEA knowledge on system components from previous projects and efficiently identify FMEA elements to re-validate after updates to PSE artifacts that come from heterogeneous stakeholder views. Efficiently identifying FMEA elements for re-validation requires capabilities to *(i)* trace or propagate a change in a PSE artifact *(ii)* a shared PSE object, such as a PPR asset, which reflects the common knowledge in the project team, and *(iii)* keep track of the change states of shared PSE objects and of FMEA elements. However, in current best-practice knowledge management in PSE, FMEA elements and PSE artifacts represent the knowledge required for FMEA re-validation incompletely. Furthermore, their meaning is difficult to interpret automatically, which makes FMEA re-validation inefficient and prone to error. Therefore, FMEA re-validation may become ineffective in agile PSE, reducing the actual benefit that would be expected from conducting FMEA early.

This paper reports on the use case *FMEA Re-Validation after Changes to Engineering Artifacts*, derived from car manufacturing with automated robot work cells, and identifies a set of requirements for FMEA re-validation capabilities. To address these requirements, we developed the *FMEA+PPR approach* that consists of *(i)* a meta model to represent the required knowledge for efficient FMEA re-validation, and *(ii)* a process to map FMEA elements to PAN concepts. The approach provides a foundation for the efficient analysis of which FMEA elements to re-validate after changes to PPR assets and PSE artifacts.

A feasibility study created a FMEA+PPR model instance that represents the required knowledge for analyzing the impact of changes in multi-view engineering artifacts on FMEA models. For a large robot work cell, the study indicated that the FMEA+PPR model's size is considerable requiring an effective approach to select the most relevant FMEA concepts for modeling with tool support.

In the evaluation, we compared the FMEA+PPR approach to two traditional best-practice approaches in PSE that relate FMEA elements (i) to engineering artifacts in a team work space or (ii) to engineering objects in a tool suite database. The study results indicate that the FMEA+PPR method is feasible and more effective than the alternative approaches. These results encourage evaluating the FMEA+PPR approach in a broader context regarding usability and scalability in agile PSE scenarios of different size and complexity.

Future Work

Empirical Validation. We plan to investigate the usability and usefulness of the FMEA+PPR approach in various agile PSE settings, e.g., making implicit domain expert knowledge sufficiently explicit in FMEA with PSE models to automate analyses for the quality assurance and reuse.

Scalability. Due to the comprehensive scope of FMEA and PSE tasks, a model's complexity may grow considerably with the number of data elements and links. This will require research on the scalability of FMEA+PPR models.

Security. The linked FMEA and PSE model aggregates knowledge both on how to attack product and production process quality by manipulating the production system components. Therefore, the FMEA+PPR model requires research on security concerns, e.g., using the knowledge to identify and mitigate risks from security attacks on a production system.

Acknowledgement. The financial support by the Christian Doppler Research Association, the Austrian Federal Ministry for Digital and Economic Affairs and the National Foundation for Research, Technology and Development is gratefully acknowledged. This work has been partially supported and funded by the Austrian Research Promotion Agency (FFG) via "Austrian Competence Center for Digital Production" (CDP) under contract nr. 881843. This work has also received funding from the Teaming.AI project, which is part of the European Union's Horizon 2020 research and innovation program under grant agreement No 957402.

References

1. VDI Guideline 3682: Formalised process descriptions. VDI/VDE (2005). https://www.vdi.de

2. VDI Guideline 3695: Engineering of industrial plants - Evaluation and optimization. VDI/VDE (2009). https://www.vdi.de

3. IEC 62714:2014 Engineering data exchange format for use in industrial automation systems engineering - automation markup language (2014). https://www.iec.ch

4. Atkinson, C., Tunjic, C., Möller, T.: Fundamental realization strategies for multi-view specification environments. In: 2015 IEEE 19th International Enterprise Distributed Object Computing Conference, pp. 40–49 (2015)

5. Biffl, S., Lüder, A., Gerhard, D. (eds.): Multi-Disciplinary Engineering for Cyber-Physical Production Systems. Springer, Cham (2017). https://doi.org/10.1007/978-3-319-56345-9

6. Biffl, S., Lüder, A., Meixner, K., Rinker, F., Eckhart, M., Winkler, D.: Multi-view-model risk assessment in cyber-physical production systems engineering. In: MODELSWARD, pp. 163–170. SCITEPRESS (2021)

7. Biffl, S., Lüder, A., Rinker, F., Waltersdorfer, L., Winkler, D.: Engineering data logistics for agile automation systems engineering. In: Security and Quality in Cyber-Physical Systems Engineering, pp. 187–225. Springer (2019)

8. Biffl, S., et al.: An industry 4.0 asset-based coordination artifact for production systems engineering. In: 23rd IEEE International Conference on Business Informatics. IEEE (2021)

9. Bihani, P., Drath, R., Kadam, A.: Towards meaningful interoperability for heterogeneous engineering tools via AutomationML. In: 25th IEEE International Conference on Emerging Technologies and Factory Automation, pp. 1286–1290. IEEE (2019)

10. Chuang, P.: Incorporating disservice analysis to enhance perceived service quality. Ind. Manag. Data Syst. **110**(3), 368–391 (2010)

11. Davis, F.D.: A technology acceptance model for empirically testing new end-user information systems: Theory and results. Ph.D. thesis, Massachusetts Institute of Technology (1985)

12. Egyed, A., Zeman, K., Hehenberger, P., Demuth, A.: Maintaining consistency across engineering artifacts. Computer **51**(2), 28–35 (2018)

13. Foehr, M.: Integrated consideration of product quality within factory automation systems. Ph.D. thesis, Otto-v.-Guericke University Magdeburg, FMB (2013). http://dx.doi.org/10. 25673/3977

14. Galati, F., Bigliardi, B.: Industry 4.0: emerging themes and future research avenues using a text mining approach. Comput. Ind. **109**, 100–113 (2019)

15. Grangel-González, I., Halilaj, L., Auer, S., Lohmann, S., Lange, C., Collarana, D.: An RDF-based approach for implementing industry 4.0 components with Administration Shells. In: 21st IEEE International Conference on Emerging Technologies and Factory Automation, pp. 1–8 (2016)

16. Himmler, F., Amberg, M.: Data integration framework for heterogeneous system landscapes within the digital factory domain. Procedia Eng. **69**, 1138–1143 (2014)

17. Illés, B., Tamás, P., Dobos, P., Skapinyecz, R.: New challenges for quality assurance of manufacturing processes in industry 4.0. In: Solid State Phenomena, vol. 261, pp. 481–486. Trans Tech Publications (2017)

18. Kattner, N., et al.: Inconsistency management in heterogeneous models - an approach for the identification of model dependencies and potential inconsistencies. In: Design Society: International Conference on Engineering Design, pp. 3661–3670. Cambridge University Press (2019)

19. Leng, J., et al.: Blockchain-empowered sustainable manufacturing and product lifecycle management in industry 4.0: a survey. Renew. Sustain. Energy Rev. **132**, 110112 (2020)

20. Lüder, A., Baumann, L., Behnert, A.K., Rinker, F., Biffl, S.: Paving pathways for digitalization in engineering: common concepts in engineering chains. In: 25th IEEE International Conference on Emerging Technologies and Factory Automation, pp. 1401–1404. IEEE (2020)

21. Lüder, A., Biffl, S., Rinker, F., Behnert, A.K.: Engineering data logistics based on AML. In: AutomationML, De Gruyter, pp. 579–602 (2021). https://doi.org/10.1515/9783110745979-034

22. McDermott, R.E., Mikulak, R.J., Beauregard, M.R.: The Basics of FMEA. Taylor & Francis Group, Boston (2009)

23. Meixner, K., Lüder, A., Herzog, J., Winkler, D., Biffl, S.: Patterns for reuse in production systems engineering. Int. J. Softw. Eng. Knowl. Eng. **31**, 1623–1659 (2021)

24. Meixner, K., Rinker, F., Marcher, H., Decker, J., Biffl, S.: A domain-specific language for product-process-resource modeling. In: 26th IEEE International Conference on Emerging Technologies and Factory Automation, pp. 1–8. IEEE (2021)

25. Omicini, A., Ricci, A., Viroli, M., Castelfranchi, C., Tummolini, L.: Coordination artifacts: environment-based coordination for intelligent agents. In: 3rd International Conference on Autonomous Agents and Multiagent Systems, pp. 286–293. IEEE Computer Society (2004)

26. Plattform Industrie 4.0, ZVEI: Part 1 - The exchange of information between partners in the value chain of Industrie 4.0 (Version 3.0RC01 Review). Standard, German BMWI (2020). https://bit.ly/37A002I

27. Rinker, F.: Flexible multi-aspect model integration for cyber-physical production systems engineering. In: Krogstie, J., Ouyang, C., Ralyté, J. (eds.) Doctoral Consortium CAiSE 2021. CEUR Workshop Proceedings, vol. 2906, pp. 31–40. CEUR-WS.org, Aachen (2021)

28. Rinker, F., Meixner, K., Kropatschek, S., Kiesling, E., Biffl, S.: Risk and engineering knowledge integration in cyber-physical production systems engineering. In: 2022 48th Euromicro Conference on Software Engineering and Advanced Applications (SEAA), accepted (2022)

29. Rinker, F., Waltersdorfer, L., Meixner, K., Biffl, S.: Towards support of global views on common concepts employing local views. In: 24th IEEE International Conference on Emerging Technologies and Factory Automation, pp. 1686–1689. IEEE (2019)

30. Rinker, F., Waltersdorfer, L., Meixner, K., Winkler, D., Lüder, A., Biffl, S.: Continuous integration in multi-view modeling: a model transformation pipeline architecture for production systems engineering. In: MODELSWARD, pp. 286–293. SCITEPRESS (2021)

31. Sarna, M., Meixner, K., Biffl, S., Lüder, A.: Reducing risk in industrial bin picking with pprs configuration and dependency management. In: 26th IEEE International Conference on Emerging Technologies Factory Automation. IEEE (2021)

32. Schleipen, M., Drath, R.: Three-view-concept for modeling process or manufacturing plants with AutomationML. In: 14th IEEE International Conference on Emerging Technologies and Factory Automation, pp. 1–4. IEEE (2009)

33. Schleipen, M., Lüder, A., Sauer, O., Flatt, H., Jasperneite, J.: Requirements and concept for plug-and-work. at-Automatisierungstechnik 63(10), 801–820 (2015)

34. Scippacercola, F., Pietrantuono, R., Russo, S., Esper, A., Silva, N.: Integrating FMEA in a model-driven methodology. In: DASIA 2016-Data Systems In Aerospace, vol. 736, p. 10 (2016)

35. Shafiq, S.I., Sanin, C., Szczerbicki, E., Toro, C.: Virtual engineering factory: creating experience base for industry 4.0. Cybern. Syst. 47(1–2), 32–47 (2016)

36. Shafiq, S.I., Sanin, C., Toro, C., Szczerbicki, E.: Virtual engineering object (VEO): toward experience-based design and manufacturing for industry 4.0. Cybern. Syst. 46(1–2), 35–50 (2015)

37. Sharma, K.D., Srivastava, S.: Failure mode and effect analysis (FMEA) implementation: a literature review. J. Adv. Res. Aeron. Space Sci. 5, 1–17 (2018)

38. de Victor, B., Souza, R., Cesar, R., Carpinetti, L.: A FMEA-based approach to prioritize waste reduction in lean implementation. Int. J. Qual. Reliabil. Manag. 31(4), 346–366 (2014)

39. Spreafico, C., Russo, D., Rizzi, C.: A state-of-the-art review of FMEA/FMECA including patents. Comput. Sci. Rev. 25, 19–28 (2017)

40. Stamatis, D.H.: Risk Management Using Failure Mode and Effect Analysis (FMEA). Quality Press (2019)

41. Star, S.L.: The structure of ill-structured solutions: boundary objects and heterogeneous distributed problem solving. In: Gasser, L., Huhns, M.N. (eds.) Distributed Artificial Intelligence, pp. 37–54. Elsevier (1989)

42. Strahilov, A., Hämmerle, H.: Engineering workflow and software tool chains of automated production systems. In: Biffl, S., Lüder, A., Gerhard, D. (eds.) Multi-Disciplinary Engineering for Cyber-Physical Production Systems, pp. 207–234. Springer, Cham (2017). https://doi.org/10.1007/978-3-319-56345-9_9

43. Tunjic, C., Atkinson, C.: Synchronization of projective views on a single-underlying-model. In: Proceedings of the 2015 Joint MORSE/VAO Workshop on Model-Driven Robot Software Engineering and View-based Software-Engineering, pp. 55–58 (2015)

44. Vogel-Heuser, B., et al.: Interdisciplinary engineering of cyber-physical production systems: highlighting the benefits of a combined interdisciplinary modelling approach on the basis of an industrial case. Des. Sci. 6, e5 (2020)

45. Wieringa, R.J.: Design science methodology for information systems and software engineering. Springer (2014)

46. Wortmann, A., Barais, O., Combemale, B., Wimmer, M.: Modeling languages in Industry 4.0: an extended systematic mapping study. Software and Systems Modeling 19(1), 67–94 (2020)

47. Wu, Z., Liu, W., Nie, W.: Literature review and prospect of the development and application of fmea in manufacturing industry. The International Journal of Advanced Manufacturing Technology pp. 1–28 (2021)

PSCS4CPP: A Generative PSCS Implementation for C++

Maximilian Hammer[(✉)] [ID], Ralph Maschotta [ID], Alexander Wichmann,
Tino Jungebloud [ID], Francesco Bedini [ID], and Armin Zimmermann [ID]

Systems and Software Engineering Group, Computer Science and Automation Department,
Technische Universität Ilmenau, Ilmenau, Germany
{maximilian.hammer,ralph.maschotta,alexander.wichmann,
tino.jungebloud,francesco.bedini,armin.zimmermann}@tu-ilmenau.de
https://www.tu-ilmenau.de/sse

Abstract. Since the early 2000s, Model-driven engineering has aimed to accomplish executable UML models. With fUML and PSCS, the Object Management Group (OMG) published standardized specifications of precise semantics for certain parts of UML in the form of metamodels, which form an execution environment. A certain characteristic of these environments is that static information about a model is analyzed and evaluated during runtime. With composite structures being a concept for describing structural properties of a model, the majority of execution semantics specified by PSCS concern analysis and processing of such static information about the model's fine-grained structure. Thus, the PSCS specification appears suitable for a generative realization approach. Using Model-To-Text-Transformation to generate source code, which serves as an input for the actual execution environment, the runtime level of model executions can be relieved by outsourcing analysis and processing of static information to the level of code generation. By inserting this preprocessing step, the performance of the actual model execution at runtime can be improved. This paper introduces an implementation of the PSCS specification for C++ based on code generation using Model-to-Text-Transformation. This also includes a generative approach to realize an extension mechanism of the fUML and PSCS execution environments by introducing user-defined semantic execution strategies. The proposed PSCS implementation was developed as a part of the *MDE4CPP* project. Moreover, this paper presents a set of test models validating the correct functionality of the implementation as well as a performance benchmark. Finally, analysis results of an application example for the presented realization are evaluated and discussed.

Keywords: Model driven software development · Composite structures ·
Executable UML · Code generation · PSCS · fUML · UML · C++

1 Introduction

One of the key suggestions of the model-driven paradigm is to describe, represent and analyze complex (software-)systems on higher levels of abstraction using domain-specific modeling languages. Beyond that, such models are further processed to

© Springer Nature Switzerland AG 2023
L. F. Pires et al. (Eds.): MODELSWARD 2021/2022, CCIS 1708, pp. 84–108, 2023.
https://doi.org/10.1007/978-3-031-38821-7_5

generate artifacts (e.g., source code) automatically (and possibly incrementally) throughout the whole development process. By that, model-driven approaches aim to increase flexibility, reusability, and efficiency of development processes [7,20]. In the domain of systems and software engineering, OMG's Unified Modeling Language (UML) has been established as a de facto standard for modeling languages [8].

Although Model-driven Engineering (MDE) is a more generic term for a paradigm and related techniques, Model-driven Architecture (MDA) is a standardized approach to MDE techniques provided by the Object Management Group (OMG). One of the main objectives of MDA is the ability to execute UML models. That means being able to create executable applications directly from conceptual models, either by complete transformation or by simulating the models using an execution environment [14]. However, UML was designed as a descriptive language that should be widely applicable for modeling abstractions for all sorts of systems and software. Because the creators of UML aimed for it to be a tool for describing conceptual models rather than being some sort of compilable programming language, UML lacks precise semantical specification of its modeling concepts and metamodel elements [1]. This circumstance intuitively contradicts the idea of being able to execute UML models like compilable source code. As a result, the necessity for formalizing UML's fine-grained semantical aspects arises. The activity diagram being one of the most widely used UML concepts for modeling behavior in the industry [8], was seen as an appropriate starting point for this standardization process. In 2011 OMG released the initial version of the fUML specification (Semantics of a Foundational Subset for Executable UML Models), which specifies precise execution semantics for a minimal subset of UML activities and classes [13]. fUML, therefore, makes it possible to execute fine-grained behavior modeled using UML activities. Subsequently, the ability to include fine-grained structural aspects of a model within the execution was aimed at. In 2015 the OMG extended fUML by PSCS (Precise Semantics of UML Composite Structures), which specifies runtime semantics for UML composite structures, which is primarily of interest for this paper [7,15].

Composite structures are used to model the structure of systems as complex part-whole relationships. Such composite structures (metaclass *StructuredClassifier*) can be described as a topology of parts (metaclass *Property* whose *AggregationKind* is composite) that are linked through connectors (metaclass *Connector*) to form the internals of their owning element (e.g., a *Class* or a *Component*) in terms of a network. A classifier may also define interaction points (metaclass *Port*) to model communication interfaces between itself (or its internal parts) and its environment. Ports are dedicated parts that encapsulate the behavior of their owning classifier (metaclass *EncapsulatedClassifier*) and specify its provided and required interfaces [7,17].

The PSCS specification defines runtime semantics for executable UML models that include *StructuredClassifiers*, as well as *EncapsulatedClassifiers*. Like fUML, PSCS provides a metamodel that describes an execution environment to realize those runtime semantics defined in the specification. In terms of structural semantics, PSCS specifies the lifecycle management of composite structures at runtime (i.e., creation and destruction of instances of composite structures). In terms of behavioral semantics, PSCS defines how instances of composite structures communicate with each other. More precisely, the behavioral semantics of PSCS specify how communication, either synchronously using operation calls or asynchronously using signals, is forwarded through a network of interconnected runtime objects [7, 19]. Additionally, OMG's UML semantics specifications (which include PSCS) introduce the mechanism of so-called *Semantic Strategy* classes to realize the concept of UML's semantic variation points. These semantic strategies are extension points for implementers of the fUML and PSCS specifications to be able to define varying runtime behavior themselves, where semantics are intentionally undefined or not further specified in UML (e.g., choice, scheduling, or polymorphism semantics) [18].

PSCS (as well as fUML) is designed platform-independent and makes no assumptions about the environment it is implemented in. All of PSCS's functionality is encapsulated in its metamodel classes which form a pure virtual machine for executing models [19].

The PSCS implementation presented in this paper aims to pursue a generative approach to improve the performance of model execution. The goal is to make use of auto-generated, model-specific source code to form the basis of the model execution as an input for PSCS's actual execution environment. Respectively, this results in a realization of structural aspects of the PSCS semantics in a way that omits runtime computation caused by the analysis and processing of static, structural model information. Since static aspects of a model are known at generation time and do not change as long as the underlying model does not change, related processing can be outsourced from the execution environment itself to the process of code generation. The described approach should reduce computation overhead during execution because the evaluation of structural model information (which is a significant part of PSCS's runtime functionality) is done only once during generation instead of multiple times at runtime during the actual model execution [7]. This paper is an extended version of [7]. In addition to the claims stated above, which are also presented in [7], this paper contributes a generation-based mechanism to extend the behavioral semantics of PSCS (and also fUML) by utilizing the semantic strategy pattern provided by the specification(s) to implement application-specific execution behavior. By realizing this mechanism using source code generation, the execution environment can be extended by application- and/or model-specific execution strategies without having to adapt the underlying metamodels themselves. This approach avoids the creation of dependencies between the otherwise model-independent execution environment and the respective models it should execute. The design of the mechanism also implies better reusability and interchangeability of strategies created within this process, as they work like plug-ins.

The remainder of this paper is structured as follows. Section 2.1 shows the realization workflow of the PSCS implementation introduced by this paper, including selected design challenges and how they were solved. Section 3 presents a validation of the presented implementation. This includes validation of the implementation's conformance to the original specification, a performance evaluation, and an academic example that utilizes the addressed extension mechanism. The results of the validation process and possible future work are ultimately discussed in Sect. 4.

2 Methodology

This section describes the design workflow and the components that were implemented to realize a model-driven implementation of the PSCS specification. First, the general structure and workflow of the framework, which the presented implementation was realized as a part of, is introduced. Subsequently, implementation details of the realized structural and behavioral PSCS semantics are presented.

2.1 General Workflow

The realization of the PSCS specification presented in this paper is based on the *MDE4CPP* project [23]. MDE4CPP aims to develop an open-source framework for Model-driven Software Development (MDSD) for C++. The framework consists of different components. It is based on the *Eclipse Modeling Framework* (EMF) as a foundational toolset for creating and analyzing models as well as developing the source code generation facilities required for the implementation of PSCS presented by this paper [7].

Furthermore, MDE4CPP provides model-driven implementations for the meta models of UML and fUML (which are required for implementing PSCS). 'Model-driven' in this case means that these models are not implemented 'by hand' but rather exist as models themselves within the framework. The corresponding C++ libraries are then created using source code generation as well. Eclipse's Ecore model is used as the meta meta model because it is well integrated into EMF. Moreover, MDE4CPP provides generators for Ecore models as well as UML/fUML models [10], which are implemented using the open-source code generator tool Acceleo [4, 7].

For realizing the PSCS in MDE4CPP in the same model-driven manner as described above, the corresponding meta model forming a new component within the framework is required. First, a machine-readable representation in the form of an XMI model provided by OMG was manually converted into an Ecore model. Because Ecore's structure is realized mostly equivalent to EMOF (Essential Meta Object Facility) [21], it only provides capabilities to describe a model's structure but not its behavior. To solve this issue, the model's behavior was implemented using annotations that carry the functionality of the model classes in the form of C++ source code. Annotations in Ecore are a text-based mechanism that allows the modeler to add information about specific elements to the model that would otherwise not be representable within Ecore. Based on the implemented PSCS Ecore model, a C++ library of the model was generated using MDE4CPP's *Ecore4CPP* generator [7,23].

In order to outsource parts of PSCS's functionality to code generation, those semantical aspects that are suitable to do so have to be identified. Again, structural semantics and behavioral semantics should be considered separately from each other. After an evaluation of the structural semantics of PSCS, two main aspects were chosen to be implemented generation-based:

1. Instantiation of composite structures, which includes: Recursive instantiation of parts and ports; Instantiation and extraction of links acting as connections between runtime objects, respectively creating and retrieving runtime topologies; Object creation based on default values, which are modeled using instance specifications

2. Destruction of objects in the context of composite structures, which includes: Recursive destruction of part and port instances; Destruction of corresponding links, respectively cleanup of runtime topologies after object destruction

[7] Details on how those aspects were realized are further explained in Sect. 2.2.

As the behavioral semantics of PSCS concern dynamic structural aspects during model execution, such functionalities of the PSCS meta model are not suitable for being substituted by static code generation. Still, even the behavioral semantics offer possibilities to make use of source code generation, to enhance expandability of PSCS in this case. After an evaluation of the behavioral semantics, it was decided that functionalities that concern dynamic aspects of a model at runtime shall remain in the meta model. Though the fUML and PSCS strategy pattern was chosen to be implemented as a generation-based extension mechanism. This mechanism is further described in Sect. 2.3.

The corresponding functionalities were implemented as extension modules for the existing generators UML4CPP [10] and fUML4CPP [1], which produce model-specific source code for the generated model libraries that substitutes the functionalities which were outsourced from the meta model. Other functionalities of PSCS remain in the meta model, respectively the model library generated from the corresponding PSCS Ecore model, which is linked with the generated model-specific source code during compilation to produce executable applications [7]. To be able to include application-specific semantic strategy classes to user-defined UML models, we designed two UML profiles which are further described in Sect. 2.3. Figure 1 depicts the whole process.

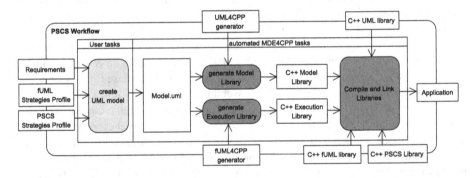

Fig. 1. Resulting workflow for executable PSCS models and integrated components. Orange: Tasks that have to be done by the user; Blue: Tasks that are automated by the MDE4CPP framework. (Color figure online)

2.2 Structural Semantics

While the behavioral semantics of PSCS concern dynamic aspects of a model which have to be evaluated at runtime, PSCS's structural semantics mainly focus on the analysis and evaluation of static information of a model. That is, for example, evaluating how composite structures and their internal topologies have to be instantiated, depending on the definition of their structural properties in the model (e.g., their parts and ports, their connectors, involved multiplicities, etc.). The fact that such information is static for a model and does not change during execution gives us the ability to outsource its analysis and evaluation to a step of preprocessing before the actual execution happens and thus decrease the amount of data processing required at runtime [7].

Major challenges of a generation-based realization of these semantics were the porting of PSCS's concept of links, that connect runtime objects to form a topology, to the level of source code generation as well as the resulting requirements for memory management. Details on how those challenges were solved will be explained in this section.

Generation-Based Realization of Runtime Links. On the model level, a composite structure is an entity that contains an internal network formed by parts and ports connected via connectors. In PSCS, runtime instances of such connectors that interconnect specific runtime objects during model execution are represented by so-called links (metaclass *CS_Link*). Links are instances (*objects* in the term of programming languages) of the aforementioned metaclass and explicitly carry information about which objects they connect. C++ itself does not provide any concept for generically connecting arbitrary objects with each other. Such a concept was developed as part of the presented PSCS implementation. That way, it was possible to implement PSCS's object instantiation, and destruction semantics on the level of automated source code generation [7]. Consider the example classes of Fig. 2a.

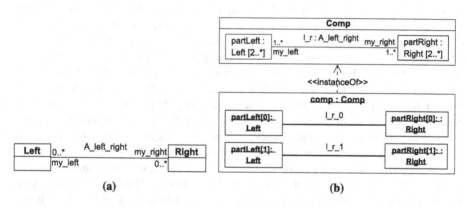

Fig. 2. (a) Class diagram showing two classes *Left* and *Right* associated bidirectionally via association *A_left_right*, and (b) Composite structure diagram of class *Comp* with parts of classes *Left* and *Right* from (a) that are connected via connector *l_r* typed by the association from (a) (upper) as well as an instance *comp* of class *Comp* (lower). Source: [7].

Because of association *A_left_right*, class *Left* has an attribute *my_right : Right* and class *Right* has an attribute *my_left : Left*. Assume that we want to model a simple composite structure *Comp* as depicted in Fig. 2b. When creating the instance *comp : Comp*, we can represent its internal links implicitly by letting objects that should be connected refer to each other, using the end properties of the association that types the corresponding connector. To implicitly represent the link *l_r_0* of instance *comp* (see Fig. 2b) for example, we must generate source code that creates a bidirectional reference between objects *comp::partLeft[0]* and *comp::partRight[0]*. To achieve that, we let *comp::partLeft[0]::my_right[0]* point to *comp::partRight[0]* as well as *comp::partRight[0]::my_left[0]* point to *comp::partLeft[0]*. By representing the information about connected objects implicitly depending on which objects refer to each other, topologies of connected objects can be created without having to instantiate any explicit link instances. This concept was used to implement a code generator that generates source code to instantiate different kinds of runtime topologies based on the model's definition by establishing bidirectional references as described above. The PSCS specification defines four kinds of topologies (so-called *connector patterns*) whose generator-based instantiation is supported by the implementation presented by this paper:

– Empty Pattern: A topology without objects and hence without connections.
– Unconnected Pattern: A topology without connections between its participating objects.
– Array Pattern: A topology consisting of 1-to-1 connections between the corresponding parts/ports that form a sequential order of connected objects (Fig. 2b depicts an array pattern).
– Star Pattern: A topology in which each object of one part/port is connected to each object of the other part/port, forming a complete bipartite graph between the connected properties [7].

As the PSCS execution environment still requires explicit links when processing link information, a generation-based adapter functionality between the generation-based components and the metamodel level of a model execution was developed. This adapter functionality works as follows: When accessing link information about connected objects at runtime, the PSCS execution environment invokes the adapter functionality via a standardized interface (which is generated for every executable model). The adapter functionality creates explicit link objects (required in the PSCS metamodel) based on implicit link information (used in the generation-based components). In contrary to the original PSCS specification, the creation of explicit links is done if and only if the PSCS execution environment requires them (e.g., to evaluate potential targets during an invocation delegation). The described mechanism was implemented as an extension of the model-specific execution library produced by the fUML4CPP generator (see Sect. 2.1). By realizing the adapter functionality generation-based and hence model-specific it can be ensured that only links that may be useful for a specific execution step are processed at runtime [7].

Memory Management. In contrast to programming languages like Java with the Java Virtual Machine (see [12]) or C# with the .NET Common Language Runtime (see [6]), C++ does not have an automated garbage collection functionality. This means that in C++, the programmer has to manually maintain memory deallocation, hence when objects can safely be deleted. The C++-11 standard introduced so-called *shared pointers* to reduce the complexity of this task. On the one hand, such shared pointers guarantee that memory is not deallocated as long as it is referenced from somewhere. In other words, no object that is managed by shared pointers is deleted as long as there exists at least one shared pointer instance that references the object [22]. On the other hand, shared pointers guarantee that objects are deleted only when they are not referenced (i.e., not needed) anymore. The MDE4CPP framework, as a part of which the PSCS implementation presented by this paper was realized, uses these shared pointers for its memory management. The usage of shared pointers within the concept for implicitly representing links, which was introduced in the previous section, however, results in problems concerning automated memory deallocation. Connected objects that hold mutual references to each other inevitably produce circular dependencies. This causes issues when trying to delete an object that is involved in such a connection. If an instance of a composite structure's part shall be deleted during model execution, it would not truly be deleted (in terms of memory deallocation) as long as it is connected to other objects, meaning that other objects hold references to it. This leads to both memory leaks as well as semantically incorrect behavior during a model execution [7].

In cases where the aspects to be modeled require circular references between objects (e.g., when implementing a composite pattern where both the parent and child class refer to each other), it is suggested to use *weak pointers* for the back-reference [22]. Without losing conceptual reasonability, however, this solution is only applicable if a clear parent-child hierarchy between involved classes can be determined (as one of the directed references would be considered 'weaker' than the other). In our case, no such hierarchy between the connected objects can be indentified because connected parts and ports are usually coequal on the conceptual level. Hence there is no identifiable 'back direction' within the circular dependencies. Using weak pointers for one of the bidirectional references would also have solved the issue for one 'direction' only. That is why the usage of weak pointers would not have been a sufficient solution for the implementation presented by this paper. To solve the issue sufficiently, a mechanism that generates model-specific deletion routines for each model class was developed. When the deletion routine of an object is invoked, all references of connected objects that refer to the object that is to be deleted are destroyed. After this process, there is only one shared pointer left that manages our object. This last reference can now safely be deleted, which ultimately results in the deallocation of memory that holds the object. Hence true deletion [7].

2.3   Behavioral Semantics

As the behavioral semantics of PSCS mainly concern non-static aspects of a model (i.e., properties that can change during model execution), they are less suitable for substitution with static source code generation. However, one aspect that can be seen as a part of the behavioral semantics of fUML and PSCS and which is suitable for a generation-based realization is the semantic strategy pattern. The UML itself contains so-called semantic variation points. Such variation points occur in the situation where UML intentionally leaves certain semantics undefined and leaves the realization of the corresponding behavior to the implementer [17]. Typical situations where this concept is utilized are, for example: realization of invocations of polymorphic operation calls, scheduling of event dispatching from an event pool (e.g., First-In-First-Out vs. Last-In-First-Out), access to properties of an interface, or propagation of invocations (more precisely, operation calls or signals) with multiple possible targets [18, 19]. Leaving the actual semantics of such situations undefined may be sufficient for UML itself, being a descriptional language that focuses on a precise syntax rather than semantics. For the purpose of creating execution environments, however, the corresponding runtime behavior of such variation points has to be defined. To realize this, fUML first introduced the concept of semantic strategies (also referred to as semantic strategy pattern), which is extended by subsequent UML execution semantics specifications like PSCS. In order to make this concept both generic and easily extendable, the corresponding metamodels contain abstract base classes, each defining the runtime behavior of a particular semantic variation point. These base classes can be specialized by implementers of the specifications, fitting certain application-specific needs. The metamodels also contain a default specialization for each abstract semantic strategy, implementing trivial default behavior [18,19]. The usual way of extending a UML execution environment with application-specific strategies would be to extend the corresponding metamodels by user-defined specialization classes. This, however, could result in the emergence of dependencies between specific application models and the execution environment's metamodels, which would otherwise be entirely independent of specific models that should be executed by it. For example, this can happen when an application-specific strategy requires model-specific types or behavior. The authors of this paper hold the opinion that the independence between these two components of a model execution should be preserved, as it supports modularity and obeys the principle of loose coupling. For the PSCS implementation presented by this paper, this was accomplished by designing and realizing the semantic strategy extension mechanism in a generation-based manner. Rather than extending the metamodels with application- and model-specific strategy classes, this mechanism allows to specify custom strategy classes in the respective models, generating source code and integrating the resulting strategy classes in the execution environment using interfaces specified by the metamodels as entry points. Technical details on how the mechanism was implemented and how it works are presented in this section.

Semantic Strategies Profiles. In order to be able to realize generation-based semantic strategies, the authors of this paper chose to utilize the mechanism of UML stereotypes. These stereotypes serve the purpose of indicating that a specific class of a model represents a specialization of an fUML or PSCS semantic strategy base class. Another possibility to accomplish that could have been to use UML generalization dependencies, making the custom strategy classes *real* specialized classes of the metamodels' base classes. As the fUML specification states, that if the execution environment should be extended by custom strategy classes, "[...] a specification must be provided for this variation via a specialization of the appropriate execution model class [...]" [18], this approach could be interpreted as the more desirable one. The stereotype approach was chosen for this implementation instead because we aimed for a noticeable separation of domain-specific extensions of execution semantics (which is conceptionally part of the metamodel level) from the behavioral specification on the actual model level. The decision that custom strategy classes should be implemented as a part of application-specific models as described above was a tradeoff. On the one hand, this concept preserves the independence of the execution environment from model-specific aspects. On the other hand, the strict separation between execution semantics and behavior of a certain model itself becomes fuzzy. To still emphasize that this conceptual separation exists, we found the concept of UML-stereotypes to be more suitable for the specific realization

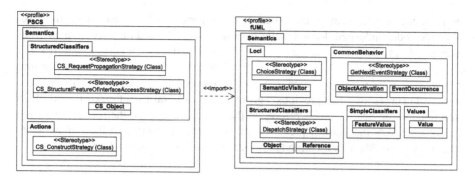

Fig. 3. Profile diagram for the fUML and PSCS strategies profiles.

presented here, where custom strategy classes (i.e., extensions of the execution environment) are contained in the actual models themselves. Concerning the source-code level however, the resulting fuzziness of the separation is somewhat resolved during the process of code generation (see Sect. 2.3, *Generation-based, model-specific semantic execution strategies*).

For the addressed purpose, two different profiles were created: an fUML strategies profile as well as a PSCS strategies profile. These profiles are depicted in Fig. 3 as a profile diagram. On the one hand, each profile contains stereotypes representing the base classes for the semantic strategies defined in the corresponding specification. On the other hand, the profiles also define types of the corresponding metamodels, which are required to specify custom strategy classes in user-defined models (e.g., for typing parameters). As stated in Sect. 2.1, the metamodels of fUML and PSCS are realized as ecore models in MDE4CPP. This makes it impossible to reuse fUML- and PSCS-types in UML models as ecore *EClass*es and UML *Class*es are not compatible. Because of that, these types had to be defined as UML *Class*es inside the profiles in order to be accessible for other UML models. In order to comply with the namespace structure of the metamodels, the internal package structure of the profiles is the same as those of the fUML and PSCS metamodels.

Generation-Based, Model-Specific Semantic Execution Strategies. In this section, the generative characteristics of the presented mechanism are described. After creating a UML model containing one or more custom strategy classes, the next step is to generate C++ source code from that model. As shown in Fig. 1, two C++ libraries are created as a result of this process: a *model library* which maps the structural aspects of the model (i.e., types, properties, associations, operations, etc.) to corresponding C++ artifacts, as well as an *execution library*. The model-specific execution library serves as an adapter between the model library and the C++ library of the execution environment [1]. In order to resolve the fuzzy separation between application-specific model behavior and execution semantics, which was introduced on the level of modeling, it is evident that the resulting C++ classes of user-defined semantic strategies should be a part of the execution library rather than the model library. Besides that, the MDE4CPP framework aims to be loosely coupled. For this scenario, that refers to the *structural* model library being compilable (and thus utilizable for external applications) without the presence of an execution environment being necessary (i.e., neither on the level of source code, undesired dependencies between the model and the execution environment should exist). During the generation process, the stereotype concept described in the previous section is transformed into C++ inheritance. That means that the custom strategy C++ classes are generated as derived classes of the corresponding base classes contained in the (somewhen previously generated) C++ libraries of the fUML and PSCS metamodels (see Sect. 2.1). Therefore, on the source-code level, the realization of the semantic strategy mechanism presented by this paper conforms to the requirements defined by the fUML specification (see 2.3, *Semantic Strategies Profiles*).

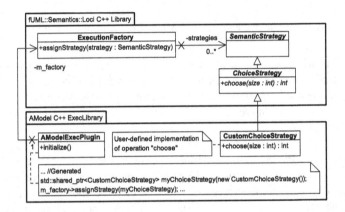

Fig. 4. An example of the connection between a model-specific execution library (containing a custom strategy class as well as the model's execution plugin) and the library of the fUML execution environment.

Integration. In order to apply a custom strategy during model execution, it must be registered at the current execution environment during its initialization process at the beginning of the execution. In MDE4CPP, the initialization of the current execution environment is handled by the *execution plugin* of a model. The execution plugin class is part of the execution library of the corresponding model and thus generated specifically for every executable model. In general, the initialization process of an fUML/PSCS execution environment mainly consists of instantiating the metamodel classes which *manage* the execution (for details, see [18]). In particular, these are the *Locus*, *Executor* and *ExecutionFactory*. The execution plugin of a model holds references to an instance of each of the mentioned classes. Within the scope of assigning semantic strategies to an execution environment, the ExecutionFactory is of interest. It holds a list of all strategies that will be applied during the current model execution. During initialization, instances of the desired strategy classes are created and registered at the current ExecutionFactory by invoking the operation *ExecutionFactory::assignStrategy* for each strategy instance. Because the execution plugin (which handles the initialization process) is generated model-specific, the registration of any desired, user-defined strategies can be generated here. At this point, the connection between model-specific semantic strategies and the fUML/PSCS execution environment is established. Figure 4 depicts the described structure on the source-code level as well as an excerpt of the generated initialization code. The *ChoiceStrategy* of fUML was extended by the custom specialization class *CustomChoiceStrategy* in this example.

3 Validation

This section first describes how the correct functionality, as well as conformance of the presented PSCS implementation to OMG's specification, were validated using a set of test models. An example model is described in Sect. 3.1. Furthermore, Sect. 3.2 presents a performance evaluation, including execution time and memory footprint of the PSCS implementation presented by this paper compared to a C++ reference implementation of PSCS as well as a Java reference implementation of fUML [7]. Finally, an academic example model focusing on the realization of model-specific execution semantics described in Sect. 2.3 is presented in Sect. 3.3. This example model addresses the use case of a load balancing mechanism of a client-server-like environment.

3.1 Conformance

A set of test models combined with corresponding unit tests was implemented to validate the correct functionality of the presented PSCS implementation as well as its conformance to the original specification. The used test models are suitable for validation as they are based on the PSCS test suite, which is provided by OMG and described in the specification document itself. In the specification, it is stated that passing all test cases defined in the aforementioned test suite is sufficient for proving the conformance of a tool that implements the specification [19]. However, not all models of the test suite could be implemented and tested against since the asynchronous communication semantics of PSCS are not yet supported by MDE4CPP and, therefore, currently excluded from the presented implementation (and hence from the validation process).

The realized set of test models consists of four different test suites, each addressing certain units of functionality specified by PSCS:

1. Instantiation of topologies of runtime objects based on composite structures.
2. Destruction of runtime objects which exist in the context of composite structures (i.e., instances of composite structures themselves or part/port objects of such instances).
3. Synchronous communication through a network of runtime objects connected through links via delegation of operation calls.
4. Synchronous communication via delegation of operation calls (as in point 3) using the *onPort* attribute of metaclass *InvocationAction*.

The presented PSCS implementation was tested against all models of the four test suites described above. As a result, all test cases were passed, and correct functionality could successfully be validated. As an example, the following section describes one of the test models of test suite 4. This model was chosen for an explanation because it combines test cases for all the functionalities mentioned above. The original test model's description can be found in [19] on pages 94 and 95 [7].

Example. The example model that is explained below addresses synchronous communication between instances of composite structures. More precisely, when the model is executed, an operation call is invoked in an initial caller object. The call is then forwarded through a network of port objects connected through links to a target object, where it is ultimately executed [7].

Figure 5 shows a class diagram of the example model. Every class realizes interface *I*, which defines the operation *assignP*. Only class *B* has an attribute *p* of type *int*. Hence, class *B* is modeled as the only class that truly implements the operation *assignP*, which means that only class *B* will define a method for the operation [7].

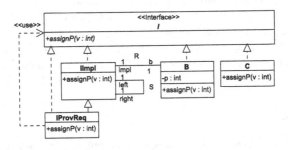

Fig. 5. Class diagram for test model. Adapted from [7].

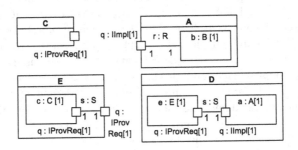

Fig. 6. Composite structure diagram for test model. Adapted from [7].

Figure. 6 depicts class *C* from Fig. 5 as well as three newly-introduced classes A, E and D as composite structure diagrams. Classes A, C and E have ports of type *IImpl* (which stands for I_Implementation) or *IProvReq* (which stands for I_Provided_Required) from Fig. 5. The types of a port specify its provided and required interfaces. In our example, class *IImpl* provides interface *I*, because it has an interface realization relationship (metaclass *InterfaceRealization*) with *I*. Class *IProvReq* both provides and requires *I* because it is inherited from *IImpl* (which determines provision) and at the same time, it uses (metaclass *Usage*) interface *I* (which determines request). When an operation call arrives at a port object, its provided and required interfaces determine how the call is further delegated from that port [7]. If the corresponding port provides the respective interface, the operation call is delegated into the object that owns the port instance. If the respective interface is required by the port, the operation call is delegated to the environment of the owner object. If the interface is both provided and required by the port, the direction of delegation depends on the source of the arriving operation call. If the operation call was received from outside of the port's owner, it is delegated into the owner object. Otherwise, the operation call is delegated to the environment [19].

Besides its structural aspects, the example model also contains a test behavior called *actTestCallDelegation* which is shown in Fig. 7 as an activity diagram. First, an instance *d : D* is created. Further, an operation call for *assignP* is invoked in *d::e::c* with port *C::q* being set for the *onPort* attribute (not depicted) of action *assignP()* on Port *q* inside of activity *actSetP*. Instance *d* is returned by activity *actTestCallDelegation* to evaluate certain postconditions after its execution.

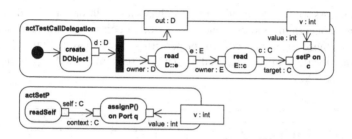

Fig. 7. Activity diagram for test model. Adapted from [7].

The presented PSCS implementation is tested against the model to validate correct functionality. The expected result is as follows: First, the operation call of operation *assignP()* invoked on port textitd::e::c::q should be delegated to port *d::e::q* via a link that was created from connector *E::s* (see Fig. 6). Next, the call should be dispatched out of *d::e* because the port *d::e::q* both provides and requires interface *I*. The fact that the source of the incoming operation call on port *d::e::q* is received from inside its owner determines that the call is further delegated to the environment of *d::e*. Looking at Fig. 6 we can see, that the call should be forwarded to port *d::a::q* over a link that was created from connector *D::s*. Finally the operation call must be dispatched inside *d::a* (because port *d::a::q* requires interface *I*) and delegated to *d::a::b* over a link that was created from connector *A::r* where it is ultimately executed. If the invocation was delegated correctly, then after activity *actTestCallDelegation* has finished, property *d::a::b::p* must be set to the value *v* that was provided into the activity. In this case, *v* is chosen as 4 [7]. The output of the example model's unit test routine is shown below:

```
Test model : Feature on both Required and Provided Interface
-- Running test case: Feature on both Required and Provided Interface --

d->a->b->p = 4
Operation call forwarded out of c through c::q, out of e through e::q
into a through a::q to a::b : true

Test case successful : true
-- End of test case --
```

3.2   Performance Evaluation

This section presents a performance evaluation of the presented PSCS implementation. Because there is no third-party open-source C++-implementation of PSCS available by now, a C++ reference implementation was developed in the context of the *MDE4CPP* project. This reference implementation was used for comparative evaluation. Furthermore, the open-source Java fUML reference implementation by *Model Driven Solutions*[1] was used as a third-party UML execution environment to reproduce certain PSCS-specific semantics for this benchmark [7]. It should be noted here that other third-party implementations of PSCS, such as *Papyrus/Moka* (see [5]) developed by the Eclipse Foundation, exist and might be compared against in the future.

Test Models. As the PSCS functionalities enhanced within the presented implementation mainly concern instantiation and destruction of composite structures, a test case that addresses these issues was chosen for performance evaluation. Figure 8 shows the class diagram for the realized test models. The internals of class *A* represent an array pattern (see Sect. 2.2).

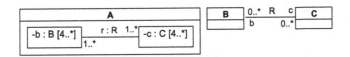

Fig. 8. Classes used in the performance evaluation test models. Class *A* is depicted using a composite structure diagram. Adapted from [7].

When the test models are executed, instances of class *A* shall be created and destroyed iteratively in a loop. This behavior is modeled by using the corresponding actions to create and destroy objects (metaclasses *CreateObjectAction* and *DestroyObjectAction*). The instantiations and destructions themself are then handled by the implemented PSCS semantics at runtime [7].

Because such semantics are not part of fUML, they have to be reproduced using activities in the fUML test model. The test model executed by *Model Driven Solution*'s Java fUML reference implementation includes corresponding activities. Figure 9 depicts the activity *actCreateParts*, which instantiates parts *A::b* and *A::c*. It does so by creating four instances of classes *B* and *C* each and adding them to the feature values of the corresponding parts using *AddStructuralFeatureValueActions*.

The activity *actCreateArrayPattern*, which is depicted in Fig. 10, is then used to instantiate the connections between those instances as defined by the array pattern. The realization of links as described in Sect. 2.2 is reproduced by activity *actCreateArrayPattern* by adding each part instance to the corresponding feature value of its linked instance. The main loop activity of the fUML test model is shown in Fig. 11.

On the model level, the PSCS implementation presented by this paper uses a simple *CreateObjectAction* for instantiation. The creation of part and port objects as well as links between them is then handled by the constructor of the auto-generated model

---

[1] see https://github.com/ModelDriven/fUML-Reference-Implementation.

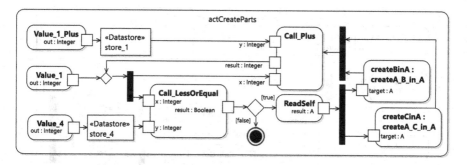

Fig. 9. Activity *actCreateParts* creates 4 instances each for parts *A::b* and *A::c*. Adapted from [7].

classes during execution. No further actions or declarations of any kind are necessary [7].

For actual instantiation (not only creation) of an object, the original PSCS specification additionally requires the call of an empty constructor operation using a *CallOperationAction*. An 'empty' operation denotes an operation with no defined method (i.e., no Activity, OpaqueBehavior, StateMachine, etc., is assigned to the operation's behavior). 'Constructor operation' means, that the UML stereotype <<*Create*>>, which is defined in the UML Standard Profile (see [17]), has to be applied to it. Conforming to the PSCS specification, such a special operation serves as an indication for the execution engine that when it is called, an instance of its owning class has to be instantiated based on the defined instantiation semantics [7, 19]. The corresponding test model was adapted for the PSCS reference implementation that was developed for comparative evaluation.

Creation and Deletion Benchmark. To compare execution times between the PSCS implementation presented by this paper and the fUML and PSCS reference implementations mentioned above, the test models described in Sect. 3.2 were executed with different numbers of loop iterations: 1000, 2500, 5000, 10000, 50000 and 100000. The number of loop iterations is equal to the number of instances of composite structure *A* from Fig. 8 that are created and destroyed during model execution. The resulting execution times shown in Fig. 12a are arithmetical mean values calculated from 10 model executions each. The x-axis represents the number of iterations used for the model executions. Each region is split by the different execution environments that were used. The y-axis represents the average execution times in milliseconds [7].

The model execution of the PSCS implementation presented by this paper runs faster than the executions of both reference implementation test models. This result was expected as the presented PSCS implementation outsources functionalities for checking and evaluating model information to the level of code generation. For both reference implementations, those functionalities are executed by their respective execution environments. This produces computation overhead at runtime compared to the presented implementation. Execution times of the fUML test model executed by *Model Driven Solution*'s Java fUML reference implementation are higher compared to those of the PSCS reference implementation. On the one hand, this could be explained by general performance advantages of C++ over Java. On the other hand, a pure fUML model was

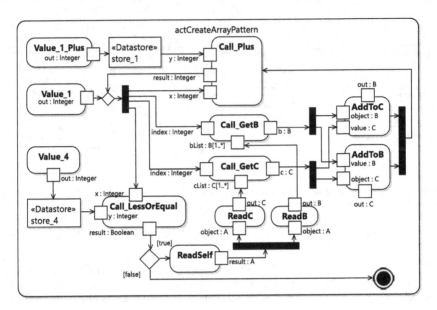

Fig. 10. Activity *actCreateArrayPattern* reproduces the links between the instances of parts *A::b* and *A::c* by adding each instance of *A::b* to the feature value of feature *C::b* of the corresponding instance of *A::c* and vice versa. Adapted from [7].

used to reproduce PSCS-specific semantics. Because of that, the model is larger and contains much more behavior that has to be executed by the corresponding execution engine than the PSCS test models [7].

Memory Footprint. Memory usage during test model execution was measured in the same manner as the measurement of execution time described in Sect. 3.2. Figure 12b depicts the arithmetical mean values of peak RAM usage from 10 model executions each. The Java fUML reference implementation uses significantly more RAM than both C++ PSCS implementations. The reason for this behavior might be the additional RAM usage caused by the Java virtual machine. The PSCS implementation presented by this paper requires the least amount of RAM. This can be explained by the fact that the instantiation and destruction semantics used by this implementation are directly translated to model-specific C++ code during generation. Thus, overhead produced by the execution engine of the PSCS reference implementation (which leads to a slightly higher RAM usage) is saved during the execution of the presented PSCS implementation. Moreover, the RAM usage of this implementation (as well as the compared PSCS reference implementation) is constant for each number of iterations that was tested. This indicates that no memory leaks exist [7].

3.3   Example: Network Traffic Load Balancing

In the previous sections, the presented PSCS implementation was evaluated regarding its conformance to the original specification as well as its performance. In this section, an exemplary use case of user-defined, model-specific semantic execution strategies is

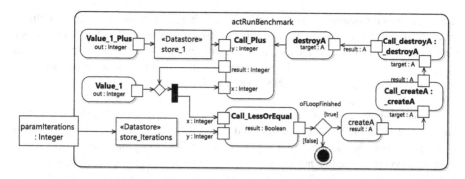

Fig. 11. Activity *actRunBenchmark* iteratively creates, instatiates and destroys instances of composite structure *A* from fig. 8. Adapted from [7].

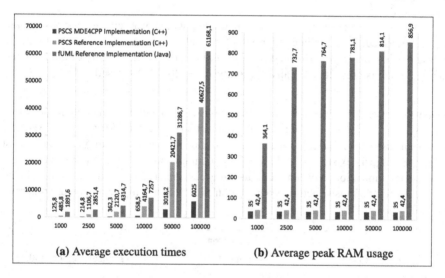

Fig. 12. (a) Average execution time in milliseconds, and (b) average peak memory usage in megabytes per number of created/destroyed objects. Source: [7].

presented, and the corresponding generation-based extension mechanism is evaluated. As stated in Sect. 1, the behavioral semantics of PSCS mainly concern how communication (i.e., operation calls or signals) should be propagated through a network of linked objects. Of course, such semantics require some *forwarding mechanism*, which selects a specific propagation target if multiple equally qualified target objects exist. In PSCS, this mechanism is realized by a semantic strategy called *RequestPropagation-Strategy*. The default realization of this strategy provided by the metamodel, *Default-RequestPropagationStrategy*, implements a trivial default propagation behavior. That is, the first one amongst a list of potential targets will always be chosen. Therefore, the number of reasonable use-cases for this default behavior is somewhat limited, and complex network model analyses are not representable at all. The mechanism described in

Sect. 2.3 makes it possible to extend the *RequestPropagationStrategy* with user-defined behavior, driven by an elaborate modeling mechanism which allows, amongst other things, the integration of model-specific attributes and their values in the logic of such strategies. This allows a more sophisticated propagation of synchronous operation invocations through components connected in a network.

As an exemplary application, a widely used and well-understood technology named *Traffic Load Balancing* (TLB) was selected. Load balancing focuses on a setting that frequently occurs in modern information systems: incoming network traffic needs to be distributed efficiently across a group of backend server machines that process the requests (e.g., web-based services, serving thousands of concurrent requests from clients). Load balancing aims to increase the response time of the overall system by utilizing its overall capacities to a decent degree while ensuring that no server is overloaded or idling.

First, the design of the TLB system model, which was created for this example, is described. This includes both structure and internal behavior. Subsequently, a simulation-like analysis performed to validate the correct functionality of the load balancing system is presented. Finally, the analysis results are discussed.

System Design. Concerning the strucutre of the TLB model, the general encapsulating class *System* is composed of three subcomponents (i.e. parts): *client : Client, server : Server* and *services : Service*. Whereat the latter has a multiplicity of *50.. ** (i.e. at least 50 *Service* objects exist). Each of these parts contains corresponding ports, in order to enable communication between them during execution. The respective ports are linked using connectors. This structure is depicted in Fig. 13 as a composite structure diagram.

Fig. 13. Composite structure diagram of the TLB system, parts *client, server* and *services* as well as their respective ports.

In order to enable the propagation of requests from the client instance to the server instance and subsequently to one of the service instances via corresponding port instances during execution, the respective ports must be typed in a way that they either require or provide corresponding interfaces. This principle of *direction control* of possible request propagations is explained in Sect. 3.1. Figure 14 depicts the structure of the TLB model in the form of a class diagram.

To describe the model's internal system behavior, the three main components are considered separately. *Client*: The client produces requests with an exponentially distributed request rate (used as a synonym for arrival rate here). On the model level, a

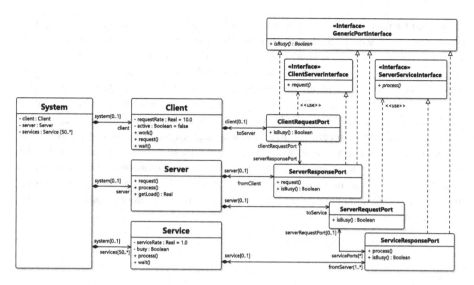

Fig. 14. Class diagram of the TLB system: major classes *System*, *Client*, *Server* and *Service* as well as additional port specification classes and interfaces.

request is a call of operation *Client::request* via port *Client::toServer*. The call is then delegated by the PSCS request propagation mechanism. *Service*: The services represent the components where client requests are processed. A single service can only process one request at a time and does not have a queue. Thus, a service object can be in one of two states: Either *busy* or *free*. The service rate of the services is also exponentially distributed. *Server*: The server is used as an intermediate relais component. When it receives a client request (i.e., the operation call that was delegated from the client is executed), it sends out an operation call of *Server::process* via the instance of port *Server::toService* which is then delegated to the *Service::fromServer* port instance of one of the service objects. The actual load balancing is done by a user-defined specialization class of the PSCS *RequestPropagationStrategy* class. This specialized semantic strategy implements the behavior that determines to which target service object an operation call should be delegated. Conceptually it does so by evaluating the state of the *service pool*. The strategy iterates the list of connected ports and checks their state by invoking *GenericPortInterface::isBusy*. While all other port types return *false* by default, *ServiceResponsePort* queries the busy-state of its owner object. The first non-busy port instance that is found is then selected as the target. If all services are busy, the request is lost. As per queueing models, the systems realizes an M/M/K/K queue (using Kendall's notation, see [11]) with K being specified as 50 here [9].

Analysis & Results. To analyze the system's behavior when the model is executed, an observation loop was implemented. The purpose of the analysis was to observe the system's load during model execution and evaluate to what extent the results concerning mean load fit the theoretical values. This simulation-like process was parameterized as follows: The process consists of 60 separate model executions. Each execution was carried out for 600 s (s). The sampling interval for system utilization (i.e., the percentage of busy services) was 10 milliseconds (ms). The expectation of the service rate for all services was specified as 1/s and was fixed for all executions. The expectation of the request rate was incremented by 1 for each model execution, starting with 1/s up to 60/s. Figure 15 shows the mean load of the system in percent for each model execution visualized by the blue graph. The red graph depicts the theoretical mean loads for each execution. These values were calculated using *Little's Law* (see [9]). The mean number of requests in the system can be calculated with a given mean request rate and a mean service time. As the services do not have a queue, the mean service time can directly be derived from the mean service rate. Moreover, the mean number of requests in the system is equal to the mean number of busy services. Based on that, the theoretical mean system load can be calculated by dividing the mean number of busy services by the total number of services.

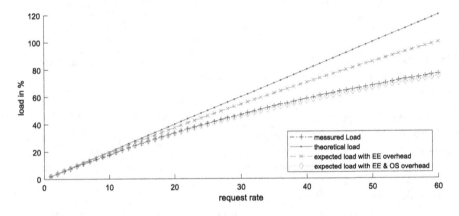

Fig. 15. Analysis results from 60 model executions, request rates [1..60]/s. Blue: Measured mean system load; Red: Theoretical mean system load; Magenta: Expected mean system load considering overhead of execution environment (EE); Green: Expected mean system load considering overhead of EE and operating system. (Color figure online)

When observing the courses of the blue and the red graph in Fig. 15, one can recognize that for lower request rates, the values of theoretical mean load and measured mean load are very similar to each other. As the request rate grows, however, the measured mean load diverges from its theoretical course. This phenomenon can be explained by the temporal overhead that emerges during specific parts of the model execution.

A major fragment of this overhead is caused by the fUML/PSCS execution environment itself. This mainly results from computationally complex processes for executing activities, object simulation, operation dispatching, and others that are inherent to the fUML and PSCS specifications. The execution time of these processes was measured isolated from the rest of the execution and was estimated to be around 3.4 ms on average.

Putting the thread that runs the client's main loop to sleep until the next request should be made was identified as another major cause for runtime overhead. This analysis was run on a Windows machine. The Windows scheduling algorithm does not guarantee that threads which transit from *wait* state (e.g., because it was put to sleep) back to *ready* state will return to execution immediately. A thread might rest in *ready* state for some time before it is selected by the scheduler to be executed [24]. The execution time of the sleep procedure was measured isolated from the rest of the execution as well. Of course, this overhead is not constant and is unpredictable for a specific sleep procedure. It was estimated to be around 6.6 ms on average.

As these overheads occur during each iteration of the client's main loop, they adulterate the expected interval between two request events which is derived from the exponentially distributed request rate. This causes the actual request rates during execution to be smaller than the expected request rates, thus causing smaller values of the measured mean loads than the calculated ones. Of course, the influence of these overheads on the real request rate depends on the choice of the expected request rate. For example, an expected request rate of 1/s results in a mean interval of 1 s between two requests. In this case, an aggregated overhead of 10ms per interval seems rather insignificant. If, on the other hand, an expected request rate of 100/s is chosen, the resulting actual request rate is only half of the expected one. This has a significant influence on the actual mean system load. The remaining two graphs in Fig. 15 visualize this effect. The magenta graph depicts the expected mean load with the overhead produced by the execution environment taken into account. The corresponding values were also calculated using *Little's Law* with the expected request rate being adjusted by the overhead. The green graph depicts the expected mean load in consideration of the aggregated overhead produced by the execution environment as well as the operating system. It becomes clear that if the expected request rate for calculating the theoretical mean system load is adjusted by the overhead, the graphs of the expected mean loads and the measured mean loads align very well. This shows that the system behaves as expected if the influence of computational overhead caused by the model execution itself is considered.

4   Conclusion

This paper presented a model-driven implementation of OMG's PSCS specification in C++, pursuing a generative approach. In the proposed solution, specific parts of the PSCS execution model are substituted with auto-generated, model-specific source code. By omitting computational overhead at runtime produced by repeatedly evaluating and processing static (i.e., runtime-independent) structural model information and outsourcing these parts of model processing to pre-runtime code generation, the performance of the actual model execution is improved. Beyond that, the presented implementation includes a generation-based realization of the fUML/PSCS extension mechanism of semantic execution strategies. This realization enables the modeling of user-defined execution strategies that may utilize application-specific models' types, properties, or behaviors. Due to the generative approach, the independence between application-specific models and the execution environment, as well as the principle of loose coupling, are preserved. That way, the modeler can flexibly extend the execution semantics of fUML/PSCS regarding model- and application-specific needs.

The generation-based PSCS implementation presented by this paper was validated concerning correct functionality and conformance, as well as examined considering performance. A set of test models and associated unit tests, described in Sect. 3.1, based on OMG's original PSCS test suite, was realized for functional validation. The results of testing the presented PSCS implementation against these models showed correct functionality and conformance to the original PSCS specification [7].

A significant improvement of execution times by substituting runtime computation of the PSCS execution model with pre-runtime computation via code generation could be demonstrated during the performance evaluation presented in Sect. 3.2. The memory footprints of the evaluated test model executions prove that the usage of C++ combined with the memory management described in Sect. 2.2 leads to lower RAM usage compared to the Java fUML reference implementation [7].

Finally, an example of application was presented, making use of the proposed model-driven extension mechanism for custom semantic strategies. This example comprises a load balancing process in a client-server-like model. The subsequent analysis of the system with differing parameterization, described in Sect. 3.3, showed that the system behaves as expected if computational overhead produced by the execution environment itself, as well as the operating systems, are taken into account. These results show that the presented realization of extending the fUML and PSCS execution semantics by user-defined strategies is functional. Moreover, it enables models with more elaborate execution behavior when it comes to semantic variation points. Thus, for example, it makes complex network-like communication processes representable in UML and executable as well as analyzable using fUML and PSCS.

Future Work. By now, the presented implementation excludes PSCS semantics concerning asynchronous communication, e.g., signal and event processing, active classes and objects, as well as concurrency. These semantics are yet to be realized in order to provide a full implementation of PSCS.

The results of this paper display the possibilities of exploiting automated source code generation to reduce runtime computation of model execution engines. Based on these findings and the experiences we made, we aim to develop model-driven execution engines for fUML, PSCS, and also PSSM that rely more on code generation and also conform (functionality-wise) to the underlying specifications [7]. As the MDE4CPP framework generates source code libraries from UML models which contain C++ representations of the model classes, such execution environments would not require runtime simulation of concepts like objects, attribute values, inheritance, or invocation of (possibly polymorphic) operations because they are handled by C++ inherently. Taking this idea one step further, the execution of UML acitivies could be substituted with source code generation by first transforming activities into their textual representation, Alf (Action Language for Foundational UML, see [16]) code respectively, and subsequently translating Alf to C++ code. Corresponding approaches to the latter have been described in [2, 3].

References

1. Bedini, F., Maschotta, R., Wichmann, A., Jäger, S., Zimmermann, A.: A model-driven fuml execution engine for c++. In: Proceedings of the 5th International Conf. on Model-Driven Engineering and Software Development. pp. 443–450. MODELSWARD 2017, SCITEPRESS. https://doi.org/10.5220/0006206904430450

2. Ciccozzi, F.: On the automated translational execution of the action language for foundational UML. Softw. Syst. Model. **17**(4), 1311–1337 (2016). https://doi.org/10.1007/s10270-016-0556-7

3. Ciccozzi, F., Cicchetti, A., Sjödin, M.: Towards translational execution of action language for foundational uml. In: 2013 39th Euromicro Conference on Software Engineering and Advanced Applications. pp. 153–160 (2013). https://doi.org/10.1109/SEAA.2013.31

4. Eclipse Foundation: Acceleo, see http://www.wiki.eclipse.org/acceleo (2018)

5. Eclipse Foundation: Eclipse Papyrus, see http://www.eclipse.org/papyrus/ (2019)

6. ECMA International: ECMA-335: Common Language Infrastructure (CLI), 6th Edition. http://www.ecma-international.org/wp-content/uploads/ECMA-335_6th_edition_june_2012.pdf (2012)

7. Hammer., M., Maschotta., R., Wichmann., A., Jungebloud., T., Bedini., F., Zimmermann., A.: A model-driven implementation of pscs specification for c++. In: Proceedings of the 9th International Conf. on Model-Driven Engineering and Software Development - MODELSWARD, pp. 100–109. INSTICC, SciTePress (2021). https://doi.org/10.5220/0010267801000109

8. Hutchinson, J., Whittle, J., Rouncefield, M., Kristoffersen, S.: Empirical assessment of mde in industry. In: Proceedings of the 33rd International Conf. on Software Engineering. p. 471–480. ICSE '11, Association for Computing Machinery, New York, NY, USA (2011). https://doi.org/10.1145/1985793.1985858

9. Jain, R.: The Art of Computer Systems Performance Analysis: Techniques for Experimental Design, Measurement, Simulation, and Modeling. Wiley, 1. ed. (1991)

10. Jäger, S., Maschotta, R., Jungebloud, T., Wichmann, A., Zimmermann, A.: An emf-like uml generator for c++. In: 2016 4th International Conf. on Model-Driven Engineering and Software Development - MODELSWARD (2016)

11. Kendall, D.G.: Stochastic Processes Occurring in the Theory of Queues and their Analysis by the Method of the Imbedded Markov Chain. Ann. Math. Stat. **24**(3), 338–354 (9 1953). https://doi.org/10.1214/aoms/1177728975

12. Lindholm, T., Yellin, F., Bracha, G., Buckley, A., Smith, D.: The Java®Virtual Machine Specification, Java SE 14 Version. https://docs.oracle.com/javase/specs/jvms/se14/jvms14.pdf (2020)

13. OMG: Semantics of a Foundational Subset for Executable UML Models (FUML) Specification, Version 1.0. http://www.omg.org/spec/FUML/1.0/PDF/ (2011)

14. OMG: MDA Guide Revision 2.0. http://www.omg.org/cgi-bin/doc?ormsc/14-06-01.pdf (2014)

15. OMG: Precise Semantics of UML Composite Structure (PSCS) Specification, Version 1.0. www.omg.org/spec/PSCS/1.0/PDF (2015)

16. OMG: Action Language for Foundational UML (Alf), concrete syntax for a UML action language, version 1.1. http://www.omg.org/spec/ALF/1.1/PDF/ (2017)

17. OMG: Unified Modeling Language, Specification, Version 2.5.1. http://www.omg.org/spec/UML/2.5.1/PDF (2017)

18. OMG: Semantics of a Foundational Subset for Executable UML Models (FUML) Specification, Version 1.4. http://www.omg.org/spec/FUML/1.4/PDF (2018)

19. OMG: Precise Semantics of UML Composite Structure (PSCS) Specification, Version 1.2. http://www.omg.org/spec/PSCS/1.2/PDF (2019)
20. Stahl, T., Völter, M.: Modellgetriebene Softwareentwicklung: Techniken, Engineering, Management. dpunkt.verlag, 1. edn. (2005)
21. Steinberg, D., Budinsky, F., Paternostro, M., Merks, E.: EMF: Eclipse Modeling Framework 2.0. Addison-Wesley Professional, 2. edn. (2009)
22. Stroustrup, B.: The C++ Programming Language. Addison-Wesley, 4. edn. (2013)
23. Systems and Software Engineering Group: Model Driven Engineering for C++ (MDE4CPP), see http://sse.tu-ilmenau.de/mde4cpp (2016)
24. Yosifovich, P., Russinovich, M.E., Solomon, D.A., Ionescu, A.: Windows Internals, Part 1: System Architecture, Processes, Threads, Memory Management, and More, 7th edn. Microsoft Press, USA (2017)

Dependency Graphs to Boost the Verification of SysML Models

Ludovic Apvrille[1], Pierre de Saqui-Sannes[2]([⊠]), Oana Hotescu[2],
and Alessandro Tempia Calvino[3]

[1] LTCI, Telecom Paris, Institut Polytechnique de Paris, Paris, France
[2] ISAE-SUPAERO, Université de Toulouse, Toulouse, France
`pdss@isae-supaero.fr`
[3] LSI, École Polytechnique Fédérale de Lausanne, Lausanne, Switzerland

Abstract. Model-Based Systems Engineering has often been associated
with the Systems Modeling Language. Several SysML tools offer formal
verification capabilities, and therefore enable early detection of design
errors in the life cycle of systems. Model-checking is a common formal
verification approach used to assess the satisfiability of properties. Thus,
a SysML model and a property can be injected into a model-checker
returning a true/false result. A drawback of this approach is that the
entire SysML model is used for the verification, even if the property
targets a sub-system of the model. In this paper, it is suggested to rely on
dependency graphs to avoid applying model checking to the entire system
when only a subset of the latter needs to be taken into account. We
formalize SysML models and properties, then we present new algorithms
to generate and reduce dependency graphs, so as to perform verification
on reduced models. A case study on Time-Sensitive Networking is used
to demonstrate the efficiency and limits of this approach. The algorithms
described in the paper are fully implemented by the free software TTool.
Our method enables an improvement in run time between 3% and 90%
depending on the state space to be traversed to verify the property.

Keywords: MBSE · SysML · Formal verification · Model checking ·
TSN

1 Introduction

Over the past two decades, Systems Engineering has transitioned from document
centric approaches to model based ones. The 'MBSE' acronym was coined to
denote a form of systems engineering where models serve as references for a set of
activities as various as requirement capture, use-case driven analysis, and system
design. With a system life cycle made up of a requirement capture, analysis and
design steps, one major concern is to detect design errors as early as possible in
the life cycle of the system.

Checking a model against design errors can be achieved using formal verification techniques. The latter have first been developed for formal methods, such
as timed automata, Finite State Machines, and Petri Nets, just to mention a

© Springer Nature Switzerland AG 2023
L. F. Pires et al. (Eds.): MODELSWARD 2021/2022, CCIS 1708, pp. 109–134, 2023.
https://doi.org/10.1007/978-3-031-38821-7_6

few. Formal verification techniques such as model checking have more recently been adapted to semi-formal languages, in particular SysML [8, 10, 36, 38].

As far as SysML is concerned, a model-checker takes a SysML model and a property as input, and outputs a true/false result. To make model checking practicable, the designer of the SysML model must be able to identify the properties to be verified and to express them in a form that is processable by the model checker. Model checking SysML models further requires to interpret the results output by the model checker, and to eventually relate the true/false answers to the original SysML Model. With its in-built model checker, TTool [43] handles the two issues. First, the properties are expressed in a CTL-like language and located in specific comments inside the SysML model. Second, the results of model checking the SysML models are reported in the comments containing the properties, by indicating which property holds or not.

Despite of its user-friendliness in terms of properties expression and verification, TTool shares one limitation with other SysML model checkers: the verification process uses the entire model as input, even if the property of interest concerns only a sub-part of it, thus leading to extra verification time, and possibly to combinatorial explosion. The purpose of this paper is to address this issue in the context of SysML and to assess the efficiency of the proposed approach by using TTool as a prototyping platform. The proposed approach relies on the following statement: many parts in the block and state machine diagrams of the SysML model are two by two dependent. For instance, a dependency does exist between two blocks $B1$ and $B2$ that synchronize by respectively sending and receiving a message m.

In the current paper, it is argued that dependencies may be expressed using a graph that we call *dependency graph*. It is further proposed to compute a reduced model of the SysML model that is sufficient to prove the property of interest. Because the resulting model is smaller, the proof is expected to be faster, as illustrated in this paper with a case study.

The current paper sketches the dependency graph generation algorithm and relies on a case study to show the efficiency of its implementation in the free software TTool [36, 43], both for the proof of reachability and liveness properties.

The current paper extends a paper co-authored by the same authors and published at Modelswards 2022 conference [5]. The current paper differs from [5]. The related work section has been substantially extended with recently released papers. Algorithms 2 and 3, at the root of this new contribution, have been substantially improved and their implementation in TTool has been updated. Last but not least, the TNS (Time Sensitive Networking) protocol [21] has been selected as a case study for it is the successor of the AFDX protocol addressed in [5]. More complete performance measures, based on the next algorithms, are provided: they better demonstrate the interest of our approach.

The current paper is organized as follows. Section 2 formally defines a subset of SysML. Section 3 introduces dependency graphs. It also presents the algorithms implemented by TTool to generate dependency graphs from SysML models. Section 4 discusses a case study based on the IEEE 802.1 TSN protocol. Section 5 surveys related work. Section 6 concludes the paper and outlines future work.

2   SysML

The Systems Modeling Language (SysML [30]) is an international standard [30] at OMG (*Object Management Group*) and originates from joint efforts of OMG and INCOSE (*International Council on Systems Engineering*) to define a modeling language for systems engineers. Version 1.6 of SysML enables covering the requirement capture, analysis and design steps in the life trajectory of systems.

The main objective of the design phase is to define the architecture of the system using the Block Definition Diagrams (BDD) and the Internal Block Diagrams (IBD) defined by the SysML standard [30]. In this paper, the BDD and IBD are merged into a Block Instance Diagram (BID). Each block instance in the BID has a behavior expressed in the form of a SysML state machine diagram.

2.1   Block Instance Diagram

A Block Instance Diagram contains a set of block instances that can be composed together, and associated through port relations.

Definition: Block Instance. A block instance is a 7-tuple $B = \langle id, A, M, P, S_i, S_o, smd \rangle$ where:

- id is a String that names the block instance.
- A is an attribute list. The attribute types include Integer, Boolean, Timer, and user-defined Records. An attribute may be defined with an initial value.
- M is a set of methods.
- P is a set of ports.
- S_i and S_o are sets of input and output signals.
- smd is a state machine diagram.
- B_p represents the parent block to which B belongs. B_p can be empty.

Definition: Block Instance Diagram. A Block Instance Diagram models the architecture of a system as a graph of interconnected block instances. More formally, a Block Instance Diagram D is a 3-tuple $D = \langle \mathcal{B}, connect, assoc \rangle$. We denote by $\mathcal{S}_i$ the set of all input signals of $\mathcal{B}$, by $\mathcal{S}_o$ the set of all output signals of $\mathcal{B}$ and by $\mathcal{P}$ the set of all ports of $\mathcal{B}$.

- $\mathcal{B}$ is a set of block instances.
- $connect$ is a function $\mathcal{P} \times \mathcal{P} \rightarrow \{No, synchronous, asynchronous\}$ that returns the communication semantics between two ports ($\emptyset$, synchronous or asynchronous).
- $assoc$ is a function $(\mathcal{P}_{\mathcal{B}_1} \times \mathcal{S}_o \times \mathcal{P}_{\mathcal{B}_2} \times \mathcal{S}_i) \rightarrow Bool$ that returns true if an output signal $\mathcal{S}_o$ of block $\mathcal{B}_1$ is associated to an input signal $\mathcal{S}_i$ of block $\mathcal{B}_2$ via 2 ports $p1, p2$ of respectively of $\mathcal{B}_1$ and $\mathcal{B}_2$, and if these two ports are connected (*i.e.*, $connect(p1, p2) = true$);

2.2   State Machine Diagram

Each block instance contains one finite state machine that supports states, transitions, attribute settings, inputs and outputs operations on signals, and temporal operators such as delays and timers.

Definition: State Machine. A finite state machine depicted by a SysML state machine diagram is a bipartite graph $\langle s_0, S, T \rangle$ where

- S is a set of states (s_0 is the initial state).
- T is a set of transitions.

Definition: State Transition. A transition is a 5-tuple $\langle s_{start}, after, condition, Actions, s_{end} \rangle$ where:

- s_{start} is the initial state of the transition.
- $after(t_{min}, t_{max})$ specifies that the transition is enabled only after a duration between t_{min} and t_{max} has elapsed.
- *condition* is a Boolean expression that conditions the execution of the transition. This Boolean expression can use block attributes.
- *action* $\in$ {*variable affectation, send signal, receive signal*} represents the action attached to the transition. The action can be executed only once the transition has been enabled, *i.e.*, when the *after* clause has elapsed and the *condition* equals *true*. *send signal, receive signal* can use its signals, or the signals of the parent block B_p, or the signals of the parent block of B_p, and so on.
- s_{end} is the final state of the transition.

2.3   Formal Verification with TTool

A SysML model is made up of one or several diagrams expressed in a graphic fashion for SysML V1 [30] or by a combination of graphics and text for SysML V2 [30]. Whatever the version of SysML, a SysML tool must offer a diagram editor. The open source Papyrus tool [32] offers a complete editor that strictly follows the SysML standard [30]. Other SysML tools commonly support variants of the OMG-based SysML syntax, and offer extensions to supports various classes of systems. Examples of tools applied to real-time systems include Cameo Systems Modeler [29], Rhapsody [34], If-Omega [13], and TTool [43].

SysML diagrams editors usually save SysML diagrams in a form that becomes processable by external tools or in-built modules in charges of checking the SysML diagrams, especially the block and state machine diagrams, against design errors. Simulation enables early debugging of SysML diagrams by randomly firing transitions. Model checking goes one step further with a more systematic and mathematically grounded analysis of the SysML models.

TTool [6,43] is a free and open source framework for the design and verification of embedded systems. The TTool model checker [11] inputs SysML models enriched with safety properties to be verified and outputs a yes-no answer for each property. In practice, the TTool model checker takes as input (1) a block instance diagram and the state machine diagrams modeling the inner workings of the blocks, and (2) properties formally expressed using a CTL-based language. TTool's model checker computes properties expressed inside the SysML model and returns the feedback in the same SysML model. Users of TTool are therefore not obliged to use external tools or to inspect the inner workings of the model checker.

The benefits and potential of using TTool for model-checking SysML models have been discussed in [6,36]. The remainder of the current paper explains how the model checker of TTool has recently been extended with the purpose to reduce the amount of time allocated to model checking of SysML models.

3   Dependency Graphs

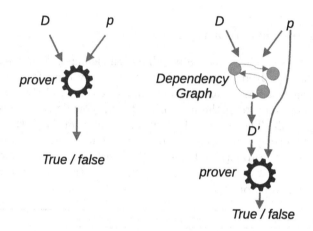

Fig. 1. Proofs without/with dependency graphs [5].

This section shows how dependency graphs can be used in the scope of the verification problem addressed by the paper. A classical verification process takes as input a design, a property, and outputs false or true, as illustrated by the left part of Fig. 1. Basically, a design is made up of a (1) a SysML block instance diagram and its associated state machines, and (2) a set of properties. Using a dependency graphs is expected to decrease the complexity of the proof with regards to the proof without using dependency graphs. This section first gives a definition related to systems' verification. Then, dependency graphs are introduced along with algorithms, and illustrated on a toy system.

3.1   Definition of a System

Definition 1. *A **System** has a Design and a set of Properties to be verified, as defined in [11] .*

$$S = \langle D, P \rangle \tag{1}$$

3.2   Proving a Property over a System

Definition 2. *Let us define* **prover** *as a function that takes a Design D and a Property p as input. The prover function returns true if p is satisfied by D (also denoted as $D \models p$), false otherwise.*

$$prover(D, p \in P) = \begin{cases} true & \text{if p is satisfied by D} \\ false & \text{Otherwise} \end{cases} \qquad (2)$$

The objective of this work is to decrease the complexity of the $prover()$ function (2).

3.3   Decreasing the Proof Complexity

To prove a property, a prover considers all design elements, even if some of these elements are not involved in this proof, as depicted by the left part of Fig. 1.

The right part of Fig. 1 illustrates the main idea behind the paper's contribution: to eliminate parts of the models that may slow down the proof without impacting its result. The proposed solution, detailed in Algorithm 1, is (i) to compute a dependency graph DG from the input model D, (ii) to reduce DG to DG_p according to property p to be proven, (iii) to rebuild a model D_p from DG_p and finally (iv) to use DG_p and p as input for the $prover$ to figure out if $D_p \models p$, and by deduction if $d \models p$.

Algorithm 1. Use of dependency graphs to simplify proofs.

    Data: D, P
    Result: $\forall p \in P, result_p = prover(D, p)$
1   $DG = computeGraph(D)$
2   **foreach** $p \in P$ **do**
3 | $DG_p = reduceGraph(DG, p)$
4 | $D_p = graphToModel(DG_p)$
5 | $result_p = prover(D_p, p)$
6 **end**

The section now formalizes the different stages of Algorithm 1.

3.4   From a Design to a Dependency Graph

We now assume that a design $d \in D$ is a block instance diagram B. A dependency graph DG can be computed from $D = B$ (Algorithm 2):

$$DG = computeGraph(D)$$

For each smd of $B \in Bl$, for each element of the state machine (states, transitions, send/receive actions), we generate one vertex v_e in DG (line 4).

Then, the algorithm looks for all couples of *read* and *write* operators connected through the same channel (line 7, $cond_1$). If the channel is synchronous, the two operators must belong to different blocks. For all such couples, a new vertex is added for each element (line 9, v_1 and v_2, and an edge is created in line 10 between the vertex of the writer (v_1) to the vertex of the reader (v_2). Then, the new vertices v_1 and v_2 are connected to the rest of the graph as follows. (i) Edges from the element vertex (*e.g.*, $vertex(elt_1)$ and $vertex(elt_2)$ created at

---

Algorithm 2. Building a dependency graph from a model.

Data: D

Result: DG

1   $DG = emptyGraph$

2   **foreach** smd of Bl of D **do**

3   **foreach** $elt \in smd$ **do**

4 | $DG \uplus vertex(elt)$

5   **end**

6   **foreach** $elt_1, elt_2 \in smd^2$ **do**

7       $c = connect(\ block(elt_1),\ signal(elt_1), block(elt_2),\ signal(elt_2))$
        $cond_1 = isSending(elt_1) \wedge isReceiving(elt_2) \wedge c! = "No" \wedge c ==$
        synchronous $\implies block(elt_1)! = block(elt_2)$

8   **if** $cond_1$ **then**

9         $DG \uplus v_1 = vertex(elt_1\_to\_elt_2)$

10        $\uplus v_2 = vertex(elt_2\_to\_elt_1)$

11        $\uplus edge(v_1, v_2)$

12        $\uplus edge(vertex(elt_1), v_1)$

13        $\uplus edge(v_1, vertex(next(elt_1)))$

14        $\uplus edge(vertex(elt_2), v_2)$

15        $\uplus edge(v_2, vertex(next(elt_2)))$

16        $cond_2 = isSending(elt_1) \wedge isReceiving(elt_2) \wedge$
         $connect(block(elt_1), signal(elt_1),$
         $block(elt_2), signal(elt_2)) == "synchronous"$

17        $cond_2 \implies DG \uplus edge(v_2, v_1)$

18   **else**

19 | $link(elt_1, elt_2) \implies DG \uplus edge(vertex(elt_1), vertex(elt_2))$

20   **end**

21   **end**

22   // Optimization: removing empty transitions

23   **foreach** $elt \in smd$ **do**

24   **if** $elt == "empty\ transition"$ **then**

25        $DG = DG\ vertex(elt)$

26   **foreach** $l = link(elt_1, elt)$ **do**

27         $DG = DG\ edge(l)$

28         $DG \uplus edge(vertex(elt_1), vertex(next(elt)))$

29   **end**

30   **end**

31 **end**

---

line 4) are respectively connected to v_1 and v_2. (ii) Edges are created from v_1 / v_2 vertices are respectively connected to the vertex of the next element of elt_1 and elt_2 (lines 12 to 15). Last, if the communication between the two operators is synchronous ($cond_2$, line 16) then an edge is also added from the reader to the writer: indeed, the latter must wait for the former to be ready to perform the (synchronous) write operation. If the two selected elements do not correspond to a pair (writer, reader), then an edge is simply added between their respective vertices according to the links specified in their state machines (line 19).

Further, if a transition is empty, then its corresponding vertex can be seen as a simple logical dependency: so it can be captured with an edge. This optimization is taken into account at the end of the algorithm by the optimisation stage: the algorithm removes useless vertices, and updates edges accordingly.

Finally, the dependency graph is built upon control flow dependencies (transitions of the state machines) and communication dependencies (asynchronous, synchronous).

Let us use a toy example to illustrate the construction of a dependency graph with a simple sensor monitoring system. Two sensors provide data to a remote filtering system. The role of the filtering is to decide to store data in a data center, or to drop them.

Blocks *Sensors* and *DataCenter* are synchronously connected by their respective ports to convey signals *value* and *stored* (Fig. 2). The two sub-blocks *Sensor1* and *Sensor2* can use both signals. *Filter* and *Center1* blocks are connected with a *query* signal via an asynchronous port connection. The state machines are given in Fig. 3. *Sensor1* and *Sensor2* have the same state machine diagram. Note that in these state machines, actions for sending or receiving messages are depicted with a dedicated graphical operator. Nonetheless, sending or receiving a message is considered as an action of a transition between two states.

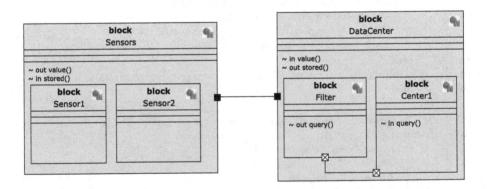

Fig. 2. Internal block diagram of the sensor system.

The resulting dependency graph of this toy system (Fig. 4) was built using TTool. The graph shows start states of blocks in green, stop states in red, other states in grey, and communication actions in blue. All double arrows between communication states depict possible synchronous communications between a sender and a receiver using the same signal, *e.g.*, between states 37 and 38. On the contrary, an asynchronous communication has a unique dependency arrow from the writer to the reader, *e.g.*, between states 29 and 30. The *Filter* block can synchronize on signals "value" and "stored" either with Sensor1, or with Sensor2: the graph depicts these two logical dependencies. Last but not least, *Filter* can stop in two different situations: either after getting a value and dropping it, or after storing the data in the center and informing sensors about the fact that the data has been stored. This explains why *Filter* has two different stop states.

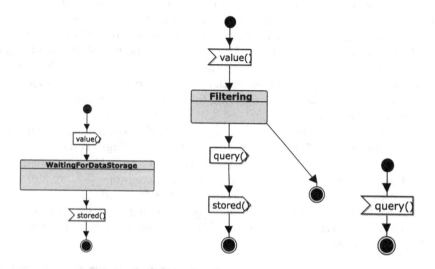

Fig. 3. State machine diagrams: sensors (left), Filter (middle) and Center1 (right).

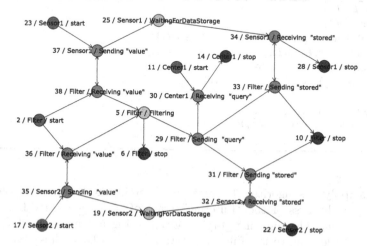

Fig. 4. Dependency graph of the toy system. (Color figure online)

3.5   Reducing a Graph with Regards to a Property

As explained before, reducing the graph w.r.t. to a property decreases the proof complexity. Yet, if a property refers to the whole graph then there is no reduction. Parts of the graph that are not related to the property can instead be pruned: this is the objective of graph reduction.

Graph reduction consists in marking the vertices related to the selected CTL property p, and then removing all vertices that are not marked, *i.e.*, that are not on a path between start vertices and property vertices. CTL properties explicitly refer to a list of elements in D. In TTool, CTL properties can either relate to a state of a block, (*e.g.*, $E <> Block_1.state_1$ means the reachability of $state_1$ in $Block_1$) or can refer to attributes of blocks, (*e.g.*, $A[]Controller.pressure > 0\&\&Controller.pressure < Controller.threshold$ expresses that in all the system states, the *pressure* attribute of block *Controller* must be between 0 and *threshold*). Another CTL property, called *leads-to* and denoted as "$expr_1 -> expr_2$" expresses that the if $expr_1$ is reached then $expr_2$ will eventually be reached. Currently, the reduction works for $A <> expr$ and $E <> expr$ properties with $expr$ referring to an sending/receiving action or the the state of a state machine.

Algorithm 3 first computes V_p, the list of vertices corresponding to the elements referenced by a CTL property p (*e.g.*, states, sending/receiving actions). Then, each vertex v of DG is added to the reduced graph DG_p if there exists a path from v to at least one vertex in V_p. For liveness properties, we also have to add all the vertices that are connected by one edge to all the vertices v on the path V_p, in order to take into account the beginning of paths not leading to v_p. Finally, if two vertices of DG are in DG_p, then all edges between these two vertices are also added to DG_p.

Algorithm 3. Reduction of dependency Graphs: reduceGraph().

Data: D, DG, p
Result: DG_p
1 $next(v)$ denotes $\{v_1 \in DG/edge(v, v1) \in DG\}$
2 $V_p = listOfVertices(D, p)$
3 **foreach** *vertex* $v \in DG$ **do**
4 | $path(v, V_p) \rightarrow DG_p \uplus v \uplus next(v)$
5 **end**
6 **foreach** *vertex* $v1, v2 \in DG^2$ **do**
7 | $e = edge(v1, v2) \neq \emptyset \rightarrow DG_p \uplus e$
8 **end**

Let us apply this algorithm to the graph given in Fig. 4 and to the following property: the liveness of the "Filtering" state of *Filter*, *i.e.*, in CTL: $A <> Filter.Filtering$. The resulting graph is given in Fig. 5. The graph shows that only the path leading to the Filtering state have been kept, thus cleaning the initial model from useless elements, *e.g.*, the *Center1* block, the behaviour of sensors after sending "value", and the behavior of *Filter* once the Filtering state has been reached.

3.6   Back to a (SysML) Model from a Dependency Graph

Since a dependency graph references all the model elements, it is possible to reconstruct the initial model from a dependency graph. As our prover takes as input a model (and a property), once the dependency graph has been reduced according to a given property, we can rebuild a new model from the reduced graph. The new model is reduced with regards to the original one, which means it contains fewer, or the same number of elements as the original model does.

Let us come back to our toy system. As said in the previous subsection, the reduced dependency graph shows that both the structure (blocks and their connections) and the behaviour (state machines) have been impacted. As shown in Fig. 6, the Center1 block has been removed, and the declaration and connection of signals "stored" and "query" has also been removed.

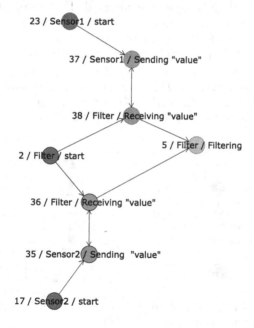

Fig. 5. Dependency graph of the toy system after reduction.

Similarly, the states machines have less states and sending/receiving actions, as shown in Fig. 7. Moreover, the state machine of *Center1* has been removed since its behaviour is now empty.

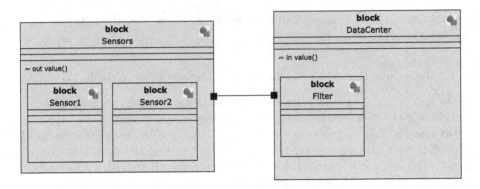

Fig. 6. Internal block diagram of the sensor system after reduction.

3.7 Dependency Graphs for Model Updates

Figure 8 depicts another usage of dependency graphs. The goal is to avoid reproving properties after a SysML model was updated. Those properties impacted by the model update are the only ones that need to be proven again. For this, as shown on the left part of Fig. 8, a property p is first proved on a design D using a dependency graph DG. Then, D is updated as D'. To know whether p must be proved again on D', the dependency graph DG' is generated and then compared with DG. If DG is equivalent to DG' according to a bisimulation relation, then the proof of p made on D is still valid for D'. Otherwise, p must be proved for D'. This approach is summarized by algorithm 4 (which is implemented by TTool).

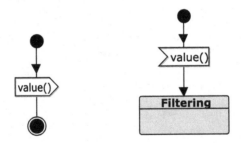

Fig. 7. State machine diagrams built from the reduced dependency graph. From left to right: Sensor1 (and Sensor2) and Filter. Center1 has been remove because its behaviour is now empty.

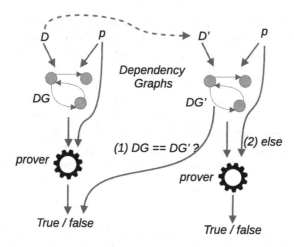

Fig. 8. Decreasing proof complexity using dependency graphs [5].

4   Case Study

The purpose of this section is to evaluate the gain when using model-checking with dependency graphs with regards to model-checking without dependency graphs. Here, model-checking relates to the internal model-checker of TTool.

The selected case study is an industrial Ethernet-based Time-Sensitive Networking (TSN) [21] that serves as communication mean for distributed safety-critical applications.

Algorithm 4. Use of dependency graphs to simplify proofs.

   Data: D, D', P
   Result: DG
1 $DG' = computeGraph$
2 **foreach** $p \in P$ **do**
3      $DG = computeGraph(D, p)$
4      $DG' = computeGraph(D', p)$
5   **if** $DG \equiv DG'$ **then**
6 | $result_{p'} = result_p$
7   **else**
8 | $result_{p'} = prover(DG', p)$
9   **end**
10 **end**

4.1   Time-Sensitive Networking

Time-Sensitive Networking (TSN) [21] is a set of standards defined by IEEE 802.1 Working Group to provide deterministic services through IEEE 802

Ethernet networks, *i.e.*, guaranteed packet transport with bounded low latency, low packet delay variation, and low packet loss. Deterministic real-time communication is a crucial requirement in modern embedded systems and cyber-physical systems, *e.g.*, safety-critical industrial, automotive and avionics networks.

The topology of such networks consists of a set of end systems and communication switches. Each end system has a network interface interconnected with communication switches via full-duplex physical links. A TSN network architecture is depicted in Fig. 9. The network supports unicast and multicast communications between a set of applications distributed over a number of end systems.

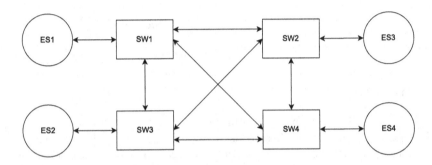

Fig. 9. A TSN network architecture.

Reliability and Fault Tolerance. To achieve determinism, TSN enables transmission of Time-Triggered (TT) flows with bounded end-to-end delay guarantees. TT flows share the network with less critical non-TT flows. Since TT flows carry safety-critical traffic, if a TT flow cannot be delivered correctly (*e.g.*, because of a fault) and in a timely manner, disastrous consequences may occur in safety-critical systems.

The reliability of TT flows may be compromised by two types of faults: *permanent faults* and *transient faults*. Permanent faults may cause link or switch failure and disturb the transmission service, while *transient faults* include packet losses or bit-flips caused by electromagnetic interference, and may compromise the transmission of a message without affecting successive messages. For fault tolerance, TSN enhances redundancy with Frame Replication and Elimination for Reliability (FRER) (IEEE 802.1CB) [20]. According to FRER, multiple routes that do not share any common switches, are allocated for each TT flow. Frames are replicated at the source and transmitted through separate paths to the destination as depicted in Fig. 10. Duplicates are eliminated at destinations.

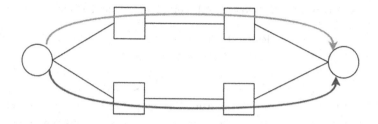

Fig. 10. Frame Replication and Elimination for Reliability (FRER).

In the past few years, several research work on Time-Sensitive networking has been using model-based approaches to formally verify properties of the network. In [16,27], the UPPAAL model checker is used for timing analysis of TSN, while in [14,35], network models described in MARTE, respectively EMF are proposed to serve for automatic generation of TSN network configurations. As for the FRER mechanisms on which we focus in this paper, most of the existing research work focus on time scheduling and routing in case of faults and propose optimal or heuristic-based algorithms to compute flows schedules in case recovery is needed, such as presented in [24,45]. In this paper, we do not focus on aspects related to the timing requirements of flows. Instead, we focus on the behavior of the network when dealing with a failure. We will address the timing analysis of flows in a future work.

4.2 TSN FRER Model in SysML

Our aim is to model the FRER mechanism for TSN with SysML and TTool, and then to verify properties on the SysML model. This model is intended to be used as a decision helper for dimensioning TSN networks for safety-critical applications.

Our model considers a communication scenario with two emitting end systems and a receiving end system. End systems are interconnected by three switches and six communication links. Emitting end systems inject data flows into the network on different priority levels as described in Table 1. In our model, we consider flows with only 3 levels of priority (0 - high, 2 - low) of the 8 priority levels available in TSN. High priority level is intended for the transmission of safe-critical flows that also require fault tolerance. So, in our example, the FRER replication/elimination mechanism is applied for flows F10 and F20 of priority 0 for which two different paths are established in the network.

Table 1. TSN flows profile considered in the model.

Emitting ES	Flow	Priority	Period	Path	FRER
ES1	F10	0	20	EmittingES1 − > Switch1 − > ReceivingES	Yes
				EmittingES1 − > Switch2 − > ReceivingES	
	F11	1	5	EmittingES1 − > Switch1 − > ReceivingES	No
	F12	2	5	EmittingES1 − > Switch2 − > ReceivingES	No
ES2	F20	0	20	EmittingES2 − > Switch3 − > ReceivingES	Yes
				EmittingES2 − > Switch2 − > ReceivingES	
	F21	1	5	EmittingES2 − > Switch3 − > ReceivingES	No
	F22	2	5	EmittingES2 − > Switch2 − > ReceivingES	No

Figure 11 depicts the SysML internal block diagram of the case study presented in this section. The model is made up of (1) blocks that describe the end systems, (2) switches, and (3) communication links of the network. Each emitting end system is modelled by a set of blocks representing the emission of flows, the classification of flows by priority, the replication of flows in case of safety-critical traffic, and the scheduling mechanisms for the selection of messages on the output ports. The switch model focuses on mechanisms for switching, for priority filtering and for selecting messages based on the Time Aware Scheduling scheduling policy of TSN. The receiving end system is defined by two blocks: one block corresponds to the elimination of duplicate messages in case of redundant transmission and the second block models the reconstruction of flows from the received sequence of messages. Examples of state machines of blocks *FrameReplication* and *FrameElimination* related to the FRER mechanism are given in Fig. 12, respectively Fig. 13[1].

4.3   Property Verification with (and Without) Dependency Graph

Let us now apply the approach of Fig. 1 and Algorithm 1 to a set of properties (Sect. 4.3) we ought to prove on our model. We then compare the proof time with and without dependency graphs and discuss the results.

Evaluated Properties. We have studied the reachability and liveness of states corresponding to frame generation and sending, frame routing and frame receiving:

1. State *Sending1* in the *FrameGeneration*
2. State *Queue0* in *PrioritySelection2*
3. State *Filter2* in block *PriorityFiltering1*
4. State *SendingMessages* in block *FrameReplication_0*
5. State *HandlingMessage1* in block *SwitchFabric1*
6. State *TestingSequence* in block *FrameElimination*
7. State *MessageToFIFO11* in block *PriorityFilteringEndSystem*

---

[1] The complete model can be retrieved under TTool− >Examples− >TSN.

8. State *ForwardMessage* in block *CommunicationLink22_0*

These states were selected in order to cover the different networking mechanisms (frame generation, frame replication and elimination, priority filtering and selection, message switching).

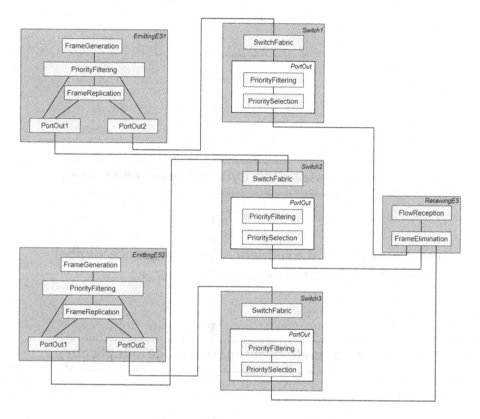

Fig. 11. TSN model with FRER.

Results. Table 2 compares results for reachability and liveness analysis. The results do not take into account the time to generate the dependency graph, which is around 10 ms: this generation is made once for all the verification process, thus this time is negligible. But obviously, the time to reduce the dependency graph is taken into account.

The left part of the table concerns the verification time without using a dependency graph, while the right part relies on the dependency graph, and its reduction to the property of interest, for performing the verification. In this table, the verification addresses two kinds of CTL properties, related to states listed at the beginning of this subsection:

- $E <> Block.state$: the reachability of a state, *i.e.* there exists at least one execution path that goes through this state, *i.e.* all execution paths have go through this state at some point.

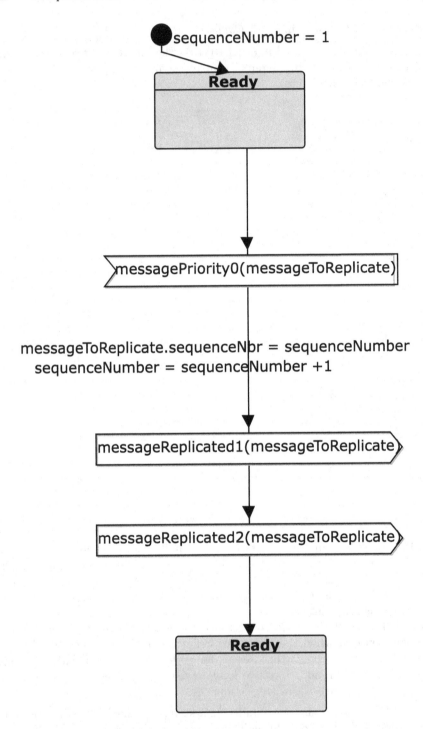

Fig. 12. Example of state machine diagram: block FrameReplication.

For the case with dependency graph, we provide the time to reduce the dependency graph, which is not negligible for some properties, and we compute the gain, that is:

$$gain = (totalNoDG - totalWithDG)/totalNoDG.$$

Verification times were obtained on a macbook pro running "Big Sur" with 2.3 GHz 8-Core Intel Core i9 and 32 GB of RAM. The oracle JRE 11 was used to execute TTool build 14145 date: 2022/06/30 03:22:06 CET. To avoid Just-In-time compilation delays and load of the machine, each verification was run 10 times and the lowest value was used.

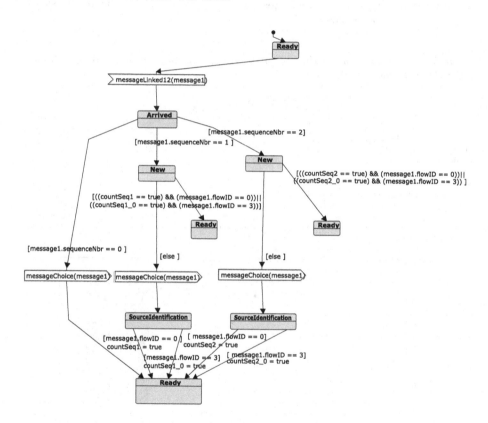

Fig. 13. Example of state machine diagram: block FrameElimination.

Results demonstrate a systematic gain, which is more obvious for liveness that for reachability. The gain is far better when the verification process is long: this is exactly what we expect since very short verification (*i.e.*, a few ms) do not need to be accelerated while a gain of 80% is obtained for long verification (a few seconds), as depicted in Fig. 14. Thus, for proving one simple property like reachability, it is not worth using dependency graphs. On the contrary, when verification takes more time, like for liveness properties, using dependency graphs always brings a gain.

As a whole, the full verification process takes more than 21 s without the dependency graph, and around 4 s with the dependency graph, including the time to generate the dependency graph and to reduce it to different graphs.

Extension to More Complex Properties. In this case study, some properties cannot be expressed as simple reachability or liveness properties. Two properties we ought to verify are:

- Property 1: **arrival of messages**. At least one of the duplicate messages must arrive at destination.

Table 2. Execution duration (in ms) of the reachability and liveness proof with and without dependency graph.

Block/State	Proof duration (ms)							Gain
	No DG			With DG				
	Reachability	Liveness	Total	Reachability	Liveness	Graph reduction	Total	
FrameGeneration/Sending1	7	284	291	6	187	40	233	18%
PrioritySelection2/Queue0	13	16035	16048	11	1939	30	1980	88%
PriorityFiltering1/Filter2	9	343	352	7	249	40	286	18%
FrameReplication_0/SendingMessages	7	566	573	7	359	33	135	30%
SwitchFabric1/HandlingMessage1	11	81	92	7	57	25	89	3%
FrameElmination/TestingSequence	11	984	995	9	718	20	747	24%
PriorityFilteringEndSystem/MessageToFIFO11	8	2768	2776	5	206	34	245	91%
CommunicationLink22_0/ForwardMessage	8	191	199	7	112	23	142	28%
Total	74	21252	21325	59	3827	255	4141	81%

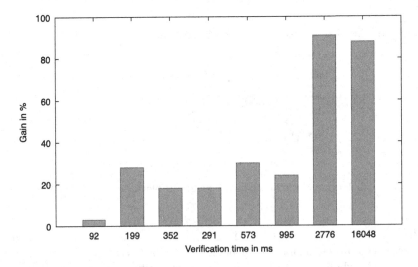

Fig. 14. Gain in function of the verification time. The higher the gain is, the more the use of dependency graphs saves verification time.

- Property 2: **order of messages**. Messages that take separate paths may arrive earlier on a path than another message that was sent after, thus leading to out of order situations. Depending on the service policy, the out of order can have an impact on the worst case delay analysis as shown in [41].

In TTool, CTL properties can be captured with so-called "safety pragmas". Figure 15 illustrates the CTL properties related to the two properties listed above: the three first pragmas correspond to the first property, while the last one captures the last property with a "leads-to".

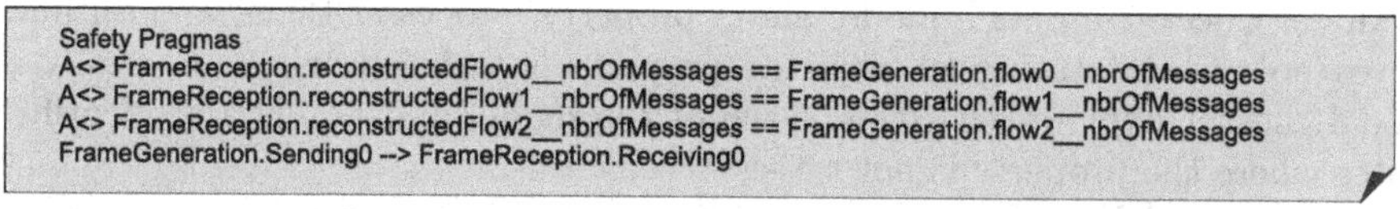

```
Safety Pragmas
A<> FrameReception.reconstructedFlow0__nbrOfMessages == FrameGeneration.flow0__nbrOfMessages
A<> FrameReception.reconstructedFlow1__nbrOfMessages == FrameGeneration.flow1__nbrOfMessages
A<> FrameReception.reconstructedFlow2__nbrOfMessages == FrameGeneration.flow2__nbrOfMessages
FrameGeneration.Sending0 --> FrameReception.Receiving0
```

Fig. 15. More advanced properties captured with safety pragmas.

Currently, the graph reduction algorithm (Algorithm 3) cannot handle these properties:

- Property 1 uses block attributes. To handle this property, our algorithm would need to identify all the vertices of the dependability graph susceptible to modify the value of all the attributes related in the property.
- Property 2 uses a lead-to, currently not supported. Handling a leads-to property, $e.g.$, $expr1 - - > expr2$, would mean to identify not only the paths starting from the initial state, but also all paths from all elements of $expr1$ to all elements of $expr2$.

5 Related Work

Formal verification of models and programs has been the subject of many papers and books. Since the current paper relies on dependency inside SysML models to optimize verification of these models, this state of the art section specifically surveys papers that include discussions and proposals for optimizing model verification.

We may first distinguish between two formal verification approaches: static analysis [3,7] and state space enumeration [4,36]. The former relies on the structure of the model and avoids explicit enumeration of the states the systems may reach from its initial state. The latter explicitly characterizes the states the system may reach from its initial state. A direct consequence is that state space enumeration faces the well-known explosion problem, which in practice means the graph of reachable states may turn impossible to compute.

Many solutions have been investigated to lower the state explosion risk by partly exploring the state space of the system without loss of property verification capacity. For instance, in [9], Bourdil $et~al.$ explore symmetries in systems modeled by Time Petri Nets and implement their proposal in the TINA tool [42]. The current paper explores another avenue in the context of SysML, by looking for dependencies inside the block and state machine diagrams defined by SysML models.

Besides the way the model's state space is traversed to compute a reachability graph, efficiently storing the states of the graph is also an issue. Work in this area has been pioneered by Holzman and implemented into SPIN [17]. Such type of optimized state storage is not yet implemented by the TTool tool considered in the current paper.

SPIN falls in the family of verification tools that we term as 'model checkers'. A Model Checker inputs a model and a property, processes them, and outputs a 'yes/no' answer stating whether the property is satisfied or not. Basically, a model checker explores the state space of the model and potentially identifies states where the property is not satisfied.

Using a model checker first requires to express the properties to be verified. It is a common practice to express the properties in the form of logic formulas expressed, *e.g.*, using Temporal Logic. Property expression is not an easy task and automatic generation of the properties to be verified is an issue [15].

As far as the model checker has been catered with a set of properties and a model, the model checking process may start, raising the following question: understanding the reasons why one or several properties are not satisfied. Identifying counter examples is an issue [22].

More generally, tracing verification results back to the initial model is a complex issue, and regularly the subject of questions asked for to researchers who present their model checkers in papers or talks. As far as the models are expressed in SysML, difficulties in tracing verification results back to the SysML model stems from the fact that SysML tools use external model checkers [26,34] that had been developed for formal methods such as Petri nets. Translation from UML/SysML to state/transition models has been formalized in the context of Petri nets [12,19,33,40], automata for NuSMV model checker [44], timed automata [37] for UPPAAL model checker, hybrid automata [1], model checker NuSMV [28], model checker nuXmv [39], probabilistic model checker PRISM [1,31], and a theorem prover [23]. Translation from UML to process algebra has been investigated for RT-LOTOS [4] and CSP [2]. The family of correct by construction specification has been addressed with B [25]. Other contributions such as [46], target a better understanding of verification results output, especially when the property of interest is not satisfied.

Conversely the TTool tool considered in the current paper includes a native model checker and returns yes/no answers inside the SysML model, for properties that are themselves expressed inside the block diagram of the SysML model. In terms of performances, the native model checker of TTool favorably compares to the performance of the first version of TTool where the latter was interfaced with UPPAAL [11].

To be more precise with respect to TTool, let us add that TTool applies model checking to the block and state diagrams of SysML. This is a common point with other research work published, *e.g.*, practice [4,12,37]. Nevertheless, some authors apply formal verification to SysML activity diagrams [19,31,39].

6   Conclusions

The expected benefits of using an MBSE approach includes early detection of design errors in the life cycle of systems. One or several models are checked against their expected properties using a model checker that takes the models and the properties as inputs, and answers stating whether each property holds or not.

Such a model checking approach has been implemented for SysML. The TTool software implements a user-friendly approach where the properties to be verified are expressed inside the SysML model and their evaluation is reported at the same place in the SysML model. Thus, users of TTool work at the SysML level with no need to learn about the inner workings of the model checker.

The model-checker of TTool, its performance, and its increased user-friendliness had already been discussed in [11,36]. The current paper proposes a new optimization for the model checking of SysML models. The goal is to avoid a prover to handle a large model when only a subset of it is necessary to evaluate a property. The proposed idea relies on dependencies internal to blocks (control flows) or between blocks (communications).

An early paper [5] by the authors of the current paper used an AFDX (Avionics Full DupleX [18]) network to demonstrate the benefits of relying formal verification of SysML models on dependency graph generation. The current paper optimizes the dependency graph generation algorithm and illustrates the proposed approach using a new generation of real-time network: TSN (Time-Sensitive Networking).

Future work includes the definition of a bisimulation relation to compare dependency graphs. Handling more CTL properties, like leads-to, is also part of our future work. We also intend to use new case studies to demonstrate the efficiency of our approach at larger scale. Last, we intend to support the new syntax (including the textual syntax) and semantics of SysML V2.

Acknowledgement. François Genauzeau has contributed to the SysML diagrams presented in this paper.

References

1. Ali, S.: Formal verification of SysML diagram using case studies of real-time system. Innovations Syst. Softw. Eng. **14**(6), 245–262 (2018). https://doi.org/10.1007/s11334-018-0318-5
2. Ando, T., Yatsu, H., Kong, W., Hisazumi, K., Fukuda, A.: Formalization and model checking of SysML state machine diagrams by csp#. In: Computational Science and Its Applications (ICCSA), pp. 114–127 (2013). https://doi.org/10.1007/978-3-642-39646-5_9

3. Apvrille, L., de Saqui-Sannes, P.: Analysis Techniques to Verify Mutual Exclusion Situations within SysML Models. In: SDL 2013: Model-Driven Dependability Engineering. SDL 2013. Lecture Notes in Computer Science, vol 7916. Springer, Berlin, Heidelberg (2013). https://doi.org/10.1007/978-3-642-38911-5_6

4. Apvrille, L., Courtiat, J.P., Lohr, C., de Saqui-Sannes, P.: TURTLE: a real-time UML profile supported by a formal validation toolkit. IEEE Trans. Software Eng. **30**(7), 473–487 (2004)

5. Apvrille, L., de Saqui-Sannes, P., Hotescu, O., Calvino, A.T.: SysML Models Verification Relying on Dependency Graphs. In: 10th International Conference on Model-Driven Engineering and Software Development. Vienna, Austria (2022). https://doi.org/10.5220/0010792900003119, https://telecom-paris.hal.science/hal-03575960

6. Apvrille, L., de Saqui-Sannes, P., Vingerhoeds, R.A.: An educational case study of using SysML and ttool for unmanned aerial vehicles design. IEEE J. Miniaturization Air Space Syst. **1**(2), 117–129 (2020)

7. Ayache, J.M., Courtiat, J.P., Diaz, M.: Rebus, a fault-tolerant distributed system for industrial real-time control. IEEE Trans. Comput. C-**31**(7), 637–647 (July 1982). https://doi.org/10.1109/TC.1982.1676061

8. Baduel, R., Chami, M., Bruel, J.-M., Ober, I.: Validation in an industrial context: Challenges and experimentation. In: European Conference on Modelling Foundations and Applications, Toulouse, France (June 2021)

9. Bourdil, P., Berthomieu, B., Dal Zilio, S., Vernadat, F.: Symmetry reduced state classes for time Petri nets. In: 30th Annual ACM Symposium on Applied Computing), pp. 1751–1758. ACM (2015)

10. Brisacier-Porchon, L., Hammami, O., Boutemy, R.: Modeling a uav in practice: A comparison between rhapsody and capella. In: IEEE International Symposium on Systems Engineering (ISSE), pp. 1–8 (2021). https://doi.org/10.1109/ISSE51541.2021.9582553

11. Calvino, A.T., Apvrille, L.: Direct model-checking of SysML models. In: Proceedings of the 9th International Conference on Model-Driven Engineering and Software Development (Modelsward'2021), Vienna, Autrichia (online) (2021)

12. Delatour, J., Paludetto, M.: UML/PNO: A way to merge UML and Petri net objects for the analysis of real-time systems. In: Oriented Technology: ECOOP'98 Workshop Reader. pp. 511–514 (1998). https://doi.org/10.1007/3-540-49255-0_169

13. Dragomir, I., Ober, I., Percebois, C.: Contract-based modeling and verification of timed safety requirements within sysml. Softw. Syst. Model. **16**(2), 587–624 (2017). https://doi.org/10.1007/s10270-015-0481-1

14. Farzaneh, M.H., Kugele, S., Knoll, A.: A graphical modeling tool supporting automated schedule synthesis for time-sensitive networking. In: 2017 22nd IEEE International Conference on Emerging Technologies and Factory Automation (ETFA), pp. 1–8. IEEE (2017)

15. Gao, H., Dai, B., Miao, H., Yang, X., Duran Barroso, R.J., Walayat, H.: A novel gapg approach to automatic property generation for formal verification: The gan perspective. ACM Transactions on Multimedia Computing, Communications, and Applications (February 2022). https://doi.org/10.1145/3517154

16. Guo, W., Huang, Y., Shi, J., Hou, Z., Yang, Y.: A formal method for evaluating the performance of tsn traffic shapers using uppaal. In: 2021 IEEE 46th Conference on Local Computer Networks (LCN), pp. 241–248. IEEE (2021)

17. Holzmann, G.J.: The SPIN Model Checker: Primer and Reference Manual. Addison-Wesley (2004)

18. Hotescu, O., Jaffrès-Runser, K., Scharbarg, J.L., Fraboul, C.: Multiplexing avionics and additional flows on a qos-aware AFDX network. In: 2019 24th IEEE International Conference on Emerging Technologies and Factory Automation (ETFA), pp. 282–289. IEEE (2019)
19. Huang, E., McGinnis, L., Mitchell, S.: Verifying sysml activity diagrams using formal transformation to Petri nets. Syst. Eng. **23**(1), 118–135 (2019)
20. IEEE: IEEE Standard for Local and metropolitan area networks-Frame Replication and Elimination for Reliability (2017)
21. IEEE: 802.1Q - IEEE Standard for Local and Metropolitan Area Networks-Bridges and Bridged Networks. www.standards.ieee.org/ standard/802 1Q–2018.html (2018)
22. Kaleeswaran, A., Nordmann, A., Vogel, T., Grunske, L.: A systematic literature review on counterexample explanation. Inform. Softw. Technol. **145** (2022). https://doi.org/10.1016/j.infsof.2021.106800
23. Kausch1, M., Pfeiffer1, Raco1, D., Rumpe, B.: Model-based design of correct safety-critical systems using dataflow languages on the example of SysML architecture and behavior diagrams. In: AVIOSE'2021, Software Engineering 2021 Satellite Events, Bonn, Germany (virtual), pp. 1–22. Lecture Notes in Informatics (LNI), Gesellschaft für Informatik (2021)
24. Kong, W., Nabi, M., Goossens, K.: Run-time recovery and failure analysis of time-triggered traffic in time sensitive networks. IEEE Access **9**, 91710–91722 (2021)
25. Laleau, R., Mammar, A.: An overview of a method and its support tool for generating B specifications from UML notations. In: ASE2000. Fifteenth IEEE International Conference on Automated Software Engineering, pp. 269–272 (2000). https://doi.org/10.1109/ASE.2000.873675
26. Leroux-Beaudout, R., Pantel, M., Ober, I., Bruel, J.M.: Model-based systems engineering for systems simulation. In: Symposium On Leveraging Applications of Formal Methods, Verification and Validation (ISoLA 2018), Limassol, Cyprus (2018)
27. Lv, J., Zhao, Y., Wu, X., Li, Y., Wang, Q.: Formal analysis of tsn scheduler for real-time communications. IEEE Trans. Reliab. **70**(3), 1286–1294 (2020)
28. Mahani, M., Rizzo, D., Paredis, C., Wang, Y.: Automatic formal verification of SysML state machine diagrams for vehicular control system. SAE Tech. Paper (2021). https://doi.org/10.4271/2021-01-0260
29. Modeler, C.S.: www.3ds.com/products-services/catia/products/no-magic/cameo-systems-modeler/ Retrieved May 16 2022 (2022)
30. OMG: OMG Systems Modeling Language. Object Management Group, www.omg.org/spec/SysML/1.5 (2017)
31. Ouchani, S., Ait Mohamed, O., Debbabi, M.: A formal verification framework for SysML activity diagrams. Expert Syst. Appl. **41**(6) (2014). https://doi.org/10.1016/j.eswa.2013.10.064
32. Papyrus: www.eclipse.org/papyrus/ Retrieved May 16 2022 (2022)
33. Rahim, M., Boukala-Loualalen, M., Hammad, A.: Hierarchical colored Petri nets for the verification of SysML designs - activity-based slicing approach. In: 4th Conference on Computing Systems and Appli. (CSA 2020). Lecture Notes in Networks and Systems, vol. 199, pp. 131–142. Algiers, Algeria (dec 2020), www.publiweb.femto-st.fr/tntnet/entries/17274/documents/author/data
34. Rhapsody: www.ibm.com/fr-fr/products/architect-for-systems-engineers Retrieved May 16 2022 (2022)

35. Samson, M., Vergnaud, T., Dujardin, É., Ciarletta, L., Song, Y.Q.: A model-based approach to automatic generation of tsn network simulations. In: 2022 IEEE 18th International Conference on Factory Communication Systems (WFCS), pp. 1–8. IEEE (2022)

36. de Saqui-Sannes, P., Apvrille, L., Vingerhoeds, R.A.: Checking SysML Models against Safety and Security Properties. Journal of Aerospace Information Systems pp. 1–13 (Nov 2021)

37. Schafer, T., Knapp, A., Merz, S.: Model checking UML state machines and collaborations. Electron. Notes Theor. Comput. Sci. **55**, 357–369 (2001). https://doi.org/10.1016/S1571-0661(04)00262-2

38. de Souza, F.G.R., de Melo Bezerra, J., Hirata, C.M., de Saqui-Sannes, P., Apvrille, L.: Combining stpa with sysml modeling. In: IEEE International Systems Conference (SysCon), pp. 1–8 (2020). https://doi.org/10.1109/SysCon47679.2020.9275867

39. Staskal, O., Simac, J., Swayne, L., Rozier, K.Y.: Translating sysml activity diagrams for nuxmv verification of an autonomous pancreas. In: SESS22), pp. 1–6 (2022)

40. Szmuc, W., Szmuc, T.: Towards embedded systems formal verification translation from SysML into Petri nets. In: 25th International Conference Mixed Design of Integrated Circuits and System (MIXDES), pp. 420–423 (2018). https://doi.org/10.23919/MIXDES.2018.843687

41. Thomas, L., Mifdaoui, A., Boudec, J.Y.L.: Worst-case delay bounds in time-sensitive networks with packet replication and elimination. arXiv preprint arXiv:2110.05808 (2021)

42. TINA: Time Petri net analyzer. www.projects.laas.fr/tina// Retrieved October 31 2020 (2020)

43. TTool: www.ttool.telecom-paris.fr/ Retrieved May 11 2022 (2022)

44. Wang, H., Zhong, D., Zhao, T., Ren, F.: Integrating model checking with sysml in complex system safety analysis. IEEE Access **7**, 16561–16571 (2019). https://doi.org/10.1109/ACCESS.2019.2892745

45. Zhou, Y., Samii, S., Eles, P., Peng, Z.: Reliability-aware scheduling and routing for messages in time-sensitive networking. ACM Trans. Embedded Comput. Syst. (TECS) **20**(5), 1–24 (2021)

46. Zoor, M., Apvrille, L., Pacalet, R.: Execution Trace Analysis for a Precise Understanding of Latency Violations. In: International Conference on Model Driven Engineering Languages and Systems (MODELS). Fukuoka (virtual), Japan (Oct 2021). https://telecom-paris.hal.science/hal-03349254

Decomposable and Executable Models for Verification of Real-Time Systems

Callum McColl[1] , Vladimir Estivill-Castro[2(✉)] , Morgan McColl[1] ,
and René Hexel[1]

[1] School of Information and Communication Technology, Griffith University, Brisbane,
Australia
[2] Departament de Tecnologies de la Informació i les Comunicacions,
Universitat Pompeu Fabra, 08018 Barcelona, Spain
`vladimir.estivill@upf.edu`

Abstract. Decomposition allows for managing complexity. We show that executable models of behaviour are significantly more decomposable when using a time-triggered semantics than an event-driven semantics. Therefore, we adopt logic-labelled finite machines LLFSMs and show that deterministic static schedules are derived to guarantee value-domain properties and time-domain properties. We illustrate that such a decomposition goes a long way in avoiding the combinatorial space explosion that occurs when attempting to formally verify executable behaviour models. We argue for parametrised machines to foster decomposability and analyse what aspects jeopardise taming the size of Kripke structures for formal verification. We provide three case studies to show that we can transform the models into small, timed Kripke structures and that components can be verified separately by the nuXmv model checker to achieve formal system verification.

Keywords: Systems engineering · Decomposition · Real-time Systems ·
Timing properties · Formal Verification

1 Introduction

Decomposition is a dominant technique in the systems engineering literature, as humans reason (within limited intuition) about complex systems (that are beyond human intuition) by using abstraction and decomposition [9, 13]. Despite this prominent role, decomposition is mostly fruitful if the converse concept of composition effectively contains complexity. If composition synergies result in too many subsystem interdependencies and interactions, system design gets derailed. Abstraction focuses on the essential information and is usually manifested by models. Thus, a model is a physical, mathematical, graphical, or otherwise logical representation of a system for understanding, communicating, explaining, or designing specific aspects of interest of that system [48]. Model-based systems engineering (MBSE) is a formalised methodology where models are at the centre of system design. MBSE is used to support the requirements, design, analysis, verification, and validation associated with the development of

Supported by organization x.

L. F. Pires et al. (Eds.): MODELSWARD 2021/2022, CCIS 1708, pp. 135–156, 2023.
https://doi.org/10.1007/978-3-031-38821-7_7

complex systems. Since modelling is also essential for tackling complexity, there has been a rapid uptake of digital-modelling environments, notations and standards, leading to a massive uptake of MBSE [26].

Real-time systems are a particularly challenging type of complex system. They are information processing systems with hardware and software components that interact with their environment, reacting to inputs within predictable and specific time constraints. Therefore, a real-time computer system must not only provide correct results (value domain), but must deliver these results within a given deadline (time domain). When the consequences of delayed responses are severe, the associated deadlines are called hard deadlines. If serious harm to assets or human beings can emerge, the system is safety-critical. We note that, although reactive systems constantly respond to stimuli from their environment, they are not real-time systems unless time constraints are imposed for the occurrence of a response.

A challenging aspect of system engineering, and in particular, software systems, is system verification. Validation is the process of checking whether the specification captures requirements, while verification confirms that the software meets specifications. Today, most real-time systems involve one or more digital controllers, and thus system verification ensures that the software will meet its deadlines. While testing is essential in software development, testing only establishes the existence of faults when a test fails. Formal verification (and in particular, model-checking), by contrast, can confirm the absence of faults. However, if models are verified, this could amount to validation, mainly if the models use a notation or language that must be humanly interpreted to construct an implementation. Executable and verifiable models directly result in the system's implementation, thus achieve this higher level of reliability.

We present executable models of behaviour as logic-labelled finite state machines (LLFSMs). These models of concurrent behaviour are encapsulated to minimise interactions and enable system design by decomposition while ensuring system correctness by composition. Our approach allows a high-level design that is formally verifiable and reduces semantic gaps by ensuring unambiguous semantics of model execution. We further show how our approach minimises the challenge of combinatorial explosion that often prevents model-checking. Most importantly, we show how we can verify properties in the time domain. This is achieved because we can perform a static, worst-case execution time analysis of the time-triggered and deterministic schedule of the LLFSMs. Our unambiguous semantics allows the direct faithful construction of Kripke structures suitable for an off-the-shelf model checker.

This paper is based on our earlier discussion [33] where we argued that executable models remove the risk that human translation introduces errors when system specifications are implemented. Model-checking verifies abstractions, but if a formal verification of a model does not correspond to its implementation, it is informative but potentially worthless. Section 2 provides further details on the distinction between modelling tools to conform a specification (and thus perform validation) and the gaps that appear when attempts are made to transform those abstract models into concrete, executable models. Section 3 discusses aspects of using event-driven models that result in severe challenges for verification of both specification and executable models. In particular, we show how event-driven systems create dependencies that prevent composition, as scheduling of jobs and timing system response become widely interdependent. Section 4 presents a series of measures by which LLFSMs offer controlled concurrency while avoiding overly large Kripke structures and thus, enabling model checkers. In this paper we incorporate new material (see Sect. 5), where we show that parameterised machines enable significant decomposition, emulating pure functions. We analyse what aspects jeopardise minimising the size of Kripke structures for formal verification.

The subsequent sections demonstrate our contributions with three small, but key case studies prevalent in the literature that are highly illustrative of formal verification in both the value and time domain. These are two more case studies than in the earlier paper [33]. These case studies also show that the analysis assists in and facilitates the design of a static, deterministic schedule. Section 9 provides final remarks.

2   The Gap Between Mathematical and Executable Models

Arguably the formalism to describe specifications of real-time systems and safety-critical systems is timed-automata [2,3]. Timed-automata are defined [10] mathematically. A logic-labelled finite-state machine (LLFSM) has a finite set S of states one of which, S_0, is designated as the initial state. In an LLFSM, each transition holds a Boolean expression g (named a guard)[1]. However, in a timed-automaton, there is a finite set X of clocks that count time (their value increases simultaneously and uniformly with the passing of time). The transitions of a timed-automaton are labelled by triples (g, a, r) where g is a guard, a are actions, and $r \subset X$ is the set of clocks that are reset when the transition fires.

Typically, an arrangement[2] of timed-automata specifies the behaviour of a system by indicating the current state of each timed-automaton.[3] A transition (g, a, r) fires as soon as its guard becomes true (since transitions can have expressions that involve comparing a clock, for example $x = 1$ is true at the exact point in time that the clock x reaches 1, and no later). All actions a execute instantaneously with zero delay, and all clocks in r are set to zero.

Timed-automata are perfectly adequate for specifying certain requirements. The abstract models of arrangements of timed-automata can be formally verified by a semantics that builds the region automaton. Systems that perform timed-automaton model-checking are well-known, most notably UPPAAL [31].

Time must be treated as a first-order quantity that can be reasoned upon to verify that a system will be able to meet its deadlines [47]. However, timed-automata make some particular assumptions that imply a semantic gap from specification to implementation. It is unclear how all the actions a can be implemented so they all run in and last zero time. Some of these actions typically involve the use of a channel and signalling between several timed-automata in the arrangement. It is unclear how the implementation can wake up sleeping timed-automata with zero time delay when they are recipients

---

[1] Transitions can be labelled by expressions in any decidable logic [8].

[2] An arrangement of finite-state machines in an array of finite-state machines where copies are allowed [12, Definition 1]. It is not a multi-set because the order matters.

[3] The literature of timed-automata refers to the states as locations.

of a signal. As a result, attempts to derive executable models from time-automata face serious challenges, and have resulted in researchers noticing semantic gaps [6,42].

Such is the importance of executable models for MBSE that many attempts have been made to derive executable models within the UML community. UML profiles such as MARTE [4], and specific languages and tools such as AADL [20] enable requirements engineering of real-time systems, but the event-driven nature and the adoption of run-to-completion (RTC) semantics prevails around UML. Many remaining issues [33] prevent the RTC semantics from deploying *executable* [40] and *formally verifiable* models without semantic gaps [6]. Some progress [5,54] has been made by introducing severe restrictions to specific subsets of UML. Others [27,28] significantly simplify RTC semantics, Even in July 2022, Papyrus[TM] [22] (the most UML 2 compliant tool), only offers an incomplete Moka prototype for executing UML state charts and it is possible to create identical diagrams with and without race conditions[4]. *Papyrus Real Time* (Papyrus-RT) UML models exhibit discrepancies with their nuXmv simulation [42], even in the value domain (let alone the time domain), and the (non real-time) C/C++ code of Papyrus-RT requires a runtime system (RTS) and a C/C++ Development Toolkit (CDT) that use non-real time Linux concurrency features. These implementations are significantly distant from the ideal mathematical behaviour of timed-automata models.

Thus, MDSE fails to guarantee time-related correctness properties.

3   Event-Triggered vs. Time-Driven Semantics

Safety-critical real-time systems largely are cyber-physical systems interacting with the environment. They are sometimes also named reactive systems [23], as they must react to changes in the environment, although reactive systems do not need to meet deadlines. Because changes in the environment are typically modelled as events, there has been a large penetration of event-driven programming and event-driven state-charts were introduced to model reactive systems [24]. There is a tendency to equate reactive systems with event-driven systems, although in the real-time [29] and networking literature [38], time-triggered models and systems are considered the best-practice alternative [21].

There are two important aspects the event-driven model abstraction sets aside. First, since events may originate from the environment, they are not in the sphere of control of the computer system. Second, events occur on a dense (or continuous) time line and may originate while the computer system is processing other events. Thus, the event-driven models leave unspecified what happens to events that occur while the computer system is processing other events. Some formalisms simply consider that such simultaneous events never occur, while others (e.g. time-automata) assume event communications channels must relay their signals simultaneously and in zero processing time. Some suggest events concurrent with the handling of an event are to be placed on a queue to be processed later. However, there are different approaches as to the capacity of these event queues. Some modelling assumes the queue is unbounded, while others attempt to incorporate a more realistic position of a bounded queue. Other alternatives for situations such as an event shower is to drop events.

---

[4] www.youtube.com/watch?v=P1KX2dBjmO8.

Because with real-time systems, correctness in the value domain must be complemented with correctness in time, temporal verification is essential, but hard. Model-checkers must consider all timing combinations of all possible tasks across all potential schedules. The combinatorial explosion that emerges from considering all possible ordering of events and their processing of an event queue results in approaches for formal verification that significantly simplify the assumptions regarding event-handling [7], dangerously widening the semantic gap.

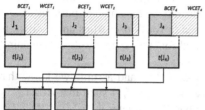
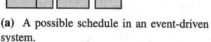

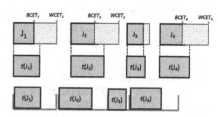

(a) A possible schedule in an event-driven system.

(b) The predefined schedule of a time-triggered alternative.

Fig. 1. An illustration that contrasts a possible event-driven schedule of four jobs with a predefined time-triggered schedule.

We now illustrate that reasoning about time-domain compliance of event-driven systems requires to consider all combinations of all possible events and event handlers [29]. Consider Fig. 1a, where we suggest there are 4 tasks depending on parameters run within their *worst-case execution time (WCET)*. The system based around when events arrive results in flexible, but non-deterministic scheduling that requires considering all possible combinations to confirm proper behaviour. Moreover, although not shown in Fig. 1a, verification should also include the analysis of all configurations of all event queues. However, what Fig. 1a does display is that the analysis also explodes through the number of possible time points where a job may start and when it may finish. In particular, the starting times of later jobs are dependent on the finishing times of earlier jobs. These is precisely the type of inter-dependency that derails composition. By contrast, a time-triggered approach (Fig. 1b) allocates a time-interval for each job, long enough to accommodate the *WCET* of this job. The simplifications is dramatic in several aspects. First, the schedule becomes deterministic and predictable, making it easy to test for and reproduce a fault. By contrast, in event-driven systems, it is particularly hard to reconstruct the timed sequence of events that cause a failure. Second, the combinatorial explosion caused by re-ordering jobs disappears, dramatically reducing the state space that model-checkers need to explore. Third, the possible values where tasks can start is also massively reduced to only a few possibilities, again reducing the state space for verification. Finally, the sphere of control changes from the environment to the system, enabling a much more resilient management of concurrency. We stress here the effect this has on composition. Verification must confirm that the system can meet all timing deadlines for any chain of events, where each job J_i responding to an event takes an execution time $t(J_i)$ somewhere between the best ($BCET_i$) and worst-case execution time ($WCET_i$). Each time point in $[BCET_i, WCET_i]$ must be considered, depending on the ordering of events. The ordering of events becomes even more important when subsystems communicate using events. Communication with events significantly impacts composition.

In a hierarchy of software subsystems sharing a single processor, an event may be of interest to multiple components; consider, for example, a system and a subsystem. If, as a result of the event, the subsystem generates more events (placed in queues), there are delays and the handling of those events and their timing depends on their ordering. This requires verifiers to consider all combinations for all deadlines. Using region automata, the modelling approach with timed automata [1] breaks up the range of possible execution times into sub-ranges. The sub-ranges are used to verify properties under different combinations of time limits. However, the potential for state-space explosion remains, as we now illustrate.

Consider a sequence of events $e_0 \rightarrow e_1 \rightarrow \ldots \rightarrow e_n$ and assume we know that the processing of an individual event e_i takes some time $t(J_{e_i})$ such that $BCET_{e_i} \leq t(J_{e_i}) \leq WCET_{e_i}$. Thus, the sequence would be handled no later than $\sum_{i=0}^{n} WCET_{e_i}$. However, what guarantees can be established regarding any potential delays in responding to event e_i, for each i? The following lemma can be verified by induction.

Lemma 1. *For all* i,

$$\sum_{j=0}^{i} WCET_{e_i} - \sum_{j=0}^{i} BCET_{e_i} \leq \sum_{j=0}^{i+1} WCET_{e_i} - \sum_{j=0}^{i+1} BCET_{e_i}.$$

In other words, the range of possible time points increases monotonically with more events. Moreover, the overall amount of processing time for the sequence of events is t. While, for the first event, the matter is simple and is processing time is $t(J_{e_0})$, the order of events that arrive during handling this or other events is arbitrary. We note that when event e_i arrives somewhere during the handling of the previous $i - 1$ events, then event e_i waits on a first-in first-out queue anywhere between $\sum_{j=0}^{i} BCET_{e_j}$ and $\sum_{j=0}^{i} WCET_{e_j}$ with numerous partitions possible for the handling of earlier events.

Therefore, *the amount of possible clock values that a verifier must consider to confirm bounds on the delay for handling an event increases with the length of the event sequence*. Furthermore, even optimistically assuming that the overhead of event queuing allows the calculation of all the *BCET* and *WCET* bounds for each job, the fact that events trigger subsequent events results in a multiplicative effect (and thus, further combinatorial state explosion) that blocks the potential of formal verification of the event-driven approach.

4   Introducing Controlled Concurrency

The state explosion and the arbitrary possible order of an event-driven system is the result of the uncontrolled concurrency of events emanating from the environment. While event-driven systems are versatile, easier to develop and successful in many applications, they are a best effort approach that may fail in the worst case [30].

Our alternative to composable and executable models that can be formally verified starts by using arrangements of logic-labelled state machines (LLFSMs). We already mentioned that LLFSMs are also state machines with a set of states S and a designated state s_0 as the initial state. Importantly, transitions are not guarded by events, instead they are only guarded by Boolean expressions. LLFSMs could be considered UML state-charts where transitions are only labelled by guards, or timed-automata where there are no clocks. At first sight, this may seem a restriction, but LLFSMs are Turing complete (equivalent to developing in any general purpose programming language), even if the action language (the language to code actions in the states) is as simple as IMP [52] (which happens to be compatible with NuSMV and nuXmv).

However, this subtle change has profound implications to execution semantics [12]. First, and most importantly, execution becomes deterministic [18] placing the management of concurrency of the arrangement, and not the environment. The sphere of control is internalised into the system. A machine is no longer asleep, waiting for an event to awaken it, and the system is not required to immediately process all events as they occur. What is required is that each LLFSM be scheduled with sufficient frequency that it attends to the current state of the environment with the necessary response rate.

Although the states of an LLFSM can have *OnEntry*, *OnExit*, and *Do* sections, akin to UML state-charts, in LLFSMs these sections are strictly syntactic sugar for the convenience of the modeller. Their semantics allow a reduction to LLFSMs that have no such sections [12]. Moreover, the semantics of LLFSMs is not only mathematically defined (as with timed-automata), it is also operationally defined [12]. This means that there are no semantic gaps between the assumption in the mathematical world where mathematical objects live (such as instantaneous rely of signals) and the actual execution in a digital processor. Thus, LLFSMs in an arrangement are scheduled in a round robin fashion, each having the opportunity to execute a *ringlet* [18]. Consider a ringlet the unit of work that executing the current state of the machine in turn.

Explaining the crucial elements of such unit of work is also instrumental on why this approach will provide control over the state explosion and composability. We start by saying that such a unit of work (the ringlet) consists of evaluating, in predefined sequence, the labels of those transitions departing the current state. As long as the result of evaluating a label is false, the ringlet moves on to the next transition. If all labels turn out to evaluate to false, the ringlet terminates there. If a label evaluates to true, then the corresponding transition fires, the actions[5] in the target state are executed and the target state becomes the new, current state of the machine.

We will not elaborate how sections of a state such as *OnEntry*, *OnExit*, or *Do* are included if these features are added to LLFSMs[6] However, a crucial point of functionality is the communication between LLFSMs in the same arrangement. This is achieved by control-status pairs of shared variables. Thus, it is important to explain that LLFSMs have three types of variables to respond to the environment and to communicate. Sensor variables are those whose value the environment may modify at any point in dense time. Actuator variables are those that the system writes to and have a physical effect. Finally, we refer to whiteboard variables as all shared variables.

---

[5] The actions can be represented in a model-based action language that can be converted to a particular programming language by model-to-text transformations [12].

[6] Again, model-to-model transformation replace LLFSMs with sections to LLFSMs without sections following a precisely defined semantics [12].

Naturally, an LLFSM or a state can have local variables, but these only exist in the scope of a machine or state respectively, and do not require any concurrency considerations. Thus, we have reached another crucial point in the separation of concerns that allows composability. The execution of a ringlet is preceded by the creation of a context, taking a snapshot of all shared variables. The ringlet is evaluated in the context of this snapshot. In particular, all the expressions labelling transitions are evaluated in a context isolated from any outside effect, including the environment's potential modifications of sensor variables. Once the ringlet terminates, the context is written into the shared variables before the execution token is passed to any other machine. Because each ringlet is essentially being executed atomically [35], there is no need for any concurrency control mechanisms such as semaphores, monitors, or the like.

This elimination of concurrency concerns also significantly simplifies the analysis of potential states with respect to an event-driven system, which could require attending to some event, while actions of a state are still executed or where a guard may be evaluated in a different context to that of a previous guard. Note also that there is always a debate in event-driven models as to whether, a guard should be evaluated when the event is extracted from the event-queue or when the event arrives. The former could result on an obsolete guard while the latter violates the RTC semantics for the current event.

Several earlier publications have shown that this has an impact on the Kripke structure that needs to be considered by LLFSM model-checkers [34]. However, until now, such formal verification was restricted to the value domain. However, a ringlet may require different time for execution, depending on which (or whether a) transition fired.

5   Improving Communication

It is now widely accepted that modular systems lead not only to correct systems, but to maintainable systems. Moreover, modularity also results in extendibility, reusability, and compatibility. All these quality attributes of modularity result from the central idea of information hiding that enables each module to implement a separable part of the whole with a simple interface. Classical metrics of the virtues of a module are its high cohesion and its low need for coupling with others. Modular system design is thus sustained by decomposability and composability. In the case of state-machines, the most dominant form of composability is the one proposed by STATEMATE [24] and adopted by OMT [41] and the UML [49]. That is the notion of a state machine being a sub-machine of another machine (also known as AND-composition [43]).

While the AND-composition is a mechanism for composition of state machines with many merits, it has as many drawbacks [15, 17, 45] from the perspective of modularity and even more if the resulting models are to be verifiable. First, the formal semantics of such AND-composition is a state machine whose states are the Cartesian product of the states of the components [14]. This aspect alone immediately implies combinatorial state explosion of the Kripke structure for the model checker. Another serious issue is that AND-composition creates simultaneous listeners for the same event and despite the approach that uses inheritance to attempt to resolve the semantics ambiguities created by this, there continues to be semantic gaps on this aspect [33]. Another alternative for composition of logic-labelled finite-state machines derives from the subsumption architecture [11] where a higher level machine can subsume or suspend a lower level machine. This composition mechanism also creates some interdependencies.

Consider the two LLFSMs in Fig. 2. The Sub LLFSM counts to five starting from zero on a local variable count. When count reaches 5, it transitions to a terminal state named Suspend. This is a deterministic behaviour. However, the Super LLFSM restarts[7] the Sub-machine and repeatedly reads a sensor variable random_Number. If this sensor variable ever has the value zero, Super moves to its terminal Suspend_Sub state where it suspends Sub. Thus, Sub executes an implicit transition to its Suspend state (which happens to be its terminal state).

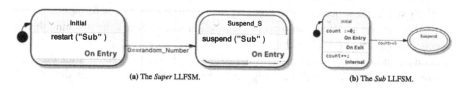

(a) The *Super* LLFSM.   (b) The *Sub* LLFSM.

Fig. 2. A Super machine that restarts and then suspends a Sub-machine.

The behaviour of the Super machine has profound impact on the behaviour of Sub. In isolation, one can formally verify that the variable count will iterate through every element of the ascending sequence $\{0, 1, 2, 3, 4, 5\}$. However, with a resume from Super, the statement that in all execution paths count will eventually reach 5 is now false for the composition with Sub.

5.1   Parameterisation

There is a long and persistent line [25] that repeatedly highlights how pure functions facilitate composability and systematically lead to program correctness.

> *"Functional programming departs dramatically from this state of impediment by promoting purity: the result value of an execution depends on nothing other than the argument values, and no state may change as program execution proceeds. Consequently, it becomes possible to specify program behaviours independently of the rest of the system."* [25].

Thus, enabling LLFSMs to work as behaviour without side-effects improves the mechanisms for modular design. We now detail how the capacity of LLFSMs to behave as functions [16] enables decomposability and therefore arrests exponential explosion, facilitating formal verification.

A pure-function LLFSM is an LLFSM with parameters that does not interact with effector or actuator variable, neither stores state (can only be restarted and not resumed,

---

[7] For simplicity here we would say that *restart* is the same as a UML *resume* except that the history state is the initial state.

and any context of local variables has these undefined). If the function is to work on some input, the designer should pass values of sensor variables as actual parameters at the time of the call. Similarly, if the LLFSM calculation are to be reflected in an actuator variable, the result of the pure function is progressed at the time of function conclusion. This effectively creates a snapshot-semantics between the caller and the callee LLFSM.

Such parametrisation allows functional abstraction and functional decomposition (two classical terms in software analysis and design), behaviour factorisation, and re-use. Moreover, schedule management of LLFSMs (which, as we have argued, operates on a static cyclic time-triggered schedule) can easily accommodate two types of calls.

1. First, one that is analogous to the notion of a subroutine, which implies the call is blocking. The caller does not advance until the callee completes, allowing the caller's slot in the schedule to be taken by the callee. In the case of further calls (the callee becoming a caller), the top of an execution stack defines the machine that is occupying the original caller slot.
2. Second, a non-blocking call, where the caller continues to execute after the call. Here, a static schedule shall be designed to reserve ahead the required slots for all callees.

In both forms, when a call happens, the caller provides the values of the parameters and resets the current state of the callee to the callee's initial state. The caller completes its ringlet normally and on the callee's turn, the callee also executes, in standard fashion, the ringlet of its current state. Note that the reserved-slot approach facilitates treating all LLFSMs uniformly. When a callee has not been called, it marks as its current state its suspended state. When an inactive LLFSM receives a turn, it executes an essentially empty ringlet. With reserved slots, it is possible to make several calls from the same caller in the same calling ringlet.

Parameterised LLFSMs designed as functions that terminate shall eventually reach an accepting state. It is also possible to use this mechanism to launch LLFSMs that become first class citizens in the system loop, in the sense that they do not terminate until system shutdown. For terminating callees, the scheduler detects the callee in an accepting state and enables access to the returned value(s). For non-blocking calls, the caller can test whether the callee has completed, and typically, only after such verification, the results is accessed. However, the callee may be designed to intermediate return results that are accessed by the caller at the caller's leisure, while the callee further refines the results. In all this cases, coupling is minimised and transparent. The callee is straightforward to formally verify, independent of the caller. Decomposition is even more profound when the caller cannot access the result until callee termination, significantly simplifying the work of the model-checker for the caller of a pure LLFSM. The only concern in computing the next Kripke state is to know the results of the pure LLFSM for the actual parameters. But now, since the Kripke structure does not need to represent *how* the results are completed, verification of the caller is independent of the callee. The callee can be analysed in accordance with contract-programming, that is, with respect to pre-conditions, post-conditions, and invariants.

If LLFSMs are designed with side effects, such as using values from the environment in a sensor variable, their behaviour is not pre-defined. The model-checker must use a Kripke structure with non-determinism for the sensor variable. Not only is verification in the value-domain jeopardised, but verification in the time-domain is essentially inaccessible, as the duration or number of scheduled cycles of the callee may include a large number of possibilities, all in combination with the possibilities of caller behaviour.

Asynchronous calls also offer cancellation by the caller. That is, the caller may stop and discard the call (however, this irregular halting clearly results in no guarantees on verified post-conditions of by the callee; the verification of the caller must in this case consider an unavailable return value). Cancellation simply takes the callee to its suspended state where, as before, it shall perform no actions, even if it receives a turn. Note that there is no conflict with cancelling a call that has already completed. Thus, the caller can still query if a call terminated, even if it also requested and has confirmation that it is cancelled. However, if a machine has been asked to cancel, it shall request cancellation of all further callees for which it acted as a caller. However, this is an interaction with the scheduler and it only lasts for the duration of the corresponding ringlet. The schedule management of an cancellation signal shall not take more than one scheduler cycle. This is to avoid semantic issues arising from a cancelled LLFSM not yet having acted on the cancellation signal but being called again. Secondly, we want to keep all scheduling deterministic and retain the capability of computing the WCET for each LLFSM by computing the WCET across all its possible ringlets.

6   First Case Study

To illustrate composability and more importantly, formal verification in the time-domain, we present here a case study not shown in the original paper [33]. This case study has been extensively studied in system design, using approaches such as *Behavior Trees* [53], Modelica [36,37], stateWORKS [50], and the UML [46,51], the literature of behaviour modelling [44], and naturally, formal verification [19]. In our case, it is illustrative of the requirements of a timing-critical, cyber-physical system that interacts with its environment and critically, must promptly react at any point in time. Our case study is commonly named the microwave oven, where the crucial aspect is that opening the door is timing-critical, as it must switch off the magnetron without noticeable delay to prevent harmful exposure to microwave radiation. This is analogous to notorious cases where software faults have actually exposed humans to excessive radiation, such as the Therac-25 X-Ray machine [32].

The system contains two sensors, a button (that increments the timer) and a sensor that detects whether the door is open or not, as well as three actuators, one that controls magnetron, one that controls the light, and one that controls the bell. The software system consists of four LLFSMs that execute concurrently (Fig. 3).

Using the standard round-robin sequential schedule of the arrangement in Fig. 3 and explicitly enumerating the Kripke structure for verification results in over one million Kripke states. This is illustrative of how a small model may result in a large exploration space for a model checker. However, we now proceed to show that the analysis of decomposability enables modular (and thus independent) verification.

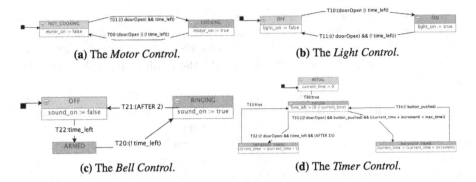

(a) The *Motor Control.*   **(b)** The *Light Control.*

(c) The *Bell Control.*   **(d)** The *Timer Control.*

Fig. 3. Executable model of an arrangement of four LLFSMs that fulfill the requirements of the Microwave case study.

Coupling that may exist between LLFSMs in an arrangement is mainly due to interaction through variables. Although there are no race conditions with LLFSMs, for each LLFSM M_i, the environment consists of the other LLFSMs as well as the physical environment. If only M_i can write to a variable v (and none of the other LLFSMs), in the value domain, M_i can be verified independently of the other LLFSMs. Figure 4 shows the dependencies between LLFSMs and the variables (local variables are excluded naturally, as they never have a scope that involves more than one LLFSM).

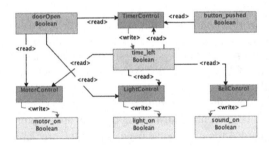

Fig. 4. The read and the write relationships between each LLFSM and the variables in the microwave arrangement.

Thus, if we explicitly generate the individual Kripke structures of the LLFSMs of the arrangement, we obtain the measurements in column (A) of Table 1.

Decomposition shows a massive reduction on the load of the model checker. There is one more improvement that we can apply to this analysis. While sensor variables can indeed change at any point in time, variables such as time_left cannot. The variable time_left is a whiteboard variable, written only by the LLFSM *Timer Control.* So when we consider this variable, we should incorporate that, contrary to those dictated by the physical environment, this variable will not change its value at any point in time other than after completion of the *Timer Control* schedule. This halves the size of the Kripke structure, as shown in column (B) of Table 1.

Table 1. The size of the Kripke Structures for the arrangement of the microwave.

LLFSM	(A) All variables treated like physical sensors.	(B) Variables considered per round.	(C) Read/Write role of variables is considered.
Timer Control	1,024	512	512
Bell Control	54	54	22
Motor Control	62	62	28
Light Control	62	62	28

A further, more precise classification of those other variables can be made when decomposing the model for analysis. Variables that are read-only are treated as sensors, while those only written to would be actuators. Actuator variables are in the sphere of control of the LLFSM, and thus, their values do not need to be considered. Applying this aspect results in Kripke spaces for the model-checker that are further reduced (column (C) of Table 1).

6.1   Enabling Time-Domain Verification

To enable decomposition within the time domain, the timing of one part of the system must not impact the timing of another part of the system. We therefore create a predictable, static time-triggered table-driven schedule. We start the design of such a schedule by analysing the timing of each LLFSM. This step consists of obtaining the *WCET* for each LLFSM, i.e. the longest time one LLFSM takes to execute one ringlet during its turn. To this end, we determine the maximum execution time across all states of the LLFSM, considering all execution paths, e.g. all but one (or none) of the transition labels evaluating to true. Determining the *WCET*, i.e. the worst-case delay that can be caused by a single LLFSM ringlet, can be performed analytically, if one is aware of the details of the compiled executable and the specifications of the target hardware. We first show this from an empirical perspective. Using swift as the action language and a translation of the model on a quad-core Intel i7 MacBook Pro Laptop with 16 GB of memory, running macOS Monterey 12.2, we found that the four LLFSMs of the microwave example have the following *WCET*s: timer control 80 ms, bell control 50 ms, motor control 30 ms, light control 30 ms. Allowing for a 10 ms overhead in between, the following static (cyclic) schedule can be defined, starting the timer control at 10 ms, the bell control at 100 ms (10+80+10), the motor control at 160 ms (100+50+10), and the light control at 200 ms (160+30+10), resulting in a total schedule cycle length of 230 ms.

The corresponding LTL formula that formally verifies the safety property for switching the power off if the door is open has the form shown in Fig. 5 (using NuSMV or nuXmv as a model checker).   This establishes that for the all sequential implementations, the door must remain open for just over one full loop around the schedule. In fact, the worst-case happens when doorOpen detects OPEN just after the motor control took a snapshot of sensor variables, execution loops over the full arrangement and then back to the motor control, whose transition fires to set motor_on to false.

Parallelisation provides an avenue to reduce this further, when, for example, we assume a guaranteed response time of 230 ms were insufficient. Since we have several

```
LTLSPEC
--R5 Keeping the door open for a period long enough causes the cooking to stop.
NAME FR5:= G (      -- At all future states:
  (G[0,4] doorOpen) --  if the door stays open for at least 5 Kripke states,
  ->                -- then:
  (F[0,5]           -- after a maximum of ten Kripke transitions,
    !MotorControl.motor_on) -- the cooking has stopped.
  )
```

Fig. 5. Time-domain property for the microwave.

CPU cores, and the decomposition analysis reveals that the three LLFSMs do not depend on each other, the motor, the light, and the bell (but not the timer) can be scheduled in parallel. Thus, to maximise parallelism, we would use three cores. On the first core, we schedule the timer at 10 ms and the motor at 100 ms (10+80+10), with a total *WCET* of 130ms. The other two cores can schedule one LLFSM each at 100 ms (so they do not overlap with the timer control), resulting in the longest cyclic schedule of 150 ms.

The important point about this case study is that scheduling becomes a classic cooperative scheduler which allows much simpler implementation, as the tasks (the slices for each LLFSM) are never unexpectedly interrupted. Moreover, the time-triggered system can be used with a watchdog timer, implementing a hard reset if one LLFSM monopolised the CPU (a reason sometimes given to justify preemptive scheduling) or in case of a fault.

7 Second Case Study

We now present a case study that illustrates other challenges in formal verification of time-domain properties, while remaining small enough to describe here. The first issue is when the system uses, performs calculations, or branches based on, a clock value. This implies that the correctness of values (value-domain properties) depends on timely execution. That is, value-domain verification must consider the potentially large range of values of a clock sensor variable. Time-domain verification would also be complex since the duration of tasks will become dependent on the environment. Moreover, the system as a whole loses decomposability since the timing of tasks influences the clock values read by other tasks.

To illustrate this, we analyse the embedded software of a sonar sensor system. These types of systems are fundamental, typically safety-critical, real-time components of larger systems that include automotive driver-assist systems, and autonomous robots, or vehicles. A sonar sensor estimates the distance to an object by actively emitting a sonar pulse and detecting the time it takes for the reflected pulse to come back. The distance d is computed by a simple formula $d = (t_{air} \times c)/2$, where t_{air} is the measured time and c is the constant for the speed of sound. Note that now, the value d is a time-domain dependant calculation, and t_{air} is a value read from the environment. The further the obstacle is away, the larger is the value of t_{air}. At first glance, the software module should wait until the pulse returns to perform the distance calculation. This would imply that the execution time of a module is dependent on the environment, putting it out of the sphere of control of the computer system. If other tasks depend on that, the scheduling itself would be at the mercy of the environment. Moreover, the accuracy of the value d is dependent of the timing of the execution of the system (and seemingly on the state of the environment).

In our case, we actually consider a system where more than one sonar is placed on the vehicle, greatly aggravating the dependency problem of time-dependent control completely disrupting task scheduling. Given that these sensor systems typically are used for obstacle avoidance, we get a hard deadline based on the maximum vehicle velocity the system needs to handle. Using a pre-emptive schedule is not scalable for performing the corresponding formal verification for the reasons explained earlier. Therefore, we apply here our time-triggered approach. We will see that our executable models are simple and result in deterministic timing, with tight bounds on the measurement error.

We introduce the idea with a simple LLFSM that measures a time interval by counting schedule cycles. That is, the machine calculates a time interval by multiplying the number of schedule cycles that have elapsed since measuring began with the SCHEDULE_LENGTH. Figure 6 illustrates how we can increment a counter every time the LLFSM executes its ringlet. This transforms a sensor variable dependent on the environment into a discrete counter value, preventing state explosion for the model checker.

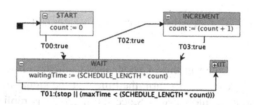

Fig. 6. Machine that reduces the analysis of all possible moments in dense time when to stop into discrete values.

This decoupling also facilitates decomposition, allowing our case study to be more sophisticated, through an array of such distance sensors. The executable model is based on Fig. 6, but now several calls to the API of the sensors are required. A version [33] offers all data types when `swift` is the action language. We present here a version with a generic action language (Fig. 7). This LLFSM controls one distance sensor and is replicated for each physical sonar sensor. The state machine works as follows. In the set-up states, appropriate GPIO pins are prepared for reading and writing. Counting of ringlets happens in the states called `WaitForPulseStart`, `ClearTrigger`, and `Wait_For_Pulse_End`. In these states, the variable `num_loops` is incremented in each ringlet. Waiting is terminated when the signal is received back, in which case a valid distance is calculated, or by reaching the maximum number of loops.

For demonstration purposes we implemented this as a real-time system with 3 physical sensors, running on an **Atmel ATmega32U4** microcontroller, operating at 16MHz. In this case, the design of a static schedule results in distance estimates obtained by

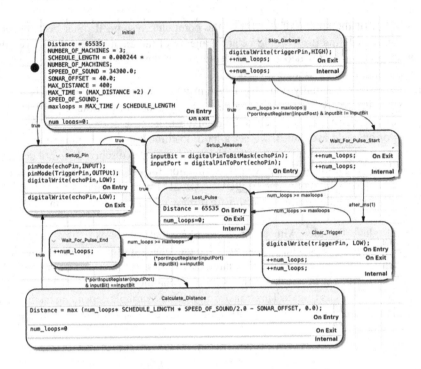

Fig. 7. A LLFSM that controls a distance sensor device.

counting the ringlets executed in the LLFSM. If the schedule is sequential, and one ringlet of each machine executes its turn, the time that the signal travels is a function of the duration of the schedule's cycle. Since the machine is replicated three times, the *WCET* is the same for all, and the schedule cycle is simply $3 \times WCET$. Our measurements of the *WCET* (including dispatch overhead) is $244\,\mu s$. Therefore, a time-triggered, sequential schedule can start the first instance at 0, the second instance at $244\,\mu s$ and the third at $488\,\mu s$. The total static schedule cycle is then $732\,\mu s$. This produces distance estimates with a precision of 13 cm.

The point here is that this demonstrates a reliable, deterministic real-time system, with a static schedule and a constant bound on the error of the estimated distances. Moreover, the system can be formally verified, and value-domain properties as well as time-domain properties can be established, even for systems beyond the three used in our experiments. That is, formal verification scales, but precision degrades as the number of sensors increases.

However, as in our earlier case study, the analysis of the interactions between the LLFSMs allows parallel (static) schedules. In this system, all instances of the LLFSM are independent of each other. Thus, all LLFSMs can be dispatched at time 0 in a static schedule of length $244\,\mu s$, which improves the precision to 3.3 cm.

To demonstrate the feasibility and scalability that our decomposition analysis produces, we have released in github.com/mipalgu/SonarKripkeStructures the explicit Kripke structures as source files for nuXmv as well as `graphviz` illustrations of these structures. These explicit Kripke structures are timed transition systems to enable formal verification of LTL properties in the value domain as well as in the time domain. In particular, we verified the nuXmv LTL formula that asserts that the machine completes within 35 ms by calculating a distance (or return maximum distance value in the case of no obstacles). This LTL formula is as follows.

```
LTLSPEC
G                                    -- It is globally true
  pc = "Sonar23-Setup_Pin-R" ->      -- If the set up is completed, then
    time_until                       -- the time to reach
      ( pc = "Sonar23-LostPulse-W" |   -- the state of lost pulse or
        pc = "Sonar23-CalculateDistance-W" -- the state that computes the distance
      ) <= 35000                     -- is less or equal than 35ms
```

8 Third Case Study

In this case study we examine parameterised LLFSMs and the scalability issue while completing verification in the time-domain. The scenario is a robot with a number n of legs symmetrically positioned around its body (typically a hexapod with $n = 6$) [16]. Gaits of the robot, where the legs are placed equidistant from the centre of the robot as if they were on a regular n-gon, are easy to derive from a single LLFSM. The single LLFSM is replicated so that each copy controls a leg. The legs are numbered 0 to $n - 1$ and the controlling LLFSM has one parameter, representing the leg number it is controlling. Each gait has essentially two phases, one for the odd legs and one for the even legs. For instance, if the robot is to spin clockwise, the even-numbered legs get raised and the odd-numbered legs come down. Then, the odd legs use their joint to push the robot clockwise by performing a counter-clockwise turn of the body joint. In this step, the even legs spin in the opposite direction (but in the air), back to when they would be able to push again, once lowered. Then, the odd legs are raised and the even ones are lowered. The fourth phase now sees the even-numbered legs doing the push, while the odd-numbered legs revert to their starting position. By parameterising which of the odd or even legs to start with, or when and how to turn, the robot can now also spin counter-clockwise or walk in a straight line in any direction (orientation). The latter case is achieved through reverting the role of the even and odd-numbered legs on the left and right sides of the robot. Another parameter we pass to the leg-controller machine is the speed of the gait.

Importantly, this parameterisation only works if we can ensure that the legs are synchronised in time, analogous to a crew of rowers. Figure 8 shows the states of the controlling LLFSM. The INITIAL state has no code and details for the C++ code inside the other states [16] is not shown here, since it consists of essentially five C++ instructions that calculate the gait motion from its input parameters as described above. Suffice it to say that the code as well as the resulting *WCET* of the 4 states in the cycle that raises, waits, lowers, and pushes the legs, are brief and extremely similar. The initial state just starts the 4-phase loop at opposite ends for even-numbered legs than for odd-numbered legs. What we emphasise here is that, in the cycle of the states, the timed transitions that get triggered are essentially the same, greatly simplifying reasoning about the behaviour of the LLFSM, both in the value domain as well as in the time domain.

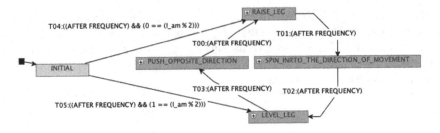

Fig. 8. Executable model of the parameterised LLFSM that controls an n-legged, symmetric robot.

There are several important aspects that this case study illustrates. First, the analysis shows that all copies of the controller machine are independent of any side-effects and are only influenced by the parameters that have been set to begin with, but do not required any subsequent communication or synchronisation. That is, the parameterised executable model can be independently verified for a large number of properties, and its integration, together with all the other copies (instances), into an arrangement of LLFSMs does not invalidate the independently-verified properties. This way, we can construct succinct, timed Kripke structures for the control machine and show that, if the leg-control machine is in one of its loop states, it takes no longer than the *WCET* of the state plus 3 Kripke state transitions plus FREQUENCY to arrive in the follow-up state of the loop control cycle. This is the guaranteed upper bound that we can calculate our overall *WCET* from. Moreover, we can also show that, if the control machine just transitioned into its loop state, it will require at least the *WCET* of the arriving state plus 3 Kripke state transitions plus the FREQUENCY to move to the next state.

Typically, the execution of the code in each state (the *WCET*) is much smaller than the FREQUENCY dictated by the physical properties of the robot, its actuators, and the environment in which it operates. It is important to point out that, while this arrangement of LLFSMs perfectly parallelises, even in the worst case, i.e. in a sequential schedule with only one CPU, where not all legs are told exactly at the same time to raise, push, lower, or spin, we can build a schedule that results in a well-designed, predictable behaviour of the robot. This is because as per the analysis above, our arrangement of n copies of this parameterised LLFSM enables us to construct a static and cyclic time-triggered schedule and show that the requirements for the 3 Kripke transitions plus the *WCET* is much slower than the FREQUENCY with which state transitions are performed. That is, the first leg has just made a negligible displacement when the last leg (the sixth) receives its motion command.

This case study demonstrates the important additional aspects in which the LLFSM analysis and formal verification can assists with the design. For example, in this case the Kripke construction assumes there are Internal (*Do*) and *OnExit* sections for the states. However, all Internal and *OnExit* sections of all states are empty. So if we were to use a scheduler for LLFSMs with no sections, the corresponding Kripke structure would remove this overhead (although such overhead is extremely small relative to the frequency, and thus negligible in real-world examples such as the present case study).

For argument's sake we point out that, if the number of legs was extremely large (compared to the level of parallelisation available), the analysis would show a deterioration on synchronisation of the legs. We argue that in reality, even with a slow, single-core microcontroller this would constitute a physical impossibility for any common-sense robot design. Nevertheless, this demonstrates that the model can be used to explore a larger number of legs that move for a narrower wedge, and derive the resulting speed of movement to enable different gaits.

9   Conclusions

"Engineers (in particular, software engineers) have been motivated to find a way to confront the intrinsic and increasing complexity of their endeavors." [39]

Executable models that are formally verifiable in the value domain and in the time domain facilitate high-level design, a choice of implementation, reliable execution, and the necessary validation to deliver dependable systems. Typically, unbounded complexity, semantic gaps, and combinatorial state explosion substantially reduce the utility of model-driven software engineering for even moderately complex real-time systems. We have shown how decomposability is crucial and demonstrated several solutions that enable high level, executable models of real-time systems. Our novel approach analyses how to facilitate decomposability and allows verification in both the value and time domains. We showed that we can systematically analyse arrangements of LLFSMs producing deterministic, static, time-triggered schedules that enable controlled concurrency and worst-case execution time guarantees. We can achieve this because we can create succinct timed Kripke structures that are fit for formal verification, including verification of timing properties. We leap further and enable parallel, non-preemptive scheduling of LLFSMs, where verification is feasible as the corresponding, faithful Kripke structure has bounded size. We illustrated our approach through three case studies where we obtain formal verification in the time domain.

References

1. Alur, R., Courcoubetis, C., Dill, D.: Model-checking in dense real-time. Inf. Comput. **104**(1), 2–34 (1993). https://doi.org/10.1006/inco.1993.1024
2. Alur, R., Dill, D.: Automata for modeling real-time systems. In: Paterson, M.S. (ed.) ICALP 1990. LNCS, vol. 443, pp. 322–335. Springer, Heidelberg (1990). https://doi.org/10.1007/BFb0032042
3. Alur, R., Dill, D.: A theory of timed automata. Theoret. Comput. Sci. **126**(2), 183–235 (1994). https://doi.org/10.1016/0304-3975(94)90010-8
4. André, C., Mallet, F., de Simone, R.: Modeling time(s). In: Engels, G., Opdyke, B., Schmidt, D.C., Weil, F. (eds.) Model Driven Engineering Languages and Systems, pp. 559–573. Springer, Berlin Heidelberg, Berlin, Heidelberg (2007)
5. Berthomieu, B., et al.: Real-time model checking support for AADL. CoRR abs/1503.00493 (2015). http://arxiv.org/abs/1503.00493

6. Besnard, V., Brun, M., Jouault, F., Teodorov, C., Dhaussy, P.: Unified LTL verification and embedded execution of UML models. In: Proceedings of the 21th ACM/IEEE International Conference on Model Driven Engineering Languages and Systems, pp. 112–122. MODELS 2018, ACM, New York (2018). https://doi.org/10.1145/3239372.3239395

7. Bhaduri, P., Ramesh, S.: Model checking of statechart models: survey and research directions (2004). http://arxiv.org/abs/cs.SE/0407038

8. Billington, D., Estivill-Castro, V., Hexel, R., Rock, A.: Requirements engineering via non-monotonic logics and state diagrams. In: Maciaszek, L.A., Loucopoulos, P. (eds.) ENASE 2010. CCIS, vol. 230, pp. 121–135. Springer, Heidelberg (2011). https://doi.org/10.1007/978-3-642-23391-3_9

9. Blanchard, B.S., Fabryck, W.J.: Systems Engineering and Analysis, 5th edn. Prentice Hall, NJ (2011)

10. Bouyer, P., Laroussinie, F.: Model Checking Timed Automata, pp. 111–140. ISTE (2010). https://doi.org/10.1002/9780470611012.ch4

11. Brooks, R.: A robust layered control system for a mobile robot. IEEE J. Robot. Autom. **2**(1), 14–23 (1986). https://doi.org/10.1109/JRA.1986.1087032

12. Carrillo, M., Estivill-Castro, V., Rosenblueth, D.A.: Verification and simulation of time-domain properties for models of behaviour. In: Hammoudi, S., Pires, L.F., Selić, B. (eds.) MODELSWARD 2020. CCIS, vol. 1361, pp. 225–249. Springer, Cham (2021). https://doi.org/10.1007/978-3-030-67445-8_10

13. Dickerson, C., Mavris, D.N.: Architecture and Principles of Systems Engineering. CRC Press, Auerbach Publications, Taylor & Francis Group, Boca Raton, FL (2010)

14. Drusinsky, D.: Modeling and verification using UML statecharts - a working guide to reactive system design, runtime monitoring and execution-based model checking. Elsevier (2006)

15. Estivill-Castro, V., Hexel, R.: Simple, not simplistic - the middleware of behaviour models. In: Filipe, J., Maciaszek, L.A. (eds.) ENASE 2015 - Proceedings of the 10th International Conference on Evaluation of Novel Approaches to Software Engineering, pp. 189–196. SciTePress (2015). https://doi.org/10.5220/0005371101890196

16. Estivill-Castro, V., Hexel, R.: Verifiable parameterised behaviour models - for robotic and embedded systems. In: Hammoudi, S., Ferreira Pires, S., Selic, B. (eds.) Proceedings of the 6th International Conference on Model-Driven Engineering and Software Development, MODELSWARD, pp. 364–371. SciTePress (2018). https://doi.org/10.5220/0006573903640371

17. Estivill-Castro, V., Hexel, R.: The understandability of models for behaviour. In: Hammoudi, S., Pires, L.F., Selić, B. (eds.) MODELSWARD 2019. CCIS, vol. 1161, pp. 50–75. Springer, Cham (2020). https://doi.org/10.1007/978-3-030-37873-8_3

18. Estivill-Castro, V., Hexel, R., Rosenblueth, D.A.: Efficient modelling of embedded software systems and their formal verification. In: 2012 19th Asia-Pacific Software Engineering Conference, vol. 1, pp. 428–433 (2012). https://doi.org/10.1109/APSEC.2012.21

19. Estivill-Castro, V., Rosenblueth, D.A.: Model checking of transition-labeled finite-state machines. In: Kim, T., Adeli, H., Kim, H., Kang, H., Kim, K.J., Kiumi, A., Kang, B.-H. (eds.) ASEA 2011. CCIS, vol. 257, pp. 61–73. Springer, Heidelberg (2011). https://doi.org/10.1007/978-3-642-27207-3_8

20. Feiler, P.H., Lewis, B., Vestal, S., Colbert, E.: An overview of the SAE architecture analysis & design language (AADL) standard: a basis for model-based architecture-driven embedded systems engineering. In: Dissaux, P., Filali-Amine, M., Michel, P., Vernadat, F. (eds.) Architecture Description Languages, pp. 3–15. Springer, Boston (2005). https://doi.org/10.1007/0-387-24590-1_1

21. Furrer, F.: Future-Proof Software-Systems: A Sustainable Evolution Strategy. Springer Vieweg, Berlin (2019)

22. Guermazi, S., Tatibouet, J., Cuccuru, A., Seidewitz, E., Dhouib, S., Gérard, S.: Executable modeling with fUML and Alf in Papyrus: Tooling and experiments. In: Mayerhofer, T., Langer, P., Seidewitz, E., Gray, J. (eds.) Proceedings of the 1st International Workshop on Executable Modeling co-located with ACM/IEEE 18th International Conference on Model Driven Engineering Languages and Systems (MODELS 2015). CEUR Workshop Proceedings, vol. 1560, pp. 3–8. CEUR-WS.org (2015)

23. Harel, D., Pnueli, A.: On the development of reactive systems. In: Apt, K, R. (ed.) Logics and Models of Concurrent Systems, pp. 477–498. Springer, Berlin Heidelberg (1985). https://doi.org/10.1007/978-3-642-82453-1_17

24. Harel, D., Politi, M.: Modeling Reactive Systems with Statecharts: The STATEMATE Approach. McGraw-Hill, New York, NY (1998)

25. Hu, Z., Hughes, J., Wang, M.: How functional programming mattered. National Science Review 2(3), 349–370 (2015). https://doi.org/10.1093/nsr/nwv042

26. ICOSE: Systems engineering vision 2035 - engineering solutions for a better world, Technical Report ISIS-1-98, International Council on Systems Engineering, Department of Electronics and Computer Science (2022)

27. Jin, D., Levy, D.C.: An approach to schedulability analysis of UML-based real-time systems design. In: Proceedings of the 3rd International Workshop on Software and Performance, pp. 243–250. WOSP 2002, Association for Computing Machinery, New York (2002)

28. Kabous, L., Nebel, W.: Modeling hard real time systems with UML the *OOHARTS* approach. In: France, R., Rumpe, B. (eds.) UML 1999. LNCS, vol. 1723, pp. 339–355. Springer, Heidelberg (1999). https://doi.org/10.1007/3-540-46852-8_25

29. Kopetz, H.: The time-triggered model of computation. In: Proceedings 19th IEEE Real-Time Systems Symposium, pp. 168–177 (1998). https://doi.org/10.1109/REAL.1998.739743

30. Kopetz, H.: Real-Time Systems: Design Principles for Distributed Embedded Applications, 2nd edn. Springer Publishing Company, Incorporated (2011)

31. Larsen, K.G., Pettersson, P., Yi, W.: UPPAAL in a nutshell. Int. J. Softw. Tools Technol. Transfer 1(1–2), 134–152 (1997). https://doi.org/10.1007/s100090050010

32. Leveson, N.G.: The Therac-25: 30 years later. Computer 50(11), 8–11 (2017). https://doi.org/10.1109/MC.2017.4041349

33. McColl, C., Estivill-Castro, V., McColl, M., Hexel, R.: Verifiable executable models for decomposable real-time systems. In: Ferreira Pires, L., Hammoudi, S., Seidewitz, E. (eds.) Proceedings of the 10th International Conference on Model-Driven Engineering and Software Development, MODELSWARD 2022, pp. 182–193. SCITEPRESS (2022). https://doi.org/10.5220/0010812200003119

34. McColl, C., Estivill-Castro, V., Hexel, R.: An OO and functional framework for versatile semantics of logic-labelled finite state machines. In: The Twelfth International Conference on Software Engineering Advances, pp. 238–243 (2017)

35. McColl, C., Estivill-Castro, V., Hexel, R.: Versatile but precise semantics for logic-labelled finite state machines. Int. J. Adv. Softw. 11(3), 227–238 (2018)

36. Myers, T., Dromey, R.G.: From requirements to embedded software - formalising the key steps. In: 20th Australian Software Engineering Conference (ASWEC 2009), pp. 23–33. IEEE Computer Society (14th-17th April 2009). https://doi.org/10.1109/ASWEC.2009.37

37. Myers, T., Dromey, R.G., Fritzson, P.: Comodeling: from requirements to an integrated software/hardware model. Computer 44(4), 62–70 (2011). https://doi.org/10.1109/MC.2010.270

38. Park, P., Coleri Ergen, S., Fischione, C., Lu, C., Johansson, K.H.: Wireless network design for control systems: a survey. IEEE Commun. Surv. Tutor. 20(2), 978–1013 (2018). https://doi.org/10.1109/COMST.2017.2780114

39. Pastor, O., Pierantonio, A., Rossi, G.: Teaching modeling in the time of agile development. Computer 55(06), 73–76 (2022). https://doi.org/10.1109/MC.2022.3144929

40. Pham, V.C., Radermacher, A., Gérard, S., Li, S.: Complete code generation from UML state machine. In: Ferreira Pires, L., Hammoudi, S., Selic, B. (eds.) Proceedings of the 5th International Conference on Model-Driven Engineering and Software Development, MODEL-SWARD 2017, Porto, Portugal, February 19–21, 2017, pp. 208–219. SciTePress (2017)

41. Rumbaugh, J.R., Blaha, M.R., Lorensen, W., Eddy, F., Premerlani, W.: Object-Oriented Modeling and Design. Prentice-Hall (1991)

42. Sahu, S., Schorr, R., Medina-Bulo, I., Wagner, M.: Model translation from papyrus-RT into the NUXMV model checker. In: Cleophas, L., Massink, M. (eds.) SEFM 2020. LNCS, vol. 12524, pp. 3–20. Springer, Cham (2021). https://doi.org/10.1007/978-3-030-67220-1_1

43. Samek, M.: Practical UML Statecharts in C/C++, Second Edition: Event-Driven Programming for Embedded Systems. Newnes, Newton, MA, USA (2008)

44. Shlaer, S., Mellor, S.: Object Lifecycles. Yourdon Press, New Jersey (1992)

45. Simons, A.: On the compositional properties of UML statechart diagrams. In: Rigorous Object-Oriented Methods 2000. Electronic Workshops in Computing (eWiC), New York (2000)

46. Sommerville, I.: Software engineering, 10th Edition. International computer science series, Addison-Wesley (2016). https://www.worldcat.org/oclc/65978675

47. Stankovic, J.A.: Misconceptions about real-time computing: a serious problem for next-generation systems. Computer **21**(10), 10–19 (1988). https://doi.org/10.1109/2.7053

48. Stevens, R., Brook, P., Jackson, K., Arnold, S.: Systems Engineering. Coping with Complexity. Prentice Hall Europe, London (1998)

49. The Object Management Group: Information technology - Object Management Group Unified Modeling Language (OMG UML), Infrastructure. ISO/IEC 19505-1:2012(E), ISO (2012)

50. Wagner, F.: Modeling Software with Finite State Machines: A Practical Approach. Auerbach Publications, New York (2006)

51. Wagner, F., Wolstenholme, P.: Modeling and building reliable, re-useable software. In: 10th IEEE International Conference on Engineering of Computer-Based Systems (ECBS 2003), pp. 277–286. IEEE (2003)

52. Winskel, G.: The Formal Semantics of Programming Languages: An Introduction. MIT press (1993)

53. Winter, K., J., H.I., Colvin, R.: Integrating requirements: The behavior tree philosophy. In: Fiadeiro, J.L., Gnesi, S., Maggiolo-Schettini, A. (eds.) 8th IEEE International Conference on Software Engineering and Formal Methods, SEFM 2010, pp. 41–50. IEEE Computer Society (2010). https://doi.org/10.1109/SEFM.2010.13

54. Zhang, F., Zhao, Y., Ma, D., Niu, W.: Formal verification of behavioral AADL models by stateful timed CSP. IEEE Access **5**, 27421–27438 (2017). https://doi.org/10.1109/ACCESS.2017.2770323

Comparing Goal-Oriented Analysis Techniques: A Controlled Experiment

Carlos Cano-Genoves(✉), Silvia Abrahão, and Emilio Insfran

IUMTI, Universitat Politècnica de València, Valencia, Spain
{carcage1,sabrahao,einsfran}@dsic.upv.es

Abstract. Background: Goal models are usually used during the early phases of requirement elicitation, since they help to understand the motivations underlying the system to be developed. Goal-oriented analysis techniques help analysts reason and make decisions regarding the analyzed goal model. Aims: In this paper, we present an empirical evaluation of two goal-oriented analysis techniques: i) VeGAn, which we proposed in a previous work, and which follows a value-driven approach and a fuzzy logic approach and ii) GRL-Quant, which follows a value-neutral approach and a quantitative approach. Method: We conducted an experiment with a population of 64 Computer Science undergraduate students. The participants were asked to analyze a goal model with one of the techniques and to answer a questionnaire to assess their perceptions. The techniques were compared with respect to the accuracy of goal model element prioritization, the participants' prioritization time, and their perceptions of the quality of the analysis results (perceived satisfaction), ease of use, usefulness, and intention to use. Results: The results of the experiment show that both techniques are very similar since no significant differences could be found in most of the variables analyzed. However, the participants perceived the results of VeGAn more satisfactorily than those of GRL-Quant, although the prioritization accuracy of GRL-Quant was better for one particular system. Conclusions: This paper provides new insights have emerged from this study, and also opportunities to improve both techniques. The experiment provides preliminary results on the usefulness of both goal-oriented analysis techniques, but further research is required in order to strengthen these results.

Keywords: Goal-models · Goal-oriented analysis techniques · Controlled experiment

1 Introduction

In order to identify and understand the intention of the stakeholders regarding the system to be developed, goal models are often used. These models not only represent the motivations and intentions of the stakeholders, but also provide some insight into some of the functional and non-functional requirements they are interested in and how they might be achieved. Due the size and complexity of goal models, goal-oriented analysis techniques are often used as they can help analysts to make decisions by providing an assessment of the satisfaction of goals, evaluating alternatives or identifying conflicts.

© Springer Nature Switzerland AG 2023
L. F. Pires et al. (Eds.): MODELSWARD 2021/2022, CCIS 1708, pp. 157–178, 2023.
https://doi.org/10.1007/978-3-031-38821-7_8

Although there are many goal-oriented analysis techniques that use different approaches (systematic propagation, simulation, planning, or techniques based on multiple-criteria decision-making), most of them assume a value-neutral approach in which all goals are equally important. In addition, quantitative and qualitative approaches are commonly used.

Whereas the use of a value-neutral approach may incur that the results of the goal-oriented analysis may be of little value. The use of quantitative or qualitative approaches can cause problems. On the one hand, the results of a qualitative approach may not be useful due to lack of precision, this can occur if the result indicates that two goals are "very important" without indicating which is more important than the other. On the other hand, the over-precision of quantitative approaches can cause problems when prioritizing because there are too many possible values and it can be difficult to decide which is the most appropriate.

In order to deal with the problems of using a value-neutral approach and a quantitative/qualitative approach we introduced VeGAn also known as GATHA in a previous work [7]. On the one hand, it follows the principles of Value-Based Software Engineering [5] where the value is used at the forefront of software engineering decisions. On the other hand, it uses a fuzzy logic based approach instead of a quantitative/qualitative one. The fuzzy logic uses *fuzzy numbers*, which represent range of values, that we use for the prioritization and then for the propagation of the importance. In this way, the use of fuzzy logic solves the existing difficulty of assigning specific single values (e.g. 37, 38, 39) to determine the importance of intentional elements (quantitative approaches), and avoids the problem of losing precision due to a small set of alternatives (e.g. low, medium, high) (qualitative approaches).

In a previous work [6], we presented a controlled experiment whose objective was to compare VeGAn with GRL-Quant [3]. The reason why it was decided to compare with that technique is because both techniques are based on the same goal modeling language and because the authors and the technique are well-known within the goal-oriented analysis community. In the previous work, the techniques were compared with respect to the prioritization accuracy, prioritization time and perceived satisfaction using both techniques. In this paper, we extend the controlled experiment including three new perception-based variables perceived ease of use, perceived usefulness and intention to use from the [10] so that the controlled experiment analyzes a total of 6 variables.

Specifically, this paper has three main goals. First, we want to further investigate whether the use of a fuzzy logic based approach can be used to analyze goal models without having the problem of the lack of precision of the qualitative approach, nor the excess of precision of the quantitative approach that causes difficulties when prioritizing. Due to this, one of the variables to be analyzed in the controlled experiment is the prioritization accuracy, in order to see if the fuzzy logic has a precision similar to the quantitative one despite having a simpler qualitative-like prioritization. Second, we want to compare whether the results of a technique that follows the VBSE principles provides more satisfactory results, for which we are analyzing the perceived satisfaction variable. Finally, we also want to highlight that although there are several goal-oriented analysis techniques, there is a lack of empirical evaluations that compare them.

This paper is structured as follows. Section 2 discusses related literature concerning existing studies comparing goal-oriented analysis techniques and empirical studies. Section 3 provides the background to the goal-oriented analysis techniques compared in this work, while Sect. 4 introduces the design and execution of the experiment carried out to compare GRL-Quant and VeGAn, whose results are subsequently presented in Sect. 5. Section 6 discusses the threats to validity. Finally, Sect. 7 presents our conclusions and future work.

2   Related Work

Although many goal-oriented analysis techniques have been proposed, very few studies have been conducted in order to compare them. Of those that do, two studies [15, 16] should be highlighted. In Horkoff and Yu [15], the authors performed a snowballing search that yielded 25 goal-oriented analysis techniques which were classified. The authors then compared these techniques according to a set of criteria.

In a subsequent study, Horkoff and Yu [16] performed a comparison of seven goal-oriented analysis techniques. In this comparison, the goal-oriented analysis techniques were applied to three different goal models and the results obtained by the techniques were compared under the premise that the techniques should be reliable if the results obtained for all of them are similar. The main difference between this comparison and ours is that we are interested in not only the precision of the results but also the participants' perceptions of the results of the analysis performed.

With regard to empirical studies performed in the goal-oriented analysis area, most of them analyze a single goal-oriented analysis technique. For example, Ernst, Mylopoulos, and Wang [12] performed an experiment in order to evaluate the scalability of a run-time monitoring framework that analyzes goal models, while Liaskos, Jalman, and Aranda [18] performed an experiment in order to evaluate whether the Analytic Hierarchy Process (AHP) approach can be used to quantitatively assess contribution relationships in goal models.

Very few empirical studies involving participants have been carried out in order to reason about their perceptions with regard to the usefulness of goal-oriented analysis techniques results. For example, Horkoff and Yu [14] performed an experiment in order to compare the manual analysis of a goal model with an automated analysis through the use of an interactive evaluation procedure that they proposed. The results showed that the participants better identified conflicts when using the interactive procedure.

In this paper, we involve participants so as to empirically evaluate two goal-oriented analysis techniques. We compare the use of a quantitative scale with that of a qualitative scale with which to prioritize goal models and we then go on to compare the participants' perceptions as regards the goal model analysis results.

3   Goal-Oriented Analysis Techniques Compared

3.1   GRL-Quant

GRL-Quant [3] is a goal-oriented analysis technique based on propagation whose goal is to evaluate the satisfaction of the intentional elements of the goal model. The technique uses *forward propagation* to calculate satisfaction, that is, it calculates how an intentional element or set of them has an impact on the satisfaction of the rest of the model elements. This technique has two activities.

The *Prioritization* is the first activity of the technique and consists of assigning importance to the elements of the stakeholders. Each of the stakeholders has the possibility (it is not mandatory) to assign an importance to each of its elements. In the event that no importance is assigned, the element is not considered to calculate the actor's satisfaction. Because the technique uses a quantitative approach, when prioritizing, an importance should be assigned within the range of the quantitative scale from 0 to 100.

The *Propagation* is the second activity of the technique and consist of selecting an intentional element or set of them, and then automatically propagate through the relationships so as to discover their impact over the satisfaction of the rest of the model elements. The satisfaction of the intentional elements is a number belonging to the quantitative scale from -100 (fully denied satisfaction) to 100 (totally satisfied). The propagation rules used by the GRL-Quant technique for each for the relationships are:

- AND decomposition links: The satisfaction of the decomposed intentional element is equal to the minimum satisfaction of the elements that compose it.
- OR decomposition links: The satisfaction of the intentional element decomposed is equal to the maximum satisfaction of the intentional element into which it is decomposed.
- XOR decomposition links: It propagates the elements as an OR decomposition, but only an intentional element of the decomposition can be initialized at the time of propagation.
- Contribution links: The satisfaction of the intentional element contributed is the satisfaction of the intentional element that contributes, multiplied by the weight of the contribution divided by 100.
- Dependency links: The satisfaction of the intentional element depender is equal to the minimum satisfaction of the depender and the dependee.

In order to be able to compare GRL-Quant with VeGAn we have made two minor modifications to the technique.

On the one hand, we have automated propagation so that it is not necessary to propagate from each intentional element individually to calculate its satisfaction score. In the event that an element were to break down, its satisfaction depended on the elements that compose it. The propagation has been automated to fix the scalability issue of the technique that negatively affects the time required to perform an analysis and therefore reducing the time needed to perform the experiment. Although we have automated the propagation, feedback is still provided on how the satisfaction has been calculated.

On the other hand, we have added a third activity to the technique, *Evaluation*, for the purpose of comparison. This activity consists of assigning a degree of agreement with the satisfaction score obtained for each intentional element. In order to do this, the stakeholders must compare the satisfaction of each intentional element with that of the rest of its elements, evaluating whether or not they are satisfied with the result.

For example, in the Fig. 1 the intentional element T.G1 (Provide course) has been evaluated as "Strongly Agree" because it is the most important intentional element for that actor (importance = 100) and, in turn, it is also the one that provides the most satisfaction (15.94). However, if there were another intentional element that provided

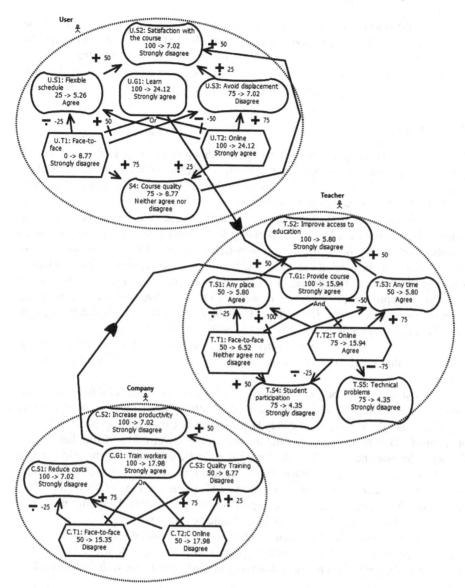

Fig. 1. Analysis result of a participant using the edX system with the GRL-Quant technique from [6].

more satisfaction than T.G1, the stakeholder might not be satisfied with this satisfaction and their evaluation of it would be different.

Figure 1 shows an analysis result obtained for the GRL-Quant technique by a participant in one of the systems used in the experiment. The number on the left-hand side of the arrow is the assigned importance, while the number on the right-hand side is the calculated satisfaction score. This score represents the satisfaction of the stakeholder with the result obtained by applying GRL-Quant. The text that appears below it is the result of the evaluation phase, i.e., the perceived satisfaction assigned by the participant to each intentional element, whose values can be one of the following: Strongly agree, Agree, Neither agree nor disagree, Disagree or Strongly disagree.

3.2 VeGAn

VeGAn (Value-based goal-oriented analysis technique) [7] is a goal-oriented analysis technique based on propagation and Fuzzy Multiple-Criteria Decision-Making (FMCDM) whose goal to calculate how valuable each intentional element of a goal model is. This technique has three activities.

The *Prioritization* is the first activity of the technique and consists of each of the stakeholders assigning a level of importance and a level of confidence to each of its intentional elements. While the level of importance represents how important an intentional element is, the level of confidence represents the confidence regarding the importance assigned to the intentional element prioritized. Because this technique uses a fuzzy logic approach, prioritization is similar to a qualitative scale. The scale of the level of importance is *Very High, High, Medium, Low and Very Low*, and the scale of the level of confidence is *Possibly More, Confident and Possibly Less*.

The *Propagation* is the second activity of the technique and its objective is to calculate the value provided by each intentional element. This activity consists of four tasks.

The first task of the propagation is the *Fuzzification of actors and intentional elements*, where the importance level is fuzzified, transformed to a fuzzy number (range of possible values). For example, the Very Hight importance level corresponds to the fuzzy number of (80, 100) meaning that the importance is between 80 and 100, but without knowing the exact number. Then the confidence level assigned during the prioritization activity is used to reduce the uncertainty (the range of possible values) of the importance level by means of polarization with the LSP (Logic Scoring of Preference) [11] technique. For example, the level of importance Very High (80, 100) after polarizing with the level of confidence Possibly More would be (90, 100).

The second task of the propagation is the *Link propagation*, where the impact (influence) that an intentional element has on the rest of the intentional elements is calculated. This task is similar to the propagation activity of GRL-Quant, but with different rules:

– Decomposition links: The impact of the intentional element is distributed between the intentional element that is composed, taking into account its weight for the intentional element that is decomposed. Furthermore, the impact of the intentional elements of an AND decomposition is propagated to the intentional element that is composed. If the decomposition is of type OR or XOR, only the impact of the most valuable child will be obtained.
– Contribution links: The impact of the intentional element that contributes is the impact of the element contributed multiplied by the weight of the contribution divided by 100.

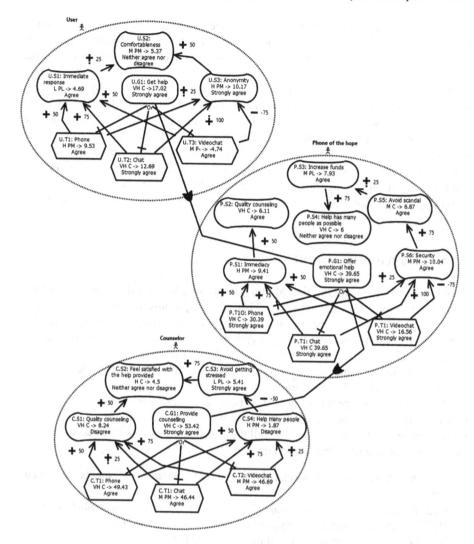

Fig. 2. Analysis result of a participant using the Hope system with the VeGAn technique from [6].

- Dependency links: The impact the of intentional element depended on has the maximum impact on the element that depends.

The third task of the propagation is the *Fuzzification of propagation*, where the impact calculated in the previous task is fuzzified.

The fourth task of the propagation is *FTOPSIS*, where the FTOPSIS (Fuzzy Technique of Order Preference Similarity to the Ideal Solution) [8] technique is employed to calculate the value of each intentional element. FTOPSIS takes as input the importance of the intentional elements (calculated in the first task of the propagation) and the relationship between the intentional elements (calculated in tasks 3 of the propagation).

The evaluation is the third activity of the technique and consists of assigning a degree of agreement with the value obtained for each intentional element. This activity can help detect problems in the prioritization of intentional elements, in the weights that the different links of the goal models may have, or in the propagation activity.

Figure 2 shows an analysis result obtained for the VeGAn technique by a participant in one of the systems of the experiment. The codes on the left-hand side of the arrow are the acronyms of the assigned importance level (i.e., VH, H, M, L, VL) and confidence level (i.e., PM, C, PL) while the number on the right-hand side of the arrow is the calculated value. For example, "VH C -> 6" from the intentional element P.S4 means that this element has a Very High level of importance, a Confident level of confidence and a calculated value of 6. The text that appears below it is the result of the evaluation phase (e.g., the perceived satisfaction assigned by the participant to the P.S4 element is "Neither agree nor disagree").

4   Controlled Experiment

On the basis of the Goal-Question-Metric (GQM) template [4], the goal of the experiment is to analyze GRL-Quant and VeGAn for the purpose of assessing them with respect to the accuracy of the prioritization (i.e., prioritization accuracy), the participants' prioritization time, and their perceptions regarding the quality of the analysis results (perceived satisfaction), perceived ease of use, perceived usefulness, and intention to use from the point of view of novice software engineers in the context of Computer Science undergraduate students.

We focused on the profile of novice software engineers, despite the fact that experienced analysts and practitioners would have been preferred because our goal was to get preliminary understanding of how well these techniques may help decision-making. The research questions addressed were:

- RQ1: Which technique allows analysts to prioritize intentional elements more accurately?
- RQ2: Which technique allows analysts to prioritize intentional elements faster?
- RQ3: Which technique is perceived to provide better analysis results?
- RQ4: Which technique is perceived to be easier to use?
- RQ5: Which technique is perceived to be more useful?
- RQ6: Which technique is most intended to be used in the future?

4.1   Context Selection

The context of this study is the analysis of two goal models through goal-oriented analysis techniques by novice software engineers. The context is defined by the goal-oriented analysis technique selected, the experimental objects (i.e., goal models to be analyzed), and the selection of participants.

Experimental Objects: Two experimental objects were selected from the following two goal models in literature [17, 19]:

- O1 - Hope: The system's goal is to provide users with an online counseling service for those who are experiencing a crisis. This system is shown in Fig. 2.
- O2 - edX: The system's goal is to provide an online education platform that facilitates access to education. This system is shown in Fig. 1.

Selection of Participants: The participants comprised 64 Computer Science undergraduate students at the Universitat Politècnica de València. The experiment was a class exercise on a Requirements Engineering course, which included an introduction to the GRL-Quant and VeGAn techniques. The participants had no previous experience of goal models and goal-oriented analysis before attending this course. We verified this assumption by means of a pre-questionnaire intended to determine the respondents' demographics and experience with goal models and goal-oriented analysis. All the participants were volunteers and were aware of the practical and pedagogical purposes of the experiment, but the research questions were not disclosed to them. The participants were not rewarded for their effort.

4.2   Variable Selection

The main independent variable (or factor) was the goal-oriented analysis technique, which was a nominal variable that could assume two possible values: GRL-Quant and VeGAn. The secondary independent variable (or cofactor) was the experimental object, which had two possible values: Hope and edX.

There are two types of dependent variables: performance-based and perception-based variables. Performance-based variables assess how well participants perform the experimental task. In our case, these variables were: prioritization accuracy and prioritization time.

The **Prioritization Accuracy (PA)** variable was used to measure the completeness (if all the intentional elements were prioritized) and correctness (if the importance conforms to the expected importance). This variable was measured by using an information retrieval-based approach [13] that has previously been utilized in other SE experiments [1, 2, 22, 23] to compare models with a Golden Solution (i.e., the correct set of relative importance assigned by a domain expert) regarding each intentional element. One of the materials provided to the participants was an Annex with a description of Personas [9] (one for each stakeholder of each system) to assist the participants in assigning the relative importance to the elements in the goal model, so that the assignment was not so subjective. As an example, if the behavioral pattern of a Persona suggests that the stakeholder is *shy*, when the participant assigns a relative importance to an intentional element such as "anonymity", an importance of 100 or 75 (GRL-Quant), or Very High/High (VeGAn) should be assigned.

We, therefore, used the harmonic mean of recall and precision, attaining a balance between the completeness and correctness of the importance assigned to each intentional element within a goal model by employing the following equation:

$$\text{F-measure}_e = \frac{|P_{element} \bigcap GS_{element}|}{|P_{element}|} \qquad (1)$$

where $P_{element}$ indicates assigned importance elements of a given goal model by a participant and $GS_{element}$ indicates the known correct set of expected importance assigned that can be easily derived by means of a Golden Solution. Since the golden solution for both GRL-Quant and VeGAn might have been biased by the expert's experience and the elements of a goal model can have several prioritization solutions, we considered only these first solutions as a baseline, which could evolve if the participants added new correct solutions.

The **Prioritization Time (PT)** variable was measured as the total time (in minutes) taken by a participant to prioritize (assign importance assign importance (and confidence in the case of VeGAn)) to all the intentional elements of the goal model.

Perceived-based variables assess how well the participants perceived the goal-oriented analysis technique used. In our case, these variables were: Perceived Satisfaction (PS), Perceived Ease of Use (PEOU), Perceived Usefulness (PU) and Intention To Use (ITU).

The **Perceived Satisfaction (PS)** measured how satisfied the participant was with the analysis results obtained after using the technique. The participant, therefore, had to evaluate the propagation result obtained for each intentional element by using a 5-point Likert scale, ranging from 1 (strongly disagree) to 5 (strongly agree).

The remaining perception-based variables were based on the Technology Acceptance Model (TAM) [10], which is a widely applied and empirically validated model:

- **Perceived Ease of Use (PEOU):** the degree to which analysts believe that using a goal-oriented analysis technique will be effort-free.
- **Perceived Usefulness (PU):** the degree to which analysts believe that using a specific goal-oriented analysis technique will increase their job performance within an organizational context.
- **Intention To Use (ITU):** the degree to which analysts have the intention to use a specific goal-oriented analysis technique in the future.

Table 1 shows the items defined to measure the perception-based variables of PEOU, PU and ITU. These three variables were measured by using a Likert scale survey with a

Table 1. Items in the survey.

Item	Item Statement
PEOU1	I found the goal-oriented analysis technique simple and easy to follow
PEOU2	The goal-oriented analysis technique is easy to learn
PEOU3	I think becoming skillful at using this goal-oriented analysis technique is easy
PEOU4	It was easy for me to remember how to analyze a goal model with this technique
PU1	I found this goal-oriented analysis technique useful
PU2	I believe this goal-oriented technique would reduce the time and effort required to analyze a goal model
PU3	I believe that this goal-oriented analysis technique has the mechanisms required to analyze goal models
PU4	I believe that the results obtained with this technique are clear, concise and unambiguous
ITU1	If I have to use a goal-oriented analysis technique in the future, I think I will consider this technique
ITU2	I would recommend using this goal-oriented analysis technique

set of closed and open questions. The aggregated value of each subjective variable was calculated as the mean of the answers to the variable-related questions.

4.3 Hypotheses

The null hypotheses of the experiment can be summarized as follows:

- $H1_0$: PA (GRL-Quant) = PA (VeGAn)
- $H2_0$: PT (GRL-Quant) = PT (VeGAn)
- $H3_0$: PS (GRL-Quant) = PS (VeGAn)
- $H4_0$: PEOU (GRL-Quant) = PEOU (VeGAn)
- $H5_0$: PU (GRL-Quant) = PU (VeGAn)
- $H6_0$: ITU (GRL-Quant) = ITU (VeGAn)

The goal of the statistical analysis was to reject these hypotheses and possibly accept the alternative ones (e.g., $H1_1 = ñH1_0$). All the hypotheses are two-sided because we did not postulate that any effect would occur as a result of the use of these goal-oriented analysis techniques.

4.4 Experimental Design and Task

The experiment was planned as a between-subjects with a confounding effect, i.e., each participant was assigned a single treatment. One treatment was created for each combination of goal-oriented analysis technique (GRL-Quant, VeGAn) and system (O1, O2), so there are four different treatments. To reduce the domain/system effect, two experimental objects were employed. Since none of the participants repeated any goal-oriented analysis technique or system while conducting the experiment, the design adopted reduced potential learning effects. Table 2 shows the experimental design.

Table 2. Experimental design from [6].

	Run 1 (Control group)	Run 1 (Experimental group)
Treatment	GRL-Quant, Hope	VeGAn, Hope
	GRL-Quant, edX	VeGAn, edX

Prior to the experiment, the participants attended a training session concerning the use of the goal-oriented analysis techniques and performed an exercise. During the experiment, the participants were asked to carry out the experimental task and no time limit was imposed. The tasks to be carried out for both techniques were the following:

1. **Goal Model Understanding:** The participants had to read a description of a goal model and answer a set of control questions. These questions helped the participants to focus on understanding the goal model and the analysis techniques and allowed us to control their comprehension of the problem. These questions did not influence the execution of the experiment or the results.

2. **Intentional Element Prioritization:** The participants had to assign an importance level to each intentional element of the goal model. To do this, the participant had to understand the needs and goals of the stakeholders, through the use of the Persona technique [9], and prioritize the intentional elements. This task made it possible to obtain information about the PA and PT variables.

3. **Goal-oriented Analysis:** The participants used an Excel file with macros that automated the calculation of satisfaction / value of each intentional element, given the level of importance (and confidence in the case of VeGAn).

4. **Evaluation:** The participants evaluated the analysis results obtained using the technique by assigning a degree of agreement with the results obtained to each intentional element of the model. As in the prioritization task, the participants had to use the Persona technique to understand the stakeholders' needs and goals. This task made it possible to obtain information about the PS variable.

5. **Questionnaire:** The participants had to fill in an online survey concerning their perceptions of the goal-oriented analysis technique they had used. This task collected information related to the PEOU, PU and ITU variables.

The documents supporting the experimental task training included:

- Four types of booklets addressing the four possible combinations of both goal-oriented analysis techniques and experimental objects (GRL-Quant-O1, GRL-Quant-O2, VeGAn-O1, VeGAn-O2). The description of the experimental task was outlined in these booklets.
- Two appendices that provide a thorough explanation of each goal-oriented analysis technique.
- One appendix containing the Personas used to describe each stakeholder and assist participants to understanding their requirements, goals and points of view.
- Four Excel files containing macros that cover the four combinations of both goal-oriented analysis techniques and experimental objects, allowing the propagation of both techniques to be automated.
- A post-task experimental questionnaire with closed and open questions that would allow the participants to express their opinion of the ease of use and usefulness of the technique, and their intention to use that technique in the future. We also included two open questions in order to obtain the participants' feedback as regards the changes that they would make in order to improve the techniques and their reasons for using a particular technique in the future.

The experiment materials, including the survey questionnaire, are available at https://doi.org/10.5281/zenodo.7185125. The material is in Spanish, which is the mother tongue of the participants in the experiment.

4.5 Data Analysis

The results were collected using the booklets (in order to ascertain the time needed to prioritize (PT)), the Excel files provided (in order to discover the prioritization accuracy (PA) and perceived satisfaction (PS)), and the questionnaire (in order to obtain PEOU, PU and ITU). We used descriptive analysis, violin plots and statistical tests to analyze the data collected from the experiment. As is usual, in all the tests, we accepted a probability of 5% of committing a Type-I error, i.e., rejecting the null hypothesis when it is actually true.

The data analysis was carried out by employing the following steps:

1. We first carried out a descriptive study of the measures for the dependent variables.
2. We analyzed the characteristics of the data in order to determine which test would be most appropriate to test our hypotheses. Since the sample size of the experiment was less than 50, we applied the Shapiro-Wilk and Brown-Forsythe Levene-type tests in order to verify the normality and homogeneity of the data.
3. We analyzed whether there was any interaction between the independent variables. We used ANOVA when the data was normally distributed and the variances were homogeneous, and the Kruskal-Wallis test when the ANOVA assumptions were not met.
4. This depended on the results of step 3:
   - When an interaction was detected, we performed a post-hoc analysis to determine which treatments were significant. A Mann-Whitney test or a t-test was used for this purpose, depending on the normality of the data distribution.
   - When an interaction between the independent variables was not detected, we combined the data and compared the treatments by using a two-way ANOVA or the Mann-Whitney test (when the ANOVA assumptions were not met).

5   Results

In this section, we discuss the experimental results by quantitatively analyzing the data according to the hypotheses stated. The results were obtained by using SPSS v20 and R v4.0.1. A qualitative analysis based on the feedback obtained from the open questions of the post-task questionnaire is also provided.

5.1   Descriptive Statistics and Exploratory Analysis

Table 3 summarizes the results of the goal model analysis task performed, divided by Technique and System, as well as the results of the technique regardless of the system in the *All* row. The table shows that when the participants prioritized the edX system they had more accuracy with the GRL-Quant technique. However, the results of the VeGAn technique were perceived more satisfactory (PS) than those of GRL-Quant. In addition, the participants had more intention to use (ITU) the VeGAn technique than the GRL-Quantitative. With respect to the remaining variables (PT, PEOU and PU), there are no differences between the techniques or the systems. The overall comparison of the two techniques without splitting by system is visually represented in Fig. 3, Fig. 4, and Fig. 5 by means of violin plots.

The visual representation of the variable Prioritization Accuracy (PA) shown in Fig. 3 suggests that there is a difference between both techniques in favor of GRL-Quant, but the Table 3 suggests that this only happens when analyzing the edX system since the mean of GRL-Quant is 74 and that of VeGAn 59.2. Regarding the variable Prioritization Time (PT) the data suggest that both techniques are similar, since the mean

Table 3. Summary of descriptive analysis grouped by technique extended from [6].

Variable	Technique	System	Mean	Median	Standard Deviation
PA	GRL-Quant	Hope	62.2	64	7.44
		edX	74.5	76	9.17
		All	68.4	67	10.3
	VeGAn	Hope	59	58	9.10
		edX	58.9	59	7.41
		All	59.2	58.5	8.17
PT	GRL-Quant	Hope	17.1	15.5	7.72
		edX	16.2	16	7.39
		All	17	16	7.47
	VeGAn	Hope	18.6	18.5	5.23
		edX	17.3	17	6.45
		All	18	18	5.85
PS	GRL-Quant	Hope	3.38	3.52	0.41
		edX	3.39	3.30	0.37
		All	3.38	3.45	0.38
	VeGAn	Hope	3.69	3.86	0.51
		edX	3.64	3.85	0.56
		All	3.71	3.86	0.48
PEOU	GRL-Quant	Hope	4.31	4.50	0.67
		edX	3.78	4.12	0.97
		All	4.04	4.37	0.86
	VeGAn	Hope	4.32	4.25	0.35
		edX	4.1	4.25	0.60
		All	4.16	4.25	0.56
PU	GRL-Quant	Hope	3.66	3.68	0.61
		edX	3.51	3.75	0.76
		All	3.58	3.75	0.68
	VeGAn	Hope	3.84	3.75	0.49
		edX	3.56	3.62	0.76
		All	3.66	3.75	0.81
ITU	GRL-Quant	Hope	3.51	3.50	0.81
		edX	3.37	3.50	1.05
		All	3.44	3.5	0.93
	VeGAn	Hope	3.90	4.00	0.55
		edX	3.75	4.00	0.70
		All	3.76	4.00	0.80

of GRL-Quant is 17 and that of VeGAn is 18. The practical meaning of this is that the participants prioritizing accuracy was higher when analyzing the edX system with the GRL-Quant technique, but the time spent by the participants when prioritizing was similar.

With regard to the participants' Perceived Satisfaction (PS) and Perceived Ease of Use (PEOU), Fig. 4 and Table 3 suggest that there is a difference in the PS variable in favour of VeGAn, since the means are 3.38 and 3.71 for GRL-Quant and VeGAn, respectively, but there is no difference in the PEOU variable, since the means are 4.04

and 4.16, respectively. These results indicate that the perceived satisfaction was higher for VeGAn but the perceived ease of use was similar when using both techniques.

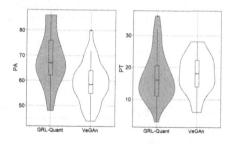

Fig. 3. Violin plot of PA and PT variables split by technique from [6].

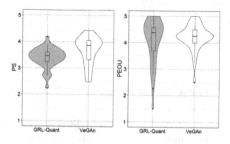

Fig. 4. Violin plot of PS and PEOU variables split by technique extended from [6].

With regard to the participants' Perceived Usefulness (PU) and Intention To Use (ITU), Fig. 5 and Table 3 suggest that there is no difference in the PU variable, since the means are 3.58 and 3.75 for GRL-Quant and VeGAn, respectively, but there is a difference in the ITU variable in favour of VeGAn, since the means are 3.44 and 3.76, respectively. These results indicate that the perception on usefulness in both techniques were similar but the intention to use of VeGAn was higher.

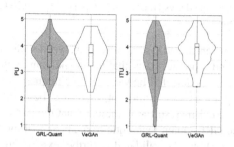

Fig. 5. Violin plot of PU and ITU variables split by technique.

5.2   Hypotheses Testing

Table 4 shows the results obtained after testing the effects of the technique, system, and their interactions for the Prioritization Accuracy (PA), Prioritization Time (PT) Perceived Satisfaction (PS), Perceived Ease of Use (PEOU), Perceived Usefulness (PU) and Intention To Use (ITU).

Table 4. Summary of statistics for the dataset extended from [6].

Variable	Interaction	Technique	In favor of	System	In favor of
PA	0.000 *	0.000 #	GRL-Quant	0.203 #	-
PT	0.970 $	0.557 $	-	0.399 $	-
PS	0.009 *	0.000 #	VeGAn	0.973 #	-
PEOU	0.371 *	0.935 #	-	0.111 #	-
PU	0.716 *	0.588 #	-	0.424 #	-
ITU	0.386 *	0.091 #	-	0.826 #	-

$ ANOVA; *Kruskal-Wallis; # Mann-Whitney

Testing Prioritization Accuracy. In order to analyze the PA variable a post-hoc analysis was required because the Kruskal-Wallis test detected an interaction between the system and the technique (p-value = 0.000). The post-hoc analysis shown in Table 5 detects two interactions, both interactions happens when the edX system is analyzed with the GRL-Quant technique.

Table 5. Test results for the post-hoc analysis for PA from [6].

Interaction	Combination	p-value	In favor of
Technique over System	GRL-Quant vs VeGAn with edX	0.000 #	GRL-Quant
	GRL-Quant vs VeGAn with Hope	0.357 $	-
System over Technique	edX vs Hope with GRL-Quant	0.001 #	edX
	edX vs Hope with VeGAn	0.264 $	-

$ ANOVA; # Mann-Whitney

Table 3 shows that when the edX system was analyzed with the GRL-Quant technique the participants had more accuracy that when analyzing with VeGAn. However, no significant difference was detected between the techniques when system Hope was analyzed. The null hypothesis $H1_0$ could not, therefore, be rejected except when the edX system was analyzed. This result may indicate that the participants' accuracy was greater when using the GRL-Quant technique to analyze goal models of domains like edX, but this assumption should be validated in further experiments.

These findings might be explained to the fact that both techniques prioritize in different ways. While VeGAn uses a qualitative scale (Very High, High, Medium, Low, Very Low, Very Low), GRL-Quant employs a quantitative scale (from 0 to 100).

Testing Prioritization Time. Since an interaction between system and technique was not detected by the ANOVA analysis (p-value = 0.970), it is not necessary to carry out a post-hoc analysis. In addition, the analysis also does not detect a significant difference between the technique and the system. The null hypothesis $H2_0$ could not consequently be rejected, since the time taken by the participants to prioritize was similar when using both techniques. These findings might be explained by the fact that the prioritization of both techniques is quite similar and that the difference between them does not affect the time required to prioritize.

Testing Perceived Satisfaction. In order to analyze the PA variable a post-hoc analysis was required because the Kruskal-Wallis test detected an interaction between the system and the technique (p-value = 0.009). The post-hoc analysis shown in Table 6 detects two interactions in favour of VeGAn. The null hypothesis $H3_0$ could consequently be rejected in favor of VeGAn, since both interactions show that the participants perceived the analysis results obtained by the VeGAn technique to be more satisfactory, regardless of the system. These findings might be explained by the fact that both techniques analyze differently, as show in Sect. 3.

Table 6. Test results for the post-hoc analysis for PS from [6].

Interaction	Combination	p-value	In favor of
Technique over System	GRL-Quant vs VeGAn with edX	0.027 $	VeGAn
	GRL-Quant vs VeGAn with Hope	0.014 #	VeGAn
System over Technique	edX vs Hope with GRL-Quant	0.663 #	-
	edX vs Hope with VeGAn	0.850 #	-

$ ANOVA; # Mann-Whitney

One of the possible reasons for this is that the techniques analyze differently, and that VeGAn takes more factors into account such as the importance of the stakeholders or their confidence level as regards the assigned relative importance.

Testing Perceived Ease of Use, Perceived Usefulness and Intention to Use. The Kruskal-Wallis test performed did not detect an interaction between technique and system for the variable PEOU (p-value = 0.371), PU (p-value = 0.716) or ITU (p-value = 0.386). Furthermore, no significant difference was detected for the technique used as regards the variables PEOU (p-value = 0.935), PU (p-value = 0.588), ITU (p-value = 0.091), or for the system as regards the variables PEOU (p-value = 0.111), PU (p-value = 0.424) and ITU (p-value = 0.826). The null hypotheses $H4_0$, $H5_0$, $H6_0$ could not, therefore, be rejected since the difference between both techniques in terms of PEOU, PU and ITU was not statistically significant. The practical meaning of this is that the participants' perceptions of the perceived ease of use of, the perceived usefulness of and intention to use both techniques were similar to those shown in the violin plots depicted in Figs. 4 and 5.

The analysis of the answers to the open questions in the post-experiment questionnaire revealed that the participants had some difficulties when using both techniques with the Excel files provided. For example, participant ID23 said that *"During the evaluation, I would have liked to know the range of results in order to avoid ambiguities."* while participant ID58 said that *"The interface used to assign the importances could be improved."*.

The analysis also showed that the participants found both techniques to be useful. For example, participant ID44 said *"I find this model analysis technique very useful because it does not take a lot of knowledge to use it which makes it very suitable for all types of people."*. Finally, the analysis also showed that the participants intended to use both techniques. For example, participant ID29 said *"I intend to use it since I have found it very comfortable to use."* while participant ID48 said that *"I think I would use it because it is easy to learn and use, and the results obtained are clear."*

5.3   Summary of the Results

A summary of the results obtained is provided in Table 7. The most prominent result is that the participants perceived the analysis results obtained by VeGAn to be more satisfactory.

Table 7. Summary of results extended from [6].

Hypotheses	Status	In favor of
$H1_0$: PA	Could not be rejected*	GRL-Quant analyzing edX
$H2_0$: PT	Could not be rejected	-
$H3_0$: PS	Rejected	VeGAn
$H4_0$: PEOU	Could not be rejected	-
$H5_0$: PU	Could not be rejected	-
$H6_0$: ITU	Could not be rejected	-

Although there are some interaction effects between technique and system that affect the prioritization accuracy (PA) variable, these interactions only occur when the GRL-Quant technique is used to analyze the edX system. Nevertheless, hypothesis $H1_0$ could not be rejected because when we compared the prioritization accuracy of the techniques regarding the analysis of the Hope system no significant difference was detected. However, the results have shown that there is not a statistically significant difference between the two techniques, and that the participants had greater accuracy when using the quantitative scale of GRL-Quant for analyzing the edX system. Overall, these results may suggest that the qualitative scale of the VeGAn technique can be improved by experimenting with different ranges of the scale.

With regard to the prioritization time (PT), the results show that there is neither an interaction effect nor a difference in means between technique and system for this variable. In addition, no effect of system was found. Therefore, hypothesis H20 could not be rejected as no significant difference was detected between the time taken by the participants to prioritize.

Regarding the participants' perception of the satisfaction (PS) with the results, we found an interaction effect between the technique and the system, but this interaction occurred for all the combinations of technique over the system. The practical meaning is that there is a significant difference between the techniques regardless of the system, but that there is no significant difference between the systems. Therefore, hypothesis $H3_0$ could be rejected in favor of VeGAn since a significant difference was detected between the participants' perceptions in terms of their satisfaction with the analysis results. These results may suggest that the propagation phase of VeGAn which is based on a fuzzy logic approach that works with range of values obtain better analysis results than the GRL-Quant technique that is based on values.

With regard to the to the participants' perception of ease of use (PEOU), participants' perceptions of usefulness (PU) and participants' intention to use (ITU), the results show that there is neither an interaction effect nor a difference in means between technique and system for this variable. Hypotheses $H4_0$, $H5_0$, $H6_0$ could not, therefore, be rejected, as no significant difference was detected as regards the time taken by the participants to prioritize.

6   Threats to Validity

In this section, we discuss some of the issues that might have threatened the validity of this experiment.

Regarding the internal validity the design of the experiment helped mitigate the learning effect, since each participant used only one goal-oriented analysis technique. In addition, none of the participants had prior experience of goal-oriented analysis techniques. The exchange of information between the participants was avoided by using two different experimental objects and monitoring the participants during the experiment. The understandability of the materials was assessed by conducting a pilot study.

Regarding the external validity the representativeness of the results could have been affected by the experimental objects used, the context and the participants selected. The experimental task can be considered realistic for small-sized projects, and they are not trivial. The experiment was conducted with students with no experience in goal-oriented analysis techniques who received only limited training in the techniques. However, their profile was not very different to that of junior software analysts. Experiments in industrial contexts are, therefore, required in order to increase our awareness as regards these results.

With regard to the measures used to quantify the dependent variables, the prioritization accuracy (PA) was measured using an information retrieval-based approach together with the Persona [9] technique in order to avoid any subjective evaluation.

In the case of the prioritization time (PT), we asked the participants to write down their starting and finishing times when they accomplished the prioritization time. The supervisors validated this information. The subjective variables are based on TAM [10].

The main threat is the validity of the statistical tests applied. This threat was alleviated by using commonly accepted tests employed in the empirical SE community [21], but more replications are needed in order to confirm these results. These results could be owing to the fact that GRL-Quant and VeGAn calculate the results differently and that VeGAn takes more factors into account, such as the importance of the stakeholders or confidence with the assigned importance. The reliability of the questionnaire as regards assessing the subjective variables was tested using the Cronbach's alpha test. For the experiment, questions related to PEOU, PU and ITU obtained a Cronbach's α coefficient of 0.696, 0.789 and 0.756, Most of the results were higher than the threshold level (0.70) [21]. In addition, as indicated by Loewenthal [20], the α coefficient of 0.6 could be acceptable if the objective is scale development.

7   Conclusions

The results of the experiment suggest that both techniques (GRL-Quant and VeGAn) are very similar, since no significant differences could be found in Prioritization Time (PT), Perceived Ease of Use (PEOU), Perceived Usefulness (PU), and Intention To Use (ITU), that is, four of the 6 variables analyzed. Regarding the Prioritization Accuracy (PA) variable, an unexpected result has been obtained since an interaction has been detected when GRL-Quant was used on the edX system. We did not anticipate this interaction, since we expected VeGAn to have greater prioritization accuracy owing to the scale it uses (qualitative), which is closer to natural language. We shall further investigate this result in order to understand the reasons behind it and to improve VeGAn. With respect to the Perceived Satisfaction (PS) variable, the results show that the participants perceived the results of VeGAn more satisfactorily than those of GRL-Quant.

From a research perspective, these results may be of interest since we compared the accuracy of the prioritization of intentional elements and perceived satisfaction when using a technique based on a quantitative propagation (i.e., GRL-Quant) or a technique based on a qualitative propagation with fuzzy multiple-criteria decision-making (i.e., VeGAn). Moreover, the participants' use of the Persona [9] technique helped them understand better the stakeholders' point of view. In this way, the participants could be considered as surrogates for actual stakeholders when performing these kind of studies. Of course, if the VeGAn or GRL-Quant technique are used in a context with practitioners and customers, the prioritization should be performed by the actual stakeholders, and we would also need to study how the technique behaves in this scenario.

As future work, we plan to implement a tool that will provide technological support to the VeGAn technique. Given the high number and complexity of calculations, we consider that this tool will potentially make it possible to reach a large number of users of goal models interested in a value-driven analysis of their models. We additionally plan to carry out replications of this experiment in order to be able to verify and generalize the results obtained. Finally, we also plan to compare VeGAn with other goal-oriented analysis techniques in order to see whether or not there are significant differences among them.

Acknowledgements. This work was supported by the grant TIN2017-84550-R (Adapt@Cloud project) funded by MCIN/AEI/10.13039/501100011033 and the "Programa de Ayudas de Investigación y Desarrollo" (PAID-01-17) from the Universitat Politècnica de València.

References

1. Abrahão, S., Gravino, C., Insfran, E., Scanniello, G., Tortora, G.: Assessing the effectiveness of sequence diagrams in the comprehension of functional requirements: results from a family of five experiments. IEEE Trans. Software Eng. **39**(3), 327–342 (2012). https://doi.org/10.1109/TSE.2012.27

2. Abrahão, S., Insfran, E., Gonzalez-Ladron-de Guevara, F., Fernandez-Diego, M., Cano-Genoves, C., de Oliveira, R.P.: Assessing the effectiveness of goal-oriented modeling languages: a family of experiments. Inf. Softw. Technol. **116**, 106171 (2019). https://doi.org/10.1016/j.infsof.2019.08.003

3. Amyot, D., Ghanavati, S., Horkoff, J., Mussbacher, G., Peyton, L., Yu, E.: Evaluating goal models within the goal-oriented requirement language. Int. J. Intell. Syst. **25**(8), 841–877 (2010). https://doi.org/10.1002/int.20433

4. Van Solingen, R., Basili, V., Caldiera, G., Rombach, H.D.: Goal Question Metric (GQM) approach. Encycl. Softw. Eng. (2002). Wiley. ISBN: 9780471028956. https://doi.org/10.1002/0471028959.sof142

5. Boehm, B.W.: Value-based software engineering: overview and agenda. Value-based Software Engineering, pp. 3–14 (2006)

6. Cano-Genoves, C., Abrahão, S., Insfran, E.: Experimental comparison of two goal-oriented analysis techniques. In: 10th International Conference on Model-Driven Engineering and Software Development, MODELSWARD 2022, pp. 242–251. SCITEPRESS (2022). https://doi.org/10.5220/0010847000003119

7. Cano-Genoves, C., Insfran, E., Abrahão, S., Fernandez-Diego, M., González-L.G., F.: A value-based approach for reasoning with goal models. In: ISD2019 (2019)

8. Chen, C.T.: Extensions of the TOPSIS for group decision-making under fuzzy environment. Fuzzy Sets Syst. **114**(1), 1–9 (2000). https://doi.org/10.1016/S0165-0114(97)00377-1

9. Cooper, A.: The inmates are running the Asylum. In: Arend, U., Eberleh, E., Pitschke, K. (eds.) Software-Ergonomie 1999. Berichte des German Chapter of the ACM, vol. 53. Vieweg+Teubner Verlag, Wiesbaden (1999). https://doi.org/10.1007/978-3-322-99786-9_1

10. Davis, F.D.: Perceived usefulness, perceived ease of use, and user acceptance of information technology. MIS quarterly, pp. 319–340 (1989). https://doi.org/10.2307/249008

11. Dujmovic, J.J., Nagashima, H.: LSP method and its use for evaluation of java ides. Int. J. Approx. Reason. **41**(1), 3–22 (2006). https://doi.org/10.1016/j.ijar.2005.06.006

12. Ernst, N.A., Mylopoulos, J., Wang, Y.: Requirements evolution and what (research) to do about it. In: Lyytinen, K., Loucopoulos, P., Mylopoulos, J., Robinson, B. (eds.) Design Requirements Engineering: A Ten-Year Perspective. LNBIP, vol. 14, pp. 186–214. Springer, Heidelberg (2009). https://doi.org/10.1007/978-3-540-92966-6_11

13. Frakes, W.B., Baeza-Yates, R.: Information retrieval: data structures and algorithms. Prentice-Hall, Inc. (1992). https://doi.org/10.5555/129687

14. Horkoff, J., Yu, E.: Interactive analysis of agent-goal models in enterprise modeling. Int. J. Inf. Syst. Model. Design (IJISMD) **1**(4), 1–23 (2010). https://doi.org/10.4018/jismd.2010100101

15. Horkoff, J., Yu, E.: Analyzing goal models: different approaches and how to choose among them. In: Proceedings of the 2011 ACM Symposium on Applied Computing, pp. 675–682 (2011). https://doi.org/10.1145/1982185.1982334

16. Horkoff, J., Yu, E.: Comparison and evaluation of goal-oriented satisfaction analysis techniques. Requirements Eng. **18**(3), 199–222 (2013). https://doi.org/10.1007/s00766-011-0143-y

17. Horkoff, J., Yu, E.: Interactive goal model analysis for early requirements engineering. Requirements Eng. **21**(1), 29–61 (2016). https://doi.org/10.1007/s00766-014-0209-8

18. Liaskos, S., Jalman, R., Aranda, J.: On eliciting contribution measures in goal models. In: 2012 20th IEEE International Requirements Engineering Conference (RE), pp. 221–230. IEEE (2012). https://doi.org/10.1109/RE.2012.6345808

19. Liu, L., Yu, E.: Designing information systems in social context: a goal and scenario modelling approach. Inf. Syst. **29**(2), 187–203 (2004). https://doi.org/10.1016/S0306-4379(03)00052-8

20. Loewenthal, K., Lewis, C.A.: An introduction to psychological tests and scales. Psychology Press (2018)

21. Maxwell, K.D.: Applied statistics for software managers. Applied Statistics for Software Managers (2002)

22. Scanniello, G., Erra, U.: Distributed modeling of use case diagrams with a method based on think-pair-square: results from two controlled experiments. J. Vis. Lang. Comput. **25**(4), 494–517 (2014)

23. Souza, E., Moreira, A., Araújo, J., Abrahão, S., Insfran, E., Da Silveira, D.S.: Comparing business value modeling methods: a family of experiments. Inf. Softw. Technol. **104**, 179–193 (2018)

A Methodological Framework for SPL Engineering from DSML

Vincent Englebert(✉) and Maouaheb Belarbi

Faculty of Computer Science, NADI Research Institute, University of Namur,
61 rue de Bruxelles, 5000 Namur, Belgium
{vincent.englebert,maouaheb.belarbi}@unamur.be
http://www.unamur.be/info

Abstract. For the last ten years, Software Product Line (SPL) tool developers have been facing the implementation of different variability requirements and the support of SPL engineering activities demanded by emergent domains. Despite several tools exist, few works resolve SPL process for both problem and solution space. Due to these reasons, we propose a methodological framework that overcomes the limits of existing tools and holds all the phases and activities from the requirement design till the product derivation. We start by using a Domain Specific Modelling Language (DSML) for domain description, which allows system designers working closer to the system domain as they can manipulate real concepts. Thereafter, an intermediate phase converts the DSML metamodel to a tree-structured representation similar to Feature Model (FM) notation enriched with extra-information such that cardinality, attributes, constraints, documentation, etc. The objective of this FM is to be used later as a decision tree to guide the generative process of our software factory in the following way: First, the engineer annotates the variation points with variability types such that *binding time, granularity, evolution,* etc, which are crucial concerns to be considered when generating the products. Second, based upon these annotations, our framework determines the possible useful variability mechanisms that could be employed to implement the product families and the engineers choose the variability programming tactic among them. Finally, the software factory produces the guidelines to implement the realization strategy and derive the related product assets through an assembly process. We provide a real industry running example giving insight into the application of the presented approach.

Keywords: Software product line · Software factory · Variability realization technique

1 Introduction

For most software system companies, large-scale software development is complicated, expensive, slow, and unpredictable [12]. Consequently, many companies are stuck in a fire-fighting mode where the cost of developing new products to rapidly respond to the customer needs is constantly increasing. To cope with the forces described above, many researchers provide a set of work best practices to reach an agreement between

© Springer Nature Switzerland AG 2023
L. F. Pires et al. (Eds.): MODELSWARD 2021/2022, CCIS 1708, pp. 179–202, 2023.
https://doi.org/10.1007/978-3-031-38821-7_9

affording the customer requirements with less development effort and a high quality for each single software element.

In this context, successful introduction of Software Product Line (SPL) paradigm in companies can be a panacea to develop similar software systems corresponding to the same market domain at lower cost, in shorter time, and with higher quality instead of proceeding one by one from scratch [24]. To do so, SPL exploits the commonalities shared by all the products and systematically handles the variation and the different aspects among those systems. In other words, common features become part of each application derived from the product line [11], whereas, variability is the ability of software artefacts to be extended, customized or configured to use in a specific context [18]. Thereby, a selection of features leads to obtain a product that provides not only basic functionality common in most applications of the domain, but also adds in addition to the core assets extra variable characteristics to distinguish it from the other derived products.

In the literature, SPL supporters propose to invest some initial work in providing feature code basis that will be reused later to generate numerous customized products with relatively low effort [1]. The idea behind this involves two different processes melted together in the following way [17]: At first, the domain engineering describes the relevant concepts and features of the target domain presented in domain models as well as the code artefacts that will be reused to derive family products. Second, based on the requirements of a specific user, the construction of a product is performed in the application engineering level where a valid combination of features is selected from the domain models and implemented by reusing domain artefacts. The variable aspects are built on the top of the core code to handle the specificity of each application. All the steps mentioned above are carried out by SPL tools that aim to convert the customer requirements into a useful product by the creation, maintenance and coordination of the different versions of product line artefacts [8]. Hence, as a matter of course, the success of an SPL approach depends on good tool support as much as on complete and integrated SPL engineering processes [3].

Most SPL approaches typically cover the domain and application engineering to help the automation process of all software development phases e.g. analysis, design, implementation and maintenance. Unless, the empirical studies meant to investigate existing SPL tools in the literature has proven that only 6% of them cover both domain and solution space of which FeatureIDE [23] and pure::variants approaches are the most recognized [9]. For instance, these SPL approaches are suitable for modelling basic variability concepts and provide a support to represent mandatory and optional features or to include and exclude basic constraints [8]. Nevertheless, it is difficult to leverage these tools to expose extended variability characteristics such that: attributes and cardinality of the features, binding mode of different aspects of the system, and defining the meta-information given to document the product line and annotate it for a better description. Moreover, some important activities, such as the analysis of non-functional properties (NFPs) or quality attributes and the evolution of SPL's artefacts [14], are set aside from existing SPL approaches. The same could be said for variability analysis, domain implementation, or product derivation. Although SPL tool for the management process is of paramount importance, even the few tools that cover all the product line phase mainly FeatureIDE and pure::variants present additional important limitations. In fact, they demand the adoption of an implementation technique such as feature-oriented programming(FOP) [21], aspect oriented programming (AOP) [16], or annotations [10]. In addition, they depend on the development IDE (e.g., Eclipse) which makes the use of classical SPL approaches a challenging task especially for engineering fields that require the simultaneous use of several programming tactics and languages.

The lack of mature tool support is one of the main reasons that make the industry to be reluctant to adopt SPL approaches [13]. In fact, nowadays existing SPL tools are unfit to generate optimum configurations of products based on some criteria like NFPs [8]. To partly solve these issues, SPL practitioners propose to combine some of the tools [19] or integrate them which is possible to carry out a simple SPL process but still in infancy when dealing with complex product lines. Due to these reasons, we propose a methodological framework that overcomes the limits of existing tools and holds all the phases and activities from the requirement design till the product derivation. This article is an extension of [4] and details the steps of the method as well as the unified metamodel of the different modelling languages used to define the different languages used at each step.

We start by using a Domain Specific Modelling Language (DSML) for domain description, which allows system designers working closer to the system domain as they can manipulate real concepts [15]. Thereafter, an intermediate phase converts the DSML metamodel to a tree-structured representation similar to Feature Model (FM) notation [5] enriched with extra-information such that cardinality, attributes, constraints, documentation, etc. This transformation has already been explained in [4] and this paper resumes its principles. The objective of this FM is to be used later as a decision tree to guide the generative process of our software factory in the following way. First, the engineer annotates the variation points with variability types such that binding time, granularity, evolution, etc, which are crucial concerns to be considered when generating the products. Second, based upon these annotations, our framework determines the possible useful variability mechanisms that could be employed to implement the product families and the engineers choose the variability programming tactic among them. Finally, the software factory produces the guidelines to implement the strategy and derive the product assets. The main characteristics of our framework are: (1) using the DSML allows modelling variability of complex features (e.g., clonable features, variable features, composite features); (2) providing flexibility on the analysis of huge feature models; and (3) implementing final products with a combination of variability realization techniques in a cooperative and coherent way to the engineer requirements. This paper presents the architecture of the proposed framework as well as the process performed from the domain modelling till obtaining the final product assets. A running example is appealed to illustrate the work-flow and the technical details and give insight into the application of our framework.

The rest of the paper is organized as follows: An academic use case is described in Sect. 2 to sketch the different steps involved in our approach. Thereafter, Sect. 3 describes the general framework process. A BPMN diagram is made to illustrate the different steps of the process, each of them being detailed in the Sect. refsec:msf where a discussion is made to give an overview of the most important results found through this contribution. Some of relevant related works are presented in Sect. 6 to motivate our contribution by illustrating the boundaries and the lack of related literature approaches. Moreover, some potential weakness threatening our proposal are identified in Sect. 5 with some attempts to mitigate them. Finally, a conclusion and some of our perspectives are determined in Sect. 7.

2 Running Case Study

The present running example describes a real world case study developed in the context of academic teaching purpose. Thus, the use case we intend to use illustrates both theoretical and practical sides of the approach. As depicted in Fig. 1, the context of the study describes a shopping online domain that ensures the purchasing operation through known online stores such as *Amazing or Fnak* as well as *local* depot. This prototype offers its services to "normal"[1], young actors or to users who suffer from a specific *visual deficiency*. The application will be adapted at execution time to fit the constraints imposed by the user severity of visual impairment. For example, in the case of colourblind actors, the GUI will exclude the invisible colour grades i.e, green, red, yellow, etc. Meanwhile, if the user is presbyopic the interface text font and components(button, list, text-field, etc.) will be increased to adjust the display appropriately to the visual impairment index. The database of the local depot can be stored and accessed via network by renting *cloud* resources or with local database server such that *H2* engine or *MySQL* management systems. The deployment and the use of application can be performed either via web service technology to afford access to internet users either using a standalone version accessible via computer desktop. Finally, a secure payment gateway can be carried out to end the basket shopping experience with following payoff options *PayPal or Visa card* for adult users, otherwise by check gift card.

For comprehensive investigation, the initial decision entailed the selection of online shopping products for normal and disabled users to represent the later PL due to several reasons: In fact, shopping applications raise the domain real relevant challenges. Hence, they present a way to check the usability and credibility of our approach when it crashes into reality. In addition, the case study is relevant for FM context since (i) several variability points are related to heterogeneous concepts of shopping systems and (ii) many alternative and optional functionality exist.

As we have mentioned before, the presented use case will be used later to illustrate the running steps of the process. In the following section, we investigate the set of related work and their limits to pave the way to our proposal.

3 Architecture and Principles of the Bespoke Framework

The Bespoke method gets together both MDE and SPL fields and aims to cover all product generation strategies and to guide the engineer in deriving the final system applications. The aim of the method is to design a software factory and its interest

---

[1] This term should be understood in the sense: a person without specific characteristics/features.

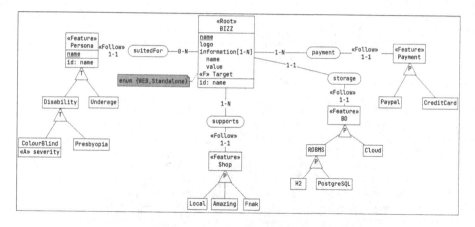

Fig. 1. The DSML metamodel of the shopping application (ER formalism [7]).

consists in providing a methodological accompaniment at each stage, documenting all the points of choice, and automating all the processes that are relevant—the others can remain manual.

The method consists of two steps. The first is to design the plans for the software factory, i.e. an assembly line capable of taking over a particular domain-specific configuration and producing the specific product in a more or less automatic way. The second is to use this factory to generate the products. While the first step is seminal, the second step is intended to be carried out for each customer who wants a customer-specific configuration. The first step guides the second one, but the latter can lead the SPL engineer to refine the first to increase the efficiency of the factory. In short, we will call *SPL Engineer* the person in charge of the first step and *Configuration Engineer* the person in charge of the second one.

Our framework consists of a series of processes (manual, automatic, or semi-automatic) that are all based on a common repository of information related to models, methods, tactics, strategies, assets, and methodological rules. The specification of this repository is shown in Fig. 2 and all the processes of our methodology are detailed in Fig. 3[2]. They will be described in more details in Sect. 4. Here we offer a bird's eye view of the method.

In Fig. 2, pane 1 depicts the metamodel of the FeatAll feature modelling language. The aim here is not to create a new language of features, but simply to have a FM language that is universal enough to be interoperable with other languages or tools such as FeatureIDE [23], Clafer [2] for instance. It was designed for the sole purpose of being a franca lingua. It allows describing features that can be decomposed into different points of variation (Group), themselves being composed of features. A complex feature must include between split-in.min-max groups and a group must include between Group.min-max features to be legal. Thus, the cardinalities $1-1, 1-N$, $N-N$ represent resp. the usual constraints XOR, OR, and AND. The closed=true

---

[2] BPMN is used here for description purposes and not as a prescriptive specification of an automatic process.

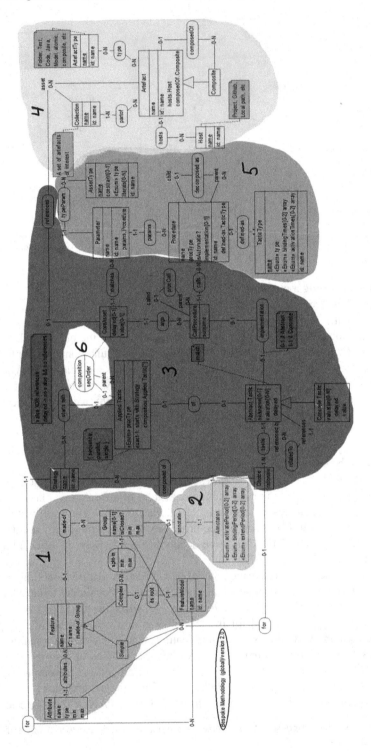

Fig. 2. Structure of the repository (ER formalism [7]). (Color figure online)

attribute means that this variation point is closed and that it will not be possible to add new features to its decomposition during the evolution of the SPL. Features can have attributes. This language has both a graphical and textual concrete syntax.

Pane 2 consists of attributes that specify more specific expectations such as requirements for the Binding Times, Activation Times, etc.

Pane 3 represents the strategies chosen by the SPL engineer to implement a product line guided by a feature model (FM). A strategy is composed of tactics, each of which is associated with a feature or a variation point (Group) with an explicit motivation (Choice.rationale). The association between a choice and a TacticType is achieved through a path Choice ↔ tactic ↔ Abstract Tactic ↔ implementation ↔ CallProcedure that denotes the root procedure of a TacticType. CallProcedure defines the operational nature of the tactic. It calls the root procedure with arguments specifying the assets or any other information useful for the application of the tactic on the project. Procedures can then be called in cascade, either sequentially or concurrently, according to the rules. A procedure can be either a manual task or an automatic process (weaving an aspect, applying a patch, fetching a file, moving a file, replacing text in a file, etc.). Note that more than one strategy can be associated with the same feature model. This makes it possible to consider several competing or candidate strategies for comparison.

Pane 4 describes all the artefacts relevant to the software factory. These can be of any nature: some will be files or folders in the development project, libraries, documentation files, scripts, aspects, etc. These artefacts can on the one hand designate existing elements (such as certain assets), or even fictitious elements representing a certain architectural vision of the computer project. In our repository, Artefacts are organised hierarchically (composedOf), and can be typed by several ArtefactTypes. It is also possible to specify the Host that stores them (Github, a path on a disk, a distribution server…). Collections are used to group artefacts together in an arbitrary way to serve the needs of a tactic.

Pane 5 represents a catalogue of tactic types. A type of tactic consists of an organization of procedures to be invoked on artefacts in order to carry out the transformation of the code necessary to take a feature into account. These types of tactics may either pre-exist the development of the software factory (in which case they are likely to be the result of the company's expertise on other projects of the same nature) or they may be defined in an ad-hoc manner according to the needs of a feature or a point of variation. Procedures take formal Parameters and can be decomposed (association composedOf) into other procedures that fit together as alternatives, in sequence or in parallel (attribute procType). Atomic procedures are either manual or automatic (attribute isAutomatic?). The former will pause the execution of the strategy and prompt the engineer to operate the procedure manually before continuing the execution. Automatic procedures just denote calls to external scripts that will sometimes invoke the weaving of an aspect, sometimes apply a patch, sometimes do a fetch from Github, sometimes copy files from one place to another, etc. These scripts are configured with the arguments passed by the tactic (associations args•matches).

And finally, pane 6 is just composed of a relationship (composition) that represents how the tactics are composed together. That plan is used to coordinate all the tactics inside a strategy.

The next script defines a type of tactic called AOP which consists of a series of calls to the AspectJ weaving tool.

```
// File AOP.tt
new AssetType AspectJFile Filename(*.aj) ;

TacticType "AOP"
    type= "Aspect Oriented Programming";
    bindingTime=compile ;
{   loop procedure aspectJ_weaving(src : Path, aspect :
        AspectJFile, bin : Path );
    proceed;
}
```

This script defines a tactic type, named JDBC, that must be realized at the link binding time. It consists in the parallel execution of 1) a series of calls to a procedure (SubsInFile) to substitute keywords (what) with text (with) in files, and 2) a procedure that will copy files (in a compressed file) to a folder.

```
// File JDBC.tt
new AssetType FileZip Filename(*.zip | *.7zip) ;

TacticType "JDBC"
    bindingTime= link ;
{   procedure parallel Insert
    {   loop procedure SubstInFile(in : File ;
                                   what : String ;
                                   with: String) ;
        procedure AppendProject(where:Directory ;
                what:FileZip) ;
    }
    proceed;
}
```

The proceed keyword explain where the phase may execute (i.e. resp. the compilation and link process for both). These two tactic types will be used later in the strategy to implement our running example.

For the sake of simplicity, we have not shown the panel for managing the DMSL part. This panel is in fact at a higher level of abstraction and would be made up of metaclasses that need to be instantiated twice, once to define the domain-specific DSML metamodel and again to define the DSML models.

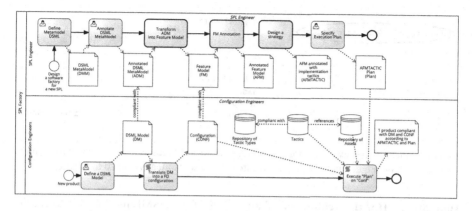

Fig. 3. Overview of the top Bespoke process.

4   The Bespoke Method

The Bespoke method is described here using the BPMN language (see Fig. 3). The engineering task of a new domain is designed on two levels. The first level is under the responsibility of the SPL engineer, who sets up the whole strategy in order to produce software products according to the best practices of the company for a particular domain. The second layer is overseen by the Configuration Engineer who models a customer's expectations in order to generate the product code that meets his/her requirements, i.e. a configuration. The following sections describe the two lanes of the BPMN schema.

4.1   The SPL Engineer Lane

The SPL engineer BPMN lane is activated when a company decides to develop a new software product line. It is therefore a domain-specific strategic activity.

Define MetaModel DSML. The SPL engineer starts by designing a DSML metamodel. He/she describes the problem space by designing the domain concepts, their relationships and system requirements in a DSML metamodel which enables a high expressiveness. The output of this task is a DSML metamodel (DMM) describing a family of products with all the concerns that can be of interest for stakeholders, i.e. users, clients, engineers, etc. This metamodel will be able to include much more information than can be found in a feature model such as requirements for traceability needs, constraints, more commercial or business aspects, etc. DSML metamodel could also describe a collection of related software components that are part of a more complex system, each of which being the result of a specific configuration. Figure 1 presents the shop domain concepts described previously. This DSML metamodel will be transformed later to a FeatAll model that will be considered as a decision tree for the product generation step. The DSML metamodel is expressed with the Entity Relationship (ER) modelling language [7].

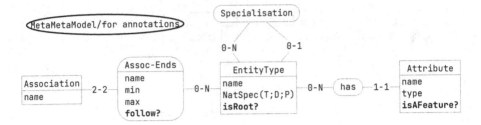

Fig. 4. Metametamodel extended for annotations. Bold attributes denotes extensions to allow engineers to annotate the model elements as information semantically related to features.

Annotate the DSML Metamodel. Taking as input the DSML metamodel (DMM), the SPL engineer annotates it manually according to the extended metametamodel (see Fig. 4) to allow its transformation into an enriched FM. That is, the engineer indicates manually the root class, the classes and their attributes that denote features as well as the roles to follow to produce the hierarchical structure of the FM from the *root class*. Since the expressiveness of a DSML and FM may not be perfectly aligned, the considered transformation is here just a best-effort process that mimics a subjective interpretation to translate a DSML into the best FM that approximates the features represented by the DSML.

In this example, the class *BIZZ* has been annotated as root so that it becomes the root of the generated FM. From there, we annotate the roles (resp. the classes) with the annotations Follows (resp. Feature) in order to make explicit the structure of the FM hidden in the ER schema. Some attributes are themselves annotated with "F" when they represent useful information for the FM—for instance, an enumeration may hide a variation point. Other attributes can be annotated with "A", they then denote attributes of the feature corresponding to the class. The other attributes are then dropped by the transformation. This mechanism makes it possible to select the information in the model that is relevant for the FM, but also to leave out the information that is not. This process results in an annotated ER model: ADM.

Both of the two aforementioned process are realized manually by the SPL engineer.

Transform ADM to a FM. The classes, associations, attributes and specialisation relationships are then traversed by this transformation process from the root class to generate a FeatAll model FM. It is depicted in Fig. 5, but for lack of space, this model includes both the feature model and the annotations commented on in the next section: the rectangular frames attached to the "clouds" (i.e. groups) are not relevant in this phase. The cardinalities and the nature of specialisation relations are preserved in the form of *min-max* multiplicities in the FeatAll FM. They allow finding AND, OR, and XOR decompositions well known in feature models. Specialisation (inheritance) relations are transformed into variation points (groups) with multiplicities that preserve the typology of the specialisation relationships (D: Disjoint, P: Partition, T: Total, *empty*: no constraint), resp. $0 - 1$, $1 - 1$, $1 - N$, and $0 - N$. When a cycle is detected, the transformation stops in order to restrict itself to the hierarchical nature of the FM. In the resulting FM, the $\triangle_i$ groups denotes auxiliary constructs produced by the transformation of the specialisation relationships.

The definition of this transformation mimics the reasoning that a human would have in this interpretation. It is therefore sometimes necessary to correct the result manually (`Normalize the feature model` process), either because the transformation has introduced artificial elements (they are judicious but redundant), or because it could not have been processed properly—this last point is discussed in Sect. 5. Due to lack of space, we have bypassed this step and the figure is therefore the raw version resulting directly from the transformation. However, this model could have been simplified by merging some artificial variation points with others, such as $\triangle 01$ with `storage`, $\triangle 03$ with `suitedFor`, $\triangle 05$ with `payment`, and $\triangle 06$ with `shops`.

FM Annotation. The FM obtained from the previous phase will now serve as a substrate to guide the code generation process. To this end, the SPL engineer will now complement the FM with annotations. These will be constraints on the appropriate times for binding or activating features, as well as on the closure of variation points. The latter is important, as some tactics are more or less suited to supporting open variation points. It will also describe the artefacts that are likely to be impacted by the implementation of this variation point/feature. As explained earlier, it can refer to artefacts present in a current project (AS-IS) or to artefacts in an architectural vision of the project to be developed (TO-BE), if the SPL is starting from scratch for example. The notable moments in the life of a project are: `analysis`, `design`, `program`, `compile`, `link`, `install`, `execute`, `init`, and `run`.

In our approach, binding and activation times are specified as possible intervals. The choice of a tactic to implement this feature/group/attribute must therefore be in accordance with this interval, or it is necessary to change it. The A (resp. B) label denotes the interval for the Activation (resp. Binding) times. When the interval is of the form $[x, x]$, then only the moment x is displayed. `Tactic` is the tactic suggested by the engineer and `Impact` represents the artefacts that will be potentially impacted by the implementation of the feature or tactic once it is known. The upper right label in the frame is just a nickname given to the annotation. The engineer is also invited to specify or confirm if a variation point is closed ? ((T),(F)).

The binding time must precede the activation time, and both must be compatible with the chosen tactic. This aspect is documented in the description of the `TacticType` that will characterize the chosen tactic (see attributes `bindingTimes` and `activationTimes` of `TacticType` in Fig. 2).

Design Strategy. This phase is the most crucial, as it is here that the SPL engineer will deploy all his/her skills in plant engineering. For each variation point, each feature or each significant attribute in Fig. 5, he/she will have to consider all possible tactics to implement the feature. To do this, he/she has a knowledge base listing the types of generic tactics (cf. `Repository of Tactic Types` in Fig. 3—its structure corresponds to pane 5 of the repository in Fig. 2) that can be reused from SPL to SPL, or from feature to feature inside a same SPL. It can also be completed dynamically with new definitions. Thus, it proposes different tactics for each and an inference engine can then validate in real time the validity of the suggestions based on their compatibility in terms of binding/activation times and possible interference at the level of the artefacts.

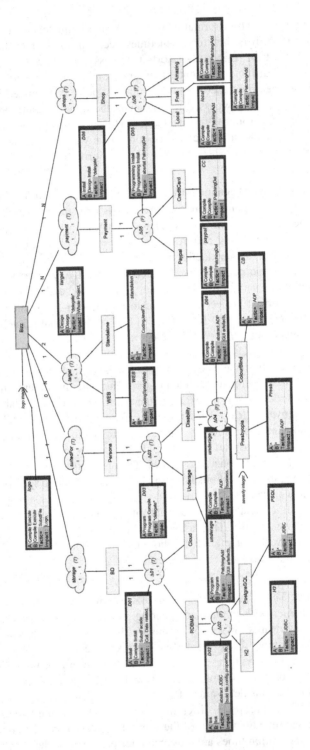

Fig. 5. The feature model with annotations (AFM).

At the same time, the engineer can also suggest the tactic to be operated on, which helps the engine to narrow down the list of alternative tactics. The engineer can then proceed by trial and error until he has a set of coherent tactics (Fig. 6).

Subsequently, precise knowledge of the tactics to be applied, their binding time and the artefacts affected by their application will make it possible to assess the validity of the overall strategy. For example, it would be inappropriate for one tactic A to modify a file (e.g. by applying a patch file) in a directory that must be updated from a Github repository by another tactic B. A simple static dependency analysis will detect this concern. This dependency will be used in the next stage to validate the execution plan. Figure 7 is a concrete notation for the pane 4 of the Bespoke repository. It is built in an iterative way as the SPL engineer develops his or her vision of the future SPL architecture and the tactics to be implemented.

Here we will go through the main choices to be made in order to implement our SPL strategy.

- Let's start with the variation point `target`. Indeed, it impacts almost the entire project at a very early binding time (`Design`), so the choice of tactic will take precedence over all others. Here, the SPL engineer opts for the Java language (`CodingJavaFX` and `CodingSpringWeb` in the child features). This code is, of course, produced manually, and these tactics simply involve importing the code from a repository to initialise the project with all the commonalities.
- For the $\triangle 02$ variation point, the binding is inherited from the parent (^) and several tactics are possible: JPA[3] and `Hibernate`[4] based on the respective ORMs as well as JDBC[5]. Here, the three tactics are quite different from a technological point of view, but the consideration of the variability will be limited to the addition of the appropriate DBMS library, the adaptation of the classpath and the use of a specific URL when establishing the connection. As the DB is very simple, the JDBC tactic is preferred. This choice will easily support the extension of the variation point with the support of other RDBMS (the group is not closed). We could import all the libraries and let the client choose the option to activate at the `execution` time. The SPL engineer has decided here to import only the necessary libraries in order to limit the weight of the executable. The properties file can/should therefore be modified at binding time for ease of use. The call of this tactic type is defined as:

```
implements Feature "H2" with TacticType "JDBC"
because "..."
call Insert {
    call SubstInFile( in= "conf.properties",
                      what ="_JDBC_", with="org.h2.Driver" );
    call SubstInFile( in= "run.bat" ,
                      what ="_JDBC_", with="/lib/h2.jar" );
    call AppendProject( where= "/lib" ,
                        what= "/assets/H2libs.zip" ) ;
}
```

---

[3] https://jakarta.ee/specifications/persistence/.

[4] https://hibernate.org/.

[5] The choice of ODBC would have been thwarted by the previous choice, unless the programming language was changed.

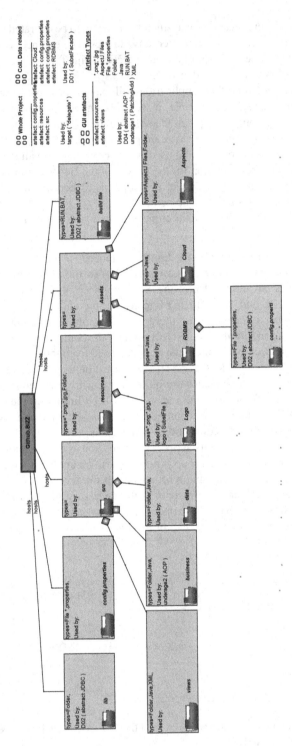

Fig. 6. Artefacts structure.

- The tactic associated with △02 is in our repository typed as a `AbstractTactic` because all the information is not yet known precisely to execute it. On the other hand, for `H2` and `PostgreSQL`, the tactic is typed as `ConcreteTactic`. They complete the abstract tactic with all the arguments necessary for their execution.
- For △01, the tactic is to hide the repository implementation behind a facade pattern and substitute the code behind it with a fetch from an asset in the Github repository. This tactic leaves all options open for the implementation of RDBMS and Cloud features.
- For `logo`, we simply decide to substitute the logo file of the project with the client's logo file at the time of compilation.
- The choice of the tactic for the △03 group is marked as `*delegate*`. No choice is made here, and the decision is deferred to the child branches.
- The adaptation of the GUI according to the nature of the disability (△04) is done by AOP and the adaptation of the CSS style sheet; here the tactic is let abstract as all the details are not yet known. The details of the aspect to be woven will be provided in the children for the concrete tactics.

  For example, for the tactic aspect, the code tip is to enlarge the size of GUI components such as text, buttons, menu items... which produces enlarged interfaces according to the "severity" attribute as we can see in Fig. 8. The colour-blind aspect customises the colour palette considered in the application interfaces and only retains the shades of grey, white and black as shown in Fig. 8. Both aspects are cumulative.

  The `Underage` feature is implemented 1) with AOP programming to modify/complete the functional aspects, and 2) by patching to correct the GUI forms (new widgets need to be added).
- For the △05 group, this point is implemented with subtractive patching. The basic code produced by the tactic chosen for `target` therefore includes all means of payment. When a feature is retained in a configuration, no effort is required. Conversely, if a payment method is not relevant, then the tactic will remove all irrelevant lines from the code. This tactic is justified on the one hand by the nature of the architecture and that the point of variation is an OR (multiplicity is $1 - N$). All payment methods can therefore be implemented simultaneously and without inconvenience. It also makes it easier to test the application. This tactic is realized at the `program` time since it must alter the source files.
- The △06 variation point for the shops is implemented by patching (`Patching-Add`), the architecture is based on a virtual shop facade class that represents a virtual shop. The patching adds to each method of the facade class the add-on specific to each shop and adds the dependent classes. This new tactic is called `PatchingAdd`. Comments with specific labels are placed inside every concerned Java method to facilitate the insertion of the code. This procedure can easily be implemented with a scripting programming language.

Once all the tactics have been chosen and validated according to the knowledge available (assets, binding times, etc.), a battle plan is drawn up. It remains to order all these processes in order to build the software factory. This is the subject of the last phase.

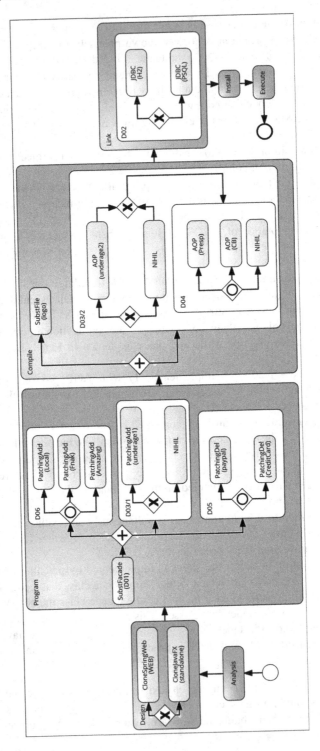

Fig. 7. The execution plan for the Bizz strategy.

Specify the Execution Plan. Finally, the SPL engineer has to order the execution of the tactics between them. This point has already been mentioned earlier. This ordering is guided on the one hand by the binding times and on the other by the artefacts used. Figure 7 explains in a BPMN diagram how all the strategies can be combined with each other in a general way while respecting their binding time. For each configuration, an execution flow in this business process will lead to the production of the product expected by the customer. This BPMN notation is used here for didactic purposes and is not supported by Bespoke. On the other hand, we have textual languages to specify tactic types, strategies and execution plans.

The scheduling of processes is a crucial and complex task, as processes can have side effects. For example, here the tactic for `underage` is applied before those for `Disability` because of their respective binding times. But if we had chosen to do the opposite, the underage GUI elements would not have been adapted to disability situations.

4.2 The Configuration Engineers Pool

The Configuration Engineer's work begins when a new customer orders a product. The requirements are collected using the DSML defined above. The result is a model (DM) which is then transformed into a specific FM configuration, i.e. CONF that must be compliant with the FM feature model produced above. Based on the selected features and the plan (PLan), the software factory knows in which tactics to apply and in which order to apply them. The execution of this plan is a semi-automatic process. Some steps will be automatic, such as applying a patch file[6] or weaving an aspect, but others may require manual intervention, such as editing code or a configuration file (Figs. 9 and 10).

5   Potential Weakness

As any study has limitations, we identify the following weaknesses: Intuitively, the SPL engineer may not define the DSML in accordance with our assumptions of the transformation process. This can be mitigated by co-creating the DSML definition and the Feature model together, with two synchronised views, in order to observe the induced effect in terms of features when editing the metamodel—this is possible with the transformation running in the background in a reactive way. Furthermore, obtaining FMs with invalid semantics cannot be avoided, as it is an immediate consequence of the engineer's competence. Similarly, we cannot guarantee that the DSML is initially well-defined. Finally, we have assumed here that DSMLs describe an application domain with a SPL as target. Not all DSMLs fall into this category (Architecture description languages, Data definition languages, Specific programming languages, etc.). This limitation cannot be considered as a weakness.

Our types of tactics are atomic and attached to a particular binding time. It is sometimes appropriate to have tactics that cut across several phases of the project, with one part of the process running at program time and another at link time, for instance. A

---

[6] See https://en.wikipedia.org/wiki/Patch_(Unix).

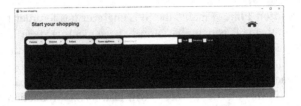

Fig. 8. Shop application for a colour-blind user.

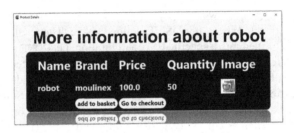

Fig. 9. Shop application for a user without disabilities.

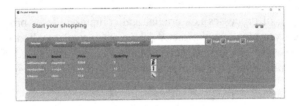

Fig. 10. Shop application for a presbyter.

solution can easily be provided, but it will bring new challenges to manage the dependencies between artefacts, though. Similarly, some tactics would benefit from being interleaved. All this is possible, with the counterpart of increased complexity. Our method has been validated on a realistic and operational case study (Bizz), some processes are tooled up, but our approach still needs serious efforts to offer an integrated and fully operational production chain.

6   Related Work

SPL phases and activities have been widely tackled by researchers, but unfortunately, few works studied how well the existing tools deal with those activities in practice. Most notable existing tools were summed up in [9] and illustrated in a roadmap built with all SPL tools. The top of Fig. 11 presents the different phases entailed during the SPL process. Existing tools that resolve only the problem space allow systems' specifications established during the domain analysis and requirements engineering phases. For example, Clafer [2] is designed as a concise notation for metamodels, feature models, and mixtures of meta and feature models. It has a concise syntax with rich semantics to allow the definition of the problem area. Whereas, the tools considered for the solution space refer to the concrete systems created during the architecture, design and implementation phases. In fact, they provide means to define the product features and the requirements for the concrete application.

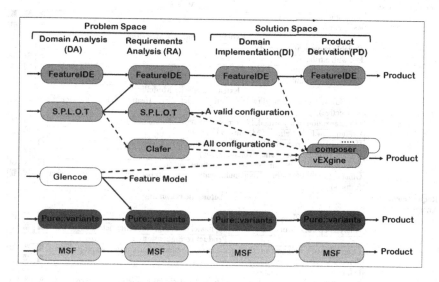

Fig. 11. Roadmap with the selected tools for an SPL process.

The tools proposed to carry out either problem or solution spaces are insufficient to provide support for the whole SPL process. To partly solve these issues, SPL practitioners can combine some of the tools or integrate them which provides a poor performance in execution time. Concretely, existing combinations are represented as solid lines, while possible combinations are represented as dashed lines. At this level, we argue that a complete SPL approach must cover both problem and solution spaces. As shown, FeatureIDE, pure::variants, and our proposed MSF are the most appropriate tools for the Domain Implementation (DI) and Product Derivation (PD) phases to support the implementation and resolution of the variability and the subsequent generation of the final product. FeatureIDE [23] is an open-source Eclipse framework with a plug-in based extension mechanism to integrate and test existing tools and SPL approaches (FeatureHouse, AHEAD, AspectJ, Antenna, etc.). Whereas, Pure::variants [22] is a commercial solution that supports all phases of the SPL process. Many extensions connect pure::variants with common systems and software engineering tools.

By reading the roadmap, we believe that our framework is spotted all over the SPL process to sustain the different activities performed for designing, analyzing, and implementing variability. It addresses two problems highlighted in the article: 1) most existing tools only support specific phases in SPL and 2) the few tools that support multiple phases require the adoption of specific technological paradigms for implementation (Feature oriented programming, FOP AOP, or annotations). Our proposal here is global, generic and technology-agnostic. Under this light, our framework is confronted in Fig. 12 to both FeatureIDE and Pure::variants tools, the only approaches that are fitted to fulfill the product line cycle.

Phase	Requirements and characteristics	FI	PV	B
Domain Analysis	**Basic Modelling**			
	Mandatory, optional, or, xor	■	■	■
	Basic constraint	■	■	■
	Extended Variability Modeling			
	Variable numerical, string, date	□	⊠	■
	FM with attributes	□	⊠	■
	FM with cardinality	□	⊠	■
	Complex constraint	□	■	⊠
	Extra-Variability Modelling			
	Multi-dimensional variability and multi-Product Lines (feature viewpoints, multi-perspective)	⊠	⊠	■
	Modularization of layer models (composition units, hierarchical levels)	⊠	⊠	■
	Evolution of FMs (refined FM, edits to FM...)	⊠	⊠	⊞
	Non-functional properties (goals, contributions, operationalisations...)	□	⊠	■
	Binding modes(time: static, dynamic; state)	□	⊠	■
	Meta-information (documentation, descriptions, annotations)	⊠	⊠	■
	Other extensions (arbitrary group multiplicity, constraints between viewpoints, abstract features)	⊠	⊠	■
Requirement Analysis	**Automatic reasoning**			
	Basic analysis of FMs (statistics, metrics)	■	■	⊠
	Analysis operations on FMs (validation, model counting, anomalies detection)	■	■	∅
	Product configuration			
	Generation of configurations (features selection, enumeration, constraints propagation)	■	■	■
	Sampling configurations	■	■	⊞
	Optimization of configurations	⊠	□	⊞
	Interactive configuration process (multi-step and partial configurations, derived features, visibility conditions)	■	⊠	■
Domain Implementation	**Variability Implementation**			
	Composition-based approach (components, feature-oriented, aspect-oriented)	■	■	■
	Annotation-based approach (parameters, stereotypes, virtual separation of concerns)	■	■	■
	Combined approach (composition and annotations)	□	□	■
	Artifacts Development			
	High abstraction level (architecture, design, models)	□	□	■
	Low abstraction level (code, functions, files)	■	■	■
	Multi-language artifacts (language independence)	□	■	⊞
Product Derivation	**Variability Resolution**			
	Product derivation	■	■	■
	Product evaluation	■	■	⊞
	Product management			
	Weaving or composition of products	⊠	□	■
	Traceability of features	■	■	■
	Evolution changes (automatic propagation of changes)	□	⊠	■

Fig. 12. Index Stability Evaluation (□: not supported – ⊠: partially supported – ■: well-supported – ⊞: feasible – ∅: incompatible. FI: FeatureIDE; PV: Pure::variants; B: Bespoke).

The table in Fig. 12 identifies the following main hints: Domain Analysis phase is in charge of modelling the domain variability. Almost all tools presented in Fig. 11 provide support for modelling the variability using FMs. Both our framework and FeatureIDE offer an excellent graphical editor to build the diagram of the FM following the notation proposed by Czarnecki [6] while pure::variants provides a great tree-based reflective editor. In all tools, mandatory, optional, and group features (*or* and *xor*) are supported. Moreover, our method can start either from a DSML or from a FM[7].

More advanced variability modelling aspects [20] have been introduced to provide a better expressiveness and a more detailed specification. Pure::variants offer a complete support for defining features with attributes, for example, to specify a utility value for each feature in the FMs. However, both FeatureIDE and Pure::variants have shortcomings to support different types of feature such that string, numerical, and data types in addition the cardinality information. Our framework overcomes these issues by using the DSML metamodel as the starting point which provides a multidimensional representation of a system and a good documentation to describe all domain concepts. All the information retrieved from this DSML will be preserved in the obtained FM enriched with cardinality, attributes, complex constraints, binding time, and quality criteria to provide an analysis for non-functional properties (NFPs). There is very poor support for extra characteristics of variability modelling in the literature, as we can notice in the table above. Only our proposed framework provides explicit support for defining variability in different dimensions such as feature viewpoints or multi-perspectives. Modifications and edits to FMs once created can be complex for FeatureIDE where modifying a part of the feature model usually can only be achieved by removing that part and adding it again. Contrarily, pure::variants allows even moving features from a branch to another in a straightforward way.

The goal of Requirement Analysis (RA) is to select a desired combination of features according to the application requirements. This phase should also consider the automatic analysis of the variability model and managing configurations of the product at the feature level. Analysis of variability is one of the most important activities in an SPL, and thus, all tools covering the RA phase provide some kind of support for automatic reasoning of FMs. Statistics and metrics about FMs are provided by almost all tools in different degrees. The requirement analysis covers model validation such that consistency, the anomalies detection and redundancy constraints. For example, FeatureIDE generates all possible configurations in order to enumerate them, and thus, with these tools it is not possible to calculate the number of configurations for large models in a reasonable time. Within pure::variants is also possible to calculate the number of configurations for each subtree under a selected feature. These concerns are outside the scope of our method, it uses the franca lingua FeatAll language and relies on tiers tools for such analyses.

Variability resolution and product derivation are achieved by all the analysed tools. A limitation in FeatureIDE is that only one composer (e.g., FeatureHouse, annotations) can be selected for an SPL application, and thus, the combination of different approaches requires building and integrating a custom composer within FeatureIDE. Apart from this, our framework, proposes to combine several variability tactics to generate final products. The tactics can be freely composed by the SPL engineer, and the procedures used are programmable add-ons. The architecture is therefore completely open to all programming paradigms and languages.

---

[7] The FM is obtained by transformation, but it could be specified/edited explicitly.

Finally, generating the final product (by resolving the variability of the artefacts according to the selection of features made in the RA phase) and validating the generated product is ensured with all the tools figuring in the table.

The objective of this work is to promote SPL engineering and overcome the limitations presented by existing approaches, without reinventing the wheel. We propose a software factory that provides multidimensional variability modelling through the use of DSML. Subsequently, the product line characteristics will be displayed by an enriched FM that supports cardinalities, attributes and complex constraints in addition to non-functional requirements. Finally, the code generation phase can combine several heterogeneous implementation tactics in order to combine their strengths and weaknesses to obtain a trade-off between the NFPs and the functional aspect of the software system.

Here, we believe that our method provides the software engineer with an awareness of all aspects of the software factory and thus a better perspective, allowing him to objectify the motivations of each choice that turns out to be crucial in the generation strategy. Our hope is that this will lead to more mature and better quality architectures.

7   Conclusion and Future Work

In this paper, we have presented a method for designing SPL. It makes it possible to capture the requirements of a particular configuration with a DSML specific to the SPL domain and transform these models into FMs that serve as decision trees to design a generative strategy for code production. Each variant is annotated with SPL-specific requirements (binding times, impact, etc.). This information can then be used to select the most appropriate tactics depending on the nature of the artefacts involved, the constraints inherent in the variant, and the annotations provided. These tactics are then arranged temporally in order to provide a generic execution plan. When a stakeholder wants a particular product, the concrete model expressed with the DSML is transformed into a set of features that will then allow the selection of appropriate tactics from the generic execution plan.

This method allows the tactics used to be catalogued by formal definitions that facilitate their reuse and application as needed. It also allows for the modelling of the artefacts manipulated to generate a product. This supports an ideation of the architecture of the future SPL with an awareness of the manipulated artefacts, their nature and their dependencies. This paves the way for future analyses to verify the validity of the generative strategy. Finally, this method has the merit of encouraging introspection on the generation methods in order to increase the mastery of them.

In the future, we will implement the whole production chain with supporting tools for each step and improve the communication between these tools in order to have the most automatic chain possible. We also want to better exploit the theoretical foundations in order to provide, in the most automatic and interactive way, better guidelines to implement the chosen generative strategy taking into account non-functional properties, and enrich the chain tool with the integration of external SPL tools.

References

1. Babar, M.A., Chen, L., Shull, F.: Managing variability in software product lines. IEEE Softw. **27**(3), 89–91 (2010)
2. Bąk, K., Diskin, Z., Antkiewicz, M.: Clafer: unifying class and feature modeling. Softw. Syst. Model. **15**(3), 811–845 (2016)
3. Bashroush, R., Garba, M., Rabiser, R., Groher, I., Botterweck, G.: Case tool support for variability management in software product lines. ACM Comput. Surv. (CSUR) **50**(1), 1–45 (2017)
4. Belarbi, M., Englebert, V.: Transforming domain specific modeling languages into feature models. In: Pires, L.F., Hammoudi, S., Seidewitz, E. (eds.) Proceedings of the 10th International Conference on Model-Driven Engineering and Software Development, MODEL-SWARD 2022, Online Streaming, 6–8 February 2022, pp. 137–146. SCITEPRESS (2022). https://doi.org/10.5220/0010772000003119
5. Berg, K., Bishop, J.: Tracing software product line variability: from problem to solution space. In: SAICSIT, vol. 5, pp. 182–191. Citeseer (2005)
6. Czarnecki, K., Helsen, S., Eisenecker, U.: Staged configuration using feature models. In: Nord, R.L. (ed.) SPLC 2004. LNCS, vol. 3154, pp. 266–283. Springer, Heidelberg (2004). https://doi.org/10.1007/978-3-540-28630-1_17
7. Hainaut, J.-L., Hick, J.-M., Englebert, V., Henrard, J., Roland, D.: Understanding the implementation of *IS*-A relations. In: Thalheim, B. (ed.) ER 1996. LNCS, vol. 1157, pp. 42–57. Springer, Heidelberg (1996). https://doi.org/10.1007/BFb0019914
8. Horcas, J.M., Pinto, M., Fuentes, L.: Software product line engineering: a practical experience. In: Proceedings of the 23rd International Systems and Software Product Line Conference, vol. A, pp. 164–176 (2019)
9. Horcas, J.M., Pinto, M., Fuentes, L.: Empirical analysis of the tool support for software product lines. Soft. Syst. Model. 1–38 (2022)
10. Hunsen, C., et al.: Preprocessor-based variability in open-source and industrial software systems: an empirical study. Empir. Softw. Eng. **21**(2), 449–482 (2016)
11. Ignaim, K.: EvoSPL: an evolutionary approach for adopting software product lines in the automotive industry (2021)
12. Kasauli, R., Liebel, G., Knauss, E., Gopakumar, S., Kanagwa, B.: Requirements engineering challenges in large-scale agile system development. In: 2017 IEEE 25th International Requirements Engineering Conference (RE), pp. 352–361. IEEE (2017)
13. Khan, F.Q., Musa, S., Tsaramirsis, G., Bakhsh, S.T.: A study: selection of model metamodel and SPL tools for the verification of software product lines. Int. J. Inf. Technol. **9**(4), 353–362 (2017)
14. Laguna, M.A., Crespo, Y.: A systematic mapping study on software product line evolution: from legacy system reengineering to product line refactoring. Sci. Comput. Program. **78**(8), 1010–1034 (2013)
15. Malaer, A., Lampe, M.: SimPL a simple software production line for end user development. In: 2008 15th Asia-Pacific Software Engineering Conference, pp. 179–186. IEEE (2008)
16. Mens, K., Lopes, C., Tekinerdogan, B., Kiczales, G.: Aspect-oriented programming workshop report. In: Bosch, J., Mitchell, S. (eds.) ECOOP 1997. LNCS, vol. 1357, pp. 483–496. Springer, Heidelberg (1998). https://doi.org/10.1007/3-540-69687-3_88
17. Nunes, I., de Lucena, C.J.P., Kulesza, U., Nunes, C.: On the development of multi-agent systems product lines: a domain engineering process. In: Gleizes, M.-P., Gomez-Sanz, J.J. (eds.) AOSE 2009. LNCS, vol. 6038, pp. 125–139. Springer, Heidelberg (2011). https://doi.org/10.1007/978-3-642-19208-1_9

18. Nuryyev, B., Nadi, S., Bhuiyan, N.U., Banderali, L.: Challenges of implementing software variability in eclipse OMR: an interview study. In: 2021 IEEE/ACM 43rd International Conference on Software Engineering: Software Engineering in Practice (ICSE-SEIP), pp. 31–40. IEEE (2021)

19. Oksanen, M., et al.: A comparison of two SPLE tools: pure: variants and Clafer tools (2018)

20. Pawletta, T., Schmidt, A., Zeigler, B.P., Durak, U.: Extended variability modeling using system entity structure ontology within Matlab/Simulink. In: Proceedings of the 49th Annual Simulation Symposium, pp. 1–8 (2016)

21. Prehofer, C.: Feature-oriented programming: a fresh look at objects. In: Akşit, M., Matsuoka, S. (eds.) ECOOP 1997. LNCS, vol. 1241, pp. 419–443. Springer, Heidelberg (1997). https://doi.org/10.1007/BFb0053389

22. Spinczyk, O., Beuche, D.: Modeling and building software product lines with eclipse. In: Companion to the 19th Annual ACM SIGPLAN Conference on Object-Oriented Programming Systems, Languages, and Applications, pp. 18–19 (2004)

23. Thüm, T., Kästner, C., Benduhn, F., Meinicke, J., Saake, G., Leich, T.: Featureide: an extensible framework for feature-oriented software development. Sci. Comput. Program. **79**, 70–85 (2014)

24. White, J., Schmidt, D.C., Benavides, D., Trinidad, P., Ruiz-Cortés, A.: Automated diagnosis of product-line configuration errors in feature models. In: 2008 12th International Software Product Line Conference, pp. 225–234. IEEE (2008)

W-Sec: A Model-Based Formal Method for Assessing the Impacts of Security Countermeasures

Bastien Sultan[1]($\boxtimes$)(ID), Ludovic Apvrille[1](ID), Philippe Jaillon[2], and Sophie Coudert[1]

[1] LTCI, Télécom Paris, Institut Polytechnique de Paris, Sophia-Antipolis, France
{bastien.sultan,ludovic.apvrille,
sophie.coudert}@telecom-paris.fr
[2] Mines Saint-Etienne, CEA-Tech, Centre CMP, F-13541 Gardanne, France
philippe.jaillon@emse.fr

Abstract. The chapter provides a detailed description of W-Sec, a formal model-based countermeasures' impact assessment method. It also introduces a new formal definition of the two SysML profiles used in SysML-Sec and W-Sec, enabling (i) for the future automation of several W-Sec stages and (ii) for the definition of consistency rules ensuring the consistency of the models written in these two distinct modeling languages. In addition, the chapter evaluates W-Sec with a new industry 4.0 case-study and discusses the strengths and the current limitations of the approach in this new application field.

Keywords: Impact assessment · Formal methods · Mutations · SysML-Sec · TTool · Cyber-Physical Systems · Safety · Security · Performance

1 Introduction

Cyber-physical systems (CPS), including industrial control systems (ICS), control physical processes involved in safety-critical industries (energy, chemical industry, etc.) [19]. Therefore, cyber attacks targeting CPS may result in extremely harmful consequences. Maintaining a high security level for these systems is thus an essential process for CPS designers and operators. CPS security is an active research field including various challenging topics. Among them, the selection of optimal countermeasures[1] mitigating the systems' vulnerabilities is a complex issue. Indeed, any modification brought to a CPS must comply with the – often drastic – safety, security and performance requirements ensuring the system's dependability.

Two of our previous contributions proposed modeling and impact assessment approaches that help in addressing this issue. On the one hand, we proposed in [26] a countermeasures impact[2] assessment method targeting the context of CPS. Relying

---

[1] A *countermeasure* refers in our works to any modification brought to a system in order to mitigate one or several vulnerabilities. It can be a modification of the system's software, hardware, processes, and/or to its physical, logical and network architecture.

[2] *Impact* refers to *positive* impacts (i.e., efficiency) as well as to *negative* impacts (i.e., regressions).

© Springer Nature Switzerland AG 2023
L. F. Pires et al. (Eds.): MODELSWARD 2021/2022, CCIS 1708, pp. 203–229, 2023.
https://doi.org/10.1007/978-3-031-38821-7_10

on CPS modeling with networks of timed automata (NTA), this method has three main drawbacks. Firstly, it is difficult to capture in a single modeling language heterogeneous aspects (such as data security, hardware architecture and discrete software behavior) at a same abstraction level. As a result, the models may lack in precision regarding some aspects (e.g., data security and low-level hardware aspects). Secondly, modeling all these aspects with a single NTA may lead to a model that is complex to understand and to verify. Last, due to the difficulty to model data security aspects with NTAs, the impact assessment of this NTA-based method does not include a fine-grained data security analysis. On the other hand, with SysML-Sec [4], we proposed a CPS design and verification method relying on two distinct SysML-based formal modeling languages. One of them targets high-level system architectural and behavioral aspects, when the other one is well suited for modeling fine-grained hardware and low-level security aspects. Yet, a drawback of SysML-Sec is that the method considers a single attacker model at the verification stage.

Therefore, we proposed in [25] a new countermeasures selection method called W-Sec, merging the strengths of our two previous contributions in order to correct the flaws we mention above. This chapter is an extended version of this work presented at the 10th ModelsWard conference. It brings to this initial paper several enhancements:

- A formal description of W-Sec is now given.
- For this purpose, the chapter provides a new mathematic definition of the models designed with the two modeling languages used in SysML-Sec and in W-Sec. This formalization is also the first step towards the automation of some W-Sec modeling stages.
- In order to ensure the modeling consistency between the two languages, the links between the both modeling views are now explicitly defined.
- W-Sec is applied to a new, more complex, real case-study, in a new context (connected factories and industrial control systems).

It is organized as follows. Section 2 presents the industrial case-study we use troughout the chapter to illustrate and evaluate the method. Then, Sect. 3 provides our new formalization of the two modeling languages. Section 4 describes both theoretical and practical aspects of W-Sec. Afterwards, Sect. 5 gives an overview of the related works. Last, Sect. 6 discusses the case-study results and the contributions W-Sec brings to our previous contributions.

2   IT'm Factory: An Industry 4.0 Case-Study

IT'm Factory is a research and training platform[3] hosted by the École des Mines de Saint-Étienne. It provides researchers and companies with a realistic connected factory case-study including typical industry 4.0 features (connected and automated packaging chain, collaborative robots, virtual and augmented reality glasses, digital twin, etc.). The case-study we present in this paper is focused on the packaging chain.

---

[3] https://itm-factory.fr/index.php/objectif_et_visite_360/.

2.1 The Packaging Chain

This chain is composed of four autonomous machines: a warehouse, a filling machine, a cobot (a collaborative autonomous articulated robotic arm) and a packer. The warehouse contains empty pots and, when operating, places them at regular intervals on the filling machine's conveyor belt. The filling machine detects the pots and fills them with grains. When a pot arrives at the extremity of the conveyor belt, the collaborative robot grabs it, closes the pot with a cap and places it on the packer conveyor belt. The packer then places it in a crate. When a crate is filled with six pots, the packer ejects it and continues the process with a new empty crate.

For supervision reasons, these machines are connected to a local network and may be supervised from a remote SCADA[4] console as well as from local control panels. Thanks to these HMIs, users can define the setpoint values for the physical processes the machines perform. Users can also supervise in real time the parameters of the machines and the number of filled pots, etc. Some values are also shared with a remote supervision system that can be connected to external networks. Figure 1 shows the physical architecture and network topology of the packaging chain, with a focus on the internal architecture of the filling machine (the warehouse's and the packer's architectures are very close to this one). The data flows are also depicted in this figure with colored/decorated arrows.

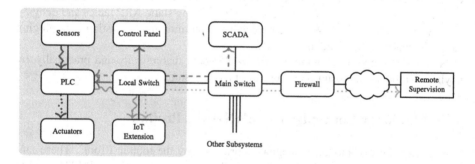

Fig. 1. Architecture of the filling machine (in the grey enclave) and its network flows. (Color figure online)

In the case-study presented in this paper, we specifically focus on the filling machine, the main switch and the SCADA remote console.

2.2 Scenarios, Attack and Countermeasures

Our case-study integrates the two main functional scenarios of the filling machine: a scenario **Sc1** where the machine is supervised from its local control panel, and a scenario **Sc2** where it is supervised from the SCADA remote console. In the both scenarios the user sends a start command to the machine and then defines the following setpoints:

---

[4] Supervisory Control and Data Acquisition system.

the speed of the conveyor belt, the filling duration of each pot (i.e., the desired grains volume), and the centering offset of the filling machine's nozzle with respect to the center of each pot during the filling phases.

In this case-study, we also consider one attack we want to protect the system from. This attack aims at falsifying the centering offset setpoints in order to make the filling machine discharging the grains on the conveyor belt. To achieve this goal, the attack scenario consists of two consecutive steps. The first one is an ARP poisoning attack targeting the SCADA console in order to reroute its outgoing traffic to the attacker's host. The second step consists in modifying the centering offset setpoint with a value greater to the pots radius, and then in forwarding the modified message to the PLC (via the main and local switches). Note that the platform is actually already protected against this attack since the control algorithms executed by the PLC perform a consistency check on the received setpoint values (contermeasure **C1**, see below). Moreover, we assume for this case-study that the SCADA console and the main switch are vulnerable to ARP poisoning. However, for the needs of our paper we consider that the platform has not its embedded countermeasures yet.

In addition, we evaluate four countermeasures aiming at mitigating this attack. **C1**, an offset setpoint check: each time the PLC receives a centering offset setpoint, it checks if it exceeds the radius of a pot. If it is the case, the received value is replaced with the the value of the radius minus 1 cm. **C2** is a cryptographic countermeasure, consisting in symmetric encryption of the communications between the PLC and the SCADA console and the local control panel. **C3** consists in defining static ARP tables and denying ARP *is-at* requests. Last, **C4** is an emergency countermeasure consisting in unpluging the filling machine from the main switch.

The following sections will describe W-Sec both theoretically and practically, by relying on models and results coming from this case-study.

3   Preliminary Concepts: TTool's SysML Profiles

W-Sec relies on two modeling languages provided by the toolkit TTool[5]. These languages are two formally defined SysML profiles: one of them, AVATAR [23], used in TTool's *System View* (or S-View), is well suited for the high-level behavioral modeling of a system. The other one, DIPLODOCUS [13], used in TTool's *Hardware/Software Partitioning View* (or HSW-View), targets the joint modeling of hardware and software aspects of a system and is well suited for a low-level modeling of a component. This section provides new mathematical definitions of the models these two SysML profiles enable to design, that enable for a formal definition of W-Sec in Sect. 4.

3.1   Preliminary Definitions

The two modeling views share some common concepts. Although these concepts have not exactly the same meaning in the both cases, we present them in a common definition for simplicity reasons.

---

[5] https://ttool.telecom-paris.fr/.

Definition 1 (Types, Attributes, Expressions and Signals).

- Types $= \{\mathbb{B}ool, \mathbb{Z}, \mathbb{N}\}$
- Attr *is a set of* attributes, *typed by type* : Attr $\rightarrow$ Types.
- Expressions *are usual integer and boolean expressions over attributes. They are typed in the usual way.*
- Profiles $= \{(t_1, \cdots, t_n) \mid n \in \mathbb{N} \wedge \forall 1 \leq i \leq n, t_i \in$ Types$\}$.
- Sign $=$ InSign $\sqcup$ OutSign *is*[6] *a set of* signals, *typed by profile* : Sign $\rightarrow$ Profiles. InSign *contains* input *signals.* OutSign *contains* output *signals.*

3.2 The System View (S)

In S-View, models rely on SysML blocks exchanging signals and having a behavior modeled with state-machine diagrams. Definition 5 provides the mathematical definition of a whole model designed in this view. Definition 4 describes a SysML block, and Definition 3 defines its state-machine diagram. Last, the syntactic correctness of such a model is given in Definition 6. These four definitions rely on basic concepts that are provided in Definition 2.

Definition 2 (S-View Basic Sets and associated Abstract Syntax).

- Meth *is a set of* methods, *typed by profile* : Meth $\rightarrow$ Profiles.
- $m(e_1, \ldots, e_n)$ *is a* method call, *where m is a method and $e_1, \ldots, e_n$ are expressions respecting the profile of m.*
- *There are four kinds of* actions*:*
    - Affectations $a := e$ *where a is an attribute and e an expression of the same type.*
    - Random affectations $a :=?$ *where a is an attribute.*
    - Send $send_s(e_1, \ldots, e_n)$, *where s is an output signal and $e_1, \ldots, e_n$ are attributes respecting the profile of s.*
    - Receive $receive_s(e_1, \ldots, e_n)$, *where s is an input signal and $e_1, \ldots, e_n$ are attributes respecting the profile of s.*
- Port *is a set of* ports.

Definition 3 (State Machine Diagram). *A* state machine diagram *is a directed (control flow) graph* $smd = (s_0, S, T)$ *where*

- *S is a set of* states, *$s_0 \in S$ is the initial state.*
- *T is a set of* transitions *$t = \langle s_{start}, after, condition, actions, s_{end} \rangle$ where:*
    - $after = (t_{min}, t_{max})$, *in $\mathbb{N}^2$, constrains the delay before firing t.*
    - $s_{start}, s_{end} \in S^2$ *are respectively the source and target states of t.*
    - $condition$ *is a boolean expression that must be true to enable t.*
    - $actions$ *is a sequence of actions/method calls, executed when t is fired.*

$attr(smd)$ *(resp.* $meth(smd)$, $sign(smd)$, $insign(smd)$, $outsign(smd)$) *denotes the set of attributes (resp. methods, signals, input signals, output signals) used in smd.*

A state machine diagram is syntactically correct if all states are reachable from s_0 (by some syntactic path on transitions).

---

[6] "$\sqcup$" denotes the disjoint union.

Definition 4 (Block Description).

A block description is a 6-uple $D = \langle A_D, M_D, P_D, S_{iD}, S_{oD}, smd_D \rangle$ *where* $A_D \subset$
Attr, $M_D \subset$ Meth, $S_{iD} \subset$ InSign, $S_{oD} \subset$ OutSign, $P_D \subset$ Port, *smd is a state*
machine diagram, and all these sets are finite.

It is syntactically correct if smd_D *is syntactically correct,* $attr(smd_D) \subseteq A_D$ *and*
$meth(smd_D) \subseteq M_D$.

The following definition derives from the *SysML block instance diagram* defined in [5].

Definition 5 (S-Model).

A system model, or S-Model, is a 5-uple $\langle \mathcal{B}, d, \mathcal{L}, \mathcal{C}, \mathcal{R} \rangle$ *where:*

- $\mathcal{B}$ *is a finite set of* blocks.
- *d is a function which associate a block description to each block of* $\mathcal{B}$.
  for $X \in \{A, M, P, S_i, S_o, smd\}$ *and* $B \in \mathcal{B}$, X_B *abbreviates* $X_{d(B)}$, *and*
  $\mathcal{P} = \bigsqcup_{B \in \mathcal{B}} P_B, \mathcal{S}_o = \bigsqcup_{B \in \mathcal{B}} S_{oB}$ *and* $\mathcal{S}_i = \bigsqcup_{B \in \mathcal{B}} S_{iB}$.
- $\mathcal{L} \subset \mathcal{P} \times \mathcal{P}$ *contains* links. *It is an irreflexive and antisymmetric partial injection.*
- $\mathcal{C} \subseteq \mathcal{L} \times \mathcal{S}_o \times \mathcal{S}_i$ *is a set of* connexions $\langle \langle p_1, p_2 \rangle, s_o, s_i \rangle$ *such that* p_1 *and* s_o *belong to the same block, and* p_2 *and* s_i *belong to the same block.*
- $\mathcal{R} \subset \mathcal{B} \times \mathcal{B}$ *is such that*
  - *its transitive closure* $\mathcal{R}^*$ *is a noetherian order.*
  - *its inverse relation* $\mathcal{R}^{-1}$ *is a function.*
  When $\langle B_1, B_2 \rangle \in \mathcal{R}$, *we say that* B_1 *"contains"/"is a superblock of"* B_2 *and that* B_2 *"is contained by"/"is a subblock of"* B_1.

Remark: the set of subblocks of a block B defines a finite tree with B as root.

Definition 6 (Syntactically Correct S-Model).

Let $\mathcal{M} = \langle \mathcal{B}, d, \mathcal{L}, \mathcal{C}, \mathcal{R} \rangle$ *be a S-Model.* $\mathcal{M}$ *is syntactically correct if and only if:*

- $\forall \langle \langle p_1, p_2 \rangle, s_o, s_i \rangle \in \mathcal{C}, profile(s_o) = profile(s_i)$
- $\forall B \in \mathcal{B}, d(B)$ *is syntactically correct and* $\forall s_x \in sign(smd_B)$,
  - $\exists! \langle \langle p_1, p_2 \rangle, s_o, s_i \rangle \in \mathcal{C}, s_x = s_o \vee s_x = s_i$.
  - $\exists B' \in \mathcal{B}, (B', B) \in \mathcal{R}^* \wedge (s_x \in S_{oB'} \vee s_x \in S_{iB'})$.

3.3 The Hardware-Software Partitioning View (HSW)

HSW-View models are mathematically close to S-View models, but present some key differences. Indeed, they rely on a couple of specific SysML block diagrams (one modeling software aspects, the other modeling hardware aspects) and on two *allocations* that explicit the links between the both block diagrams. The whole HSW-Model is defined in Definition 12. Definitions 10 and 11 define the both specific SysML block diagrams used in this view. The SysML blocks used in the software diagram are defined in Definition 9, and the activity diagrams used for modeling their behavior in Definition 8. These five definitions rely on basic concepts that are provided in Definition 7.

Definition 7 (HSW-View Basic Sets and associated Abstract Syntax[7]).

- DSign $\subseteq$ Sign *is a set of* data *signals. For any d in* DSign, $\mathit{profile}(d) = (\mathbb{N})$.
- Keys *is a set of cryptographic* keys.
- *There are six kinds of* actions*:*
    - Affectations *and* Random affectations *such as defined in Def. 2.*
    - Send *actions:*
        * $\mathit{send}_e(a_1, \ldots, a_n)$, *where* $e \in$ OutSign *and* $a_1, \ldots, a_n$ *are attributes respecting* $\mathit{profile}(e)$.
        * $\mathit{encrsend}_d(k, e)$ *where* $d \in$ OutSign $\cap$ DSign, $k \in$ Keys *and e is a (natural) integer expression.*
    - Receive *actions:*
        * $\mathit{receive}_e(a_1, \ldots, a_n)$, *where* $e \in$ InSign *and* $a_1, \ldots, a_n$ *are attributes respecting* $\mathit{profile}(e)$.
        * $\mathit{encrreceived}_d(k, e)$ *where* $d \in$ InSign $\cap$ DSign, $k \in$ Keys *and e is a (natural) integer expression.*
    - Delay*:* $\mathit{delay}(e)$, *where e is a (natural) integer expression.*

Definition 8 (Activity Diagram). *An* activity diagram *is a directed (control flow) graph* $ad = \langle s_0, S, T \rangle$ *where:*

- *S is a set of states,* $s_0 \in S$ *is the initial state.*
- *T is a set of transitions* $t = \langle s_{start}, \mathit{condition}, \mathit{action}, s_{end} \rangle$ *where:*
    - $(s_{start}, s_{end}) \in S^2$ *are respectively the source and the target states of t*
    - *condition is a boolean expression that must be true to enable t*
    - *action is an action executed when t is fired.*

$\mathit{attr}(ad)$ *(resp* $\mathit{sign}(ad)$, $\mathit{keys}(ad)$*) denotes the set of attributes (resp. signals, keys) used in ad.*

An activity diagram is syntactically correct if all states are reachable from s_0 *(by some syntactic path on transitions).*

Definition 9 (Task Description).
A task description is a 5-uple $D = \langle A_D, S_{iD}, S_{oD}, ad_D \rangle$ *where* $A_D \subset$ Attr, $S_{iD} \subset$ InSign, $S_{oD} \subset$ OutSign, ad_D *is an activity diagram, and all these sets are finite.*

It is syntactically correct if ad_D *is syntactically correct,* $\mathit{attr}(ad_D) \subseteq A_D$ *and* $\mathit{sign}(ad_D) \subseteq S_{iD} \cup S_{oD}$.

Definition 10 (Application Model).
An application model *is a 4-uple* $\langle \mathcal{T}, d, \mathcal{C}, \mathcal{K} \rangle$ *where* $\mathcal{K} \subseteq$ Keys *and:*

- $\mathcal{T}$ *is a finite set of tasks.*
- *d is a function which associate a task description to each task of* $\mathcal{T}$.
  For $X \in \{A, S_i, S_o, ad\}$ *and* $T \in \mathcal{T}$, X_T *abbreviates* $X_{d(T)}$, *and*
  $$\mathcal{S}_o = \bigsqcup_{T \in \mathcal{T}} S_{oT} \text{ and } \mathcal{S}_i = \bigsqcup_{T \in \mathcal{T}} S_{iT}.$$

---

[7] Note that in this view, data are abstracted: we do not model data values and the profile of a data signal is an integer representing the amount of transfered data. Moreover, computations (exec, wait,...) are abstracted by their complexity (a duration) in one unique "delay" operation.

– $C \subset S_o \times S_i$ *is a set of* connexions.

It is syntactically correct if and only if :

– $\forall \langle s_o, s_i \rangle \in C, profile(s_o) = profile(s_i)$
– $\forall T \in \mathcal{T}, d(T)$ *is syntactically correct and* $keys(ad_T) \subseteq \mathcal{K}$.

Architecture models rely on specific SysML blocks called *hardware nodes*. There are different kinds of hardware nodes, depending on the compoment they model: *Bus, CPU, FPGA, HWA* (hardware accelerator), *DMA Controller, Memory,* and *Bridge*.

Definition 11 (Architecture Model).
An architecture model *is a 2-uple* $\langle \mathcal{H}, \mathcal{L} \rangle$ *where:*

– $\mathcal{H} = Buses \sqcup CPU \sqcup FPGA \sqcup HWA \sqcup DMA \sqcup Memories \sqcup Bridges$ *is a finite set of* hardware nodes.
– $\mathcal{L} \subset (\mathcal{H} \backslash Buses) \times Buses$ *is a set of* links *between hardware nodes.*

Definition 12 (HSW-Model).
A HSW-Model *is a 4-uple* $\langle App, Arch, Alloc_t, Alloc_k \rangle$ *where* $App = \langle \mathcal{T}, d, C, \mathcal{K} \rangle$ *is an application model,* $Arch = \langle \mathcal{H}, \mathcal{L} \rangle$ *is an architecture model such as defined in Definition 11, and:*

– $Alloc_t : \mathcal{T} \to CPU \sqcup FPGA \sqcup HWA$ *is a total function called* task allocation.
– $Alloc_k \subseteq \mathcal{K} \times Memories$ *is the* key allocation.

It is syntactically correct iff App is syntactically correct and, informally,

– *for each signal connection there is a path from the execution node of the task of the output signal to a memory and a path from this memory to the execution node of the task of the input signal.*
– *for each key used by a task, there is a path from the execution node of the task to a memory where the key is allocated.*

(roughly speaking, a path is a sequence of linked busses and bridges between an execution node and a memory)

4   W-Sec: Theory and Practice

W-Sec relies on formal methods, since its aim is to **quantitatively** assess the impact and efficiency of security countermeasures. Verification techniques, including model-checking and simulation, are then needed for verifying safety and security properties as well as performance thresholds. Therefore formal methods take part in the four W-Sec stages: an initial modeling stage, a second modeling (mutation) stage, a verification stage and then a last modeling (enrichment) stage. This section explains these four stages both from theoretical a point of view and an applied perspective. These stages derive from the stages of our initial NTA-based impact assessment method, and bring to them several substantial improvements as discussed in Sect. 6.

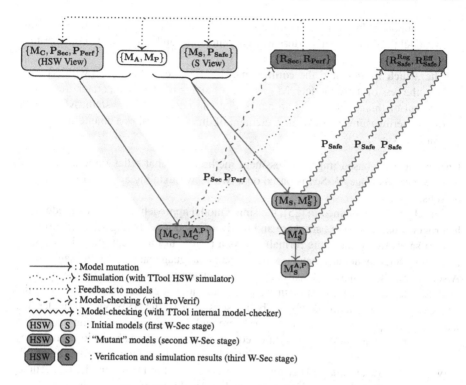

Fig. 2. The W-Sec Method (adapted from [25]).

4.1   Modeling the System Using S and HSW Views

The preliminary W-Sec stage consists in building a comprehensive modeling of the system. For this, three classes of models are designed:

- The **system models**, called S-Models (see Sect. 3), are captured in S-View. We denote with M_S the set of these system models: each element of M_S models the high-level discrete and physical behavior of the whole system[8]. Note that M_S gathers several models. Indeed, a system may operate according to different *functional scenarios*: for instance, the IT'm Factory's packaging chain can be controlled from the local control panel (first scenario), from the remote SCADA (second scenario), or from the both (third scenario). As we usually want to compute the countermeasures impact on the system according to several of these functional scenarios, we need to design one system model per scenario. Differences between these system models are usually light, e.g., the variables of some blocks are initialized with different values.

- The **components models**, called HSW-Models (see Sect. 3), are captured in HSW-View. We denote with M_C the set of these components models. M_C contains one model per modeled component[9]. As explained in [25], these models are focused on

---

[8] Systems models may also include some blocks and signals modeling the system's environment.

[9] A *component* is an equipment of the system. For instance, the components of IT'm Factory's packaging chain include the PLC, the two switches, the local control panel, etc.

the component but can also include some external tasks/hardware patterns in order to model the component's external communications and to be able to consider these external elements during the verification stage.

- The **attack models** and the **countermeasures models**. We denote with M_A and M_P the sets of these models. M_A is a set of attack models (e.g., attack trees): each element of this set describes an attack that can occur on the system. M_P is a set of countermeasures models: each element of this set describes a countermeasure we want to assess.

Unlike our NTA-based impact assessment method [26] that relies on a single model approach at this stage, W-Sec is based on a two-view modeling approach for two main reasons.

Firstly, as we explained in [25], the single model approach requires the modeling of heterogeneous items (e.g., software and hardware) and aspects (e.g., data security and system safety) with the same formalism. As a result, an important effort is necessary to express heterogeneous concepts with the same language and within the same views. Also, the resulting model typically lacks in precision with respect to one of the modeled aspects, for instance data security, and details are not given at the same abstraction level. The two-view approach tackles both issues since (i) the HSW-View provides dedicated SysML patterns for low-level hardware and data security modeling and (ii) the S-View provides a SysML profile tailored for complex systems behavioral modeling, including all the modeling capabilities of standard behavioral modeling formalisms like networks of finite automata. This approach thus enables for a better modeling accuracy with respect to both high-level (system) and low-level (components) aspects.

Secondly, gathering all aspects in a single model leads to a pointlessly complex model that may be difficult to formally verify or to simulate. Indeed, the objective consists in performing safety, security and performance analyses thanks to model-checking and simulation. To this end, some modeling aspects are essential when performing one of these three assessments while being unnecessary when performing the two others (e.g., the output values of an algorithm can be needed when analyzing its safety, while they can be useless when assessing its performance). Once again, the two-view approach addresses this issue since our modeling approach cleverly separates safety, security and performance concerns. On the one hand, **security** and **performance** assessments are indeed performed in the HSW-View: hardware modeling is obviously needed to assess a system's performance, and verifying the security properties we want to assess (i.e., integrity, authenticity and confidentiality of data when transferred between two components or processed by a component) includes hardware-related attacks (e.g., putting a probe on a bus, stealing a cryptographic key from a memory, . . .). On the other hand, **safety** assessments are carried out in the S-View, since their aim is to provide an analysis of the countermeasures regarding the overall system's functions and behavior. If safety countermeasures need to modify the HSW views, e.g., by introducing a redundancy on processor, then obviously the HSW view must be updated and performance and security reassessed. This drawback due to the separation of concerns is further discussed in Sect. 4.3.

In conclusion, the models of M_C shall only include the information that is necessary to precisely depict the software and hardware architecture of the modeled components, as well as the low-level security and performance, including algorithmic complexity, aspects. In addition, the models of M_S shall only integrate the information that is necessary to depict the high-level aspects of the system (e.g., system's functions, dynamics and system-wide network topology) and, if needed, some component-level information in order to depict the high-level behavior of the components algorithms (i.e., the evolution of their output parameters depending on their inputs).

Based on the system's safety, security and performance requirements, safety and security properties (P_{Safe} and P_{Sec}) are also designed at this preliminary stage, and performance thresholds (P_{Perf}) are also set. Due to our separation, security properties are included in the HSW-View while the S-View features safety properties. TTool offers specific pragmas to describe properties within views.

Example 1 (S-Model and HSW-Model).

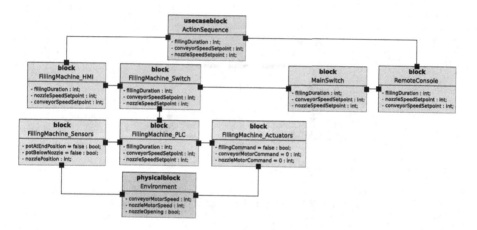

Fig. 3. S-Model: part of the block diagram modeling the filling machine.

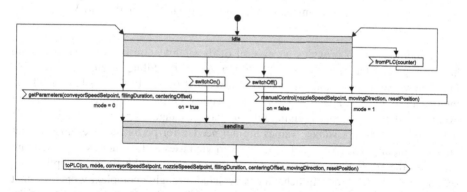

Fig. 4. S-Model: state-machine diagram modeling the behavior of the filling machine's control panel.

An excerpt of the packaging chain S-Model is given in Fig. 3 and 4:

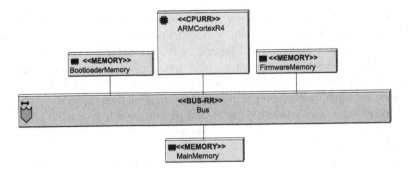

Fig. 5. HSW-Model: part of the architecture diagram of the filling machine PLC (based on the analysis presented in [1]).

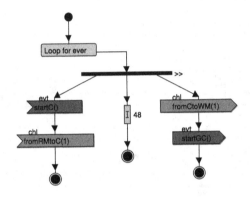

Fig. 6. HSW-Model: activity diagram of a typical task.

– Figure 3 shows the part of the block diagram modeling the filling machine. Note that only a subset of the blocks attributes and signals is displayed in this figure.
– Figure 4 shows the state-machine diagram associated with the block `Filling Machine_HMI`.

In addition, Fig. 5 provides an excerpt of the architecture diagram modeling the hardware part of the Siemens S7-1200 PLC used for the filling machine control, and Fig. 6 shows an activity diagram of a task executed by the PLC. The horizontal bar models a sequence of activities (from left to right). Purple sending/receiving refer to events, while blue sending/receiving refer to data exchanged. There, only a quantity of data is exchanged, not values: values are not needed for performance evaluation, but only the amount of values which is exchanged via buses and memories. This diagram illustrates the HSW-View modeling abstractions: apart from the signals reception and sending, the whole algorithm behavior is depicted through a complexity operator that performs 48 operations on integers. This figure has been chosen after an analysis of the source-code of the modeled task, by adding the number of add, multiply, move, etc. instructions along the most complex execution path.

At the end of this stage, the S-View then features the set of system models $\mathbf{M_S}$ and the set of safety properties $\mathbf{P_{Safe}}$, while the HSW-View features the set of components models $\mathbf{M_C}$, the set of security properties $\mathbf{P_{Sec}}$ and the set of performance thresholds $\mathbf{P_{Perf}}$ (see Fig. 2).

In order to ease the consistency between S and HSW views, the following modeling rules should be followed when it is possible:

- In the S-View, a component shall be modeled with one single block (that might, if needed, contain subblocks).
- In the HSW-View, for each HSW-Model, the attribute sets of the tasks shall be included in the attribute set of the S-Model block modeling the same component.
- In the HSW-View, for each HSW-Model, each output (resp. input) data signal modeling an external communication of the component shall match a unique output (resp. input) signal belonging to the output (resp. input) signals set of the S-Model block modeling the same component. More formally, given a component C, we denote with $\mathcal{M}_C \in \mathbf{M_C}$ its HSW-Model and with B_C the block modeling this component in models of $\mathbf{M_S}$. S_{oB_C} (resp. S_{iB_C}) is the output (resp. input) signals set of B_C. We denote with $S_{o\mathcal{M}_C}$ (resp. $S_{i\mathcal{M}_C}$) the output (resp. input) signals set of the application model of $\mathcal{M}_C$, and with $S_{o\mathcal{M}_C}^{d,ext} \subseteq S_{o\mathcal{M}_C}$ (resp. $S_{i\mathcal{M}_C}^{d,ext} \subseteq S_{i\mathcal{M}_C}$) the set of output (resp. input) *data* signals that model an external communication of the component. Then, it shall be ensured that $\forall \mathcal{M}_C \in \mathbf{M_C}, \exists f : S_{o\mathcal{M}_C}^{d,ext} \hookrightarrow S_{oB_C} \wedge \exists g : S_{i\mathcal{M}_C}^{d,ext} \hookrightarrow S_{iB_C}$[10].

4.2   Modeling the Countermeasures Deployment and the Attacks: HSW-Models and S-Models Mutations

Like in [26], the second W-Sec stage consists in altering the initial sets of models $\mathbf{M_S}, \mathbf{M_C}$ in order to enrich them with the attacks and countermeasures description provided by $\mathbf{M_A}$ and $\mathbf{M_P}$. Alterations of formal models are often called *mutations* [2,21] [24]. In our context, a mutation of a S-Model or of a HSW-Model is any alteration that preserves its syntactic correctness (see Definition 13, 14, 15).

S-Models Mutations

Definition 13 (S-Model Mutation). *Let $\mathfrak{S}$ be the set of all syntactically correct S-Models. We call S-Model mutation any (partial) function $\mu : \mathfrak{S} \rightarrow \mathfrak{S}$.*

Such a function can be seen as a composition of atomic modifications on the model, or *mutation operators* similarly to what is explained in [2] for timed automata. Concerning S-Models, these operators include:

- At S-Model level:
    1. Addition/deletion of a block
    2. Addition/deletion of a link between two ports
    3. Addition/deletion of a connexion

---

[10] $f : E \hookrightarrow F$ means that f is an injective application from E to F.

4. Addition/deletion of a block containment relation
- At block level:
  5. Addition/deletion of an attribute
  6. Addition/deletion of an input (resp. output) signal
  7. Addition/deletion of a state in the block's state machine diagram
  8. Addition/deletion of a transition in the block's state machine diagram

Formally defining each of these operators in this chapter would be pointlessly long; but we provide below, as an example, the definition of the block addition operator that is used in example 2.

Definition 14 (Block Addition). *Let $\mathfrak{B}$ be the set of all blocks and $\mathfrak{S}$ be the set of all syntactically correct S-Models. We define a* block addition *as the function*

$$add : \mathfrak{S} \times \mathfrak{B} \to \mathfrak{S}$$
$$(\mathcal{M}, B) \mapsto \mathcal{M}'$$

such that $\mathcal{M} = \langle \mathcal{B}, d, \mathcal{L}, \mathcal{C}, \mathcal{R} \rangle$ and $\mathcal{M}' = \langle \mathcal{B} \cup \{B\}, d, \mathcal{L}, \mathcal{C}, \mathcal{R} \rangle$.

Using these S-Model mutations, three sets of S-Models are derived from the set $\mathbf{M_S}$ and from the sets of countermeasures and attacks models $\mathbf{M_P}$ and $\mathbf{M_A}$.

1. $\mathbf{M_S^P}$. This set contains the initial S-Models enriched with the countermeasures descriptions. Since it is necessary to assess the impact of the countermeasures with respect to each functional scenario, each S-Model of $\mathbf{M_S}$ is mutated into $card(\mathbf{M_P})$ mutant S-Models (one per countermeasure). In other terms, if we denote with μ_{Patch} the mutation that integrates the countermeasure model *Patch* with a S-Model, $\mathbf{M_S^P} = \{\mu_{Patch}(\mathcal{M}) | \mathcal{M} \in \mathbf{M_S}, Patch \in \mathbf{M_P}\}$.

2. $\mathbf{M_S^A}$. This set contains the relevant initial S-Models enriched with the attacks descriptions: for each element of $\mathbf{M_A}$, each S-Models of $\mathbf{M_S}$ that model functional scenarios in which the modeled attack can occur is mutated into a S-Model enriched with the attack model. In other terms, if we denote with (i) μ_{Att} the mutation that integrates the attack model *Att* with a S-Model and with (ii) $\mathbf{M_{S\,Att}} \subseteq \mathbf{M_S}$ the set of S-Models that model functional scenarios in which the attack described by *Att* can occur, $\mathbf{M_S^A} = \bigcup_{Att \in \mathbf{M_A}} \{\mu_{Att}(\mathcal{M}) | \mathcal{M} \in \mathbf{M_{S\,Att}}\}$.

3. $\mathbf{M_S^{A,P}}$. This set contains the S-Models of $\mathbf{M_S^A}$ enriched with the countermeasures models: for each element of $\mathbf{M_S^A}$, $card(\mathbf{M_P})$ mutant S-Models (one per countermeasure) are produced. In other terms, if we denote with μ_{Patch} the mutation that integrates the countermeasure model *Patch* with a S-Model, $\mathbf{M_S^{A,P}} = \{\mu_{Patch}(\mathcal{M}) | \mathcal{M} \in \mathbf{M_S^A}, Patch \in \mathbf{M_P}\}$.

Example 2 (Mutations of S-Models).
Figure 7 shows the block diagram initially depicted in Fig. 3 after a mutation modeling the integration of the attack scenario introduced in Sect. 2. This mutation is the composition of: (i) a block addition, (ii) two link additions, (iii) two new connexions, (iv) two state additions and (v) seven transition additions in the RemoteConsole block. In addition, Fig. 8 shows an excerpt of the FillingMachine_PLC block's

state-machine diagram before and after a mutation modeling the offset setpoint check countermeasure. This mutation consists in (i) a transition deletion, (ii) two state additions and (iii) four transition additions.

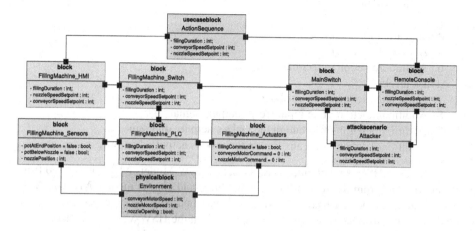

Fig. 7. M_S^A: mutation modeling an ARP spoofing and man in the middle attack.

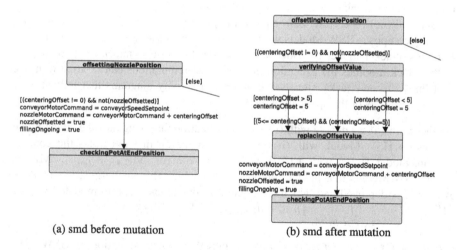

(a) smd before mutation   (b) smd after mutation

Fig. 8. M_S^P: mutation of a subpart of the PLC state-machine diagram, modeling the offset setpoint check.

HSW-Models Mutations

Definition 15 (HSW-Model Mutation). *Let $\mathfrak{C}$ be the set of all syntactically correct HSW-Models. We call HSW-Model mutation any (partial) function $\mu : \mathfrak{C} \nrightarrow \mathfrak{C}$.*

As for S-Models mutations, HSW-Models mutations are sequences of atomic operators:

- At HSW-Model level:
    1. Modification of the *task allocation* function
    2. Addition/deletion of an element in the *key allocation* set
- At architecture model level:
    3. Addition/deletion of a hardware node
    4. Addition/deletion of a link
- At application model level:
    5. Addition/deletion of a task
    6. Addition/deletion of a connexion
- At task level:
    7. Addition/deletion of an attribute
    8. Addition/deletion of an input (resp. output) signal
    9. Addition/deletion of a state in the tasks's activity diagram
    10. Addition/deletion of a transition in the tasks's activity diagram

Using these HSW-Model mutations, the set of HSW-Models $M_C^{A,P}$ is derived from the set M_C and from the sets of counteremeasures and attacks models M_P and M_A. This set contains the relevant HSW-Models[11] enriched with the countermeasures and attack descriptions. Due to the modeling approach in the HSW-View, countermeasures are often modeled with additional tasks and/or with additional complexity and encryption/decryption operators[12]. In HSW-View, attacks are modeled in two ways:

1. a Dolev-Yao attacker model is embedded in ProVerif [7], the security model-checker used in TTool. Therefore, before performing security verification, the tool automatically composes HSW-Models with a worst-case attack scenario at data level.
2. if this attacker model is inadequate to model the desired attack scenario (e.g., if the attack modifies the execution flow of a task), mutations can be used to model it thanks to new tasks, signals and actions in activity diagrams that influence the execution flow of the application model.

In other terms, if we denote with (i) μ_{Att} the mutation that integrates the attack model *Att* with a HSW-Model, with (ii) μ_{Patch} the mutation that integrates the countermeasure model *Patch* with a HSW-Model and with (iii) $M_{C\,Att,Patch} \subseteq M_C$ the set of HSW-Models that model components on which the countermeasure modeled by *Patch* is deployed and which is targeted by the attack scenario modeled by *Att*,

$$M_C^{A,P} = \bigcup_{Att \in M_A, Patch \in M_P} \{\mu_{Att} \circ \mu_{Patch}(\mathcal{M}) | \mathcal{M} \in M_{C\,Att,Patch}\}.$$

Example 3 (Mutations of HSW-Models). Figure 9 shows the mutation, in HSW-View, modeling the deployment of the offset setpoint check countermeasure. Since this countermeasure consists in performing two comparisons and at most one move instruction, the complexity operator modeling 48 integer operations is replaced with a complexity operator modeling three more operations on integers.

---

[11] i.e., the models of components on which the countermeasures described by M_P are deployed and that are targeted by the attack scenarios described by M_A.

[12] These operators are actions over transitions in the tasks activity diagrams (see Def. 7).

4.3   Computing the Impacts and Enriching the Models

Once the mutations have been applied, the third stage of W-Sec consists in computing the positive and negative impacts of the countermeasures thanks to formal verification and simulation.

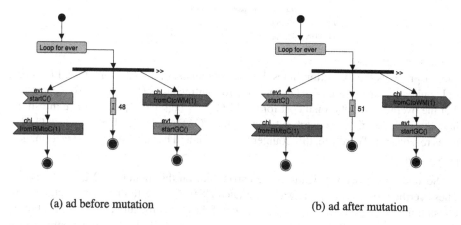

(a) ad before mutation   (b) ad after mutation

Fig. 9. $M_C^{A,P}$: mutation of an activity diagram of a task executed by the PLC, modeling the offset setpoint check.

Computing the Components-Level Performance and Security Impacts

First, simulations are performed with TTool's internal simulator on the models of M_C and on the models of $M_C^{A,P}$. The aim of these simulations is to measure, for each component targeted by a given countermeasure, the total execution time of an iteration of the application modeled in the component's HSW-Model. The set R_{Perf} contains the results of these simulations.

Example 4 (Performance Impacts)
(i) Composition of the Set M_C. We have modeled two components in the HSW-View: the filling machine's S7-1200 PLC, and the SCADA (i.e., the remote console). The whole control algorithm has been modeled in the PLC application model, whereas only an abstract setpoint message formatting and sending task has been modeled in the SCADA application model.
(ii) Assessed Countermeasure. We provide here the performance assessment results of the symmetric encryption countermeasure. Note that the full results (i.e. regarding the four countermeasures) will be provided in Sect. 6.
(iii) Chosen Performance Thresholds. In our case-study, we consider that the PLC performance threshold is given by the filling machine's sensors commutation rate. As their maximum commutation rate is equal 500 Hz, the full operating cycle of the PLC (i.e., the elapsed time between the reception of a setpoint message and the sending of the commands/supervision message) shall remain **below 2 ms**. In addition, since the

SCADA console is not safety-critical we have not set up a performance threshold for this component; notwithstanding, we still can compare the execution times after/before the deployment of the countermeasures and therefore quantify their overhead cost.

Table 1. Some performance assessment results.

	No countermeasure	Symmetric Encryption
PLC	608.5 ns	690 ns (+13,3%)
SCADA	42.5 ns	170.8 ns (+301,9%)

(iv) Results (R_{Perf}):
Table 1 provides the execution times[13], in nanoseconds, of an iteration of the PLC control application and of the SCADA message formatting and sending task. We can notice that the overall computational cost for the PLC is far below our performance threshold in both cases, and that the overhead cost for the SCADA message handling task (128.3 ns) is reasonable. Therefore, this countermeasure should be suitable from a performance perspective.

Secondly, security verifications are carried out on the models of M_C and $M_C^{A,P}$. These verifications consists in (i) an automated HSW-Models to ProVerif specifications translation [17, 18] and (ii) a model-checking of these specifications against the chosen security properties with ProVerif. The set of security results R_{Sec} is thus built at this stage.

Example 5 (Security Verification).
(i) Composition of the Set M_C,
(ii) Assessed Countermeasure: same as above.
(iii) Chosen Security Properties. Since we want to protect the system against a falsification of the network messages sent to the PLC, we have chosen to verify the data origin authenticity (*strong authenticity*) and data integrity (*weak authenticity*) for the following data channels: SCADA → Main switch and Filling machine switch → PLC.
(iv) Results (R_{Sec}):

Table 2. Some security assessment results.

	No countermeasure	Symmetric Encryption
SCADA → Main switch	Weak auth.: ✗ Strong auth.: ✗	Weak auth.: ✓ Strong auth.: ✗
Local switch → PLC	Weak auth.: ✗ Strong auth.: ✗	Weak auth.: ✓ Strong auth.: ✗

Table 2 provides the formal verification results concerning the two chosen properties. We notice that the nominal (i.e., with no countermeasure deployed) system does not protect the two studied data flows from an attacker. On the other hand, symmetric encryption in our implementation seems to enable the components for detecting any alteration of the data conveyed by the both channels[14].

---

[13] Each figure is an average of 10 consecutive measurements.
[14] Actually, symmetric encryption does not provide integrity. But our verifying environment assumed that if a ciphered message is modified by an attacker, the receiver will notice that the deciphered text is inconsistent.

Computing the System-Level Safety Impacts

The last impact assessment performed at this stage consists in verifying the models of M_S, M_S^P, M_S^A and $M_S^{A,P}$ against the chosen safety properties. The models are verified thanks to the direct model-checking algorithm of S-Models embedded in TTool [10]. Like in our NTA-based impact assessment method [26], the aim of these model-checking operations is to quantify:

- the safety regression due to each countermeasure deployment, thanks to the comparison of the model verifications performed on the models belonging to M_S and M_S^P.
- the efficiency of each countermeasure in terms of safety requirements recovery when the attack is carried out, thanks to the comparison of the model verifications performed on the models belonging to M_S^A and $M_S^{A,P}$.

Example 6 (Safety Assessment).

(i) Functional Scenarios. The two functional scenarios **Sc1** and **Sc2** (see Sect. 2) are assessed.

(ii) Assessed Countermeasure. We present here the safety assessment of the offset setpoint check.

(iii) Safety Properties. We have chosen to evaluate the following safety properties. **P1**: every pot put on the conveyor belt will eventually be filled by the machine with the volume chosen by the operator; **P2**: the machine never discharges grains outside of a pot (on the conveyor belt); and **P3**: the SCADA remote console is always kept up-to-date with the number of filled pots.

(iv) Results (P_{Perf}):

Table 3. Some safety assessment results.

	No countermeasure	Offset check
P1	✓	✓
P2	✓	✓
P3	✓	✓

(a) No attack, scenarios **Sc1** and **Sc2**

	No countermeasure	Offset check
P1	✗	✓
P2	✗	✓
P3	✓	✓

(b) With attack, scenario **Sc2**

Table 3 (a) shows that the assessed countermeasure does not cause any safety regression, neither in scenario **Sc1** nor in scenario **Sc2**: with respect to our safety requirements, this countermeasure has no negative impact. In addition, Table 3 (b) shows that when the attack is carried out, the countermeasure preserves the properties **P1** and **P2** that the nominal system was not able to preserve: this countermeasure therefore has a positive impact.

Enriching the Models

Once the assessment results are known, further W-Sec iterations may be necessary in order to refine the countermeasures models M_P. For instance, for a given countermeasure, performance results on a component might reveal that some functions cannot be executed by the component: the countermeasure model shall then be refined in order to express this issue in the S-Models thanks to more suitable mutations. Once the models M_P have been refined, the second and third W-Sec phases are performed again in order to obtain more accurate assessment results.

In addition, if one of the assessed countermeasures $Patch$ is selected to be deployed on the system, the $\{M_C, M_S\}$ model base must be modified in order to keep them up-to-date: M_S is replaced with the subset of M_S^P that depicts the deployment of $Patch$ on the system; and the elements of M_C that model a component targeted by $Patch$ are replaced with the result of the mutation integrating $Patch$ with themselves.

5   Related Works

Assessing the (negative and positive) impacts of several security countermeasures in order to find the optimal one is not really a new research topic: Brykczynski and Small [8] and Nicol [22] highlighted in 2003 and 2005 the interest of such an assessment before the deployment of a countermeasure. Subsequently, several optimal countermeasures selection methods have been proposed. Nespoli et al. [20] provided an interesting litterature survey focused on the recent (between 2012 and 2016) contributions to this topic. When it comes to evaluate the countermeasures' negative impacts, the surveyed approaches mainly focus on the monetary cost of them. However, as we explained in [25], "several of them express the impacts in terms of system downtime or impacts on the provided services, e.g. in terms of confidentiality, integrity, availability and performance. Depending on the methods, these impacts can be used as inputs of the selection method (thus they are not computed on the basis of the countermeasure description but chosen on the basis of a human analysis), or computed." Some of these approaches even explicitly assess the "collateral damages" of the countermeasures, like the one presented by Gonzalez-Granadillo et al. [14]. Nevertheless, none of them seem to enable for a precise enough countermeasures impact assessment with respect to the behavior of the system, which is critical regarding CPS. For instance, a comprehensive evaluation of a software countermeasure deployed on a PLC controlling a physical process requires, beyond the evaluation of the availability of the PLC, to quantify how the output command values of the PLC's control algorithms are affected. To the best of our knowledge, however, few contributions published after this survey propose approaches enabling for a precise and objective impact assessment of security countermeasures with respect to the systems behaviors.

Part of a patch-management approach for naval systems, we proposed in [26] a formal verification-based impact assessment method for security countermeasures. This method relies on formal modeling and verification of networks of UPPAAL timed automata [6]. Firstly, the system is modeled with a network of timed automata (NTA). Then, when a vulnerability that affect the system is discovered, the NTA is *mutated* into four sets of new NTAs modeling (i) the vulnerable system, (ii) the vulnerable system enhanced with security countermeasures mitigating the vulnerability, (iii) the realization of successful attacks exploiting this vulnerability on the original vulnerable system, and (iv) the realization of these attacks on the "patched" systems. Afterwards, the original NTA as well as the modified NTAs are formally verified against a set of safety properties. The positive and negative impacts of the evaluated countermeasures are then assessed by comparing the verification results. Formal modeling and verification for the assessment of cybersecurity-related events (countermeasures deployment, attacks) is well-suited to the context of CPS – including ICS –, and further promising contributions have been proposed by Jawad et Jaskolka in [15] regarding the impact assessment of cyberattacks, and by Jawad et al. in [16] where the authors model a botnet infrastructure with UPPAAL NTAs and evaluate the efficiency of a countermeasure thanks to simulation. Nevertheless, as we explained in [24], a drawback of our previous approach [26] is that the NTA-based modeling formalism lacks in expressiveness with respect to data security aspects: for instance, data confidentiality is here modeled in a too simplistic way, with a boolean variable modeling an illegitimate access to the component processing the data. As a consequence, the verification of the properties expressing data security requirements may lead to results that are not accurate and/or representative enough. In addition, designing a fine-grained modeling of heterogeneous aspects (e.g., hardware architecture, scheduling policy of a processor, and software behavior) of a system in a same modeling language can be time-consuming and error-prone, and the resulting model can be complex to understand as it encompasses heterogeneous aspects in a single modeling view. In addition, gathering all the modeled aspects in a single fine-grained model may also lead to a state-space explosion at verification stage due to the potential multiplication of states, variables, etc.

The aim of W-Sec is precisely to address these lacks. This requires more suitable modeling formalisms and tools that enable for designing and verifying formal models in a fine-grained way while enabling for capturing heterogeneous aspects without complexifying the models. SysML-Sec [4] provides a framework and a method for designing safe and secure embedded systems. For these needs, SysML-Sec relies on two enhanced and formally defined SysML profiles that enables for modeling high-level system architectural and behavioral aspects, as well as fine-grained hardware ones. SysML-Sec is fully supported by the toolkit TTool that provides a graphical and easy-to-use interface for designing and verifying models with the two SysML-Sec profiles: direct model-checking [9] and simulation can be performed with TTool. In addition, TTool provides two distinct modeling views (one per SysML profile) that help simplifying the system models, and is tailored for producing joint safety, security and performance analyses [3], thus spanning the three critical assessment dimensions of a countermeasure. For these reasons, have chosen TTool and its tailored formal SysML profiles as the underlying formalism and toolkit for designing a method improving our previous one [26]. In a complementary way, W-Sec also complements the SysML-Sec method. Indeed, the attack model considered in SysML-Sec is the Dolev-Yao one [11]. Therfore other kinds of attacks such as "sequences of exploitation of vulnerabilities of several components" [4] are considered out of scope. TW-Sec then widens the considered attack corpus as it considers modular attack scenarios like in [26].

6 Discussion

6.1 Regarding Our Previous Contributions

As we explained in [25], W-Sec merges contributions from SysML-Sec and [26] (see Table 4). As a result, W-Sec brings several improvements to both of the methods. With regards to [26]:

- W-Sec "reduces the models complexity since it does not rely on a single NTA but on several models that can separately be simulated and verified. These models are based on two distinct views which only contain the information needed for their respective purposes (i.e., safety assessment at system-level or security and performance assessment), and do not aggregate all this information in a single view.
- Hardware modeling relies on configurable templates already defined in TTool (CPU, memories, DMA, etc.) so it helps reducing the modeling time and effort, while giving more precision to the models with respect to the NTA approach.
- Low-level security aspects can be captured in a more fine-grained way. In addition, this low-level security modeling is facilitated thanks to TTool predefined security-related patterns (e.g., cryptographic algorithm models or hardware firewall blocks).
- Thanks to the simulation and verification tools provided by TTool, W-Sec assesses the impact of countermeasures and attacks, with respect to a widened property basis. Indeed, we can now evaluate fine and low-level security properties (e.g., related to the integrity of a data transfer, or the confidentiality of a component data)." [25]

In addition, as explained in Sect. 5, W-Sec also complements the SysML-Sec approach thanks to the consideration of modular attack scenarios.

Table 4. Comparison with SysML-Sec and [26] (table expanded from [25]).

Modeling formalism	From SysML-Sec and [12]
Two-views modeling	From SysML-Sec
Use of HSW-View for low-level component modeling	W-Sec contribution
Separation of safety concerns at system level in S-View vs. security and performance aspects at component-level in HSW-View	W-Sec contribution
Attacks and countermeasures modeling through model mutations	From [26]
S-Models and HSW-Models mutations definitions and operators	W-Sec contribution
Impact assessment approach	From [26] (composition of the sets of mutant system models, comparison of verification results)

6.2   Regarding IT'm Factory Case-Study Results

W-Sec has been evaluated with the IT'm Factory's packaging chain case-study. This evaluation provides interesting results, complementary to those discussed in [25] where W-Sec is evaluated with a rover swarm case-study. Indeed, even if these two systems have common aspects (cyber-physical systems, safety-critical systems, etc.) they also have significant differences : contrary to the rover swarm, the packaging chain is a real system, it relies on highly specific devices like PLCs, the source code of its control algorithms was provided in a domain-specific language —*ladder logic*—, etc.).

The first interesting conclusion is that the W-Sec modeling approach is well suited for modeling industrial systems, especially PLCs. Designing the PLC HSW-Models was really natural indeed, since ladder logic includes low-level instructions that can easily be converted in complexity operators (see Fig. 6). Moreover, the sequential logic of PLC algorithms is particularly consistent with the semantics of tasks and activity diagrams in HSW-Models. However, the modeling stage is still an engineering task that may require a lot of time depending on the modeled system. Given the relative semantic proximity between ladder logic and our modeling formalism, the (partial) automation of the models generation from PLC source-code is an interesting research direction we intend to investigate.

Also regarding the modeling stage, we have been able to optimize the S-Models to avoid combinatorial explosion at verification stage, while this issue occurred in the rovers case-study [25]. Yet, both the rover swarm and the packaging chain necessitate "environment" blocks that compute the evolution of the physical parameters of the systems, leading to potential highly-complex state space graphs. This shows that W-Sec can be suitable for complex systems of systems, provided the S-Models are wisely designed.

Four countermeasures were evaluated in this case-study. They target different components, implement different mechanisms and belong to two categories: software patches (**C1**, **C2** and **C3**) and hardware temporary workaround (**C4**). For each of these countermeasures, we were able to provide appropriate models with HSW and S-Models mutations that seem well suited for the countermeasures modeling needs. Notwithstanding these encouraging results, applying these mutations still requires human intervention and thus can be time-consuming. We are currently working on a mutation language and compiler that will enable for automating this process: the new formalization provided in Sect. 3 is a good step towards this automation.

Table 5. Full safety assessment results.

	P1	P2	P3
Sc1	✓	✓	✓
Sc2	✓	✓	✓
Sc2 + Attack	✗	✗	✓

(a) without countermeasure

	P1	P2	P3
Sc1	✓	✓	✓
Sc2	✓	✓	✓
Sc2 + Attack	✓	✓	✓

(b) **C1** (offset check)

	P1	P2	P3
Sc1	✓	✓	✓
Sc2	✓	✓	✓
Sc2 + Attack	✗	✓	✓

(c) **C2** (encryption)

	P1	P2	P3
Sc1	✓	✓	✓
Sc2	✓	✓	✓
Sc2 + Attack	✓	✓	✓

(d) **C3** (static ARP table)

	P1	P2	P3
Sc1	✓	✓	✗
Sc2	✗	✓	✗
Sc2 + Attack	✗	✓	✗

(d) **C4** (unplugging)

Table 6. Full performance assessment results.

	No countermeasure	C1	C2	C3	C4
PLC	608.5 ns	610.7 ns	690 ns	608.5 ns	608.5 ns
SCADA	42.5 ns	42.5 ns	170.8 ns	40.6 ns	42.5 ns

Table 7. Full security assessment results.

	No countermeasure	C1	C2
SCADA → Main switch	Weak auth.: ✗ Strong auth.: ✗	Weak auth.: ✗ Strong auth.: ✗	Weak auth.: ✓ Strong auth.: ✗
Local switch → PLC	Weak auth.: ✗ Strong auth.: ✗	Weak auth.: ✗ Strong auth.: ✗	Weak auth.: ✓ Strong auth.: ✗

	C3	C4
SCADA → Main switch	Weak auth.: ✗ Strong auth.: ✗	Weak auth.: ✗ Strong auth.: ✗
Local switch → PLC	Weak auth.: ✗ Strong auth.: ✗	Weak auth.: ✗ Strong auth.: ✗

The third W-Sec stage (i.e., impact assessment) provided results that are presented in Tables 5, 6 and 7. As in [25], these results shows the relevance of a joint safety/ security/ performance assessment of countermeasures. Indeed, a mere safety analysis would lead to chose the countermeasures **C1** and **C3**: the security analysis yet shows that the system with these countermeasures is still vulnerable to a Dolev-Yao attacker on the two critical data channels studied. Similarly, a single performance analysis would lead to select **C3** and **C4**, although the safety verification results show an important regression for **C4**. Finally the security analysis alone favors **C2**, which leads to a safety regression on one property with respect to **C1** and **C3**.

Relatedly, these results illustrate a current lack of our method. Indeed, comparing the assessment results to find the optimal countermeasure may be a difficult problem since it requires to rank very different properties between them (e.g., is it more important to ensure that no grain can be discharged on the conveyor belt, to minimize the duration of a PLC algorithm iteration or to ensure that one of the communication channels is protected with integrity?). We tried to address a similar problem in [26], but the proposed metrics was based on the definition of a strict total order on the importance of properties and functional scenarios (called *missions*), that may lack in realism [24]. An interesting research direction could be to affect weights to functional scenarios and properties, enabling for a non-strict ordering of properties and scenarios and defining evaluation formulae based on these weights.

Concerning the results again, note that it is necessary to put the SCADA performance results into perspective: unlike the PLC HSW-Model, the SCADA console HSW-Model is not based on a real system description nor on a real algorithm. We have arbitrarily considered that the supervision application runs on a standard host (Core i5 CPU), and we have modeled a fictitious algorithm creating a network message and sending it. Therefore, the SCADA performance results are far less likely than the PLC ones that are based on the real system. They should only be seen as complementary results that illustrate how the method can deal with several HSW-Models.

7   Conclusions and Future Works

Extending the works presented at ModelsWard 2022 [25], this chapter provides a detailed and formalized description of W-Sec, a formal model-based method for assessing the safety, security and performance impacts of security countermeasures. It also defines three consistency rules that help ensuring the consistency of the models used in the method. For those purposes, it also provides new mathematic definitions of the two SysML profiles used in SysML-Sec and W-Sec. W-Sec has now been evaluated with two case-studies, a rover swarm and a connected factory's packaging chain: the chapter presents the results of the latter and discusses the relevance of the method for this new application field. It also discusses the current limitations of W-Sec, and gives several research perspectives.

We are currently investigating two of them. Firstly, the automation of the second (mutation) W-Sec stage: the mathematic definitions given in Sect. 3 enable for formally defining each mutation operator and designing a mutation language. A compiler for this language is currently being implemented in TTool. Secondly, we are studying the semantic links between the ladder logic language, used for programming Siemens PLCs, and the two SysML profiles we use. This is the first step towards the automation of the first (modeling) W-Sec stage in the context of industrial control systems. A third interesting research perspective we intend to investigate is the design of tailored metrics enabling for an easy comparison of the impact assessment results. We also plan to evaluate W-Sec with further attack and countermeasures scenarios on our connected factory case-study.

References

1. Abbasi, A., Scharnowski, T., Holz, T.: Doors of Durin: The Veiled Gate to Siemens S7 Silicon. BlackHat Europe (2019)
2. Aichernig, B.K., Lorber, F., Ničković, D.: Time for mutants — model-based mutation testing with timed automata. In: Veanes, M., Viganò, L. (eds.) TAP 2013. LNCS, vol. 7942, pp. 20–38. Springer, Heidelberg (2013). https://doi.org/10.1007/978-3-642-38916-0_2
3. Apvrille, L., Li, L.W.: Harmonizing safety, security and performance requirements in embedded systems. In: 2019 Design, Automation & Test in Europe Conference & Exhibition (DATE), pp. 1631–1636. IEEE (2019)
4. Apvrille, L., Roudier, Y.: SysML-Sec: a SysML environment for the design and development of secure embedded systems. In: APCOSEC 2013. Yokohama, Japan (Aug 2013). https://hal.telecom-paris.fr/hal-02288385
5. Apvrille, L., de Saqui-Sannes, P., Hotescu, H., Tempia-Calvino, A.: SysML models verification relying on dependency graphs. In: MODELSWARD, pp. 174–181 (2022)

6. Behrmann, G., David, A., Larsen, K.G.: A tutorial on UPPAAL. Formal methods for the design of real-time systems, pp. 200–236 (2004)
7. Blanchet, B.: An efficient cryptographic protocol verifier based on prolog rules. In: 14th IEEE Computer Security Foundations Workshop (CSFW-14), pp. 82–96. IEEE Computer Society, Cape Breton, Nova Scotia, Canada (Jun 2001)
8. Brykczynski, B., Small, R.A.: Reducing internet-based intrusions: effective security patch management. IEEE Softw. 20(1), 50–57 (2003)
9. Calvino, A., Apvrille, L.: Direct model-checking of SysML models. In: Proceedings of the 9th International Conference on Model-Driven Engineering and Software Development - Volume 1: MODELSWARD, pp. 216–223. INSTICC, SciTePress (2021). https://doi.org/10.5220/0010256302160223
10. Calvino, A.T., Apvrille, L.: Direct model-checking of SysML models. In: 9th International Conference on Model-Driven Engineering and Software Development, pp. 216–223. SCITEPRESS-Science and Technology Publications (2021)
11. Dolev, D., Yao, A.: On the security of public key protocols. IEEE Trans. Inf. Theor. 29(2), 198–208 (1983). https://doi.org/10.1109/TIT.1983.1056650
12. Enrici, A., Apvrille, L., Pacalet, R.: A model-driven engineering methodology to design parallel and distributed embedded systems. ACM Trans. Design Autom. Electron. Syst. (TODAES) 22(2), 1–25 (2017)
13. Enrici, A., Li, L., Apvrille, L., Blouin, D.: A tutorial on TTool/DIPLODOCUS: an open-source toolkit for the design of data-flow embedded systems. Tech. rep. (2022)
14. Gonzalez-Granadillo, G., Garcia-Alfaro, J., Alvarez, E., El-Barbori, M., Debar, H.: Selecting optimal countermeasures for attacks against critical systems using the attack volume model and the RORI index. Comput. Electr. Eng. 47, 13–34 (2015)
15. Jawad, A., Jaskolka, J.: Analyzing the impact of cyberattacks on industrial control systems using timed automata. In: 2021 IEEE 21st International Conference on Software Quality, Reliability and Security (QRS), pp. 966–977 (2021). https://doi.org/10.1109/QRS54544.2021.00106
16. Jawad, A., Newton, L., Matrawy, A., Jaskolka, J.: A formal analysis of the efficacy of rebooting as a countermeasure against IoT botnets. In: 2022 IEEE Conference on Communications, ICC (2022)
17. Li, L.: Safe and secure model-driven design for embedded systems. Ph.D. thesis, Université Paris-Saclay (Sep 2018)
18. Lugou, F., Li, L.W., Apvrille, L., Ameur-Boulifa, R.: SysML models and model transformation for security. In: 2016 4th International Conference on Model-Driven Engineering and Software Development (MODELSWARD), pp. 331–338. IEEE (2016)
19. McLaughlin, S., et al.: The cybersecurity landscape in industrial control systems. Proc. IEEE 104(5), 1039–1057 (2016)
20. Nespoli, P., Papamartzivanos, D., Mármol, F.G., Kambourakis, G.: Optimal countermeasures selection against cyber attacks: a comprehensive survey on reaction frameworks. IEEE Commun. Surv. Tutorials 20(2), 1361–1396 (2017)
21. von Neumann, J., Burks, A.W., et al.: Theory of self-reproducing automata, vol. 1102024. University of Illinois press Urbana (1966)
22. Nicol, D.: Modeling and simulation in security evaluation. IEEE Secur. Priv. 3(5), 71–74 (2005). https://doi.org/10.1109/MSP.2005.129
23. Pedroza, G., Apvrille, L., Knorreck, D.: Avatar: a sysml environment for the formal verification of safety and security properties. In: 2011 11th Annual International Conference on New Technologies of Distributed Systems, pp. 1–10. IEEE (2011)
24. Sultan, B.: Maîtrise des correctifs de sécurité pour les systèmes navals. Ph.D. thesis, Ecole nationale supérieure Mines-Télécom Atlantique Bretagne Pays de la Loire (2020)

25. Sultan, B., Apvrille, L., Jaillon, P.: Safety, Security and Performance Assessment of Security Countermeasures with SysML-Sec. In: Proceedings of the 10th International Conference on Model-Driven Engineering and Software Development - MODELSWARD, pp. 48–60. INSTICC, SciTePress (2022). https://doi.org/10.5220/0010832300003119
26. Sultan, B., Dagnat, F., Fontaine, C.: A methodology to assess vulnerabilities and counter-measures impact on the missions of a naval system. In: Katsikas, S.K., et al. (eds.) Cyber-ICPS/SECPRE -2017. LNCS, vol. 10683, pp. 63–76. Springer, Cham (2018). https://doi.org/10.1007/978-3-319-72817-9_5

Managing Schema Migration in NoSQL Databases: Advisor Heuristics vs. Self-adaptive Schema Migration Strategies

Andrea Hillenbrand and Uta Störl

University of Hagen, Hagen, Germany
andrea.hillenbrand@studium.fernuni-hagen.de
uta.stoerl@fernuni-hagen.de

Abstract. Schema-flexible NoSQL databases are increasingly popular backends in the agile application development as they allow developers to write code assuming a new database schema that is different from the current one. If the application is in production already, non-functional requirements for application performance and cost efficiency are routinely part of service-level agreements (SLAs). Co-evolving the schema with the application code then requires subtle management decisions regarding the migration of variational legacy data that is persisted in the production database. Eventually, project managers have to deal with the repercussions of schema evolution in order to comply with SLAs, especially if stipulated metrics compete with each other in tradeoffs. To this end, we present a *NoSQL Schema Migration Advisor* that supports the schema migration management in NoSQL databases in two distinct ways: If the migration situation can be elicited, a heuristic is offered to estimate the impact of schema evolution by means of choosing a migration strategy and pace code releases accordingly. If this information is not sufficiently or not readily available, self-adaptive schema migration strategies are presented that can automatically curate variational data such that competing metrics can be balanced out in order to comply with SLAs, if possible, making management interventions superfluous.

Keywords: Databases · NoSQL · Data migration · Schema evolution · Schema migration · Automated curation · Variational data · Self-adaptive migration · Migration advisor

1 Introduction

Schema-flexible NoSQL databases allow developers to write application code in iterations, since a tentative, new database schemas can be assumed that is different from the current one. Then, new software releases can be planned and deployed without extra application downtime for the schema migration. Eventually, it has to be addressed how to handle the variational data that is persisted in the database, especially if it is in

This work has been funded by the German Research Foundation (project grant #385808805). We thank Jan-Christopher Mair, Kai Pehns, Tobias Kreiter, Shamil Nabiyev, and Maksym Levchenko from Darmstadt University of Applied Sciences for their contributions to *MigCast* and *Darwin*.

L. F. Pires et al. (Eds.): MODELSWARD 2021/2022, CCIS 1708, pp. 230–253, 2023.
https://doi.org/10.1007/978-3-031-38821-7_11

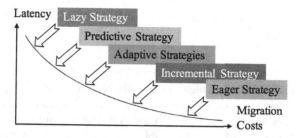

Fig. 1. Tradeoff between competing metrics in schema migration; adapted from [16] and published in [18].

production already. In such an agile development setting that deploys application code iteratively, managing the consequences of a flexible schema evolution comes up repeatedly, oftentimes in unison with changing non-functional requirements from service-level agreements (SLAs). In addition to the financial pressure, a crucial issue to overcome in this context is a timely handling of the schema evolution problem despite its complexity, i.e., forecasting the impact of schema evolution on relevant SLA-required metrics despite the fact that they are influenced by a multitude of factors.

Due to this mismatch, there seem only two approaches pragmatic in general. First, a *heuristic* allows an adequate solution in form of an approximation based on the correlations between migration situation characteristics and the impact of schema evolution. To realize this, we have investigated the schema evolution problem in terms of performance and financial metrics using a Monte Carlo method of repeated sampling [17,21]. In this present paper, we distill a heuristic that makes full use of the gathered knowledge on these correlations in order to forecast the impact of schema evolution in all possible migration situations. Although the existence of such a knowledge-based heuristic saves project managers time, monitoring the metrics and applying the heuristic repeatedly still requires resources and presupposes a suitable reaction time.

Moreover, this elicitation of the migration situation and application of a heuristic is inconvenient especially at the beginning of a software project, just when stakeholders are most busy and presumably workflows still inefficient. But reorganizing a database schema is often necessary due to newly emerging functional requirements. In [17], we have identified schema modification operations (SMOs) that affect data entities of multiple types as the most definite cost driver of schema evolution, e.g. copying or moving attributes between the types. Furthermore, we have found in our probabilistic experiments that, depending on the schema changes, measurements of metrics can vary by factor 900 in case of high cardinalities of the entity-relationships, sometimes resulting in exceptionally high migration costs and tail latencies. This uncertainty gets worse if the migration situation is unknown or future migration scenarios are hard to predict.

We have presented a second approach in [18] featuring self-adaptive schema migration strategies that can automatically curate variational data if this information is not sufficiently or readily available. Then, competing metrics can be balanced out to comply with SLAs, if possible, then making continuous management interventions superfluous. We also included in [18] a prototype of these self-adaptive migration strategies integrated in our schema migration advisor tool *MigCast*. Both solutions of the schema evolution problem, we now integrate into a consistent *NoSQL Schema Migration Advisor* in this present paper.

Contribution. We contribute a *NoSQL Schema Migration Advisor* that offers two solutions to the schema evolution problem: First, if the migration situation can be elicited, a heuristic is distilled based on a Monte Carlo method of repeated sampling in order to estimate the impact of schema evolution and choose a migration strategy as well as pace the code releases accordingly, if possible. Second, if this information is not sufficiently or readily available, self-adaptive schema migration strategies are presented that can automatically curate variational data such that competing metrics can comply with SLAs, if possible, then making continuous management interventions superfluous. This way, the necessity of navigating a heuristic repeatedly in order to deal with the impact of schema evolution can be overcome, which is especially crucial during busy times of the project management.

2 Definitions and Architecture

Migration strategies vary with respect to how much and when they migrate and thus curate legacy data that is structured according to earlier schema versions. The *eager* migration strategy migrates all of the variational data right away at the release of software code implying schema changes. This produces maximal charges with the service provider if the database is in production already and hosted in a cloud setting. The advantage of this investment into a structurally homogeneous database instance is that a migration-induced runtime overhead is avoided, which is especially crucial for the performance of cloud-hosted applications [3,7,10]. On the other hand, if budgetary savings are favored in the SLAs at the opportunity cost of application performance, then a *lazy* strategy minimizes these *migration costs*, since data remains unchanged in the event of schema changes. The drawback of this is though, that a considerable latency overhead is introduced [23,31]. The metrics *migration costs* and *latency* thus compete in a tradeoff where alternative strategies in between *eager* and *lazy* approaches can resolve this tradeoff at different opportunity costs, which is depicted schematically in Fig. 1.

In this paper, we define and use the following *metrics*: We refer to the time that a *read access* takes as *data access latency*, i.e. the time from the query to retrieving the requested data entity. Latency competes in a tradeoff with the monetary charges that are occasioned by migrating the data with a cloud service provider, which we refer to as *migration costs*. The costs are based on actual and recent tariffs by leading cloud service providers.[1] The migration costs consist of *on-release* and *on-read migration costs*, which together make up the *cumulated migration costs*. *On-release* migration costs are caused when entities are migrated in the event of SMOs that change the database schema. In contrast, *on-read* migration costs are caused when entities are accessed that exist in older versions than the current schema required by the application code.

---

[1] The *MigCast* pricing model is specified at USD 0.2 per 1M I/O-Requests and is based on Amazon DocumentDB (AWS) for US-East. It can be viewed at https://aws.amazon.com/en/documentdb/pricing/, visited on February 2, 2022.

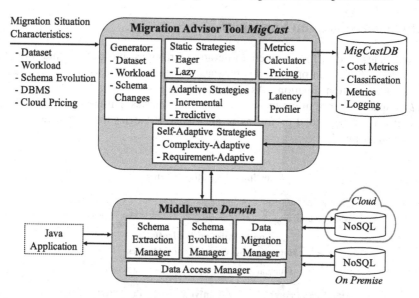

Fig. 2. Architecture of the *MigCast*, a NoSQL schema migration advisor tool based on the schema management middleware *Darwin*; in contrast to non-self-adaptive strategies, self-adaptive strategies automatically change the extent of schema migration according to the monitored metrics (note the arrow back from the *MigCast* database); illustration adapted from [17].

In contrast to the above cost metrics, we use the following *classification metrics* as commonly defined [38], in particular in [20]: By *precision*, it is referred to the fraction of correctly predicted entities among the total predicted entities, i.e., $p := \mathrm{tp}(\mathrm{tp} + \mathrm{fp})^{-1}$ where tp is the number of true positives and fp the number of false positives. *Recall* is defined by the fraction of correctly predicted entities among the accessed entities, i.e., $r := \mathrm{tp}(\mathrm{tp} + \mathrm{fn})^{-1}$ where fn is the number of false negatives. The traditional F_1-measure is the harmonic mean of precision p and recall r, i.e., $F_1 = 2pr(p + r)^{-1}$. The F_1-measure emphasizes values closer to zero compared to the arithmetic or geometric means. The F_1-measure keeps an equal importance for each metric, whereas the more general F_β-measure gives one metric more importance than the other, as defined by [30]: $F_\beta := (1 + \beta^2)pr(\beta^2 \cdot p + r)^{-1}$

MigCast is our NoSQL schema migration advisor tool, which we presented in earlier work [16,19]. The architecture follows the overview of Fig. 2. *MigCast* generates the migration situations, computes the scenarios for each migration strategy throughout a sequence of schema changes according to the parameterizable *MigCast* configurations, and calculates various cost and classification metrics by means of the schema management middleware *Darwin* [35]. Specifically, the cost model of *MigCast* takes all relevant situation characteristics into account: i. intensity and distribution of data entity accesses, ii. different kinds of schema changes as regards the share of SMOs affecting single types or multiple types, and iii. the cardinality of the entity-relationships of the dataset, and calculates the monetary migration charges and the data access latency, as well as classification metrics like precision and recall in order to assess the structural heterogeneity of the database instance, while persisting all data in the *MigCast*DB database. For more details, be referred to [17,20].

3   Schema Migration Strategies

We have integrated different schema migration strategies into our schema migration advisor tool *MigCast* in order to demonstrate the effectiveness and the pros and cons in different migration situations. As illustrated in Fig. 3, the migration strategies *eager* and *lazy* span the space of opportunity costs on the metrics. Different compromises on this tradeoff can be settled by means of alternative strategies that populate the space between *eager* and *lazy*.[2]

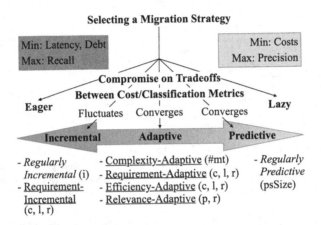

Fig. 3. Selecting a migration strategy settles on a compromise between metrics that compete in tradeoffs at certain opportunity costs; italic are strategies with adaptive features, underscored are strategies with self-adaptive features, each with their parameters in parentheses.

3.1   Non-self-Adaptive Migration Strategies

Regularly Incremental Migration. A common compromise between *eager* and *lazy* is the *incremental* strategy which fluctuates between these extremes at the disadvantage of an unstable, though not entirely unpredictable latency. With the *incremental* strategy, schema changes are usually treated like with *lazy* migration, the disarray in the database increasing accordingly. But at certain periodic increments, legacy entities in the databases are migrated to match the current schema and thus, getting rid of the runtime overhead intermittently that is caused by updating legacy entities on-the-fly when being accessed.

Regularly Predictive Migration. If the query workload concentrates on *hot* data, i.e., on data that is Pareto-distributed, the *predictive* strategy settles on a compromise with a better cost-benefit ratio of invested migration costs for improved latency. This strategy exhibits a more stable latency and can thus be selected towards a heuristic when the workload is Pareto-distributed and cost savings are just as important as avoiding tail latencies.

---

[2] We have already analyzed possible options of self-adaptation from a theoretical stance in [19, 20] and the prototype in [18].

The *predictive* strategy is controlled through adapting the cardinality of the set of entities to be migrated after an SMO, what we refer to as *prediction set size* psSize [20]. In order to keep a steady balance between metrics, we devised the *predictive* strategy which keeps hot entities in a *prediction set* and orders them according to their actuality and access frequency in an algorithm based on *exponential smoothing* [20]. Legacy entities that are not included in the prediction set, are migrated *lazily* when accessed. We view the *predictive* strategy as a strategy with adaptive features, since the psSize is parameterizable by the project manager according to the stipulated SLAs.

3.2 Self-adaptive Migration Strategies

Requirement-incremental Migration. Arguably, the simplest version of a self-adaptive strategy is an incremental migration that is initiated when a certain, configurable threshold is surpassed, which we refer to as *requirement-incremental* strategy [20] (cp. with Fig. 3). This threshold could be defined in terms of parameters like cost or classification metrics or combinations thereof. We view this strategy as having self-adaptive features as the migration adapts itself automatically according to parameterizable thresholds, yet we categorize it under the *incremental* strategies as its metrics fluctuate characteristically.

Figure 4 illustrates the *requirement-incremental* strategy throughout the releases of schema changes. Migration is initiated when the threshold for latency l_{max} is exceeded but not so the threshold for migration costs c_{max}. Thus, it follows a recurrent pattern of increasing latency until the *incremental* migration is initiated: Whereas in the first and second release, latency is below its threshold, in the third release, latency surpasses its threshold and the *incremental* migration is initiated, since the constraint of maximum migration costs holds. At release 4 with a structurally homogeneous database instance, latency has no runtime overhead for migrating legacy entities that are accessed. Latency increases again until release 6, but the migration costs have already exceeded the threshold. At release 7, a provisional budget increase to overcome the migration cost constraint allows an *incremental* migration to bring down the latency again to its minimum. This fluctuation is characteristic for all *incremental* approaches.

Complexity-adaptive Migration. Through the *complexity-adaptive* strategy we avoid tail latencies that can occur when legacy entities are accessed that have been affected by a sequence of multi-type SMOs, i.e., when operations modifying the database schema affect more than one entity type, like copy, move, split, or merge [9,25]. This usually happens during major schema changes at the beginning of a software development life-cycle (SDLC) and/or in agile development settings when the schema is reorganized. A backlog of a long sequence of consecutive multi-type schema changes can be moderated by increasing the prediction set size psSize automatically when a certain number of multi-type SMOs have accrued pertaining to that same type. Then, older and relatively frequently or recently accessed legacy entities are included in the prediction set and migrated up to the latest schema version.

This approach is a relevant self-adaptation since we have proven that multi-type complexity is a significant cost driver for both latency and migration costs compared to standard migration situation characteristics [17]. As discussed in [20], the differences of the metrics are significant for these migration situations of a higher share of multi-type SMOs. Since with the *complexity-adaptive* approach, the psSize is adapted

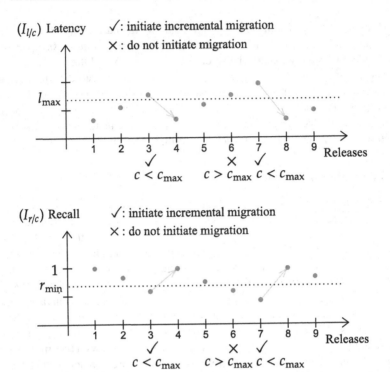

Fig. 4. The *requirement-incremental* strategy initiates migration when the threshold for latency is exceeded but not so the threshold for migration costs; adapted from [20].

automatically to react to a certain degree of disarray of the database, we consider it as *self-adaptive* (cp. with Fig. 3).

Requirement-Adaptive Migration. In the following, several metric-driven self-adaptive strategies are defined, which automatically react to disarray in the database in order to reach specified cost or classification metrics. First, we devise the algorithm of the *requirement-adaptive* migration strategy in Algorithm 1 that automatically adapts the prediction set size psSize. This strategy is parameterized by the thresholds of migration costs, c_{max}, and latency, l_{max}, as inputs. The metrics c and l are monitored and the psSize increased or decreased in order for the measurements of both metrics to comply with their thresholds, or find a suitable compromise. The monitored migration costs consist of the on-read migration costs caused by accessing legacy entities when serving the workload in between schema changes and the on-release migration costs caused by migrating legacy data due the last schema change.

As the metrics are competitors in a tradeoff, compromises can differ in the compromise as such but also in the way they are found. Whereas the first is a decision residing with the stakeholders, for the latter we outlined three feedback control systems of the *requirement-adaptive* strategy in general in [20], of which we spell out the most promising one in this paper, following [18]: The psSize of to-be-migrated legacy entities of the prediction set is adjusted to reach a balanced compromise through an average of the measured metrics in respect of their maximal thresholds, i.e., $\frac{c}{c_{max}}$ and $\frac{l}{l_{max}}$. The average can be realized through, e.g., the arithmetic mean, the geometric, or the harmonic mean. The main difference in this context is that the compromises are more or less careful in their change of the psSize. The more careful arithmetic mean has been selected to be implemented into *MigCast* in order to minimize possible fluctuations of the metrics that had become apparent with simpler feedback control systems [20].

Geometric Approach. In Fig. 5, tuple M represents the measured metrics since the past schema release with the auxiliary line β to indicate the used resources. Analogously, the red tuple T marks the thresholds of the metrics with the auxiliary line α to indicate the available resources. The red tuple can be connected to the origin, the red dotted line, and described by the function $\frac{c}{c_{max}} = \frac{l}{l_{max}}$ which expresses the compromise between the metrics. Consequently, the averages in green (F_1 for harmonic and $\varnothing$ for arithmetic means) of the share of measured metrics to required thresholds can be located on this red dotted line, with the harmonic mean F_1 as the furthest and the arithmetic mean $\varnothing$ as the compromise closest to the red tuple. Equivalently, the auxiliary lines (dashed green lines) are parallel to the red line representing different compromises.

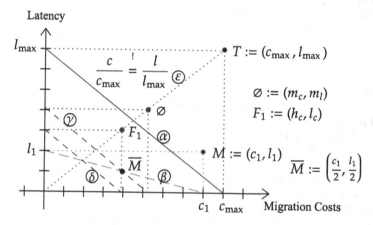

Fig. 5. The *requirement-adaptive* strategy using measured-to-required quotients to balance out the metrics: the psSize is adapted to balance out the metrics (M, line β) according to the thresholds (T, line α) through arithmetic $\varnothing$ or harmonic mean F_1 (γ and δ) such that their prospective values make up equal shares wrt. their thresholds; adapted from [18]. (Color figure online)

The intersections of the green lines with the x-axis are a geometric solution that determines how to adapt the psSize. They represent the predicted costs that are caused if the shares of the measured-to-required metrics are assumed to be equally high for both migration costs and latency, depending on their correlation being arithmetic or harmonic. Then, the green lines all turn out to be parallel to the red line, the available resources. In fact, this is an interesting way of picturing the metrics being *balanced out*: the blue line can be rotated at certain angles to be identical to the green lines. Not by coincidence does the angle, at which the blue line is rotated to become the harmonic mean, lie on the red dotted line, and the angle, at which it becomes the arithmetic mean, equals half of the measured metrics ($\frac{c_1}{2}, \frac{l_1}{2}$).

We have spelled out this approach in Algorithm 1 based on the migration costs and latency and the arithmetic mean as a compromise between the shares of measured-

---

Algorithm 1. Requirement-adaptive strategy adapts the prediction set size psSize at each release based on metrics migration costs and latency and their arithmetic mean.

Result: Updates prediction set size psSize fulfilling given requirements regarding the maximum migration costs $c_{\max}$ and maximum latency $l_{\max}$ and regarding the prioritization of these thresholds prio

Input: psSize, c, $c_{\max}$, l, $l_{\max}$, prio

Output: psSize

1 $q_c \leftarrow \frac{c}{c_{\max}}$;
2 $q_l \leftarrow \frac{l}{l_{\max}}$;
3 $\varnothing \leftarrow \frac{1}{2}(q_c + q_l)$;
4 $m_c \leftarrow \varnothing \cdot c_{\max}$;
5 $m_l \leftarrow \varnothing \cdot l_{\max}$;
6 **if** $c_{\max} \neq \emptyset \wedge l_{\max} = \emptyset$ **then**
7 $\quad$ psSize $\leftarrow$ psSize $\cdot q_c^{-1}$;
8 **else if** $c_{\max} = \emptyset \wedge l_{\max} \neq \emptyset$ **then**
9 $\quad$ **if** $l < 2l_{\max}$ **then**
10 $\quad\quad$ psSize $\leftarrow$ psSize $\cdot \frac{l_{\max}}{2l_{\max}-l}$
11 $\quad$ **else** /* $l \geq 2l_{\max}$ */
12 $\quad\quad$ psSize $\leftarrow 1$;
13 $\quad$ **end**
14 **else** /* $c_{\max}, l_{\max} \neq \emptyset$, $\neg(\mathrm{prio}(c_{\max}) \wedge \mathrm{prio}(l_{\max}))$ */
15 $\quad$ **if** $\mathrm{prio}(c_{\max})$ **then**
16 $\quad\quad$ **if** $m_c > c_{\max}$ **then**
17 $\quad\quad\quad$ psSize $\leftarrow$ psSize $\cdot q_c^{-1}$;
18 $\quad\quad$ **else** /* $m_c \leq c_{\max}$ */
19 $\quad\quad\quad$ psSize $\leftarrow$ psSize $\cdot \varnothing \cdot q_c^{-1}$;
20 $\quad\quad$ **end**
21 $\quad$ **else if** $\mathrm{prio}(l_{\max})$ **then**
22 $\quad\quad$ **if** $m_l > l_{\max}$ **then**
23 $\quad\quad\quad$ **if** $2l_{\max} \leq l$ **then**
24 $\quad\quad\quad\quad$ psSize $\leftarrow 1$
25 $\quad\quad\quad$ **else** /* $2l_{\max} > l$ */
26 $\quad\quad\quad\quad$ psSize $\leftarrow$ psSize $\cdot \frac{l_{\max}}{2l_{\max}-l}$;
27 $\quad\quad\quad$ **end**
28 $\quad\quad$ **else** /* $m_l \leq l_{\max}$ */
29 $\quad\quad\quad$ psSize $\leftarrow$ psSize $\cdot \varnothing \cdot q_c^{-1}$;
30 $\quad\quad$ **end**
31 $\quad$ **else** /* $\neg \mathrm{prio}(c_{\max}) \wedge \neg \mathrm{prio}(l_{\max})$ */
32 $\quad\quad$ psSize $\leftarrow$ psSize $\cdot \varnothing \cdot q_c^{-1}$;
33 $\quad$ **end**
34 **end**
35 **return** psSize

---

to-required metrics $\varnothing$. The algorithm is discussed in detail in [18] in each of its case distinctions for the adjustments of psSize and accompanied by geometric illustrations.

The arithmetic mean can be replaced by other means like the harmonic F_1-measure which emphasizes values closer to zero (see Fig. 5). The F_1-measure considers each metric as equally important, whereas the more general F_β-measure allows one metric to be more important than the other, by means of which a more biased compromise can be achieved in favor of one metric and at the opportunity cost of the other metric. Algorithm 1 must then be adapted and β would be an additional input to the algorithm.

Efficiency-Adaptive Migration. The *efficiency-adaptive* strategy chooses the mathematical derivative of the latency with respect to the migration costs as a measure for the improvement of latency per migration investment [20]. Figure 6 shows that efficiently spent migration costs then stay below a certain maximum of migration costs ($c < c_{max}$) and above a certain minimal efficiency ($e_{min} < e$). Conversely, a minimum of migration costs ($c < c_{min}$) should be spent mandatorily as this can be considered a very good bargain in terms of the cost-benefit ratio of the improvement of latency per migration investment ($e > e_{max}$). Therefore, an efficient compromise on the tradeoff can be located within c_{min} and c_{max}.

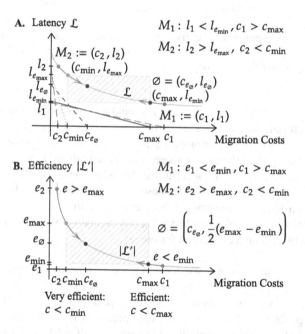

Fig. 6. Metrics competing in a tradeoff can be evaluated by an efficiency ratio of improving latency at the cost of higher migration charges (**A.**), such that latency's derivative stays within a certain span of invested costs ($c_{min} < c < c_{max}$) where latency improvement is cost-efficient ($e_{min} < e < e_{max}$) (**B.**); adapted from [20]. (Color figure online)

If, however, the efficiency drops below a certain efficiency e_{min} corresponding to $l_1 < l_{e_{min}}$, the psSize should be decreased such that the costs c fall below c_{max}, as indicated by the right blue arrows (Fig. 6). Conversely, if the efficiency exceeds a certain

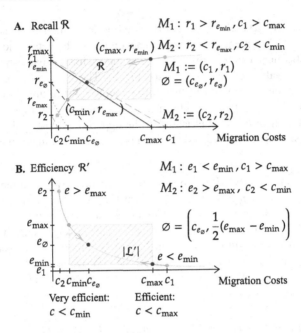

Fig. 7. Analogously, the derivative $\mathcal{R}'$ of the classification metric recall $\mathcal{R}$ stays within a certain span of a cost-efficient investment ($c_{\min} < c < c_{\max}$) of improving recall and ultimately latency; adapted from [20]. (Color figure online)

$e_{\max}$ corresponding to $l_2 >_{e_{\max}}$, the psSize should be increased such that the costs c surpass $c_{\min}$ (left blue arrows). The exact manipulation of the psSize can algorithmically efficiently be determined through a gradient descent or ascent of the derivative of the latency, taking the efficiency into account. Alternatively to the dependent metric of latency, the measurements of recall can be used together with its mathematical derivative. Then, the disarray of the database caused by schema evolution is directly quantified, which remains independent from external influences. Of course, recall is maximal if latency is minimal. The illustration of this analogous approach can be found in Fig. 7, left here without a discussion for brevity.

Relevance-Adaptive Migration. We have defined a *relevance-adaptive* strategy in [20] that aims to comply with SLAs by means of the classification metrics precision and recall as qualitative descriptors for the relevance of past migrations: If all migrated data entities of the prediction set are accessed, then precision is 100%, and if all accessed data entities have been part of the prediction set, then recall is 100%. Then, all predicted entities have been *relevant* migrations.

Although the query workload of future entity accesses cannot be predicted in general, any compromise between precision and recall stipulated in the SLAs can be considered tantamount to a certain ratio, i.e., the ratio of the accessed entities to the predicted entities, defined in [20] as α. The ratio of α can be used again in different feedback control systems based on fixed increments of the psSize, based on averages of the share of metric measurements to their required thresholds as in the geometric approach above, or by an efficiency ratio like in the *efficiency-adaptive* approach. The first, most basic approach of fixed increments of the psSize based on the ratio of α precision and recall is:

$$\text{Relevance-Adaptive}(p/r): \quad \textbf{if } \frac{p}{r} > \alpha \textbf{ then } \textit{increase } \text{psSize};$$

$$\textbf{else if } \frac{p}{r} < \alpha \textbf{ then } \textit{decrease } \text{psSize};$$

As regards the second approach of the share of metrics to their required thresholds, precision and recall would be monitored and the psSize is increased or decreased in order for the metrics to comply with the thresholds given in the SLAs as inputs to an algorithm analogous to Algorithm 1. As usual with regard to classification metrics, the harmonic F_β-measure as defined above can be assumed as correlation between the metrics, with $\beta = 1$ if both thresholds are considered equally important. If it is considered more problematic when legacy entities are accessed causing a migration on-the-fly than unnecessary migration of legacy entities that are never accessed, then β should be chosen greater than 1 (and vice versa). This would be the case if the SLA penalties for tail latencies are severe but opportunity costs of higher migration charges relatively cheap. For instance, if recall is considered twice as important, then $\beta = 2$. A detailed explication is left out here for brevity.

4 Proof of Concept: Integration into *MigCast*

We have integrated six schema migration strategies into *MigCast* in order to demonstrate the potential and effectiveness in terms of controlling the impact of schema evolution. We calculated the migration costs and measured the latency for all strategies for a common migration situation[3] throughout 12 consecutive releases of software code implying changes to the database schema. The charts of four metrics commonly stipulated in SLAs are shown in Fig. 8.

The *incremental* strategy migrates the legacy data at every fifth release, and the *complexity-adaptive* strategy is parameterized such that the psSize is doubled when four multi-type SMOs have accrued per type. A relatively high share of 75% multi-type compared to single-type SMOs has been specified in this run of *MigCast*, which is typical at the beginning of SDLCs, in order for the *complexity-adaptive* strategy to differ significantly from the *(regularly) predictive* strategy, for which the psSize is set invariably at 30%. The *requirement-adaptive* strategy is parameterized by two thresholds for migration costs (USD 20 per release) and latency (30ms per entity access), plotted in the charts as dashed lines.[4]

---

[3] The distribution of the served workload of entity accesses and the distribution and kinds of SMOs are randomized in *MigCast* within the given bounds as specified, in this case a Pareto-distributed workload of medium intensity and a high multi-type ratio of SMOs. The cost model is chosen as described on page 3. For further details of the implementation setup be referred to [17].

[4] Despite the relatively small amounts in our example of an original database instance of 10m entities and just 12 schema changes affecting parts of the database, costs can easily amount to many thousands of USD, increasing exponentially due to many influencing factors [17].

The most recent integration of the *requirement-adaptive* strategy (here in its version of measured-to-required quotients) stays consistently below the *predictive* and *complexity-adaptive* strategies with respect to on-release and cumulated migration costs. The threshold for the latency is complied with in about half on the releases, which appears as a good balancing result, since the metrics have been specified as equally important and the sum of on-release and on-read migration costs is also just above its threshold.

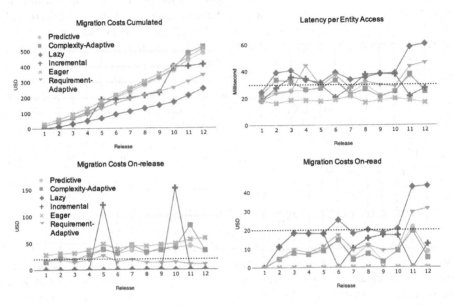

Fig. 8. Competing metrics of migration costs and latency calculated by our schema migration advisor tool *MigCast* through 12 consecutive releases of schema changes applied to a dataset of 10m entities; thresholds specified for the *requirement-adaptive* strategy: USD 20 migration costs and 30 ms latency; published in [18].

At release 4, latency is significantly higher than the threshold for the *requirement-adaptive* strategy. Consequently, the psSize is increased which is reflected in higher on-release migration costs, yet not at the same measure as the latency threshold is surpassed. The increase here is relatively moderate, because the sum of on-release cost of release 3 and on-read costs of release 4 have also already surpassed the threshold of USD 20, abiding by the measured-to-required quotient. At release 6, latency again surpasses its threshold, but now the psSize is decreased and on-release cost shrink, because the on-read costs have already exhausted the budget. At releases 11 and 12, latency peaks again, which is also visible in high on-read migration costs, and on-release costs are dialed down accordingly. Although an algorithm could be devised not considering on-read costs for the adaptation of the psSize, it can be argued that a budget strategy should include all migration costs. As a consequence, higher latency does not always translate to higher on-release migration costs.

5   A NoSQL Schema Migration Advisor

Since NoSQL databases enable the flexible persistence of data abiding by different versions of the database schema, new application releases can be deployed in iterations in order to be able to quickly adapt to frequently changing requirements. When new increments of NoSQL-backed applications are released that include database schema changes, affected data becomes legacy data and needs to be curated eventually. When deploying new features of an application that is already in production, significantly higher migration costs and/or tail latencies can occur if the database is not taken offline for the schema migration. Especially in situations typical in agile development settings, a fast-paced co-evolution of application code and database schema opens up a management problem: When the application service has to be maintained and code changes are deployed quickly to keep up with market competitors, SLA-stipulated metrics like migration costs and latency compete in a tradeoff that cannot be optimized independent from each other.

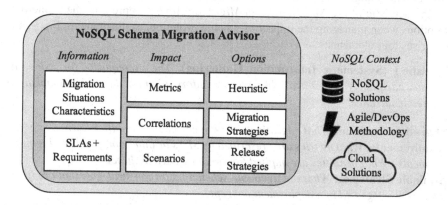

Fig. 9. Overview of the *NoSQL Schema Migration Advisor*.

In this paper, we propose a *NoSQL Schema Migration Advisor* that applies two consistent solutions to the schema evolution problem depending on the requirements for deploying new application features and on available options and information: First, if the migration situation can be elicited and non-self-adaptive migration strategies are available, a heuristic is distilled in order to estimate and to an extent even control the impact of schema evolution by means of choosing a migration strategy and pacing the code releases accordingly. Second, if this information is not sufficiently or readily available, the implementation of self-adaptive schema migration strategies complements the advisor. As shown in the prototypical implementation in the preceding section, they automatically curate variational data such that competing metrics can comply with SLAs, if possible, then making continuous management interventions superfluous. Regardless of whether the information on the migration situation is available or not, self-adaptive migration strategies are a schema management option that overcomes the necessity of navigating a heuristic repeatedly in order to deal with the impact of schema evolution.

In [17,21], the impact of schema evolution has been traced back to characteristics of the migration situations that influence the impact on key metrics for different non-self-adaptive migration strategies by means of a Monte Carlo based method of repeated sampling of our schema migration advisor tool *MigCast*, which we refer to as *MigCast in Monte Carlo* experiments. Table 3 on page 22 summarizes the correlations between influencing factors of schema evolution and impact on the metrics for the choices of the *eager, incremental, predictive, complexity-adaptive*[5] and *lazy* migration strategies. In the following, the lessons learned are condensed into a *NoSQL Schema Migration Advisor* by means of which project managers can mitigate the impact of schema evolution, if possible even pace releasing schema changes accordingly, in order to ascertain the compliance with stipulated thresholds for migration costs and latency. Then, even in a fast-paced development environment, decisions on alternative migration strategies can be based on transparent opportunity costs for competing metrics in terms of as much information on migration situations as is available.

The heuristic of the *NoSQL Schema Migration Advisor* represents the framework of options when managing the impact of schema evolution, as illustrated in Fig. 9, and comprises four elements:

Heuristic 1 (Systematic Information Gathering). *The prerequisite for using the heuristic adequately is that available, relevant information for the decision making is clarified in advance:*

Migration Situation: *What migration situation characteristics are known?*

Requirements: *What metrics are prescribed by SLAs or other non-functional requirements? What penalties are implied for violating each of these?*

Available Strategies: *What are available schema migration strategies that are (flawlessly) integrated in a deployment concept?*

Planning: *What are known migration situation characteristics expected for the near and far future, and are they prone to change or remain stable? Make precautions to notice critical metric changes quickly. Decide on a long term strategy and prepare estimates for alternatives.*

Further Strategies: *What is the reaction time for non-self-adaptive migration strategies from noticing a metric change to applying an appropriate strategy change? What effort in person hours is needed to plan, apply, and administrate migration strategies? What is the estimated time to implement further non- or self-adaptive migration strategies?*

Learning: *What are known correlations between migration situation characteristics and cost metrics of the past? Use this historic information and supplement it over time forming a knowledge base (see Heuristic 2).*

Heuristic 2 (Estimating the Schema Evolution Impact)

---

[5] The limit values for the *complexity-adaptive* strategy are in the depicted migration scenarios equivalent to the *predictive* strategy, because its advantage can only be played out at a higher share of multi-type SMOs and a lesser, Pareto-distributed query workload.

Knowledge Base: *The results of the* MigCast in Monte Carlo *experiments summarized in Table 3 (page 22) can be used as a knowledge base to calculate estimates of migration costs and latency during schema evolution.*

Estimating the Impact: *For each available non-self-adaptive migration strategy, calculate the expected values for the metrics by means of the knowledge base. (Exemplary use cases are discussed in Sect. 6.)*

Single Metric: *If latency has to be as low as possible, then the* eager *strategy optimizes this metric at a maximum recall. If migration costs have to be as low as possible, then* lazy *optimizes this metric at a maximal precision (see Fig. 3). If a single required metric just needs to meet a threshold, then estimates for all non-self-adaptive migration strategies should be considered in terms of saving opportunity costs when this is safe in respect of possible variance and variation (see Heuristic 3).*

Competing Metrics: *If both a metric and its competing metric need to be met, then estimates for all non-self-adaptive migration strategies should be determined in terms of both metrics. A migration strategy should be selected that each of their costs and opportunity costs are balanced out, i.e., their expected-to-required quotients are equal or suitable in terms of charges for violating either SLAs and in terms of possible variance.*

Variance: *Both cost metrics should be assessed in respect of their variances under different migration strategies. Variances depend on the migration situation characteristics (a use case with particular variance is discussed in Sect. 6). In general, variances turn out to be lower for strategies that continually invest into the homogeneity of the database at every release of a schema change. This is trivially the case for* eager, *but also for the* predictive *strategy despite its growing migration debt due the aging of legacy data, especially when the query workload is Pareto-distributed, as* predictive *utilizes the concentration of accesses on hot data. Then, latency does not have peaks in latency like with* lazy *and* incremental *migration strategies.*

Heuristic 3 (Matching Strategies with Migration Situations)

Variation: *Metrics for different migration strategies can be matched to migration situations throughout the releases of schema changes in order to minimize overall costs and opportunity costs.* Eager *has the lowest variation of metrics throughout the releases of schema changes,* lazy *and* predictive *still relatively low. With* predictive, *the migration costs are distributed relatively evenly between on-release and on-read costs, each of which being much stabler than with the* incremental *strategy, which has the highest variation in its metrics. Whereas the* complexity-adaptive *strategy is mostly similar to* predictive, *it is preferable to avoid tail latencies if the share of multi-type SMOs is high and the workload low.*

Workload Intensity: *The higher the workload becomes, the less the advantages of delaying migration become. Although latency becomes lower on average with higher workload, migration costs rise disproportionately, even beyond an* eager *migration. If high workload intensity is expected, preemptive schema migrations could be considered in order to profit from a lower latency right from the start. Such an investment is especially efficient if a possible localization of accesses is* *utilized, e.g., under* predictive *migration. The variation of the incremental strategy can be used in particular to match incremental rounds to phases of low workload or application downtime, if possible.*

Heuristic 4 (Deciding on Self-adaptive Migration Strategies)

Pros and Cons: *The integration of a self-adaptive migration strategy should be considered, if finding a suitable compromise between competing metrics is often required in busy project stages, if SLA-penalties are in place and/or if migration situation characteristics are unknown, hard or expensive to come by, outdated, or changing rapidly. The gain should outweigh the effort of an integration, especially as self-adaptive migration strategies should not be maintained within the application code, but require a dedicated schema management middleware to be implemented into the software stack.*

Cost or Classification Metrics: *The choice on the kind of self-adaptive migration strategy should be made according to the metrics that are prescribed. The advantage of classification metrics is that the control remains on the actual heterogeneity of the database, whereas migration costs and latency are usually directly specified in SLAs.*

6   Use Cases of the Advisor

In this section, three use cases of the *NoSQL Schema Migration Advisor* are discussed that highlight its general range of application. The impact of schema evolution on migration costs and latency can be estimated by means of Table 3 (page 22) as a knowledge base. The table shows the impact after 12 releases of schema changes for the standard parameter configuration of *MigCast in Monte Carlo* (see caption of Table 3), partitioned into *Schema Changes*, *Dataset*, and *Workload*. The table also shows the differential factors when one characteristic changes, which is discussed exemplarily in Use Cases 2 and 3.

Use Case 1 (Number of Schema Change Releases) . *If more or less schema changes than 12 are expected, the impact on the metrics can be assumed to be proportional. The cumulated migration cost of* eager *increase linearly towards USD 1289.07 at release 12, which equals the reference value of* 1.0000 *in Table 3.*[6] *Thus, per release the twelfth part of it, i.e., USD* 107, 43, *can be reckoned on average per release for eagerly migrating the legacy data. For other non-self-adaptive migration strategies, the cumulated migration costs can be estimated relative to the reference for* eager*: For instance, for* lazy *at release 6 a share of* 0.5687 *of the costs for* eager *at that release are spent, i.e.,* $0.5687 \cdot USD\ 1289.07 \cdot \frac{6}{12} = USD\ 366.55.$[7] *Estimates for migration costs and latency*

---

[6] The increase is slightly exponentially for a data growth rate of 10%, which increases the number of entities by a constant amount per release; see bottom left column of Table 3.

[7] This amount can be considered an upper limit, because the migration costs can be assumed to grow exponentially, such that in the Monte Carlo experiments not the assumed 50% but 40% need to be spent at release 6 for *lazy* due to the Pareto distribution of the entity accesses.

can be taken for all other non-self-adaptive strategies and parameter configurations analogously.

A frequent use case can be to change the migration strategy in the course of schema evolution in order to reach compliance with SLAs. Let us assume that the budget allows to spend the amount of USD 1000. For instance, for 9 of the 12 schema changes the affected legacy data can be migrated eagerly (for USD 967) in a divide-and-conquer approach, such that latency remains at an optimal throughout the 9 releases.[8] For the remaining three schema changes, a lazy approach could be applied in order to zero on-release costs in the hope that on-read costs do not surpass the budget limit. This would be a viable approach if the last schema changes coincide with a time of lower workload.

Alternatively, USD 888 could be spend throughout all 12 planned releases using a predictive strategy, resulting in a latency of factor 1.9683 compared to the minimal latency with eager (see Table 3), which is comparable to three releases of lazy migration after 9 eager releases. However, latency under predictive has increased steadily throughout the releases, resulting in a higher mean than with a prior eager migration of the legacy data up to release 9.   □

Table 1. Excerpt of Table 3 for Use Cases 1 and 2.

Schema Changes	Share of Multi-Type SMOs					
	0%		25%		100%	
Eager	0.6149	0.9905	1.0000	1.0000	1.8702	1.0000
Incremental	0.4866	1.2683	0.8058	1.8397	1.6136	2.8571
Predictive	0.3677	1.4397	0.6888	1.9683	1.4079	3.1730
Lazy	0.2880	1.6524	0.5687	2.6302	1.2196	4.5381

Use Case 2 (Reorganization of the Database Schema). If latency is critical for the success of an application, denormalization techniques are used, which require copying and moving attributes between types, often in an offline batch processing mode [32]. However, not all applications can be taken offline due to high availability requirements, nor are blue-green deployment always affordable in competitive markets [22]. When a database schema is planned to be reorganized due to changing requirements, this situation can pose a challenge to a project manager, since the share of multi-type SMOs has turned out to be a cost driver of schema evolution [17].

We assume that 12 attributes have to be moved between the types in order to react to changing requirements (other settings see the underlined parameter configuration of Table 3). With the eager strategy, migration costs of USD 2411 would have to be spent (factor 1.8702 of USD 1298, see Table 1) and with lazy, USD 1572 (factor 1.2196),

---

[8] The migration can either be done in offline batch processing, or in a blue-green deployment [22], or during a phase of low query workload, then causing higher latency intermittently.

which would be a 35% discount. We have found in our experiments that an intermittent workload in between reorganizing the database with lazy *implies an average latency of 28.59 ms per entity access, which is by factor 4.5381 greater than* eager *(see Table 1), and outliers of up to 37.87 ms.*

Furthermore, assume that no more than USD 2000 may be spent for reorganizing those 12 attributes, then the predictive *strategy can be recommended (USD 1815, factor 1.4079 in Table 1) at that* psSize, *or* lazy *for even lesser costs (USD 1572, factor 1.2196). If an SLA-stipulated maximum latency has to be complied with, e.g., 15 ms, then the* eager *strategy would be mandatory, since no other strategy features such low latency on average. If possible, migration costs should be spent casually when reorganizing the database, since the opportunity costs of a deteriorating latency for non-eager migration strategies when rewriting queries and retrieve legacy data on-the-fly, is higher for multi-type SMOs than for any other migration situation characteristic.*

Apart from this specific example, in case that metrics cannot be sufficiently balanced out by the choice of a migration strategy for impending schema changes, the project manager could also hold off on applying the changes or change their order. Since at a higher share of multi-type SMOs, lesser migration costs can be saved with a strategy delaying migrating legacy entities at a much higher latency increase than at a lower share. Thus, single-type SMOs can be matched to higher workload and multi-type SMOs can be applied in times of lower workload, if such a reordering is feasible administratively. □

Use Case 3 (Higher Cardinality of Entity-relationships). *When the database schema co-evolves with the application, performance criteria of the application in production should be kept in mind for non-*eager *migration, especially how latency increases when entities are being instantiated in higher cardinalities of the entity-relationships. Other migration situation characteristics have not led to such variances, which is why this use case of higher cardinality of entity-relationships has been selected to be discussed.*

Table 2. Excerpt of Table 3 for Use Case 3.

Dataset	Entity-Relationships					
	1:1		1:10		1:25	
Eager	1.0000	1.0000	0.9319	1.0175	0.8742	1.0032
Incremental	0.8059	1.8397	0.9170	1.7514	0.8516	1.7286
Predictive	0.6887	1.9683	0.6953	2.1302	0.6593	2.1952
Lazy	0.5687	2.6302	0.5810	2.7603	0.5556	2.8476

With the *lazy* strategy, slightly lesser migration costs are caused with higher cardinalities of 1:10 (factor 2.7603 of Table 2) and 1:25 (factor 2.8467) entity-relationships compared to the standard 1:1 (factor 2.6302). In our *MigCast in Monte Carlo* experiments, we have observed outliers in latency of up to 43 ms for 1:10 and 92 ms for 1:25

instead of outliers of 25 ms for 1:1 (see Fig. 10). This affects the arithmetic means of the latency to increase by approx. 8% for 1:25-relationships compared to 1:1. However, if time critical applications rely on a reliably low latency, the high variance of latency must be taken into account and either schema designs avoided that lead to high cardinalities or migration strategies selected that are not that prone to high variance like *eager* or maybe also *predictive*.   □

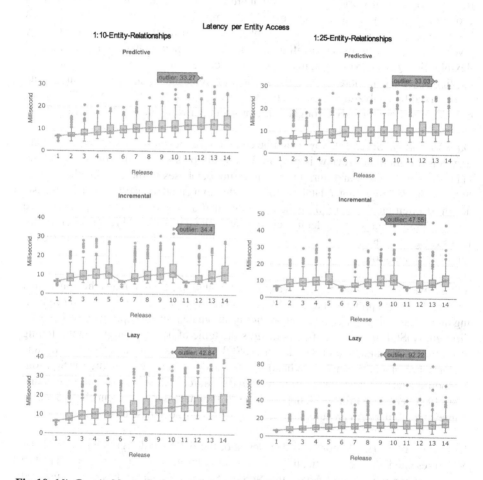

Fig. 10. *MigCast in Monte Carlo* experiments: Box-whisker plots showing latency for *lazy*, left 1:10 and right 1:25 entity-relationships, graphs show the medians and highest outliers are labeled.

7 Related Work

Schema Evolution. Frameworks managing schema changes in relational databases have been researched intensively in the past decade in [2,5,8,15]. In XML, schema evolution has been continuously investigated in [4,14]. Most recently, Klímek et al. described a framework for the management of evolution and change propagation in XML applications in [24]. In real-world applications that are backed by relational databases, schema evolution has been researched extensively in empirical studies [9,29,34,40], which has matured with the availability of public code repositories. A most recent study revealed that projects undergo different volumes of schema changes [39]. Schema-flexible NoSQL database systems have yet to come into the focus of research. Its implicit schema is declared within the application code, such that schema changes can be observed by analyzing the code [26,33]. There is evidence that the NoSQL schema evolves more continuously throughout the project than with relational databases [33].

Data Migration. Several surveys examine cloud migration, most recently in [12], where a systematic literature review is proposed from the perspective of process modeling. [11] investigates costs and duration of migrating databases to the cloud. When stakeholder consider migrating a database to be hosted in a cloud, concerns about high costs are most often cited, with tail latencies being cited as one of the issues [1]. Because *eager* migration causes considerable charges with cloud providers [11,17], other migration strategies such as *lazy* [23,31] and *proactive* [20] strategies have been proposed to remedy the situation.

Self-adaptation. A recommender system is presented in [27] that maps the conceptual data model of an application to a NoSQL database schema. Ongoing research originating in our research group focuses on providing automated schema optimization between different NoSQL data stores [6]. As regards the topic of deployment parameter tuning at runtime, [28] addresses the issue for NoSQL databases in terms of scalability and performance of data-intensive applications. A survey on parameter-tuning for SQL-on-Hadoop systems examines the throughput and resource utilization, response time, and cost-effectiveness by Filho et al. in [13]. In [37], Tsoumakos et al. present cloud-enabled frameworks to perform an automatic resizing of NoSQL database clusters.

Migration Advisors. Almost two decades ago, the database design advisor *DB2* has been presented that automatically recommends physical design features [41]. The schema design advisor tool *NoSE*, the NoSQL Schema Evaluator, has been presented in 2017 by Mior et al. in [27]. In a follow-up paper, Suárez-Otero, Mior et al. deliver a framework that provides the required database schema modifications to reflect the conceptual model change, the migrations of that data, and the subsequent changes of the application queries [36].

Table 3. Summary of the results of the *MigCast in Monte Carlo* experiments after 12 schema changes wrt. migration situation characteristics *Schema Changes, Workload,* and *Dataset*; first columns are cumulated migration costs (factor 1 equals USD 1289.07) and second columns latency (factor 1 equals 6.3 ms); reference parameter configuration of *MigCast* underlined column headings; color legend: $x < 0.5$ green, $0.5 \leq x < 1.5$ yellow, $1.5 \leq x < 2$ yellow-orange $2 \leq x < 3$ orange, $2 \leq x < 3$ red, $x \geq 4$ purple.

Schema Changes	Share of Multi-Type SMOs									
	0%		25%		50%		75%		100%	
Eager	0.6149	0.9905	1.0000	1.0000	1.2673	0.9968	1.5566	1.0222	1.8702	1.0000
Incremental	0.4866	1.2683	0.8058	1.8397	1.0845	1.9873	1.3183	2.5905	1.6136	2.8571
Predictive	0.3677	1.4397	0.6888	1.9683	0.9216	2.2698	1.1294	2.7857	1.4079	3.1730
Lazy	0.2880	1.6524	0.5687	2.6302	0.7801	3.0635	0.9553	3.9778	1.2196	4.5381

Workload	Distribution				% Accessed Data				Intensity					
	Pareto		Uniform		10%		20%		Low		Medium		High	
Eager	1.0000	1.0000	1.0156	1.0206	1.0093	1.0508	1.0000	1.0000	0.9699	1.0111	1.0000	1.0000	0.9866	1.0159
Incremental	0.8059	1.8397	0.8861	1.9730	0.7856	1.9968	0.8059	1.8397	0.7874	2.0619	0.8059	1.8397	0.8271	1.5889
Predictive	0.6887	1.9683	0.7608	2.1905	0.5658	2.3381	0.6887	1.9683	0.5588	2.4127	0.6887	1.9683	0.7801	1.5683
Lazy	0.5687	2.6302	0.6957	2.7190	0.3543	3.4444	0.5687	2.6302	0.4049	3.4984	0.5687	2.6302	0.6953	1.9190

Dataset	Data Growth Rate				Entity-Relationships					
	0%		10%		1:1		1:10		1:25	
Eager	1.0000	1.0000	1.5148	0.9889	1.0000	1.0000	0.9319	1.0175	0.8742	1.0032
Incremental	0.8059	1.8397	1.1388	1.7492	0.8059	1.8397	0.9170	1.7514	0.8516	1.7286
Predictive	0.6887	1.9683	0.8949	1.8794	0.6887	1.9683	0.6953	2.1302	0.6593	2.1952
Lazy	0.5687	2.6302	0.5420	2.6651	0.5687	2.6302	0.5810	2.7603	0.5556	2.8476

8 Conclusion

We have contributed the first *NoSQL Schema Migration Advisor*. It is based on two approaches that both solve the schema evolution problem depending on whether the migration situation can be elicited by stakeholders or project managers or not. Based on our *MigCast in Monte Carlo* experiments, a heuristic is distilled in order to estimate and, if possible, even control the impact of schema evolution by means of choosing a suitable migration strategy and pacing the code releases accordingly. If information on the migration situation is sparsely available or too costly to acquire, self-adaptive schema migration strategies are discussed and prototypically implemented into our schema migration advisor tool *MigCast*. These self-adaptive migration strategies can automatically curate variational data such that competing metrics can comply with stipulated SLAs, if possible, or balance them out. Then, management interventions to reach compliance in order to deal with the impact of schema evolution are made superfluous, which is especially important during busy times of the project management.

References

1. 3T Software Labs Ltd.: MongoDB Trends Report. Cambridge, U.K. (2020)
2. Aulbach, S., Jacobs, D., Kemper, A., Seibold, M.: A comparison of flexible schemas for software as a service. In: Proceedings of SIGMOD 2009. ACM (2009)
3. Barker, S., Chi, Y., Moon, H.J., Hacigümüş, H., Shenoy, P.: "Cut me some slack" latency-aware live migration for databases. In: Proceedings of EDBT'12 (2012)

4. Bertino, E., Guerrini, G., Mesiti, M., Tosetto, L.: Evolving a set of DTDs according to a dynamic set of XML documents. In: Proceedings of EDBT'02 Workshops (2002)
5. Cleve, A., Gobert, M., Meurice, L., Maes, J., Weber, J.: Understanding database schema evolution. Sci. Comput. Programm. **97**(P1), January 2015
6. Conrad, A., Gärtner, S., Störl, U.: Towards automated schema optimization. In: ER Demos and Posters. Proceedings of CEUR Workshop, vol. 2958 (2021)
7. Curino, C., et al.: Relational cloud: a DbaaS for the cloud. In: Proceedings of CIDR (2011)
8. Curino, C., Moon, H.J., Deutsch, A., Zaniolo, C.: Automating the database schema evolution process. VLDB J. **22**(1), 73–98 (2013)
9. Curino, C., Moon, H.J., Tanca, L., Zaniolo, C.: Schema evolution in Wikipedia - toward a web information system benchmark. In: Proceedings of ICEIS 2008 (2008)
10. Difallah, D.E., Pavlo, A., Curino, C., Cudre-Mauroux, P.: OLTP-bench: an extensible testbed for benchmarking relational databases. Proc. VLDB E **7**(4), 277–288 (2013)
11. Ellison, M., Calinescu, R., Paige, R.F.: Evaluating cloud database migration options using workload models. J. Cloud Comput. **7**(1), 1–18 (2018). https://doi.org/10.1186/s13677-018-0108-5
12. Fahmideh, M., Daneshgar, F., Beydoun, G., Rabhi, F.A.: Challenges in migrating legacy software systems to the cloud. CoRR abs/2004.10724 (2020)
13. Filho, E.R.L., de Almeida, E.C., Scherzinger, S., Herodotou, H.: Investigating automatic parameter tuning for SQL-on-hadoop systems. Big Data Res. **25** (2021)
14. Guerrini, G., Mesiti, M., Rossi, D.: Impact of XML schema evolution on valid documents. In: Proceedings of WIDM'05 Workshop. ACM (2005)
15. Herrmann, K., Voigt, H., Behrend, A., Rausch, J., Lehner, W.: Living in parallel realities: co-existing schema versions. In: Proceedings of SIGMOD (2017)
16. Hillenbrand, A., Levchenko, M., Störl, U., Scherzinger, S., Klettke, M.: MigCast: Putting a price tag on data model evol. in NoSQL D. S. In: Proceedings of SIGMOD (2019)
17. Hillenbrand, A., Scherzinger, S., Störl, U.: Remaining in control of the impact of schema evolution in NoSQL databases. In: Proceedings of ER 2021 (2021)
18. Hillenbrand, A., Störl, U.: Automated curation of variational data in NoSQL databases through metric-driven self-adaptive migration strategies. In: Proceedings of MODEL-SWARD 2022. SCITEPRESS (2022)
19. Hillenbrand, A., Störl, U., Levchenko, M., Nabiyev, S., Klettke, M.: Towards self-adapting data migration in the context of schema evolution in NoSQL databases. In: Proceedings of ICDE 2020 Workshops. IEEE (2020)
20. Hillenbrand, A., Störl, U., Nabiyev, S., Klettke, M.: Self-adapting data migration in the context of schema evolution in NoSQL databases. Distrib. Parallel Databases **40**(1), 5–25 (2021). https://doi.org/10.1007/s10619-021-07334-1
21. Hillenbrand, A., Störl, U., Nabiyev, S., Scherzinger, S.: MigCast in Monte Carlo: the impact of data model evolution in NoSQL databases. CoRR (2021)
22. Kim, G., Debois, P., Willis, J., Humble, J.: The DevOps Handbook. IT Revolution Press (2016)
23. Klettke, M., Störl, U., Shenavai, M., Scherzinger, S.: NoSQL schema evolution and big data migration at scale. In: Proceedings of SCDM 2016. IEEE (2016)
24. Klímek, J., Malý, J., Necaský, M., Holubová, I.: eXolutio: methodology for design and evolution of XML schemas using conceptual mod. Informatica **26**(3), 271 (2015)
25. Levandoski, J.J., Larson, P., Stoica, R.: Identifying hot and cold data in main-memory databases. In: Proceedings of ICDE 2013. IEEE (2013)
26. Meurice, L., Cleve, A.: Supporting schema evolution in schema-less NoSQL data stores. In: Proceedings of SANER 2017 (2017)
27. Mior, M.J., Salem, K., Aboulnaga, A., Liu, R.: NoSE: schema design for NoSQL applications. IEEE Trans. Knowl. Data Eng. **29**, 2275–2289 (2017)

28. Preuveneers, D., Joosen, W.: Automated configuration of NoSQL performance and scalability tactics for data-intensive applications. Informatics **7**, 29 (2020)
29. Qiu, D., Li, B., Su, Z.: An empirical analysis of the co-evolution of schema and code in database applications. In: Proceedings of SIGSOFT 2013. ACM (2013)
30. Rijsbergen, C.J.V.: Inf. Retrieval. Butterworth-Heinemann, USA (1979)
31. Saur, K., Dumitras, T., Hicks, M.W.: Evolving NoSQL databases without downtime. In: Proceedings of ICSME 2016. IEEE (2016)
32. Scherzinger, S., Klettke, M., Störl, U.: Managing schema evolution in NoSQL data stores. In: Proceedings of DBPL 2013 (2013)
33. Scherzinger, S., Sidortschuck, S.: An empirical study on the design and evolution of NoSQL database schemas. In: Dobbie, G., Frank, U., Kappel, G., Liddle, S.W., Mayr, H.C. (eds.) ER 2020. LNCS, vol. 12400, pp. 441–455. Springer, Cham (2020). https://doi.org/10.1007/978-3-030-62522-1_33
34. Skoulis, I., Vassiliadis, P., Zarras, A.: Growing up with stability: how open-source relational databases evolve. Inf. Syst. **53** (2015)
35. Störl, U., et al.: Curating variational data in appl. dev. In: Proceedings of ICDE 2018 (2018)
36. Suárez-Otero, P., Mior, M.J., José Suárez-Cabal, M., Tuya, J.: Maintaining NoSQL database quality during conceptual model evolution. In: IEEE International Conference on Big Data (Big Data) (2020)
37. Tsoumakos, D., Konstantinou, I., Boumpouka, C., Sioutas, S., Koziris, N.: Automated, elastic resource provisioning for NoSQL clusters using TIRAMOLA. In: CCGrid 2013. IEEE (2013)
38. Upton, G., Cook, I.: The Oxford Dictionary of Statistics. Oxford University Press, United Kingdom (2002)
39. Vassiliadis, P.: Profiles of schema evolution in free open source software projects. In: Proceedings of ICDE 2021. IEEE (2021)
40. Vassiliadis, P., Zarras, A., Skoulis, I.: Gravitating to rigidity: patterns of schema evolution-and its absence-in the lives of tables. Inf. Syst. **63** (2016)
41. Zilio, D.C., et al.: DB2 design advisor. In: Proceedings of VLDB (2004)

Author Index

© Springer Nature Switzerland AG 2023
L. F. Pires et al. (Eds.): MODELSWARD 2021/2022, CCIS 1708, p. 255, 2023.
https://doi.org/10.1007/978-3-031-38821-7

Printed in the United States
by Baker & Taylor Publisher Services